LAW AND POLITICS IN THE UNITED STATES

SECOND EDITION

Herbert Jacob
Northwestern University

 HarperCollins*CollegePublishers*

Acquisitions Editor: Leo A. W. Wiegman
Electronic Production Manager: Angel Gonzalez Jr.
Publishing Services: Ruttle, Shaw & Wetherill, Inc.
Electronic Page Makeup: RR Donnelley & Sons, Barbados
Printer and Binder: RR Donnelley & Sons Company
Cover Printer: RR Donnelley & Sons Company

Law and Politics In the United States, Second Edition

Library of Congress Cataloging-in-Publication Data

Jacob, Herbert
    Law and politics in the United States / by Herbert Jacob. — 2nd ed.
    p.   cm.
    Includes bibliographical references and index.
    ISBN 0-673-52380-2
    1. Law—United States. 2. Law and politics. I. Title.
KF380.J33 1995

349.73—dc20   94-18644
[347.3]   CIP

94 95 96 97 9 8 7 6 5 4 3 2 1

For Lynn

CONTENTS

PREFACE   vii

Part I Concepts and Framework   1

1 LAW AS POLITICS   3
   The Law   7
   The Legal System   9
   The Legal Process   17
   Outline of What Follows   18

2 THE LAW   20
   An Abstract Definition of Law   21
   The Structure of American Law   26
   The Distinctiveness of American Law   35
   Justice and Law   36
   Conclusion   37

Part II The Outer Ring: Disputants and Criminals   39

3 DISPUTANTS AND THE LAW   41
   Dispute Processing Arenas   44
   Disputes In and Out of Court   59
   Are Americans Overly Contentious?   82
   Conclusion   83

4 USING THE LAW TO PROMOTE PUBLIC ORDER AND SAFETY   86
   Victims and their Decisions to Invoke the Criminal Law   87
   Public Authorities and Invocation of the Criminal Law   91
   Offenders as Targets of the Criminal Process   93
   The Experiences of Other Countries   97
   Conclusion   99

Part III The Middle Ring: Gatekeepers   101

5 THE POLICE   103
   The Police as Agents of Social Control   103
   The Police as Gatekeepers   107
   Conclusion   116

6 LAWYERS   **118**
The Structure of the Bar   120
Implications for Gatekeeping   128
Three Examples of Gatekeeping   134
Conclusion   139

7 INTEREST GROUPS   **142**
Interest Groups in Legislatures   144
Interest Groups in the Administrative Process   146
Interest Groups in Courts   147
Conclusion   155

Part IV   Core Institutions: The Courts   **157**

8 TRIAL COURTS   **159**
Common Elements of Trial Courts   159
Criminal Proceedings   163
Civil Proceedings   175
Trial Judges   191
Conclusion   196

9 APPELLATE COURTS   **200**
The Functions of Appellate Courts   200
Structural Characteristics of Appellate Courts   202
What Appellate Courts Do   203
How Appellate Courts Work   205
Appellate Courts and the Political Arena   206

10 THE SUPREME COURT   **214**
How the Court Works   215
The Supreme Court and the Political Arena   224
Conclusion   236

Part V   Core Institutions: Legislatures and
Administrative Agencies   **239**

11 LEGISLATURES   **241**
The Legislative Process   242
Relations Between Legislatures and Courts   251
Legislative Lawmaking   253
Conclusion   254

12   ADMINISTRATIVE AGENCIES   **256**
     Implementation of Law and Policy   256
     Administrative Rule Making   260
     Administrative Adjudication   266
     Conclusion   272

Part **VI   Conclusion**   **275**

13   THE LIMITS OF LAW   **277**
     Divorce Law Reform   279
     Criminal Code Reform   290
     Conclusion   295

14   EPILOGUE   **297**
     The Crisis of Confidence   297
     The Crisis of Effectiveness   299
     Internationalization of Norms   301
     Future Challenges   302

     INDEX   **304**

PREFACE

This book introduces readers to the American legal system, but the introduction is not conventional. I emphasize the legal system's inescapable links with the political arena, because law and legal institutions are used to maintain social control, to buttress a political regime's legitimacy, and to make policy. The legal system is conceptualized broadly to include much more than courts, for they are only one of the core institutions. The others—legislatures and administrative agencies—also need to be considered, as do the users and gatekeepers. Thus, this book has chapters not only on lawyers but also on the police and interest groups, for both are significant gatekeepers. It also has chapters on legislatures and administrative agencies.

All readers of this book are users of the law and objects of legal actions. Many may become lawyers. My hope is that those who do become lawyers will be more thoughtful about the power and limits of law after reading this book.

This edition differs from the first in many ways. The discussion of appellate courts has been expanded significantly. The analysis of interest groups has been collected in a separate chapter. The emphasis on social control and legitimation is new. The book has been completely updated.

As before, I have incurred many debts. I am grateful to Northwestern University for research support and to my colleagues Wesley G. Skogan, Jerry Goldman, Jonathan Casper, and John P. Heinz for many illuminating discussions while (often unbeknownst to them) I was working on this manuscript. My Northwestern students have heard the arguments in these pages and helped me sharpen them. Max Caproni provided valuable assistance preparing the manuscript and Christian Freitag has been a wonderful research assistant throughout his undergraduate career. Several anonymous readers have steered me from errors and misplaced emphases. If there is any merit in the book, all of these people deserve part of the credit; all blame for the remaining errors of judgment or fact is mine.

Herbert Jacob
Evanston, Illinois

I

CONCEPTS AND FRAMEWORK

Law is often perceived as the opposite of politics. Law seems dignified whereas politics seems seamy. Law appears predictable whereas politics seems typified by the unexpected. Law seems to search for justice while politics seems to seek the expedient.

Such perceptions, however conventional, are nevertheless misleading, for one cannot comprehend law without understanding its roots in politics. To place law and the legal system in their social setting, we need first develop a conceptual picture of what they comprise. The legal system is comprised of diverse institutions and processes, some of which we find in the political arena as well—such as legislatures, executives, interest groups, and, indeed, law itself. Law and justice are important to the political arena in distinctive ways. Their relationships are the subject of the first two chapters of this book. In them, we develop both a conceptual framework and a vocabulary that enables us to explore the legal system more thoroughly.

1

LAW AS POLITICS

Disaster struck a young couple in Long Island, New York, one day in October 1983.[1] Their joyful anticipation of the birth of a child turned into calamitous anxiety when they learned that their daughter suffered from multiple birth defects. We know the infant only as Baby Jane Doe, the name given her in the press and in court proceedings to protect her anonymity. She suffered not only from spina bifida, a defect in the vertebral column, but also from hydrocephaly and microcephaly, commonly known as water on the brain and an abnormally small skull and cranial capacity. The couple's consultation with their physician and other doctors indicated that the child would either die quickly or linger for two years if nothing were done to correct the defects. If immediate surgery were performed and if operations were repeated throughout her life, she might live for as long as twenty years. Even with such surgery, however, her life would be difficult at best. In all likelihood, she would be subject to epileptic seizures, paralyzed from the waist down, and bedridden. She would also be severely retarded.

What should the parents do in light of these options? Before medical science made intervention in serious illnesses possible, their situation would have been simpler: They would have had no choice but to wait until nature took its course and the child died. By 1983, however, dreadful choices faced them. They could authorize vigorous medical intervention in the hope of prolonging the life of their daughter, even though her quality of life would probably always be minimal. Alternatively, they could order only passive care with the knowledge that their child would die sooner rather than later.

Traditionally such painful decisions were the sole responsibility of parents. Others might offer advice and counsel, but no one else could legally interfere with their choice. This, however, was not to be the case for the parents of Baby Jane Doe. They did con-

---

[1]This account of the Baby Doe case is based on reports that appeared in the *New York Times* from 20 October 1983 through October 1984. Key articles are found in the 29 October 1983 (I, 30:3), 13 November 1983 (I, 45:1), and 12 January 1984 (II, 5:1) issues. See also Jeff Lyon, *Playing God in the Nursery* (New York: W.W. Norton, 1985), pp. 45–55.

sult clergy and doctors, and after considering the alternatives the couple decided against radical medical intervention, a decision that unwittingly pushed them into the midst of a legal maelstrom. Within days they and the hospital in which their child was being treated found themselves charged with child neglect and abuse. Lawrence Washburn, a New Hampshire private attorney who was active in the right-to-life movement, had somehow heard of the birth of this child and of her parents' decision. He sued in New York State court to force the hospital to operate on the child.

From late October 1983 until mid-January 1984, the parents and the hospital were forced to defend themselves in both state and federal courts. The state trial court that heard the original case ruled for Washburn and ordered the operation, but after an immediate appeal a New York appeals court first suspended the trial court's decision and then reversed it. The federal government then entered the legal fight. President Reagan embraced the pro-life position in his 1984 reelection campaign and even published a book supporting this stance.[2] Consistent with those views, the U.S. Department of Health and Human Services issued administrative regulations that invited federal intervention in the care of infants such as Baby Jane Doe. Those regulations, however, had been challenged in court and ruled illegal because they had been issued without the required public hearings and public notice. In early 1984 the case of Baby Doe seemed to provide an ideal opportunity to promote the argument for federal intervention. The federal government consequently sued the hospital for access to its records on the treatment of the infant. That suit was also lost even though it was reported that the solicitor general of the United States had personally reviewed the appeal brief before it was submitted to the U.S. Court of Appeals.[3] At the same time the Department of Health and Human Services solicited public responses to new regulations it had issued ten weeks after Baby Doe's birth. Those regulations provided for much less active intervention by federal authorities, but they firmly established the federal government's interest in such incidents.

Congress also entered into the conflict. For several years opponents to abortion had been promoting legislation that would prohibit using public funds for abortions. With the prominence given to the Baby Doe case, Congress enacted a law in 1984 that expanded the definition of child abuse to include denial of care to newborns.[4] Because child abuse is not ordinarily a concern of the federal government, the law sought to force states to agree with the expanded definition by threatening them with the loss of federal grants if they did not establish procedures to prevent such abuse. Finally, in April 1985 the Department of Health and Human Services promulgated new rules as authorized by the 1984 congressional act. Those rules required that full medical services be provided all infants unless they were "chronically and irretrievably comatose," or treatment would only prolong an "inevitable death" was so extreme "that it becomes inhumane to administer it."[5] In the meantime, Baby Jane Doe's parents consented to the operation they had originally refused. The child lived; seven years later she was getting

---

[2]Ronald Reagan, *Abortion and the Conscience of the Nation* (Nashville: T. Nelson, 1984).
[3]*New York Times*, 20 November 1983, p. I, 42.
[4]Public Law 98–457; *CQ Weekly*, 22 September 1984, p. 2305.
[5]*New York Times*, 16 April 1985, p. 10.

special education and although unable to walk was classified as educable.[6] The regulations persisted and were still causing controversy in 1993.[7]

Few cases illustrate more dramatically the potential intervention of the law and politics into areas many people presume to be private. The litigation not only cost Baby Doe's parents thousands of dollars but also added to the anguish they already were suffering by observing their child's plight. Government officials and private citizens with no immediate interest in Baby Doe or her family inserted themselves into the parents' decision-making process. Some, like Washburn, acted out of ideological concern; others, like the Reagan administration officials, were motivated by the opportunity to promote their policy objectives. Some judges sided with Washburn and the federal officials; others—and they sat on the higher appeals courts—sided with the girl's parents and the hospital. Congress eventually sided with the Reagan administration's policies.

Baby Doe's case illustrates not only the vast possibilities for intervention by the law into affairs that have been traditionally considered private, but also the private disputes and political conflicts that surface in the legal and political arenas. Baby Doe's parents sought to protect their privacy and their parental right to take reasonable actions to care for their child without governmental interference. The right-to-lifers who sought to force medical treatment on Baby Doe advocated an absolute claim for the right to life for all persons as guaranteed under the Fifth and Fourteenth Amendments to the Constitution. They viewed the financial and emotional stresses imposed on parents as subordinate to the child's right to live. They also dismissed as irrelevant the claim that her quality of life should be considered in the decision to provide medical care. As the Baby Doe case illustrates, the resolution of such conflicts is the function of both the legal system and the political process.

While the Baby Doe case was especially dramatic, it was not an unusual intervention of law into everyday life, because law in the United States pervades every aspect of each person's life. It affects how people are hired, paid, fired, and retired. It governs the obligations of family and the conditions under which persons may break away from their family. It determines how much they must pay in taxes and their use of credit and the agreements they make to purchase goods and services. To an even greater degree, the law determines the shape of public institutions and their role in the political process. No sphere of life in the United States remains untouched by law.

It is therefore not surprising that law is at the center of all politics. Not only does the law affect how the political game is played, but it also is the goal of most political activity. People use politics to change or maintain a law, affect its implementation, and influence its interpretation by the courts. They focus on the law because law is an instrument of policy and a powerful agent of social control; it is a tool for compelling peo-

---

[6]Nat Hentoff, "Whatever Happened to Baby Jane Doe?" *Washington Post*, 11 December 1990, p. A23.
[7]Daryl Evans, "Cultural Law, Economic Scarcity, and the Technological Quagmire of 'Infant Doe'," *Journal of Social Issues* 49 (1993), pp. 89–113; Stephen A. Newman, "Baby Doe, Congress and the States: Challenging the Federal Treatment Standard for Impaired Infants," *American Journal of Law & Medicine* 15 (1989), pp. 1–60.

ple to obey the norms of those dominant in the political arena. This book reflects the inextricable link between law and politics: it is as much about politics as about law.[8]

SOME KEY DEFINITIONS

We first need to understand the meaning of *law, legal system, legal process, politics,* and *political process.* I use the term **law** to denote *the body of legitimately authoritative statements that have the weight of governmental power behind them.* This is what is known as a **positivist** view of the law, a term that is contrasted to a **natural law** interpretation. A natural law interpretation sees law not as the product of human (political) activities, but as a natural or divinely ordained moral order.[9] The positivist definition I use throughout this book is closely connected to the realist tradition of sociological jurisprudence, which in the United States was first most vigorously expounded by Roscoe Pound who, like many of his successors, emphasized that one needs to understand **law in action** as well as **law on the books.** Although I employ a positivist view of law here, I do not deny the enduring influence of natural law perspectives; they persistently surface in the rhetoric of litigation about diverse claims of inherent rights.

If law consists of "legitimately authoritative statements that have the weight of governmental power behind them," then it is intimately connected to **politics,** for *politics is the process by which a society makes authoritative allocations of values,* to use David Easton's terms.[10] The key word in this definition of politics is "authoritative." The allocation of values resulting from politics is not simply the product of a sale or barter in the marketplace; such values have the power of the state behind them. In modern societies in which customary law has mostly disappeared or been incorporated in legislation, almost all law is the product of a political process.

Law takes many forms, but as we employ the term in this book, it is always connected with government.[11] Laws may emanate from legislatures, and we call such laws **statutes.** Many laws in modern societies emerge from the administrative process in the form of **regulations** such as Baby Doe rules that regulate the treatment of children with severe birth defects, standards that govern the disposal of toxic waste materials, or rules that define the kinds of income that are subject to the income tax. The judicial process

[8]While hotly contested in the 1960s, this is now the conventional view of law and politics. It was first prominently expounded by Victor G. Rosenblum in 1955 in his *Law as a Political Instrument* (New York: Random House). It is also the assumption underlying Herbert Jacob, *Justice in America: Courts, Lawyers, and the Judicial Process,* 4th ed. (Boston: Little, Brown, 1984), the first edition of which appeared in 1962. For a contemporary view, see Frances Kahn Zemans, "Legal Mobilization: The Neglected Role of the Law in the Political System," *American Political Science Review* 77 (1983), pp. 690–703.
[9]For one of the most influential early statements of the positivist definition, see John Austin, *Lectures on Jurisprudence* (London: J. Murray, 1869); for an extremely influential exponent of the natural law tradition in the English and American legal history, see William Blackstone, *Commentaries on the Laws of England* (London: W. Maxwell & Son, H. Sweet, and Stevens & Sons, 1869).
[10]David Easton, *A Framework for Political Analysis* (Englewood Cliffs, N.J.: Prentice-Hall, 1965), p. 50.
[11]This definition excludes law that is based purely on custom. Compare Roberto Magabeira Unger. *Law in Modern Society* (New York: Free Press, 1976), pp. 48–58. As Victor G. Rosenblum, supra, note 6, says on page 2, "the view of law asserted here is the traditional positivist view of men like Austin, Holland, and Kelsen. Law consists of general rules of external human action subject to enforcement by the coercive authority of the State or legal order." See also Donald Black, *The Behavior of Law* (New York: Academic, 1976), p. 2.

also produces **case law** in the form of judges' decisions interpreting statutes and regulations or extending customary or **common law.**[12]

All of the institutions, private as well as public, involved in making law, interpreting it, or implementing it constitute the **legal system** of the United States. Just as **political process** refers to partisan activities and relationships surrounding the making, implementation, and interpretation of policies that authoritatively allocate values by the institutions of the political system, the **legal process** denotes the actions, both private and public, that result in the adoption, change, repeal, maintenance, or implementation of law.

Such activities do more than simply satisfy the demands of persons with specific interests who articulate their demands and flex their muscles sufficiently to persuade legislators and executive officials. The enactment, interpretation, and implementation of laws also have a profound effect on maintaining order. In the United States, the duty of government to maintain order is given high priority, as reflected in the preamble to the Constitution, which speaks not only of forming "a more perfect union" and establishing justice, but also of ensuring "domestic tranquility." The legal system, with its laws and courts, is the primary instrument used by the political process to impose social control.

The political and legal processes overlap; they are not neatly set apart as distinct entities. Both involve actions in legislatures, administrative agencies, and courts. For example, the statutes governing the payment of federal income taxes are part of the body of law as well as a product of the political process in Congress; the Internal Revenue Service is both part of the government, subject to political pressures, and part of the legal institutions implementing the tax code. There are, however, significant differences between the legal and political processes. In debates over tax reform, for example, the political process reacts mainly to elections, interest group pressures, and partisan policy preferences. The legal process responds to both specific disputes involving interpretation of the tax laws Congress has adopted and arguments about what the lawmakers intended and what the law says on its face. While political parties and elections are central elements of the political process in the United States, they are peripheral to the legal process. On the other hand, lawyers' activities are central to the legal process, but only marginal to the political process.

These terms—*law, legal system, legal process, politics,* and *political process*—are used constantly in this book, for they define its core. To begin our analysis of law and politics in the United States we need to explore the boundaries of these concepts.

The Law

The law, as we view it in this book, is the product of people working to create, abolish, implement, or interpret authoritative rules that have the force of governmental sanctions behind them. Much social science research on law focuses on how people sculpt the law to their own advantage, and it is tempting to think of the law as solely the prod-

[12]As Chapter 2 explains, not all laws have equal standing. Law embodied in a constitution is given more weight than statutory law, and statutory law is given more weight than administrative regulations. But this should not blind us to the fact that all three kinds of authoritative statements are forms of law.

uct of these efforts. Such a view would be a mistake, however, for the law has an inertia and logic of its own, inculcated by the training that all the legal professionals share and that affects the work of the legal system.

One element of this inertial force of the law may be illustrated by the manner in which the rape of a woman by her husband was treated by the law until recently. Until the early 1980s, spousal rape was a contradiction in legal terms. Under the traditional family law that all lawyers learned, the wife had a duty to agree to sexual intercourse with her husband; she had no right to refuse. If the husband used force, he was only taking what was his by right. Such a view of marital relations reflected an older, patriarchal concept of marriage and made it impossible to apply the criminal law of rape to husbands. However, by the late 1980s both social understandings and the law had changed. A married woman was no longer considered her husband's property or subordinate to him. Domestic sexual abuse had come out of the closet, and many states changed the definition of sex offenses in their criminal codes. Thus, as legal concepts changed, marital rape went from a contradiction in terms (an oxymoron) to a punishable offense.[13]

The logic of the law is another of its traits and is rooted in its very careful use of language, so careful that it appears arcane to the uninitiated.[14] This is why experts argue that a law should not be changed without careful drafting and attention to the consequences the change may have for other statutes. Words have special meanings for lawyers and judges, which, if neglected, could lead to unintended interpretations of the law. Lawyers are accustomed to close reasoning and will apply it even to a loosely drafted law. These characteristics, while not preventing all changes in the law, do force those who would alter it to bend their will to existing law. Under ordinary circumstances, they make legal change a slow and very incremental process.

The inertial characteristics of the law, which we explore more fully in Chapter 2, are reinforced by the fact that most important positions in the legal system are held by lawyers who are committed to the law as an autonomous structure of intellectual concepts. Lawyers in the United States are the product of three years of formal schooling in these concepts, and they have an enormous intellectual and emotional investment in law. Throughout their careers, attorneys' formulations of the law are continuously reinforced by professional reading, contacts, and activities.

In addition, law has a mystique, reinforced by mystifying rituals, which sets it apart from "mere" politics. More than just words on a piece of paper, the law represents the collective will of the state or nation. It simultaneously appeals to a person's sense of civic obligation and threatens serious punishment if violated. It sometimes seems to have roots in a distant past that is only dimly understood. Its expression in arcane lan-

---

[13]Jean Grossholtz, "Battered Women's Shelters and the Political Economy of Sexual Violence," in Irene Diamond (ed.), *Families, Politics and Public Policy: A Feminist Dialogue on Women and the State* (New York: Longman, 1983), pp. 59–69; Kathleen Barry, *Female Sexual Slavery* (New York: New York University Press, 1984); Allen Houston, "Spousal Rape: In More and More States, Serious Discussion of Once Unthinkable Laws," *Los Angeles Daily Journal*, 25 September 1984. Donald Brieland and John Allen Lemmon report in *Social Work and the Law*, 2d ed. (St. Paul: West Publishing, 1985), p. 238, that by 1985 only nine states still gave husbands complete immunity in alleged marital rape incidents.
[14]Lief H. Carter, *Reason in Law*, 4th ed. (New York: HarperCollins, 1993), pp. 84–96.

guage adds to its mystery. To many people the law represents a moral order that serves to teach and otherwise induce correct behavior. None of this prevents many people from viewing specific laws cynically or from making elaborate attempts to evade their impact. Yet while some may place little value on particular laws, the concept of law is usually regarded with exaggerated respect.

Attitudes toward law constitute an important dimension of what is often termed the **legal culture.**[15] Legal culture emcompasss the attitudes, habits, and shared values that pervade the manner in which people use and interpret formal law. An example of legal culture is the emphasis on social harmony, found both among American Amish communities and in Japan, which leads to a reluctance to litigate.[16] Another example is how criminal court officials in different communities in the United States have different perceptions of what is an appropriate punishment; those perceptions of "going rates" then color interpretations of the criminal code and affect the behavior of all participants in the prosecution of offenders.[17] Likewise, the frequency with which Americans take their disputes to court appears to be partially the result of attitudes and habits that are widely shared among aggrieved persons and attorneys; Robert Kagan calls this "adversarial legalism."[18] Some scholars scoff at the use of culture to explain how legal systems operate because it is very difficult to specify its effect; its use sometimes seems simply to be a catchall for everything not yet explained by other factors.[19] Nevertheless, the concept continues to be used because it refers to significant variations in the ways in which people perceive, interpret, and invoke law.

The Legal System

The term **legal system** pertains to the relationships between institutions that produce, implement, and interpret the law, the gatekeepers to those institutions, and those who wish to use the law. It includes not only the entire array of governmental institutions but also the social structures surrounding them and the social, economic, and political forces impinging on them. It includes much more than courts or even "the state." We may clarify the abstraction by separating it into its several components. Let us think of

[15]Lawrence M. Friedman, *The Legal System: A Social Science Perspective* (New York: Russell Sage Foundation, 1975).

[16]Robert L. Kidder and John A. Hostetler, "Managing Ideologies: Harmony as Ideology in Amish and Japanese Societies," *Law & Society Review* 24 (1990) pp. 895–922.

[17]James Eisenstein, Roy B. Flemming, and Peter Nardulli, *The Contours of Justice: Communities and Their Courts* (Boston: Little, Brown, 1987).

[18]Robert A. Kagan, "Do Lawyers Cause Adversarial Legalism? A Preliminary Inquiry." Paper prepared for annual meetings of the Law & Society Association, Chicago, May 27–30, 1993.

[19]Herbert M. Kritzer and Frances Kahn Zemans, "Local Legal Culture and the Control of Litigation," *Law & Society Review* 27 (1993), pp. 535–558.

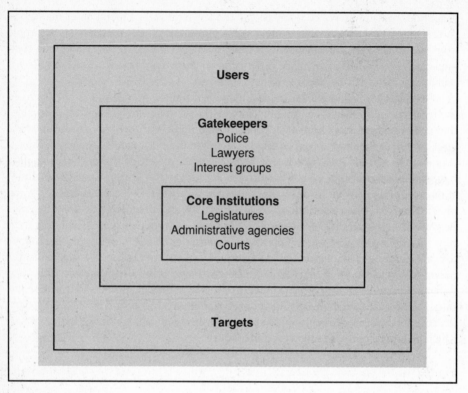

Figure 1.1
The Legal System

them as being arranged in three concentric rings, as in Figure 1.1. The outer ring consists of **users and targets** of the legal system. Here we find users such as litigants and disputants and targets of legal activity such as victims and offenders. The middle ring consists of the principal **gatekeepers**—attorneys, police, and interest groups. Finally, at the center stand **core institutions**—legislatures, administrative agencies, and courts—in which laws are produced, implemented, and interpreted. Each ring is affected by social, economic, and political forces, but the relative strengths of these forces varies.

THE OUTER RING

The outer ring of the legal system is composed of disputants, litigants, victims of crime, and criminal offenders. They either invoke the law for their own benefit or have it invoked against them. For the majority, law is an occasional tool or experience; they live under the shadow of the law without being aware of its impact.

Relatively few actions of those in the outer ring of the American legal system are politically motivated. Individual circumstances rooted in social and economic conditions generate most of the disputes that eventually become claims to administrative agencies or cases before a court. Similarly, most crimes are not political but stem from private motivations spawned by social, economic, or psychological conditions. Only one segment of this outer circle is closely connected with the political arena: those who make demands to legislators and other elected officials for a change in the law. Although an integral part of the political process, these demands also are largely generated by social and economic conditions rather than by partisan affiliation.

Yet, although disputes stem from private motivations that are rooted in social and economic conditions, the fact that people turn to law and courts has some political significance.[20] Their mobilization of law is a resort to governmental rather than private means of redressing grievances; when they go to court, they use a government facility, bare their secret grudges in a public forum, and subject themselves to the governmental authority of the judge. Disputants who resort to law and courts also bring expectations to this public arena. In the United States, there is considerable evidence that they expect to have a chance to air their grievances and be heard by a disinterested judge. In short, they expect to be treated fairly.[21] Most disputants know that when they go to court, they go to a branch of government; their individual experiences in court are one of many ways by which they come to evaluate the fairness and legitimacy of their government. Those evaluations do not usually lead directly to decisions at the ballot box, but they are part of what defines the political sphere in the United States.

THE MIDDLE RING OF GATEKEEPERS

The middle ring of the legal system consists of lawyers, police, and interest groups—the gatekeepers to the inner circle of institutions. They either help people use the law or apply it to others. Sometimes they establish barriers that keep certain individuals from employing the law. Gatekeepers are affected both by the political process and by social and economic forces. The police and interest groups are more influenced by politics; the bar is more affected by social and economic circumstances.

The police are the gatekeepers of the criminal courts; they apply the law to those they perceive as lawbreakers. Almost no one in the United States is sent to court on a criminal complaint unless the police initiate the case. Although not highly trained in the law, police must constantly apply it to concrete situations. When cruising on the highway and enforcing a speed limit of 65 miles per hour, they must decide whether to issue a summons to a driver who exceeds the limit by only 2 miles per hour or whether to reserve that sanction to drivers who exceed it by 5 or 10 miles per hour. Likewise, when called to a disturbance, they must decide whether the behavior of those at the scene warrants a warning or an arrest, and if an arrest, whether the offenders should be arrested for the trivial offense of disturbing the peace or for a more serious offense, such as assault. Because of their heavy reliance on legal sanctions, the police are known as law enforcement officers.

---

[20]Zemans, supra, note 8.
[21]Tom R. Tyler, "What Is Procedural Justice? Criteria Used by Citizens to Assess the Fairness of Legal Procedures," *Law & Society Review 22* (1988), pp. 103–136; Tom R. Tyler, *Why People Obey the Law* (New Haven: Yale University Press, 1990).

The police are themselves an administrative agency that in most localities works under the supervision of the mayor. In many cities, the position of police chief is one of the most sensitive offices in local government and one that is often drawn into the political maelstrom. An incumbent police chief is often routinely fired and a replacement hired when a new mayor takes office.[22] The police are also under political pressure to achieve results, be it in the form of reducing reported crime, controlling vice, or facilitating the flow of traffic. The size of the police budget and police officers' wages are often subject to political negotiation by an elected city council. These circumstances dictate a close relationship between policing and politics. When things go wrong, many people blame elected officials; when citizens are satisfied with the police, elected officials take the credit.

In addition, social and economic conditions clearly impinge on police work. The social structure of neighborhoods largely determines the amount of crime, and the lifestyle of a city's population influences the types of offenses to which police must be sensitive.[23] Moreover, a city's economic resources have a large impact on police budgets; in poor cities such as Newark, New Jersey, the police are likely to feel fiscal constraints much more severely than in relatively affluent areas such as San Jose, California, or Phoenix, Arizona.[24]

The legal profession performs the same kind of gatekeeping functions for civil cases as the police do for criminal cases. Except for very minor civil cases, almost no one takes a case to court in the United States without having consulted a lawyer or being represented by one. Many other activities that involve the law—such as the formulation of contracts and wills and the negotiation of damages arising from accidents—are performed in the United States with the help of lawyers. Although some lawyers engage in real estate, insurance, or other businesses, the law is the core of most attorneys' work.

Because most lawyers in the United States are in private practice, politics generally plays a small role in their work. Most private attorneys take cases when it is profitable; as long as a fee is available, they are as likely to be on one side of a controversy as on the other. There are important exceptions, however, as the Baby Doe case illustrates. The charges against Baby Doe's parents and hospital were financed by a politically oriented group, and the federal government's lawyers became involved because the issue fit the Reagan administration's political agenda. Such blatant political motivations by attorneys are, however, relatively rare.

On the other hand, lawyers' work is very much affected by the social and economic structure. As we discuss in Chapter 6, the ways in which lawyers organize their work, the services they offer and perform, and the fees they charge all are directly affected by social and economic conditions.

A third significant type of gatekeeper to the legal system is the interest group. Unlike the police and lawyers, who mostly work with courts, interest groups primarily help

[22]Herbert Jacob, *The Frustration of Policy: Response to Crime by American Cities* (Boston: Little, Brown, 1984), pp. 96–100.

[23]James Q. Wilson, *Varieties of Police Behavior: The Management of Law and Order in Eight Communities* (Cambridge, Mass.: Harvard University Press, 1968).

[24]Anne M. Heinz, Herbert Jacob, and Robert L. Lineberry (eds.), *Crime in City Politics* (New York: Longman, 1983), pp. 23–96, 193–280.

others obtain access to legislatures and administrative agencies.[25] It is very difficult for ordinary citizens, for instance, to be informed about the agenda of legislative enactments or administrative rules that might affect them. Such information is, however, routinely published in the *Congressional Record* for Congress, in the *Federal Register* for federal agencies, and in parallel publications at the state level. Interest groups have the resources to screen those publications and to alert their membership when their concerns might be involved. In addition, interest groups assist members in contacting the appropriate official for help in using a government program or invoking a benefit to which they may be entitled. Interest groups also help litigants use the courts, as we discuss in Chapter 7. All these interest group activities involve a rich blend of law and politics, with politics being the more prominent element.

Social and economic forces also influence interest group activities. Usually only those with resources are able to organize into interest groups. Direct, and chiefly economic, goals motivate most individuals and corporations to join interest groups.[26] The social structure of the United States and its free market economy have been particularly accommodating to the organization of interest groups.

THE INNER RING OF CORE INSTITUTIONS

The institutions constituting the inner ring of the legal system—legislatures, administrative agencies, and courts—are its most visible arenas. Both law and politics lie at their heart. Law is the principal product of legislatures. They pass laws to establish new agencies and to regulate existing ones. They enact laws to authorize agencies to provide public services, to permit expenditures to pay for them, and to assess taxes, which the public in turn pays to the government. All these laws must be explicitly adopted by legislatures, and many need to be reviewed periodically, sometimes every year. As politicians, legislators respond easily to partisan appeals, but in the United States party affiliation plays only a small role in their decisions to support legislative proposals. Legislators in the United States are almost never mere agents of party organizations. They are accustomed to dealing independently with the special concerns of interest groups. Because an elected official's responsiveness to constituents includes accountability to such groups, every law has its roots in politics. The other tasks that legislators perform are also closely related to their lawmaking function. The services they provide constituents, for example, usually concern the implementation of laws and regulations. Constituents often seek the help of legislators in dealing with administrative agencies in the belief that legislators have clout because they control the law that authorizes and pays for the administrators' work. Thus, politics infuses almost every aspect of a legislature's work. Legislators vote on laws according to their estimates of how their actions will affect their chances in the next election.

Although legislators in the United States are primarily politicians who need to win reelection, they also develop technical expertise in many fields and employ specialists

[25]Jeffrey M. Berry, *The Interest Group Society* (Boston: Little, Brown, 1984); David B. Truman, *The Governmental Process* (New York: Knopf, 1951).
[26]Mancur Olson, *The Logic Of Collective Action: Public Goods and the Theory of Groups* (New York: Schocken, 1970).

in many areas as staff assistants, including lawyers. The legal specialists in legislatures often share the policy biases of their employers, but they also bring a technical expertise about law to the task of legislation. They know how particular words and phrases have been interpreted by courts and how they can convey the intention of the legislature in the text of a statute. We examine this core institution more fully in Chapter 11.

The work of administrative agencies also revolves around the law; politics is a less visible but nevertheless important partner. Law is paramount to public administration because a central tenet of the American governmental system is that public agencies can do only what the law authorizes. The law governs agency procedures, and agencies in turn often enact their own regulations pursuant to the law. It is no accident that lawyers play a prominent role in American public administration. They are prominent because law is central to agency work. Public administration, however, is more than just law, for politics also plays an important role. Most administrative agencies are accountable to an executive who is elected—the president, a governor, or some other elected official. While bureaucrats are not themselves elected, they are expected to be sensitive to the needs of their superiors who do face the electorate. Moreover, they are aware that their appropriations come from a legislature that is sensitive to political forces. Bureaucrats know that their agency may be altered or abolished if it fails to satisfy the public. Like legislators, administrators are accustomed to working with interest group representatives who provide technical information in exchange for at least a hearing of their concerns and who may generate political support for their programs. Political motives are often better disguised in the work of administrative agencies than in the legislative process, but they often lie just beneath the veneer of professional behavior. City officials, for example, are fond of saying that there is no Republican or Democratic way to pave streets but only engineering specifications. However, when one looks to see who wins street pavement contracts and whose streets are paved first, one often finds that those with clout are favored.

It is, however, true that the norms and methods of particular technologies exercise considerable influence on administrative activities. One cannot understand the Public Health Service without knowing it is composed of medical doctors or the Department of Agriculture without realizing it employs many agronomists. That is because doctors, agronomists, and other professionals base their decisions on their expertise as well as on political considerations. Their training and pressure from fellow professionals often force them to consider evidence in ways foreign to politicians, as, for instance, when scientists examine the statistical evidence relating to the cancer-producing effects of a chemical. When the bureaucrats of the Department of Health and Human Services formulated their regulations concerning medical care of severely handicapped infants, they wrote with the technical understanding of physicians. But the political preferences of the Reagan administration were the motivating factor in those administrative decisions. Likewise, reflecting the preferences of their political masters, the managers of federal land in the Clinton administration sought to raise grazing fees for ranchers using federal lands, in sharp contrast to the policies of the Reagan and Bush administrations. However, in each case, the regulations had to be drafted in the language of the law and had to fit into the legal framework of authority granted to the agency. We examine this core institution more fully in Chapter 12.

The law is most prominent in the work of courts. All levels of courts are fixated on the law. Like administrative agencies, courts apply the law in their daily work. Like legislatures and administrative agencies, they sometimes make new law in the course of interpreting the old. Also like legislatures and administrative agencies, courts issue regulations—within the boundaries allowed by statutes and the Constitution—that have the force of law. Although courts are not nearly as openly partisan or politically sensitive as legislatures or even administrative agencies, they are by no means insulated from the political arena. Politics, for example, plays a large role in the selection of most judges. Just as Franklin Delano Roosevelt tried to appoint judges who would not hinder the implementation of his New Deal, so Ronald Reagan and George Bush appointed judges who would favor the conservative policies of their administrations. The more prominent the judge's position, the more visible the role that politics plays; political pressures are much more evident in the selection of a U.S. Supreme Court justice, for example, than of a federal district judge. In addition, the jurisdiction of both federal and state courts is subject to change by the legislature, and judges' salaries and the quality of their facilities depend on legislative approval. Chapters 8–10 analyze the role of courts as core institutions.

Thus, both law and politics pervade the work of each of the three core institutions of the legal system. However, by saying that politics affects these institutions we mean to indicate more than the force of elections or party activities. The term *politics* includes the entire range of activities that produces the authoritative allocations of values.

In the United States, many of these activities are split into myriad pieces. The fragmentation of politics across the three levels of government—federal state, and local—splinters the political process in ways that fundamentally affect the legal system, for each level has its own core institutions responding to its own constituencies. Moreover, within each level, politics is fragmented among the core institutions because the principle of separation of powers has guided the design of government throughout the nation. Each of the core institutions in turn is fragmented into many pieces. On the federal level, for example, there are two houses of Congress, each with dozens of committees in which many important decisions are made. And while the president is chief executive, hundreds of agencies, which he nominally supervises, often act quite independently. The political forces underlying the making, implementation, and interpretation of law are consequently often a confusing swirl of activities.

While the political arena has a powerful effect on the inner ring of the legal system, social and economic forces have a less direct impact. That is not to say that the inner ring is impervious to social and economic forces. Social and economic structures, for instance, create biases that affect the selection of high-level officials. Economic status affects the opportunity costs that attract or repel aspirants to certain positions in the core institutions; social status constructs "old boy" networks that consistently bring Wall Street lawyers and bankers and Ivy League professors into positions of prominence in Washington. In addition, both social and economic circumstances generate disputes and conflicts that force their way onto legislative, administrative, or judicial agendas and impose resource constraints on possible solutions. But for the most part, these ef-

	Law	Politics	Social & Economic Forces
Inner ring (Core institutions)	+++	++	+
Middle ring (Gatekeepers)	++	++	++
Outer Ring (Users)	+	+	+++

+, some influence; ++, moderate influence; +++, great influence

Figure 1.2
Patterns of Influence on the Three Rings of the Legal System

fects are felt indirectly because social and economic forces are mediated by the political process before they cause legislatures, agencies, or courts to change the law.

SUMMARY

Figure 1.2 shows the three segments of the legal system and the different degrees of influence from the political, social, and economic arenas to which they are subjected. For the inner ring of core institutions, law plays a very large and direct role and, together with politics, often controls the outcome, while social and economic forces set the context. The force of the two sets of factors is reversed for the outer ring: social and economic forces dominate, while political forces and the law are less immediately important. Politics, social and economic forces, and the law play roughly equal roles in the middle ring of gatekeeping institutions. Although these relationships constitute the dominant patterns of influence, variations do occur. For instance, although most litigants are not immediately responsive to political forces, this is not true when governmental agencies are litigants; they often use the law and enter the courtroom out of political motivations. Likewise, although the legal profession is molded mostly by economic and social forces, it sometimes involves itself directly in the political arena to defend a particular program, such as legal services for the poor. But such cases, although interesting, represent a deviation from the general pattern.

The Legal Process

The **legal process** consists of the activities and procedures by which people adopt, change, abolish, maintain, or implement the law. Lawyers are accustomed to thinking of the legal process purely in terms of what happens in court. Although this is an important part of the legal process, it is only one element.

Very special procedures set court proceedings apart from actions in most other arenas of the legal system. Court actions are typically adversarial in the United States, usually involving two opposing parties. The **adversarial process** seeks to uncover the truth through the presentation of conflicting claims. Lawyers, not judges, are in charge of presenting evidence; most trials depend on oral testimony rather than documentary evidence. Court proceedings consequently pay great heed to the conditions that should promote full disclosure of the facts and correct application of the law. The result is a highly developed set of rules governing evidence and judicial decision making, which we explore in later chapters. Nowhere else in the legal system are those rules so explicitly and fully developed.

However, the legal process involves more than making and applying law in the courts. Most law is *not* made in the courts but in legislatures; likewise, most law is *not* interpreted or applied in courts but, rather, in administrative agencies. Special procedures mark the work of these institutions just as they do that of the courts. The legislative process is full of public ceremony and complex rules designed to fulfill many purposes, the most important being the assurance of the legitimacy of the laws they produce. Administrative agencies must also follow special rules in their work; although they resemble private bureaucracies in many ways, the procedures of public agencies are often quite different. For example, while the management of a computer company can simply decide one morning to decrease the price of its personal computers by $200 without public notice or public hearings, the Secretary of the Interior cannot tell the Bureau of Land Management to change the price of public land leases without going through elaborate procedures.

The procedures that mark the legal process are not empty rituals. Intended to assure the public that the results are fair and just, these procedures are important in legitimizing law's claim to obedience. However, they are neither politically neutral nor do they give access to the legal system evenhandedly. The intended beneficiaries of many such rules are often obscured by their long history, but each rule tends to benefit one disputant or segment of society. For instance, rules mandating that a jury have twelve members make a judgment of guilt less likely than rules calling for a jury of only six; the rule of twelve safeguards against mistaken verdicts of guilty.[27] Similarly, the complexity of many legal procedures favors those who can hire a lawyer and makes specialized at-

---

[27]Hans Zeisel and Shari Diamond, "Convincing Empirical Evidence on the Six Member Jury," *University of Chicago Law Review 41* (1974), pp. 281–295; Peter W. Sperlich, ". . . And Then There Were Six: The Decline of the American Jury," *Judicature 63* (December–January 1980), pp. 262–279; Reid Hastie, Steven D. Penrod, and Nancy Pennington, *Inside the Jury* (Cambridge, Mass.: Harvard University Press, 1983).

torneys more effective than generalists. The rules themselves are therefore sometimes the object of political controversy. It is not surprising that the advocates of six-person juries are persons who hope for sterner administration of criminal laws and that advocates of simpler legal procedures are often representatives of those who cannot afford legal fees. At other times, the rules explicitly link the legal process with the political arena, as in the rules administered by the Federal Election Commission governing campaign financing. We explore these links in detail in later chapters.

Outline of What Follows

In the next chapter we explore in depth some of the peculiar characteristics of law in general and of American law in particular. That sets the stage for our examination in later chapters of the outer ring of the legal system—the persons and disputes that bring the law into action. We then examine the middle ring of the system, the gatekeepers, with chapters on the police, lawyers, and interest groups. This material allows us to investigate the inner ring of the legal system; in subsequent chapters we examine the judicial, legislative, and administrative institutions in which law is formulated, implemented, and interpreted. In the final part of the book, we address how all these segments of the legal system interact and how the legal system is constrained by both internal and external limits.

KEY DEFINITIONS

Law: Legitimately authoritative statements that have the weight of governmental power behind them.
Legal System: The relationships between the institutions that produce, implement, and interpret law (legislatures, administrative agencies, and courts), the gatekeepers to those institutions, and those who wish to use the law.
Legal Process: The activities and procedures that produce, implement, or interpret law.
Politics: The process by which a society makes authoritative allocations of values.
Political Process: The partisan activities surrounding the making, implementation, and interpretation of law and the authoritative allocation of values.

KEY WORDS

law	common law
positivist	legal system
natural law	political process
law in action	legal process
law on the books	legal culture
politics	users and targets
statutes	gatekeepers
regulations	core institutions
case law	adversarial process

FOR FURTHER STUDY . . .

A treatment of some of the issues discussed in this chapter is found in Lawrence M. Friedman, *Law and Society: An Introduction* (Englewood Cliffs, N.J.: Prentice-Hall 1977).

Two case studies that illustrate the many links between law and the political arena are Gerald M. Stern, *The Buffalo Creek Disaster* (New York: Vintage Books, 1976) and Richard B. Sobol, *Bending the Law: The Story of the Dalkon Shield Bankruptcy* (Chicago: University of Chicago Press, 1991).

2
THE LAW

Law is much richer than our definition—"the body of legitimately authoritative statements that have the weight of governmental power behind them"—implies. It is a many-layered concept whose complex texture must be unraveled if we are to understand the ways in which law is used in the United States. This chapter dissects the law to expose its social, economic, and political roots. We need, however, to remain aware of two levels of analysis. The first is abstract and illustrates the law's general characteristics. The second is concrete and anchors the law in specific social, economic, and political circumstances. These two levels of analysis parallel an important distinction that those who study the law recognize: the distinction between law as it is written and the living law. The law on the books is abstract and general, and it often appears deceptively clear and unambiguous. The living law reflects the intricate complexity of actual affairs and is full of equivocation and ambiguity.

Let us begin with a concrete example. As every fan of cops-and-robbers television dramas knows, when the police make an arrest, they mumble a formula known as the **Miranda warning** to the suspect. This warning comes from a 1966 decision by the U.S. Supreme Court[1] in which the Court confronted the chasm separating the buzzing complexity of police work and the spare words of the Fifth and Sixth Amendments to the Constitution. Those sections of the Bill of Rights guarantee every American the right to due process under the law, the right to refuse to incriminate themselves, and the right to legal counsel. When the police made an arrest, however, those rights often had little meaning. Under the implied or actual threat of being beaten, some prisoners confessed to crimes they had not committed. Others confessed without realizing they had certain constitutional rights. Few were told of their rights to remain silent or to consult an attorney. Ernest Miranda had been in such a situation. He was arrested in Phoenix, Arizona, on a rape charge and confessed while in custody.[2] The prosecution introduced

[1]*Miranda v. Arizona*, 348 U.S. 436 (1966).
[2]Liva Baker, Miranda: *Crime, Law and Politics* (New York: Atheneum, 1983).

his confession at his trial and it had a substantial impact on its outcome. Miranda had obtained an attorney not on arrest, but only later, when he faced trial. The Arizona trial court considered his attorney's argument that Miranda's confession was illegal, but it saw nothing unusual about the circumstances under which the police had obtained it and declared that it met the standards of voluntariness as defined by the state's criminal procedure statutes. Miranda was convicted, and his conviction was upheld by Arizona's appeals courts.

The U.S. Supreme Court saw the case differently. Having decided just two years earlier that a suspect's request for an attorney before being questioned by the police had to be honored,[3] the Court decided that the only difference in Miranda's case was that he had apparently not known to ask for a lawyer. To the majority of justices (a bare five to four majority), that seemed to violate the Bill of Rights' guarantees. Therefore, they declared, police officers must not merely comply with a suspect's request for an attorney when such a request is made, but they must also inform suspects of their constitutional rights to remain silent and to obtain counsel. Furthermore, suspects would need to be told that an attorney would be supplied free of charge if they did not have sufficient funds to hire one. As a consequence, police departments across the country devised warnings for their officers to recite to suspects and issued administrative regulations requiring the officers to deliver these warnings. Almost all officers in the United States now carry the warning on a plastic card in their pockets, which they read when making an arrest.

The Supreme Court's *Miranda* decision moved the law on the books and the living law a little closer together. However, police officers for many years complained about the complexity of the law that now confronted them. We cannot yet be certain that all confessions are truly voluntary and uncoerced, but the law contains procedural standards against which voluntariness can be measured. We now are ready to unravel the many strands of law that compose the *Miranda* warning.

An Abstract Definition of Law

We begin by reexamining and elaborating the definition of law provided in Chapter 1, namely that law is the set of legitimately authoritative rules emanating from government officials.[4] This definition implies a number of important characteristics of law.

1. *Only legitimate rules are considered to be law.* Legitimacy produces obligation. People must perceive that they ought to obey the law. In the United States, **legitimacy** is usually the product of fulfilling two requirements. The first is that law be produced by procedures that are considered legitimate because they follow established rules which themselves are considered fair. A statement made by a legislative minority is not considered law, because the prescribed procedure requires that laws be passed by a majority or plurality of legislative votes. Likewise, a statement by the president at a press conference does not have the force of law, because it has not met the requirements for issuing

---

[3]*Escobedo v. Illinois*, 378 U.S. 478 (1964).
[4]Alternative definitions of law are discussed by Jack P. Gibbs, "Definitions of Law and Empirical Questions," *Law & Society Review 2* (1968), pp. 429–446.

Model Miranda Warning

You are under arrest. Before we ask you any questions, you must understand what your rights are.

You have the right to remain silent. You are not required to say anything to us at any time or to answer any questions. Anything you say can be used against you in court.

You have the right to talk to a lawyer for advice before we question you and to have him with you during questioning.

If you cannot afford a lawyer and want one, a lawyer will be provided for you. If you want to answer questions now without a lawyer present you will still have the right to stop answering at any time. You also have the right to stop answering at any time until you talk to a lawyer.

WAIVER

1. Have you read or had read to you the warning as to your rights? _____
2. Do you understand these rights? _____
3. Do you wish to answer any questions? _____
4. Are you willing to answer questions without having an attorney present? _____

5. Signature of defendant on line below.
_____

6. Time _____ Date _____
7. Signature of officer _____
8. Signature of witness _____

Source: U.S. Department of Justice, Law Enforcement Assistance Administration, *The D.C. Public Defender Service, Vol. II: Training Materials* (Washington, D.C.: Government Printing Office, 1975), p. 58.

an executive order, such as prior notice in the *Federal Register,* where the federal government publishes legally binding administrative regulations. However, when the president issues an executive order that meets the prescribed procedural requirements, it has the same force as a congressional statute. Prescribed procedures, such as elections and the taking of an oath of office, must be used to empower officials to make laws. Thus, if a bus driver tells a passenger that he is under arrest and the passenger flees, no law has been broken by the passenger because bus drivers have not been given the power to arrest. But if the passenger flees from an arrest by a police officer, the law has been violated because the police are "sworn" officers who have been empowered to issue legally binding orders.

The second requirement for legitimacy is that law must reflect the conception of fairness and justice that is dominant in a society. Social psychologists studying perceptions of procedural justice suggest six essential components: (1) an ability to affect the decision-making process; (2) equal treatment; (3) an absence of bias; (4) the use of procedures that minimize errors; (5) the presence of procedures for correcting mistakes; and (6) a high correlation between the rule and general standards of morality and ethics.[5] It remains unclear how much compliance with these requirements is needed to make law legitimate, but the absence of many of these elements seriously erodes perceptions that a rule is binding.

These requirements are much looser than procedural regularity because it is much more difficult to point unmistakably to such things as equality of treatment, lack of bias, or coincidence with general standards of fairness. In many instances, there are conflicting assertions about what is fair or just. The legitimacy of the *Miranda* warning, for example, has remained controversial. It seems legitimate to many people who believe that the police violated common standards of fairness when they took advantage of the shock of arrest and fear of beatings to extract a confession. However, many others consider the rule illegitimate because it was announced by the Supreme Court rather than by Congress, and they had no voice in the making of the rule. This controversy parallels the opposition of many young men during the 1960s to the military draft that threatened to send them to fight what they considered an unjust and illegitimate war in Vietnam, in part because Congress had never declared war. When Congress adopted a law that made the destruction of draft cards a criminal act, some people defiantly burned their cards because they thought the law violated common standards of morality and therefore was illegitimate.

Rules that are considered unfair or unjust, and therefore not binding, invite civil disobedience. When large portions of the population defy such laws, they often are simply no longer enforced. That has been the fate of the so-called blue laws that prohibit businesses and places of entertainment from operating on Sundays. They are ignored by store owners, patrons, and the police alike and have lost their status as living law, although they remain on the books in some places. Similarly, the Eighteenth Amendment to the Constitution, which prohibited the manufacture, sale, or transportation of alcoholic beverages, was ignored by thousands of people before it was eventually repealed.

2. Laws are authoritative rules backed by the force of the State. Brute force lies at the end of the legal process that begins with a written rule, runs through the courts, and is finally enforced by a police officer armed with a pistol. Those who violate the law may be punished by loss of property or liberty. Most people voluntarily comply before such sanctions are imposed because most consider laws to be legitimate. However, it is always difficult to distinguish between compliance based on conscience and compliance based on fear of punishment. The potential for punishment is an essential element of law.

Concern about the **use of force** permeates much of the legal process. Perceptions about the legitimacy of legal procedures hinge on whether decisions to apply force were made fairly. Thus, a police officer may not lawfully shoot a suspect unless the suspect threatens the officer, or flees; the police are not to be judge, jury, and executioner. Even

---

[5]G. S. Leventhal, "What Should Be Done with Equity Theory?" in K. J. Gergen, M. S. Greenberg, and R. H. Weiss (eds.), *Social Exchange: Advances in Theory and Research* (New York: Plenum, 1980), pp. 27–55; Tom R. Tyler, *Why People Obey the Law* (New Haven: Yale University Press, 1990), pp. 115–124.

when offenders plead guilty in a court, judges insist on elaborate rituals to legitimize the impending use of force by requiring a statement in open court from the defendant that the guilty plea is voluntary, that it represents the truth, and that it is made knowing the consequences. Absent a guilty plea, U.S. criminal law requires the prosecution to prove the defendant's wrongdoing beyond a reasonable doubt. If sanctions were less awesome, the legal system would not need to spend so much attention on these elaborate safeguards.

Many of the characteristics of law described above apply to the rules of many private institutions as well as those of the State. Indeed, we sometimes speak of the law of the church, the union, or the professional association. Such "laws" also depend on perceptions of legitimacy. Like state laws, they provide for private sanctions such as excommunication, the loss of a job, or expulsion from a profession. However, the sanctions imposed by the laws of the State are more pervasive. One can resign from a private organization, stop attending a church, or find a new employer and thus escape private "laws" that seem oppressive. Short of exile, it is impossible to escape the reach of the State's laws.

3. *Laws are* **prescriptive statements**. Laws deal with what should be rather than with what is. They prescribe desired modes of behavior. They prohibit certain actions that are considered so destructive of social solidarity as to be classified as criminal. They require other activities, such as paying taxes or expending monies, to provide collective goods, such as a military defense, which cannot be otherwise attained in a society. Still other rules prescribe desired behavior of persons occupying public positions, such as members of Congress, judges, or the president; they lay down the procedures officials must follow in their public actions.

Law is thus always closely connected to a vision of how society should be structured; it always reflects moral as well as political values and goals. It is explicitly normative. Its normative character always places law in a perilous position because it runs the risk that a substantial portion of the population to which it applies does not agree with its values. That is the crux of the debate about abortion. The conflict is about whether the law should permit it, reflecting values that privilege the woman's life, or prohibit it, reflecting values that privilege the fetus's potential. Because law is normative, it also seeks to educate and persuade so that a consensus, which is absent from the abortion question, can be built or buttressed. Without a consensus on values, law has only brittle support.

The need for consensus buttresses the link between politics and law. The political process involves building support, creating coalitions, and developing consensus. The more democratic the political regime, the wider the consensus-building process must reach. Thus, the law of the State is rooted in politics; it expresses the policy objectives of the governing coalition and is the product of compromises required to build or sustain a consensus.

4. *Law is always* **allocative**. Because laws prescribe behavior, they always allocate important values in a society, some of which are symbolic some, material. Laws honor some people, such as judges for whom all must rise when they enter the courtroom; and strips respect from others by prescribing demeaning punishment. The law allocates ma-

terial values when it requires the expenditure of funds for the benefit of particular persons. Often the allocative function of laws is indirect; it gives some people an advantage in obtaining access to resources, as with the award of a franchise or a monopoly, or it facilitates efforts to obtain resources, as when it creates procedures for enforcing obligations and collecting debts.

The allocative character of law means that law is never neutral. Even when a law appears to contain only a technical procedural adjustment of current practices, it maintains its allocative characteristic. For instance, in the 1970s, all states adopted some form of no-fault divorce; the change was often supported with the argument that it simply represented a technical change in divorce law, allowing law on the books to catch up with the living law, since most divorces were uncontested and appeared to be consensual. The change, however, removed the possibility of aggrieved spouses winning vindication with the attribution of fault to the other spouse, and some critics have charged that it also had serious financial implications for divorced women.[6] This experience reflects the fact that with the adoption of each law, some people win and others lose something of importance.

Let us return to the Miranda ruling, for each of the characteristics of law is apparent in it. Its claim to legitimacy rests on its claims to fairness. The decision had a strong claim to common standards of morality and fairness, since it guaranteed notice of constitutional rights to those who might need to invoke them; it also promised equal treatment and minimization of error. The ruling was authoritative: it had the force of the federal government behind it. If police disobeyed it, the federal courts would reverse the convictions of those who had been jailed by its neglect. Miranda was also prescriptive: it told police what they ought to do when making an arrest. Finally, the Miranda ruling was allocative. It reinforced the rights of those accused of a crime and took away some intimidative powers from the police. It is important to note, however, that our definition of law is not universal. It pertains only to law in the United States and countries with similar political regimes. When anthropologists speak of the law of native societies, they do not require that it be backed by the force of the State. Moreover, in many countries, law is backed by more brute force and less legitimacy than in the United States.

Nor does our definition of law require that it be consonant with everyone's conception of justice; it need only conform to the ideal of justice held by enough members of the population to be considered legitimate. In addition, our definition of law lies much nearer to that of the legal realists than to the definitions favored by legal scholars who contend that the law is closely linked with an ideal natural law or that it consists of a scientific set of logically related imperatives. Ours is a definition sculpted to fit our examination of the intersection of law and politics.[7]

---

[6]Herbert Jacob, *Silent Revolution: The Transformation of Divorce Law in the United States* (Chicago: University of Chicago Press, 1988). See Chapter 13 for a further discussion of these issues.
[7]For a discussion of alternative definitions of law, see Robert L. Kidder, *Connecting Law and Society* (Englewood Cliffs, N.J.: Prentice-Hall, 1983), pp. 11–35.

The Structure of American Law

Law in the United States is many-layered. The layers reflect both the history of the law and the complex structure of American government. To understand it, we need to become acquainted with each layer.

THE FIRST LAYER: ITS ORIGIN BY THE LEVEL OF GOVERNMENT

Three different sets of laws exist in the United States depending on the level of government from which each comes. This is a consequence of the federal structure of American political institutions, which has left a fragmented, federal legal structure in its wake.

So-called **federal laws** are those enacted by Congress or other agencies of the federal government and are valid in all corners of the country. Article I, Section 8 of the Constitution enumerates the subjects on which the federal government may enact laws. These include such specifics as laws regulating bankruptcy, prohibiting the counterfeiting of money, and establishing post offices as well as what has become known as the **commerce clause,** which allows Congress to "regulate Commerce with foreign Nations, and among the several States, and with the Indian Tribes." The Supreme Court has generally interpreted that clause very broadly since John Marshall's 1824 decision in *Gibbons v. Ogden*.[8] Given the growth of interstate transportation and communication since the early nineteenth century, almost every economic activity has implications beyond the boundaries of a single state, and, therefore, the scope of federal law has grown enormously.

Second, each state may adopt laws for its own territory on those topics not monopolized by federal law. In the early years of American history, most law was **state law,** while federal law occupied only a tiny portion of the legal sphere. That has changed in the twentieth century. As the power of the federal government has grown, the extent of its laws has also increased. Nevertheless, some very important areas of the law are mostly or entirely state rather than federal law. Almost all family law, most criminal law, and much law governing contracts and personal injuries remains the domain of the states. On the other hand, much of the law regulating economic enterprises and personal rights has migrated to the federal arena.

A third set of laws has a still more limited jurisdiction: **local ordinances,** which are the product of local governments. Such laws are in one sense simply an extension of the authority of state governments, because local governments do not have their own constitutions but are chartered by state law. From a political perspective, however, local ordinances should be viewed as a third set of laws because they are the outcome of a quite separate political process that is centered almost entirely in local interests, history, and institutions. Although the scope of local law is quite limited, it is not insignificant. Many taxes are local, and the regulation of land use and construction is governed mostly by local ordinances. Even some criminal law emanates from local authorities.

---

[8] Wheat. 1 (1824).

The division of law among the three levels of government in the United States means that law, like politics, is highly fragmented. There is no single national legal code. In many instances, the law that applies to a particular problem is scattered among the law books of many jurisdictions. To open a business, for example, one must comply not only with local building and housing codes, but also with state and federal tax laws, employment codes, and safety standards. Moreover, law in one locale is often different from that in other places; thus the law that determines the property settlement in a divorce in Wisconsin is quite different than that in neighboring Illinois or Iowa. Where one divorces may make a large difference in the amount of money one can take away from the marriage.

THE SECOND LAYER: INSTITUTIONAL ORIGINS

Law in the United States may originate from one of four institutions. The first of these is the body that creates a **constitution;** that may be a constitutional convention, a legislature which amends the constitution by an extraordinary majority, with or without the subsequent consent of the voters, or the electorate by itself through an initiative petition. The resulting form of law is a constitution. The second institution is a legislature that enacts law in the form of **statutes;** third is an administrative agency that creates law in the form of **regulations.** Fourth is a court which establishes law in the form of **case law** that interprets constitutional provisions, statutes, or regulations.

The first three of these kinds of law form a hierarchy. At the top is constitutional law, on the second rung is statutory law, and at the bottom is administrative law. The position of judicial decisions in this hierarchy depends on the status of the court that issues the ruling. United States Supreme Court decisions are at the top; those from other appellate courts come next; trial court interpretations and the rulings of administrative tribunals are at the bottom.

Constitutional law is at the top of the hierarchy because the Constitution is the fundamental law of the land. It is much more difficult to amend than other kinds of law. The Constitution is regarded with special veneration. It is considered a compact among the citizens of the United States that specifies their rights and duties and outlines the basic elements of governmental structure. It authorizes governmental agencies that are established in conformity with its provisions to promulgate their own legal rules, but those rules must conform to the Constitution both substantively and procedurally. The substance of laws may not violate prohibitions listed in the Constitution, such as the prohibition against ex post facto laws or the prohibition against the taking of property without due process of law. In addition, other laws must be adopted in accordance with the procedural provisions of the Constitution. Thus, proposals must be adopted by both houses of Congress and signed by the president (unless his or her veto is overridden) to become law. It was this requirement that led the Supreme Court to decide in 1983 that the numerous laws Congress had passed permitting the Senate or the House (and sometimes just a committee of one or the other) to veto executive agency actions were unconstitutional. That practice, called a legislative veto, had been a useful tool because it allowed Congress to pass a general law and then maintain control over the regulations needed to implement it. However, because the Constitution does not provide for such a mechanism, the Supreme Court decided the practice was unauthorized and unconstitutional.[9]

These considerations apply not only to the U.S. Constitution, but also to the constitutions of the states. Like the U.S. Constitution, state constitutions also enjoy priority over state statutes. State statutes must conform to the constitution of their state as well as to the U.S. Constitution. For instance, some state constitutions require the state to provide equal school facilities for all children. Such a constitutional provision led the California Supreme Court in 1971 to declare unconstitutional state laws that distributed funds to schools because they violated the constitutional mandate for providing equal school facilities to all.[10] Two years later, the New Jersey Supreme Court ordered the legislature to provide local school districts with sufficient state funds to equalize their tax base so that poor districts had as much to spend as rich districts.[11] This ruling led directly to the imposition of an income tax in New Jersey for the first time.[12] Similarly, Texas spent most of the 1980s trying unsuccessfully to adopt a formula for meeting that state's constitutional guarantees for equitable distribution of education funds.[13] Local governments do not have their own constitutions. Therefore, their ordinances must conform to the state constitution and to the U.S. Constitution.

The second rung of the hierarchy consists of statutes, rules adopted by a legislature in accordance with the provisions of the constitution that authorized the establishment of the legislature. Congress is the only legislative body for the nation as a whole; in addition, each state has a legislature, and local governments have legislative bodies usually called city councils. These legislative bodies are the only ones authorized to formulate statutes. Statutes are typically, although not always, much more detailed than constitutions. A statute normally specifies a goal and a set of procedures by which that goal is to be attained. It may impose obligations or confer privileges. Often, statutes mandate actions that public officials must undertake.

The third rung in the hierarchy of U.S. laws is composed of administrative regulations. To attain the goals prescribed by statutes, administrative officials often issue regulations. Such regulations must conform to the statute that authorized them and must be issued in accordance with approved procedures. Regulations are much more detailed than statutes or constitutions. Although they are not adopted by legislatures, they have the force of law, and violations may carry penalties much like those imposed by statutes themselves.

The fourth institution that makes law in the United States is the judiciary. Courts make law (called **case law**) because every form of law is subject to court interpretation in the United States. No lawyer is comfortable with his or her understanding of a law without checking to see how it has been interpreted by the courts. Judicial interpretations bind everyone over which the court has jurisdiction until a superior body changes the law. When a trial court issues an interpretation of the law, it binds only other liti-

[9]*Chada v. I.N.S.*, 103 S. Ct. 2764 (1983); Barbara Hinkson Craig, *Chadha: The Story of an Epic Constitutional Struggle* (New York: Oxford University Press, 1988).
[10]*Serrano v. Priest*, 96 Cal. Rptr. 601 (1971).   [11]*Robinson v. Cahill*, 118 N.J. 223 (1973).
[12]Richard Lehne, in *The Quest for Justice: The Politics of School Finance Reform* (New York: Longman, 1978), gives an extended account of the New Jersey controversy.
[13]*New York Times*, 4 December 1992, p. A26.

gants appearing before that court; when a state supreme court interprets the law, its interpretation is authoritative for all who use that law within the state's boundaries. The rulings of the U.S. Supreme Court bind everyone in the country.

Courts interpret not only laws made by other institutions, but also their own past rulings. Where those rulings do not directly draw on statutory or constitutional law, the law of the courts is called **common law.** Before legislatures became the dominant law-making agency, most American law had its origin in court decisions that interpreted custom, English court decisions, or previous American court decisions. The balance between court-made law and statutory law changed during the nineteenth century. Today most law is statutory, but vestiges of court-made common law remain.

Equity also carries historical vestiges of court-made law. In England in the late Middle Ages, the courts were bound by a long tradition of pleadings that made them rather inflexible. Cases were sometimes brought for which the common law either had no remedy or the remedy seemed unfair. The king eventually allowed such cases to be brought to his chancellor, who decided them on the grounds of fairness, or equity, using quite different procedures and achieving quite different results.[14] Eventually, the king's chancellor was replaced by a new set of judges. In the United States at the time of the Revolution, separate courts handled complaints at law (i.e., common law) and at equity.[15] Now these courts have been merged.[16]

Despite this merger, some important procedural distinctions remain between actions brought at equity and complaints brought at law (whether it be common or statutory law). At equity, the remedy is directed at the person who is ordered to do something; this action is often in the form of an **injunction,** which seeks to avoid irreparable harm. Persons who refuse are considered to be personally disobeying the judge may be held in **contempt of court** and thrown in jail until they comply. At law, the legal action occurs after the harm has been done, and the remedy is compensation. For instance, if a contract has not been fulfilled, one can sue for compensation at law; if one acts in equity, one can seek specific performance of the contract. The difference is that in the action at law, one may receive compensation for not having received delivery of the contracted goods; at equity, one forces the supplier to deliver them. Incorrectly formulating a claim may result in losing the case despite having a legitimate claim for the substance of the dispute.

Important procedural differences also persist between actions at law and those at equity. Forcing payment for a judgment at law usually requires a separate action; for instance, the sheriff may seize property and sell it to cover a debt. At equity, failure to comply results in a contempt-of-court ruling and possible imprisonment. In addition, juries are not used at equity; therefore, if one wishes to have a jury hear one's case, the action must be brought at law. These distinctions may appear arcane to the nonlawyer, but they remain important when legislators or other policy makers seek to change laws. Because these historical meanings and distinctions are embedded in the minds of lawyers and judges, they retain significance.

One may recognize the four types of law by the publication in which they may be found. Statutes are published in the proceedings of legislatures; administrative regula-

---

[14]Lawrence M. Friedman, *A History of American Law* (New York: Simon & Schuster, 1973), pp. 21–23.
[15]Ibid., pp. 47–48.   [16]Ibid., pp. 346–347.

tions of the federal government are published in the *Federal Register*, those of state governments in similar volumes. Both statutes and administrative regulations are also published in codified form by legal publishers. Constitutions are often printed in all of these sources, but are always identified as such. Courts publish their decisions in their own volumes; the decisions are also collected by legal publishers in books and electronic data bases identifying the courts covered.

THE THIRD LAYER: CIVIL AND CRIMINAL

A common distinction in the law is between **civil** and **criminal** law. Civil law is distinguished from criminal law largely by the procedures that apply when a case is brought to court and by the sanctions that may be imposed.[17] One set of procedural rules is labeled civil and the other criminal, and they differ on many points. For example, judges and juries in criminal cases may convict a defendant only if the defendant's guilt is beyond a reasonable doubt. By contrast, the standard of proof in civil cases is much lower, and usually requires only a preponderance of the evidence. In a case involving a contract or marital dispute, for example, a jury or judge may decide the case in favor of one party whenever that side has more evidence in its favor, even if some doubt remains as to who is right.

Many other differences distinguish the processing of criminal and civil cases. A criminal case is brought by the government against the offender, whereas either a private party or the government may bring civil suits. Juries are almost always available to defendants in criminal cases; that is not so in many civil cases. Different sanctions also usually apply in civil and criminal cases. Civil cases typically lead to compensation or restoration of the situation that existed before the problem was brought to court. Criminal cases occasionally result in compensation, but the normal outcome is some form of punishment: community service, a fine, probation, or imprisonment. However, these differences between civil and criminal outcomes are not absolute. Some civil cases lead to an award of punitive damages, and some criminal cases may require restitution to the victim.

The distinction between civil and criminal law has many implications. Civil penalties are easier to enforce than criminal sanctions because the burden of proof is lighter. Moreover, the stigma attached to losing a civil case is much less than that attached to being convicted of a criminal offense. Thus, when legislators consider new sanctions for violations of laws such as environmental regulations or civil rights acts, these choices sometimes become determinative in the struggle to build a winning coalition. Those who want to take a stronger position may prefer criminal sanctions, but they realize that imposing such sanctions may make enforcement difficult. Those who consider the violations only "technical" matters may prefer civil sanctions, but adopting those sanctions may make enforcement more likely.

---

[17]For a nontechnical explanation of these procedures, see Geoffrey C. Hazard, Jr. and Michele Taruffo, *American Civil Procedure* (New Haven: Yale University Press, 1993).

THE FOURTH LAYER: PUBLIC AND PRIVATE LAW _____

Another common distinction lawyers make is between **public** and **private** law. Public law principally pertains to the institutions of government—their operations and inter-actions with private citizens. Constitutional, administrative, and criminal law are major areas of public law. Private law, on the other hand, centers on relationships among pri-vate citizens, such as commercial contracts and family disputes. Private law is, of course, not really private, and, in fact, relies heavily on legislation such as the Uniform Com-mercial Code and divorce laws. It usually reflects public policy in areas of great impor-tance to American society. Its provisions also intersect with the work of many public agencies other than courts, such as the Federal Trade Commission, which oversees the fairness of business transactions, and public welfare agencies, which provide care for needy citizens. Yet commercial law, family law, tort law, and the like are considered pri-vate because they do not centrally involve public agencies in their execution. In addi-tion, private law typically leaves much to the discretion of private parties. The Uniform Commercial Code, for instance, establishes general guidelines for drawing enforceable contracts, but leaves the details to private parties. Lawyers pride themselves in finding novel ways of using the provisions of the code for the benefit of their clients. Family law is, in some ways, even more private, because people are generally more hesitant to use the courts to enforce marital and other family-related arrangements than to implement commercial contracts. Consequently, many families arrange their affairs with no refer-ence to family law or even knowledge about it. Most of the arrangements are formulated in private, and because most are never deposited in a public place or opened to public inspection, they remain private. Over many years, such arrangements may alter the for-mal law as judges' decisions slowly recognize the law in action to be the law on the books. Thus while public law is always made in public arenas, much private law is the product of private processes.

THE FIFTH LAYER: SUBSTANTIVE LAW _____

Another set of categories—contracts, torts, property, and criminal law—distinguishes the law in terms of its apparent substance. As with the other distinctions, these divi-sions must be understood in light of their considerable overlap. **Contracts,** for example, are inconceivable in their American context without a concept of private property, but **property law** also concerns property. Property law deals principally with real property, such as land and buildings, while contract law addresses the exchange of other forms of property. Similarly, fraud involves both criminal and contract law. Yet each of these bodies of law possesses its own core concepts, statutes, and a distinct set of rules. For in-stance, compensation may be calculated substantially differently under tort law than under contract law. Many **torts** (which are private wrongs causing harm) do not in-volve contracts, but when a contract is breached, it may easily inflict harm.

In each of these areas of law, judges and lawyers have built an elaborate structure of interrelated concepts. Consequently, to change a seemingly small element of one of these bodies of law involves much more than changing a single section of a statute. It often also involves altering many related provisions and legal rules, which means that revising the law to achieve some policy objective without unnecessarily muddying the waters requires a high degree of legal expertise. Perhaps more significantly, when legislators change one aspect of a law, they often have to alter others, and those other changes may provoke unexpected opposition to the first change or trigger unanticipated consequences. A vivid example was the effort in 1993 and 1994 to enact a new health care system. Providing universal health care as President Clinton proposed involved changing not just health insurance law but also the laws involving worker's compensation, automobile accident insurance, taxes, and employment contracts, among many others.

THE SIXTH LAYER: LAW AS PROCEDURE

Laws, as we have already pointed out, are rules. Rules usually specify the steps that must be taken to achieve desired goals. That is certainly true of the law; procedure is one of its central elements.

The law often specifies procedures for engaging in certain activities. If those procedures are followed, the activities are considered to be lawful; if not, they are illegal and can lead to damage claims or criminal actions. For example, when a creditor trying to collect a debt goes to court, obtains a judgment after notifying the debtor, and then executes that judgment by using the sheriff's office to seize the debtor's property, the seizure is completely legal because all the procedures outlined by the law have been followed. On the other hand, if a creditor simply goes to the debtor's house and takes enough furniture to settle the specific claim, such an action is illegal and can expose the creditor to a damage suit or possibly even to the criminal charge of burglary. The difference is that the former followed the procedures specified by the law, while the latter did not.

Specified procedures are not trivial. Their principal purpose is to provide essential protection against arbitrary actions. Quite literally, procedures prevent persons from taking the law into their own hands. In the United States, the most essential procedures are captured by the phrase **due process of law.** In criminal cases, due process includes the rights to confront one's accusers, to have a jury trial, to be represented by an attorney, and to resist self-incrimination. These rights, which are guaranteed in the Bill of Rights, have been elaborated in many U.S. Supreme Court decisions and constitute a very substantial body of complex rules. Due process also regulates procedure in civil cases; **civil procedure** constitutes a core course in all law school curricula. Civil court cases involve an adversarial proceeding in which both parties must have a chance to state their case before a disinterested judge. The rules of evidence, which seek to guarantee that decisions will be made on reliable facts, must be observed.

Rules have important substantive consequences for those who use the courts. American courts generally require that cases involve real conflicts and that the parties who bring the litigation have an actual interest in the outcome. The importance of this requirement is illustrated by a 1970 Wisconsin case in which the supreme court significantly extended the rights of tenants to resist eviction when there were housing code violations in their dwelling.[18] The court case began with an action by a landlord to evict his tenant for nonpayment of rent, which the tenant had not paid because of unsanitary conditions in his apartment. However, by the time the case reached the Wisconsin Supreme Court, the tenant had already left the apartment. The only remaining thread of a dispute was the fact that court costs of $5.60 had been assessed against the tenant, who had lost the case in the lower courts. Had the landlord waived those costs, in all probability the case would not have been heard by the Wisconsin Supreme Court because the issues would have been moot. But because the landlord insisted on being reimbursed for his court costs, the court assumed jurisdiction and eventually ruled against him, establishing a rule that tenants could not be evicted for nonpayment of rent under such circumstances. It is on such technicalities that major legal cases may hinge.

In some instances, litigants carefully consider the advantages offered by the procedural differences among several courts when deciding where to take their case. It may even be possible to choose between the courts of different countries. A dramatic example of this occurred in the aftermath of the Union Carbide disaster in Bhopal, India.[19] In December 1984, a series of mishaps resulted in the release of an extremely poisonous gas at a plant of one of the company's affiliates. The gas killed more than 2000 persons and injured thousands more. A question immediately arose about where litigation might be filed to recover the damages. Indian courts were the most apparent choice because the incident occurred in that country, the corporation operating the plant was Indian, and the victims were Indian. However, Indian courts are much costlier for litigants; they operate at a much slower pace, even by American standards, with tort suits often taking a decade or longer. The chances of obtaining substantial compensation in an Indian court was much smaller because the Indian company had fewer assets than its American corporate parent, and Indian law is much less hospitable to such suits. Thus began a struggle to determine where the suits should be filed. Within hours of the disaster, American attorneys, sensing an opportunity to earn large fees, flew to India to investigate filing suits in the United States.

Lawyers must decide which of the available procedures will provide the greatest advantage to their clients, for procedures are rarely neutral in their impact on litigants. Consequently, when legislatures discuss procedural reforms, seemingly arcane procedural points may stir vigorous debate. This was the case when the Voting Rights Act of 1965 was considered for renewal in 1982. One of the major points at issue was whether federal intervention would be permitted when actions were shown to have had discriminatory consequences or whether it would be necessary to prove that those consequences had been intended by local officials, a procedural point of immense substantive significance because intent is difficult to prove. Those opposed to the change feared that requiring proof of intent would make enforcement of civil rights laws impossible.[20]

---

[18]*Dickhut v. Norton*, 45 Wis. 2d 389, 173 N.W.2d 297 (1970).
[19]The following is based on accounts of the Bhopal incident in the *New York Times*, 29–31 January 1985, p. 1, and the *Wall Street Journal*, 24 January 1985, p. 1; see also Marc Galanter, "Bhopals, Past and Present: The Changing Legal Response to Mass Disaster," *Windsor Yearbook of Access to Justice* 10 (1990), pp. 151–170.
[20]Charles S. Bullock III and Charles M. Lamb, *Implementation of Civil Rights Policy* (Monterey, Calif.: Brooks Cole, 1984), pp. 28–29.

The importance of procedure is often underestimated. Consider, for example, the experience of a widow of a prison guard who was killed in the uprising at the Attica prison in New York State in 1971. As Tom Wicker reported,[21] the woman refused to accept a worker's compensation check for $21 as reimbursement for the four meals her husband missed while he had been held hostage, because her attorney feared that acceptance would waive her right to sue. She subsequently sued the state of New York for using excessive force in quelling the riot, and eventually won a judgment against the state for $550,000. She was the only victim or survivor of the Attica uprising to win such a suit because she was the only person to refuse the worker's compensation check. The courts held that the others' election of remedy—the legal term for accepting the check—precluded them from subsequently suing the state for damages.

Procedures have another effect. They are often expensive, and generally require an attorney who knows the correct legal forms. The complexity of that task is suggested by the sixteen volumes on law library shelves containing nothing but legal forms for federal courts and agencies;[22] still more forms exist for state and local courts and agencies. In addition, lawyers must know the deadlines for each forum and the places at which each step must be performed. Fees are required for filing a case in court and for using the sheriff's office. Many procedures are also lengthy. For these reasons, the services of the law are usually more available to the wealthy than to the poor.

THE INTERACTION OF THE SIX LAYERS OF LAW

These six layers complicate the law in the United States. Lawyers use them as shorthand to call attention to some distinctive feature of the law they wish to use. I use the term *layers* to suggest the visual image of a multilayered phenomenon, as illustrated in Figure 2.1. A cross-section would reveal that any particular law has some features of many layers.

Let us return to the *Miranda* rule. It is a federal, rather than state or local, law. It rests on a judicial interpretation of the Fifth Amendment to the Constitution and, therefore, may be considered an example of constitutional case law. Its substantive niche is the criminal code rather than contracts, torts, or another area of the law. Finally, it specifies a particular procedure that police officers must use when they make an arrest. Every law may be described along these multiple dimensions.

The multilayered characteristics of the law are more than an intellectual curiosity. They help explain why the law is so bewilderingly complex to the layperson and so maddeningly cumbersome to those who wish to alter it. Much of the immediate unresponsiveness of law to political activity is a consequence of the extremely complex structure of law in the United States. The many overlays of definitions and distinctions require legislators to have deft skills to construct new legislation that will accomplish desired alterations. This complexity constitutes the core of the legal culture that would-be attorneys study for three years in law school.

---

[21]*New York Times*, 22 March 1985, p. 27.
[22]Louis R. Frumer and Marvin Waxner, *Bender's Federal Practice Forms* (New York: Matthew Bender, 1984).

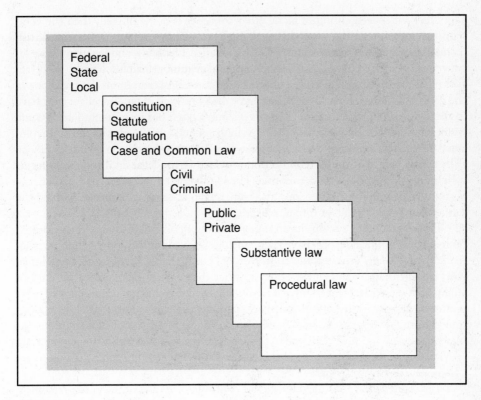

Figure 2.1
The Multiple Layers of Law

The Distinctiveness of American Law

Law in the United States is distinctive in many ways when compared to laws of other nations. It is much more complex, it is structured in an entirely different way, and has its roots in a different tradition.

The complexity of American law in part stems from the fragmentation of American government. Because of its federal structure, the United States has maintained multiple overlapping sets of laws. This means not only that 51 bodies of statutory law, but also 51 bodies of administrative regulations and case law, exist in the United States. In such countries as Germany, France, and Japan, only one national body of law exists and it operates in all corners of the country; there are relatively few local variants.

The common law tradition of the United States adds to the complexity. Courts in the United States more frequently create law by deciding cases than do courts in other countries because of the established tradition in the United States of following precedent. A decision by an appellate court not only settles the legal arguments of the case in question, but also will be used as the authority for subsequent decisions by the same court and its subordinate trial courts.

The civil code tradition of many other countries is quite different than the common law tradition of the United States, England, and other countries of the British Commonwealth.[23] Civil law countries such as France, Germany, and Japan possess a legal code constructed on the basis of certain fundamental principles. Ideally, each section of the code is logically related to other sections. Legislation forms the backbone of the code; judicial interpretations do not have the same kind of binding effect they have in the United States. This form of legal code most often has its roots in quite specific historical experiences. It is one of the most fundamental legacies of the French Revolution; the French armies of the revolutionary period carried it to the countries France then conquered. In other parts of the world, such as Japan,[24] the civil code was specifically adopted as a tool for modernization. The United States, of course, had its own revolution; French armies did not wash the French civil code on U.S. shores. Nor did the United States need to adopt it to modernize.

The common law system fits an important set of political attitudes in the United States, where political leaders have been much less programmatic and much more pragmatic than in many other countries. In part, of course, that is a reflection of a political party system that favors centrist policies rather than radical programs of the Left or Right. Consequently, legal changes have usually been incremental adaptations to solve particular problems rather than systematic reformulations based on logical deductions from fundamental premises. Such incremental changes often do not fit well into existing bodies of law, because they lead to further incremental adjustments. Incrementalism is evident in many spheres of life in the United States; it would be more difficult to accommodate in a civil law code.

The result is that the characteristics of American law (and of the entire American legal system) are not at all representative of law and legal systems of the world. The United States is the exception in almost every generalization that might be made of legal phenomena in the contemporary world. We point to many of these differences as we explore the details of the American legal system in subsequent chapters.

Justice and the Law

It is no accident that I have rarely used the word *justice* in this discussion of the law, for justice and law are not necessarily linked. People may consider some laws just, while they view others as unjust. The relationship between the law and justice is a difficult one because both philosophers and politicians often disagree on the definition of justice. It is usually defined using such words as fairness, equality, and equity, characteristics we have noted are essential for law to be legitimate. However, it is also important to note that even these terms have no universally accepted meanings. Procedural definitions of justice fail to win unanimous support because the procedures themselves are perceived to harm some in society.

[23]For a description of the practice in civil code countries, see John H. Merryman, *The Civil Law Tradition* (Stanford, Calif.: Stanford University Press, 1969).
[24]However, Japan adopted the German version of the civil code.

For instance, take the justness of the rule that requires a candidate win a majority of the vote to gain a party nomination. Used for decades by the Democratic Party in southern states, this rule often meant a runoff election was needed to determine the winner in a party primary. It was an effective device for preventing African-American candidates, or those favoring policies helpful to African Americans, from winning an election. They might win a plurality in the first primary against several white candidates but would lose in the runoff when opposed by a single opponent. The practice went virtually unchallenged until the presidential campaign in 1984, when Jesse Jackson complained of its injustice because it discriminated against African-American candidates. As with many legal procedures, whether one perceived the runoff election as just or unjust depended on whether it worked to one's own advantage.

The *Miranda* ruling provides another example of disagreement over the justness of a legal rule. The Supreme Court believed the warning to be essential for a just administration of the criminal law, but it did so by a bare majority of five of the nine justices. Some of the justices vigorously disagreed with the majority ruling, and over the years many public officials and private citizens believed the rule resulted in unjust decisions. Such critics blame the *Miranda* rule for the release of factually guilty criminals on what is perceived as a mere legal technicality when the police forget to recite the required warning. Indeed, twenty years after *Miranda,* the Supreme Court, which then had only one remaining member of the original *Miranda* majority, substantially altered the requirement in a new case. In *New York v. Quarles,*[25] the Court held that if the police delayed in giving the *Miranda* warning, the delay did not necessarily invalidate the arrest and prosecution. Thus, the Supreme Court itself changed its definition of what constituted a just procedure. Clearly, what is justice to some at one moment in history is seen differently by others at different times.

Almost the only point of unanimous agreement on the concept of justice is that justice is a powerful symbol. The word is inscribed on the walls of nearly all courthouses, where justice is often portrayed as a blindfolded woman holding a set of scales. Judges also invoke the term frequently in their decisions. In this book, however, we avoid using the word. To term a law or the outcome of a legal dispute as *just* is conclusory and states an opinion that cannot be readily substantiated with empirical analysis. Judgments about justice must be made by the reader as they are made by consumers of the law—on the basis of personal values and beliefs.

Conclusion

The law is not infinitely malleable. It is encrusted with myriad traditions that affect its use. Enacting a new policy is usually more complicated than simply drafting a new law. New law must be blended with the old if it is to have the desired consequences. It must be drafted with attention to the many-dimensioned contours of existing law and procedure. The structure of law can never be neglected in considering its role in the political

[25]*New York v. Quarles,* 467 U.S. 649 (1984).

process, and despite the subjectiveness of the concept of justice, that remains a powerful element in perceptions of the legitimacy of law.

KEY WORDS

Miranda warning	equity
legitimacy	injunction
use of force	contempt of court
prescriptive statements	civil law
allocative	criminal law
federal laws	public law
commerce clause	private law
state law	substantive law
local ordinances	contract law
constitution	property law
statutes	torts
regulations	due process of law
case law	civil procedure
common law	

FOR FURTHER STUDY . . .

An excellent historical survey of American law is Lawrence M. Friedman, *A History of American Law*, 2d ed. (New York: Simon & Schuster, 1985). A very good introduction to the distinctiveness of American law compared to law elsewhere is Mirjan R. Damaska, *The Faces of Justice and State Authority* (New Haven: Yale University Press, 1986). An introduction to civil code legal systems may be found in John Henry Merryman, *The Civil Law Tradition* (Stanford, Calif.: Stanford University Press, 1969).

To demonstrate the multiple layers of law, take several laws that are mentioned in a current newspaper and seek to identify all the layers. Consider what body promulgated them, where they fit in the organization of government, and the types of law they incorporate (e.g., civil, criminal, public, private). Then try to establish how each of the different layers affected the politics surrounding the adoption of these laws and the politics of their interpretation and implementation.

II

THE OUTER RING: DISPUTANTS AND CRIMINALS

Peple enmeshed in the legal system fall into two categories. Some deliberately use the law and the courts to achieve an objective. Others are dragged into the legal arena by a plaintiff who complains about the injury they allegedly have committed or by the police who charge a criminal offense.

Law, however, may be employed without going to court. There are many ways to handle disputes short of litigation; some of them employ much law and others use little. Even allegedly criminal acts may be handled in a variety of ways. In the following chapters, we examine the multitude of dispute resolution arenas that provide alternative ways of handling grievances and deviant acts. They are marked by enormous discretion.

A decision to use the courts or an alternative arena is neither whimsical nor free from constraint. Such choices are embedded in social contexts in terms of both the handling of disputes and the processing of criminal incidents.

In the following two chapters, we examine the paths that bring people to the legal arena and the social terrain they cross. We look at the benefits and costs that confront persons who wish to use the law. We also compare legal remedies with those offered by other social institutions. Such comparisons allow us to understand the reasons for employing the law and the consequences of using alternatives.

3

DISPUTANTS AND THE LAW

Cooperation constitutes the face of civilization we admire; conflict is the face that we must endure. The law suffuses both.

The law promotes cooperation in several ways. It helps stabilize expectations about relationships that often have become rooted in the norms of everyday life. When people rent apartments, they know what to expect from the landlord, while the landlord knows what is expected of the tenant. Thus, tenants know that they may lock the door and enjoy privacy and will not have to endure a leaky roof, glassless windows, or the lack of heat in the winter. All that and more is part of the law but is taken for granted by most tenants. On the other hand, the landlord knows that the rent will be paid each month and that the tenant will not destroy the apartment. If, however, the tenant or landlord violates these expectations, the law provides remedies and penalties: a judge may force recalcitrant landlords to provide heat or may authorize the eviction of tenants who do not pay their rent. Thus, the law promotes cooperation both by establishing firm expectations about behavior and by supporting those expectations with sanctions. Even people who are strangers can cooperate, because these expectations are based on law rather than personal relationships. In postindustrial urban societies, where each person must deal with many strangers, this function of law is vital. Without legally enforceable expectations, most people could not safely agree to accept employment from total strangers, place their assets in strange banks, drive the streets surrounded by strangers, eat food prepared by strangers, or rely on complicated products, such as automobiles, refrigerators, and computers, made by people whom they never see.

Because we often concentrate on the use of the law in settling disputes and conflicts, we tend to take the cooperative aspect of the law for granted. The law's promotion of cooperation is, however, constantly at work and constitutes a core element in the structure of social control. As sociologists such as Graham Sumner, George Herbert Mead, Emile Durkheim, and Talcott Parsons—among many others—have emphasized, law is one of many forces that keep society's members in line.[1] It is important in generating conformity and imposing social control, but it often works almost invisibly.

The law's contribution to social control is much more apparent in its role of subduing disputes. People often use the threat of invoking the law to win their point in a dispute; the mere threat may be enough to win an accommodation. As we discuss in this chapter, the invocation of courtroom procedures and judicial decisions is quite exceptional, but it casts a long shadow over many disputes that never reach the courts. Consequently, the law's role in disputes is complex and subtle. To comprehend this role more fully, we must have a more general understanding of the ways in which disputes are generated and the role of the law in resolving them.

Let us begin with a small dispute that is typical of many faced in everyday life. Some years ago, my wife and I began to be bothered by the shade our neighbor's tree was casting on our flower garden. Over the years, it became increasingly difficult to grow the flowers we liked. One morning, when I saw my neighbor working in his garden, I spoke to him across the fence and asked whether we might employ a tree surgeon to cut the tree branches that extended over our yard and were shading the flower patch. He did not say much at the time, but a few days later, I received a registered letter in which he wrote that he had consulted his corporate attorney and wished to warn me that he would hold me liable for any damage I inflicted on his tree. Further, he refused to allow me or anyone in my employ access to his yard to climb his tree to cut its branches. We were taken aback by this response and considered various ways to negotiate further. However, a few days later, I noticed the tree was sporting a small red tag that meant the city was testing it for Dutch elm disease. Within a week, the city's tree crew cut the tree down. Our flower garden had sunshine once again.

This dispute had many of the important elements of dispute processing. The fact that it involved small stakes is itself important because that is characteristic of many disputes affected by the law. Our request touched a raw nerve with our neighbor, and his response escalated the controversy to a potentially serious level. He invoked the assistance of a gatekeeper to the law, his corporate attorney; I consulted my law books. Disliking trouble, my wife and I decided to live with the unwanted shade, when an independent force intervened. However, my neighbor respected the lawful authority of the city to cut down his tree even though he objected to my less drastic proposal to trim it; he also feared that the Dutch elm disease would spread to his other elms. Thus, in the end, his threat of invoking the law and court action was irrelevant to the resolution of our dispute, although the authority the law granted to the city to remove diseased trees fortuitously provided the solution to our dispute.

Disputes such as ours arise out of **grievances.** Grievances are beliefs that a person "is entitled to a resource which someone else may grant or deny"[2] or that some harm has been done to them. My wife and I had a grievance because we felt we had a right to sunshine, which our neighbor could permit or deny; our garden was being harmed. However, not all grievances lead to disputes. Some remain unspoken; for some months we

---

[1]For a summary of their views, see Lewis A. Coser, "The Notion of Control in Sociological Theory," in Jack P. Gibbs (ed.), *Social Control: Views from the Social Sciences* (Beverly Hills, Calif.: Sage, 1982), pp. 13–22.
[2]Richard E. Miller and Austin Sarat, "Grievances, Claims, and Disputes: Assessing the Adversary Culture," *Law & Society Review* 15 (1980–81), p. 527.

had not said anything to our neighbor even though the shade of his tree bothered us. Other grievances are satisfied. Had he agreed to our proposal, no dispute would have arisen. Thus, two additional elements are required for a dispute. First, the grievance must be communicated in the form of a **claim.** Second, the claim must be denied. Only when these conditions are met can we identify a dispute.

Not all disputes involve the law or courts. Some disputes involve claims concerning entitlements granted by social custom or some other form of social norm, rather than the law. For instance, a widely observed custom specifies that the bride's family pays for the wedding. If they refuse to do so, the bride, groom, and his family may negotiate with them, attempt to apply peer pressure, or simply pay for the ceremony themselves. But no legal action can be taken to resolve such a grievance. Other disputes involve claims that the law specifically labels unenforceable in court. For instance, a hired killer's claim requesting payment by the client cannot be taken to court, nor can a child's claim for an allowance from his or her parents. Thus, for a claim to have the potential of invoking the law, it must involve matters covered by legal doctrine.

It is possible to avoid the law at every stage of the disputing process. People may decide not to air their grievances as a claim. Once a claim has been made and rejected, one party may decide to avoid further strife by abandoning the claim and letting the other party prevail. Finally, they may use nonlegal channels for advancing their claims rather than going to one of the legal arenas.

These elements of the disputing process are illustrated by Figure 3.1. As the figure makes clear, legal disputes in courts have a long history of prior activity and represent only a small portion of all potential disputes that might reach the courts. Evidence from a comprehensive study of disputes and litigation confirms this. Miller and Sarat[3] found that 41.6 percent of all households they contacted reported having had a grievance during the preceding three years. Of those whose grievances were terminated, 71.8 percent made claims, and 62.6 percent of the claims led to disputes. In 23.0 percent of the dis-

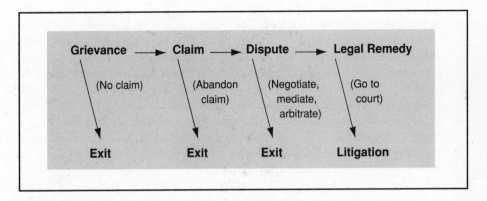

Figure 3.1
The Generation of Disputes

[3]Ibid., p. 537.

putes a lawyer was used, and in 11.2 percent of the disputes a court case was filed. These findings show attrition at each stage indicated in Figure 3.1. In general, they show a funnel effect, with few court cases emerging from the entire universe of grievances or claims.

Social and economic circumstances govern the emergence of disputes from grievances. Disputes arise from soured relationships, such as frayed friendships, strained relationships among coworkers, mistreatment in the marketplace, and hurt feelings among family members. The fact that most disputes arise from ongoing relationships is very important for the ways in which they are processed. Such relationships, as we will see, provide the basis for using nonlegal, private arenas to work out the problems. However, other disputes involve complete strangers, such as those arising from automobile accidents or defective products manufactured by a faceless corporation. In those instances, fewer informal remedies and procedures are available to resolve the dispute. In addition, a few disputes become aggregated into social conflicts and migrate to the political arena, where demands are made for collective solutions and the authoritative allocation of values. But those disputes are the exception in the United States. As indicated in Chapter 1, social and economic forces are much more prominent than political factors at the outer ring of the legal system, where disputes are generated.

Once an unmet claim has emerged as a dispute and has not been dropped (a process called **exit**), there are four ways of handling it: negotiation, mediation, arbitration, or adjudication.[4] Each has quite different characteristics.

Dispute Processing Arenas

The most frequently used process for handling disputes is **negotiation.** Negotiations may involve either the principals to the dispute or their representatives, but no outside party participates. The disputants seek some common ground for a settlement. Often such negotiations occur when the disputants share some important cultural or social identity, such as being members of the same religion, living in the same neighborhood, belonging to the same club, or working at the same place. The norms they invoke in settling their disputes are sometimes the law but more often are informal social norms. Often the norm is one of "fairness." A neighborhood grocer might decide to make a refund for spoiled meat because the customer is a "regular" and has not made many such complaints previously. It seems fair to give the refund even though the meat may have spoiled in the customer's refrigerator. At the same time, such a customer knows the grocer and feels constrained to complain only when it is apparent that the spoilage is not the customer's fault and the claim seems to be "fair." Fairness in negotiations is not defined by some legal criterion, but by a community sense of what is right. Negotiations, therefore, often involve many informal customs and social norms, and relatively little law. In many negotiations, no one mentions the law and no lawyers are involved. However, law is not excluded from all negotiations. Labor and management negotiate wage

---

[4]William L. F. Felstiner, "Influences of Social Organization on Dispute Processing," *Law & Society Review* 9 (1974), pp. 63–94.

agreements with explicit references to labor law, and lawyers typically play a central role in those discussions.

Because the principals or their representatives are the only participants in the negotiation process, they retain full control. No outsiders impose a solution. Moreover, the negotiation process is often very informal. It may consist of neighbors talking across their fence or representatives meeting in a living room. Negotiations involve no required rituals.

A second way to handle a dispute is to take it to **mediation**.[5] Unlike negotiation, mediation involves a third party. Both sides to the dispute agree to invite a disinterested outsider to bring them together in a settlement. The mediator does this by finding common grounds and interests for building a settlement. For example, the mediator may appeal to the common religious beliefs of the disputants or to their common concern for their children (in the case of a family dispute). A mediator often suggests a particular settlement, but it is up to the disputants to accept or reject it. Law is often in the background, while social norms and customs play a more prominent role. However, unlike negotiations, in mediation the disputants surrender some control over the dispute to a third party. The mediator, rather than the concerned parties, sets the agenda and controls the direction of the discussion. The mediator often plays a vigorous role in emphasizing salient aspects of the dispute.

Arbitration is a third way to handle a dispute.[6] An arbitrator, like a mediator, is a disinterested third party chosen by the disputants. However, while a mediator makes suggestions, an arbitrator makes findings that are binding on the disputants. Part of the arbitration process requires that the disputants agree beforehand to abide by the arbitrator's decision. If they later refuse to accept the decision, it may be brought to a court for enforcement. Law plays a more important role in many arbitrations, although social custom may still be prominent. Arbitrators are more likely to be professionals who specialize in settling disputes in a particular situation; for instance, a quite different group of arbitrators works in labor disputes than in disputes between diamond merchants. The law plays a more visible role because the arbitration agreement is enforceable in court. The setting for arbitration is likewise more formal than for negotiation or mediation. The need for a prior agreement to arbitrate the dispute dictates some of this formality. The potential enforceability of arbitration decisions in courts also requires that the arbitration follow agreed upon procedures. Furthermore, the role of the third party is much greater in arbitration than in mediation. Arbitrators *decide* rather than *suggest*. When parties to a dispute agree to submit it to arbitration, they also consent to give up control over the dispute resolution process and to place their fate in the hands of a third party.

Finally, disputants may take their troubles to court if they involve a claim for which there is a legal remedy. Bringing cases to court introduces a judge into the dis-

[5]Susan S. Silbey and Sally E. Merry, "Mediator Settlement Strategies," *Law & Policy* 8 (1986), pp. 7–32.
[6]Soia Mentschikoff and Ernest A. Haggard, "Decision Making and Decision Consensus in Commercial Arbitration," in June Louin Tapp and Felice J. Levine (eds.), *Law, Justice, and the Individual in Society* (New York: Holt, Rinehart & Winston, 1977), pp. 295–307; Herbert M. Kritzer and Jill K. Anderson, "The Arbitration Alternative: A Comparative Analysis of Case Processing Time, Disposition Mode, and Cost in the American Arbitration Association and the Courts," Working Papers, Disputes Processing Research Program, University of Wisconsin, mimeographed (Madison, 1983).

pute, a third party not chosen by the disputants but appointed by the government. Judges have no preconceived personal interest in the dispute; they represent the public interest and impose decisions that represent that communal concern. Because judges rule according to the law, rather than according to private norms and customs, disputants lose control over the outcome of disputes brought to court. Even when negotiations continue after the parties have gone to court, they do so in a very different atmosphere than if no court case had been filed. Often such negotiations directly involve the judge; sometimes they occur under the threat of a court-imposed solution.

Adjudication in court imposes a high degree of formality on the disputing process. Courts are governed by rituals that must be carefully followed. Court procedures also dictate the elements of the dispute that will be considered relevant. For example, in the dispute with our neighbor, the fact that we had never become close friends clearly affected our ability to negotiate. Had the dispute gone to court, however, our relationship would have been entirely irrelevant.

It is important to note that none of these procedures necessarily resolves a dispute. Disputes often linger for many years and migrate from one forum to another until they finally fade away because they lose their salience. Therefore, it is better to think of these as types of **dispute processing** rather than as alternatives for **dispute resolution.**

The alternative dispute-processing arenas differ on many characteristics. Table 3.1 summarizes and arranges the arenas according to the amount of third-party involvement. As one moves from no third-party involvement in negotiation, to binding third-party decisions in arbitration and adjudication, one also moves to different degrees of outsider participation, levels of required resources, variations in the role of law, participant control, formality, and constraint over facts. We have already discussed the differences in third-party involvement for each of these methods. We now turn to the variations in the other characteristics.

REQUIRED RESOURCES

The resources required for each arena are very important in the choice of a process for processing disputes. Each requires different amounts and types of resources for effective use. As one moves from negotiation to adjudication, the amount of required resources increases. Negotiation is potentially the least expensive. If disputants negotiate directly with one another, it may require nothing but the expenditure of personal time and attention. When representatives are used, they often are friends or acquaintances, rather than specialists. Because many negotiations are informal, the cost of information is of-

TABLE 3.1   Characteristics of Dispute-Processing Arenas

	Third-Party Involvement	Required Resources	Role of Law	Participant Control	Degree of Formality	Use of Facts
Negotiation	None	Few	Least	Maximum	Little	Unbounded
Mediation	Some	More	More	Less	Little	Bounded
Arbitration	More	More	Still more	Still less	More	Bounded
Adjudication	Most	Most	Most	Least	Most	Bounded

ten low. The parties may agree to rely on their memories, rather than requiring documentation; the presentation of information is likely to be oral and informal and, therefore also inexpensive. Only when negotiations involve specialized representatives, such as attorneys, are the costs likely to rise. Relative to other methods of dispute processing, the cost of negotiations is low.

Mediation and arbitration always use a third party. Although people may ask friends or acquaintances to play this role, they normally employ an outsider whom they must pay. In addition, arbitration often also requires hiring legal representatives for each party. Other costs are also higher in mediation and arbitration. In many cases, the disputants wish to meet on neutral ground, which means they may have to pay for a meeting room. Since an outsider is involved, more background information will be required, which means the process may take more time than would negotiation, and some of the information needed may be in the form of documents and testimony from witnesses.

Adjudication is the most expensive. Disputants must almost always hire lawyers to represent them. The judge requires formal presentation of information in the form of documentation and testimony. Trials necessitate substantial preparation, which consumes much time and money; the trial itself usually takes one or more days.

The four methods of dispute processing also differ in the types of resources required. Negotiation and mediation require that disputants share certain values. Negotiations between strangers often fail because they lack the shared values needed to find common ground on which to negotiate. Similarly, mediation has better results if the dispute involves continuing relationships. Arbitration generally requires a prior agreement about the standards to be imposed and the procedures to be used. However, adjudication does not require such commonalities. Adjudication is suited to processing disputes between strangers who share nothing but the perception that they can be forced to submit to the law of the land.

THE ROLE OF LAW

Equally important to the choice of a dispute-processing forum is the role law plays in each. Table 3.1 indicates that law plays an increasingly central role as one moves from negotiation to adjudication. The varying effects of the law have many implications.

Law may have two separate effects: it may dictate the standards applied to the dispute, and it may specify the procedures used. Legal scholars Robert Mnookin and Lewis Kornhauser[7] have suggested that many negotiations occur in "the shadow of the law." This occurs particularly when lawyers are involved, since they are trained to see problems from a legal perspective. Even when lawyers are not present, people may apply what they think are legal standards or procedures.

However, direct negotiations between the disputants may instead rely on social norms they share, which sometimes echo legal norms, but sometimes are quite different. For instance, when spouses who have children divorce, they may decide that the chil-

---

[7]Robert H. Mnookin and Lewis Kornhauser, "Bargaining in the Shadow of the Law: The Case of Divorce," *Yale Law Journal* 88 (1979), pp. 950–997.

dren should stay with the mother, because women usually take care of the children. Even though the law is gender-neutral, the social norms to which many couples adhere are not.[8]

Mediation and arbitration are likely to rely on a mixture of law and social norms. The specific blend depends on the background of the mediator, the degree to which disputants share common social norms, and the nature of the dispute. Family disputes mediated by mental health professionals are more likely to employ a mix rich in social norms, while labor disputes mediated by labor lawyers are more likely to employ a mix rich in legal norms. However, the techniques employed in all mediation rely mostly on social norms of fairness, rather than legally prescribed procedures. Since the outcome of the mediation must be accepted voluntarily by both parties, procedural irregularities cannot be appealed to a court; rather, the disputant who feels the procedure was biased may simply reject the outcome. In arbitration, however, disputants often agree beforehand to the procedures, and failure to follow them may be appealed to a court.

Courts employ the most law. Law specifies both the standards used to adjudicate the dispute and the procedures employed to reach the outcome. For instance, consider the statutory prohibition against sex discrimination in Title VII of the Civil Rights Act of 1964. In one case, the president of a forklift rental company told his manager, a woman, in front of other employees, that she was a "dumb-ass woman," proposed that they both go to the Holiday Inn to negotiate her raise, asked her to get coins from his front pocket, and indulged in many other demeaning acts and remarks. She complained to him and he promised to stop such behavior, but resumed after a few days. She quit her job and sued on the basis that he had made the work environment abusive because of her gender. The trial court and appeals court decided that, while these acts and words might offend a reasonable woman, they were not serious enough to constitute a hostile work environment. The Supreme Court disagreed, and held that these actions were within the statute's prohibition.[9] Note that the plaintiff's request for her employer to stop the abuse did not invoke the law. Only after she failed to negotiate a remedy did she use the law and go to court. In such a case, not only must the aggrieved person show that the behavior falls within the definition of some prohibition, they must also demonstrate that the behavior actually occurred according to the law's procedures which require documentary and eyewitness evidence proving the claimed harrassment by a preponderance of the evidence.

For the law to cast a shadow on bargaining or to be invoked in mediation, arbitration, or adjudication, disputants must have some knowledge of the law, and such knowledge is often limited. Knowledge about the law requires an awareness of at least three elements. First, persons must know the substance of the law; second, they must have some awareness of the applicable sanctions and remedies; third, they must have some knowledge of legal procedures.

Knowledge of the substance of the law includes a rudimentary understanding of what is permitted and prohibited. Most people possess little legal knowledge. Take, for

[8]Herbert Jacob, "The Elusive Shadow of the Law," *Law & Society Review* 26 (1992), pp. 665–690. For another example, see Robert C. Ellickson, *Order Without Law: How Neighbors Settle Disputes* (Cambridge, Mass.: Harvard University Press, 1991).
[9]*Harris v. Forklift Systems,* No. 92-1168, decided November 9, 1993.

instance, the obligations incurred when people marry, or the remedies that may be available to them in a divorce. Marriage, like many acts, involves a mixture of social and legal norms, and most people confuse the two. Baker and Emery,[10] for instance, asked marriage license applicants, law students in a family law course, and undergraduates in a psychology course to explain the ramifications of the marriage contract. They found that none of the groups, not even the law students, had substantial knowledge of the legal obligations incurred in marriage. Likewise, Jacob[11] found that when recently divorced parents were interviewed, many misstated the legal norms for child support. Such lack of knowledge makes it difficult for people to invoke legal norms even when they want to. It is the principal reason that people consult with lawyers, and explains why legal norms are less prominent when lawyers are not involved in dispute processing.

The second essential element is knowledge of the sanctions that are threatened by the law and the available remedies. Without this knowledge, the law may play no role in processing disputes because people either do not fear it or do not know what remedies it might provide. If persons whose credit cards are stolen do not know that the law limits their liability to $50, they may unwittingly pay a larger amount. Similarly, consumers who do not know that many products carry an implied warranty may not think to return a defective item for a refund.

Despite substantial research on these first two cognitive prerequisites for invoking the law in disputes, our understanding of them nevertheless remains fragmentary. It is possible, however, to discern the outline of the law's potential for influencing behavior. It is evident that substantial socialization to fundamental ideas about law occurs in childhood.[12] Children learn to recognize the prohibitive and prescriptive character of law in their early school years. Elementary school children in the United States who were interviewed often spoke of the need for law to provide order. Without it, one fourth-grade girl said, "People would go around killing other people, and they'd be stealing things, and they'd be kidnapping people."[13] Very young children appear to personalize law in the figure of an idealized police officer.[14] As they grow older, they see law in terms of more direct, personal benefits.

Evidence from studies of adults suggests that public knowledge of the details of laws is limited.[15] People seem to know more about criminal law than about civil matters.[16]

---

[10]Lynn A. Baker and Robert E. Emery, "When Every Relationship Is Above Average," *Law & Human Behavior 17* (1993) pp. 439–450.

[11]Supra, note 8.

[12]June Louin Tapp and Lawrence Kohlberg, "Developing Senses of Law and Legal Justice," in Tapp and Levine (eds.), supra, note 6, pp. 94–101.

[13]Ibid., p. 94.

[14]Judith V. Torney, "Socialization of Attitudes Toward the Legal System," in Tapp and Levine (eds.), supra, note 6, pp. 134–144.

[15]Adam Podgorecki, Wolfgang Kaupen, J. Van Houtte, P. Vinke, and Berl Kutchinsky, *Knowledge and Opinion about Law* (London: Martin Robertson, 1973).

[16]Austin Sarat, "Support for the Legal System: An Analysis of Knowlege, Attitudes, and Behavior," *American Politics Quarterly 3* (1975), pp. 11–14; Austin Sarat, "Studying American Legal Culture: An Assessment of Survey Evidence," *Law & Society Review 11* (1977), p. 451; "Legal Knowledge of Michigan Citizens," *Michigan Law Review 71* (1973), pp. 1463–1486.

Almost everyone seems to know that common crimes such as theft, burglary, rape, and murder are against the law. However, specific knowledge of the sanctions that might be imposed for such offenses is far from universal. The most comprehensive examination of public knowledge of criminal sanctions was made during the 1960s in California.[17] This study indicated that more people underestimated than overestimated sanctions and that only 30 percent of the sample could give the correct penalty for more than three of the eleven offenses about which they were asked.[18] On noncriminal matters, a study of public knowledge about laws of inheritance showed that less than half the sample knew who would inherit their property if they had no will[19]

Knowledge about law appears to be related to social status, but even high-status people often know quite little. Researchers have shown that persons with higher education and income know more about the law than those with less education and income. However, even the high-income Anglos in this study achieved only an average of 18.9 correct answers on a 30-item test, while low-income Hispanics scored an average of 12.8 correct answers.[20]

A third cognitive element is knowledge about legal procedures. Few people possess sufficient knowledge about these procedures to invoke the law without the assistance of one of the gatekeepers described in Chapter 1. Finding such gatekeepers, however, is not always simple. Persons must know where to find a lawyer, how to engage the interest of a police officer, or how to attract the concern of an interest group. These matters are discussed in detail in Chapters 5 to 7.

Knowledge about the law and its role in the alternative procedures affects calculations that people make in deciding what to do about their disputes. In choosing a dispute-processing forum, people try to estimate the potential benefits. Such calculations are complicated because much uncertainty attends the invocation of the law. Even with the law on their side, many people lose lawsuits because a crucial witness dies or performs poorly on the witness stand. Others may find (as we show in Chapter 5) that their lawyer is more interested in profit than in the client's benefit. Some disputants enter negotiations, arbitration, or adjudication confident that the law is on their side only to find that their adversary has found a countervailing legal principle that prevails. Potential law violators face similar difficulty in estimating whether the law, if violated, will be invoked against them. Experience teaches that many laws can be violated with impunity. We know that much tax evasion goes undetected and unpunished, and that many commercial practices are outside the law but never prosecuted. Much shoplifting and pilfering also goes unnoticed. But partial enforcement of the law is no defense if

[17]California Committee on Criminal Procedure, "Public Knowledge of Criminal Penalties," in Richard L. Henshel and Robert A. Silverman (eds.), *Perception in Criminology* (New York: Columbia University Press, 1975), pp. 74–90.
[18]Ibid., p. 78.
[19]Mary Louise Fellows, Rita J. Simon, and William Rau, "Public Attitudes About Property Distribution at Death and Intestate Succession Laws in the United States," *American Bar Foundation Research Journal 1978* (1978), p. 340.
[20]Martha Williams and Jay Hall, "Knowledge of the Law in Texas: Socioeconomic and Ethnic Differences," *Law & Society Review 7* (1972), p. 113.

one is caught and prosecuted. Therefore, calculation of the probable consequences of violating the law is no simpler than calculation of the probable benefits of invoking it.[21]

PARTICIPANT CONTROL

Another important difference among the four dispute-processing arenas is the degree of participant control. As Table 3.1 shows, this control is greatest in negotiation and least in adjudication. Negotiation can proceed without an outsider; therefore, the disputants can be entirely on their own. The disputants decide what norms to employ, what kinds of proof are sufficient, what outcomes will be acceptable. They also determine the schedule. No outsider makes suggestions, favors one side or the other, or follows an independent agenda. Of course, each disputant may employ a representative or consultant, such as an attorney, but at least in theory, such representatives are controlled by the disputants who hire them. In most cases, the only constraint on the outcome is its acceptability to the disputants.

The other three dispute-processing arenas involve third parties, norms that may be imposed from the outside, and procedures that may bring still other strangers into the decision-making process. In mediation, the mediator's own values often play a role in setting the agenda for the mediation process, defining the dispute, and suggesting a settlement. Greatbatch and Dingwall[22] and Staidl[23] show that mediators who are mental health professionals exercise a different kind of control, structuring the process in a way that, according to their experience and values, will lead to an acceptable agreement. Simply by making suggestions about alternative solutions, mediators influence the course of the mediation and guide disputants to outcomes they might not have considered on their own. Sometimes those outcomes are superior to what would have otherwise happened; at other times, they impose the mediator's own values on the problems of their clients.

The third party's role is still greater in arbitration. Arbitrators act much like judges. They hand down decisions and, in doing so, often invoke values that may be foreign to the disputants. To some extent, the degree to which they do so is constrained by the fact that the disputants jointly select their arbitrator and would, presumably, not choose one who would impose unacceptable values. Moreover, most arbitrators rely on personal recommendations for new clients; if they get a reputation for openly imposing personal values, new clients are likely to shun them.

Court adjudication offers the least amount of control to disputants. When they bring a dispute to court, they must accept the law of their jurisdiction, the procedures of the court, and the judge assigned to their case. Sophisticated litigants may attempt to

[21]In general, see Frank M. Gollop and Jeffrey Marquardt, "A Microeconomic Model of Household Choice: The Household as Disputant," *Law & Society Review* 15 (1980–81), pp. 611–630; for discussions of uncertainty in enforcing criminal laws, see especially Franklin E. Zimring and Gordon J. Hawkins, *Deterrence* (Chicago: University of Chicago Press, 1973).
[22]David Greatbatch and Robert Dingwall, "Selective Facilitation: Some Preliminary Observations on a Strategy Used by Divorce Mediators," *Law & Society Review* 23 (1989), pp. 613–642.
[23]Tracy Lynn Staidl, "Perceptions of Attorneys and Private Mediators Regarding the Process of Divorce," typescript, Northwestern University, Department of Political Science, May 1993.

choose their jurisdiction so that the substantive law and procedural rules are as favorable as they can be to their cause. They may engage in whatever "judge-shopping" is possible. In the end, however, they must accept the involvement of many strangers over whom they have little or no control.

Consequently, the choice of forum also involves a choice of control. Sacrificing control may be advantageous to disputants when their antagonists are more powerful than they, because forums other than negotiation may do a better job of leveling the playing field. In other instances, loss of control means imposition of norms that neither party prefers.

DEGREE OF FORMALITY

A fourth characteristic of dispute-processing forums is the degree of formality that governs the proceedings. This may appear to be only a superficial difference, but it affects some disputants' choice of forum. Negotiation, because it is informal, can take place in almost any setting in which the disputants feel comfortable. Negotiation often may span many casual meetings until a settlement is reached. Negotiations may be entirely private with no one else knowing about them. Mediation and arbitration are more likely to occur in unfamiliar settings and at specific times, if only because they involve other persons whose schedules and locations must be accommodated. Because they may occur in a quasi-public setting, such as an office, they are less likely to be entirely private.

Courts are the most formal setting. Trials take place in special public buildings and in specially designed rooms that emphasize the authority of the judge, who sits above all others. Everyone has an assigned place in the courtroom: separate tables for the attorneys for each side, an enclosed area near the judge for witnesses, a set of chairs or benches at the side for the jury. From the moment the judge enters, all the proceedings follow a set ritual.

Courtroom formality can readily intimidate disputants. It is common for witnesses and litigants to think of a trial as an ordeal. Moreover, adjudication takes place in public, where anyone may watch, and it is potential fodder for the public media.

USE OF FACTS

The last trait of dispute-processing arenas indicated in Table 3.1 is the way facts are used. In negotiation, disputants may present their story in any way they wish. The only limit is the other side's patience. The disputants discuss whatever seems relevant; they are the sole judges of relevance.

In the other three disputing processes, the third parties play a role in deciding what facts need to be exposed. Mediators do this less than arbitrators, who control fact presentations less than do judges. Mediators may suggest that only certain facts be considered relevant to reach a common ground for settlement; that is part of their task of setting the agenda and defining the issues. For instance, in a divorce mediation, the mediator may begin by asking each spouse to create a budget; this not only focuses discussion on financial matters, but also initially establishes each partner's income and expenses. The mediator may later ask for documentation of income, but perhaps not, if there is no dispute about it. Arbitrators often take a more aggressive role because the disputants already have agreed to a set of rules that often includes procedures for defining the issues and excluding irrelevant matters. They are much more likely to demand formal documentation of critical information. Courts are the most stringent in defining the relevance of facts. For example, the rules of evidence specify that if a witness heard someone else's report of an event, rather than experiencing it directly, such information is considered hearsay and is not admissible. Likewise, if a witness is to be certified as an expert, he or she must present documentation of their expertise to the judge, who decides whether to accept the information from that witness. Thus, a court employs quite different criteria to authenticate facts, and they are substantially more restrictive than those used in negotiation, mediation, or arbitration.

THE CHOICE OF FORUM

Disputants choose a forum for the features it offers. Of course, they do not lay them out as we have; rather, they choose on the basis of imperfect information, hunches, and momentary convenience.

How disputants think about their problems is especially important. If they think of it as a social problem, they are likely to seek an informal forum for resolving their grievance. If they think of it as a matter of rights and law, they are much more likely to move toward adjudication.[24] For instance, if a dinner guest never arrives, the host is unlikely to think of this as a breach of contract, even though the guest agreed to come. Many hosts would not complain, but simply would not invite the guest again. Others may telephone the missing guest and negotiate an apology. However, the grievance remains a violation of social, not legal, norms. When disputants identify a problem as having legal ramifications, it is more likely to move from negotiation or mediation to arbitration or adjudication, arenas in which the law plays a more prominent role. Thus, a grievance arising from the denial of a promotion because the candidate was a woman is likely to seen in terms of a violation of rights, and lead to a demand for arbitration or for an order from a court.

Many disputes begin in one arena and move to another. If negotiation or mediation fails, the aggrieved party may redefine the issue as one of legal rights and take the matter to court. However, disputes are not simply shifted from one arena to another. In the process of moving from informal processing (as in negotiation) to formal processing (as in adjudication), disputes are often transformed in several ways.[25] The application of law to a dispute often requires that the dispute be changed to fit into standard legal categories, because the aggrieved party must demonstrate a violation of the law, and a legal remedy must exist. In this transformation process, a dispute becomes, as Table 3.1 suggests, more bounded. The new legal case focuses only on those issues that both have sig-

[24]Jacob, supra, note 8.
[25]Lynn Mather and Barbara Yngvesson, "Language, Audience, and the Transformation of Disputes," *Law & Society Review 15* (1980–81), pp. 775–822.

nificance to the disputants and fit the categories required by the laws being invoked. For instance, it is not uncommon when women feel they are being sexually harrassed by their male coworkers for the men to claim they are unaware that their stares, their use of such terms as "honey" and "babe," and their jokes are offensive. Women may first informally negotiate with the offenders, attempting to change their behavior on the basis of social propriety and courtesy. If such efforts are rebuffed, those women may begin to think about their rights to a nonthreatening work environment and may file a grievance through their union or a complaint with management. If those efforts fail, they may go to a lawyer and file a lawsuit. With each move, the grievance becomes narrower. In negotiation and mediation, the disputants may discuss the general ambience of the workplace, including illustrations of offensive acts. In arbitration and adjudication, however, specific acts of harrassment must be documented. The dispute is thereby narrowed to the facts surrounding each time someone inappropriately used a term of endearment or made an offensive joke. The focus moves to individual instances rather than the general atmosphere of the workplace. The issue becomes whether the harrassment meets the legal standards set forth by statutes and prior court cases.

Disputes may also be broadened in some ways when they become legal cases. In the above example, the employer becomes a party to the case when it goes to court, although the original dispute was between fellow workers. Another kind of expansion occurs if the aggrieved women take their case to an organization, that then uses it to try to expand the judicial interpretation of what is illegal behavior.

Such transformations do not simply happen; they must be carefully constructed. An error in the transformation process may be fatal to the claim, either because it arouses unexpected opposition or because it fails to fit the legal categories invoked. These transformations occur regardless of whether a case is brought to court or simply broached in a lawyer's office. As soon as a disputant explicitly invokes the law, either privately or publicly, the dispute changes in an important way.

A disputant's choice of forum is consequently complex. It depends on consideration of all the factors we have discussed, a process that is still poorly understood. When disputes are between persons with ongoing relationships, negotiation or mediation is more likely, at least in the beginning, because the disputants share values and because the privacy and informality in those methods promise a degree of protection to the continuing relationship. In addition, persons who have little information about lawyers or the legal process may also begin with negotiation. Where the stakes are small, negotiation is also likely to be preferred.

The four processes are not entirely distinct. The choice of a dispute-processing forum does not simply occur at the beginning of a dispute, but may be a continuing phenomenon. Quite frequently, in the midst of adjudication, arbitration, or mediation, negotiations may occur that settle the dispute, obviating the need to continue the more formal proceedings. In other cases, negotiation or mediation may be interrupted by a court hearing and then resume.

We can observe some of these conditions at work by examining the empirical evidence on the generation of legal disputes in the United States as shown in Figure 3.2. People surveyed in 1973 and 1974 commonly used lawyers for only four sets of problems: three involved marital breakup (separation, divorce, and postdivorce) and the

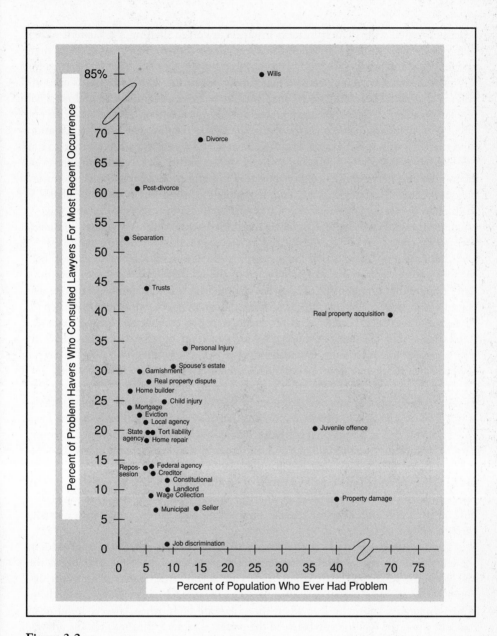

Figure 3.2
Lawyer Use in Most Recent Occurrence of Each of Twenty-Nine Problems
Source: Barbara A. Curran, *The Legal Needs of the Public: The Final Report of a National Survey* (Chicago: American Bar Foundation, 1977), p. 135

other concerned wills (which in most instances involved drafting a document rather than processing a dispute). In 17 of the 29 problems shown in the figure, fewer than one-fourth of the persons with problems engaged an attorney.[26] These data can be interpreted in two ways. Many persons may simply not define their problems as ones involving the law. Thus, landlord problems might be seen as commercial and personal problems rather than legal ones, and problems with state agencies may be viewed as political problems rather than ones involving administrative law. The other explanation (and the one principally advanced by the researcher) is that many people either do not have access to lawyers or fear going to them. Miller and Sarat have shown that even when problems become disputes, a majority of disputants use lawyers only when they have tort claims (such as from automobile accident injuries) and postdivorce claims.[27] In disputes involving consumer claims, debts, discrimination, property, claims to government agencies, and landlords, fewer than one-fourth of the disputants consulted with an attorney.

Other research suggests that many people in the United States feel uneasy or ineffective in court. In a study Jacob conducted in the mid-1960s in Wisconsin, less than half of a random sample of urban debtors who had no previous court experience displayed a high sense of "judicial efficacy."[28] Instead, most agreed with statements such as, "I can't use the courts because legal proceedings are too complicated for me to understand them," and "It doesn't do much good to go to court because the courts are biased against people like me." Such attitudes influence decisions either to invoke the law or to find some other remedy for one's problems (including simply living with them).

In addition, the Wisconsin study, which focused on delinquent debtors, suggests the existence of certain subcommunities that share information about particular problems. The study indicated delinquent debtors learned from each other about the legal procedures for declaring personal bankruptcy as a way to protect themselves. Moreover, persons with greater wealth and more education tended to be better informed about legal procedures. Finally, as we see in Chapter 6, lawyers are better organized to take care of the claims of the affluent than of the poor. Although legal aid offices exist in many places, they are often located far from where prospective clients live and are sometimes difficult to mobilize. In contrast, the person who can afford to hire an attorney usually can find one.

Thus, a combination of cognitive and situational factors plays important roles in the choice of a dispute-processing forum. When those involved know little about the law, when the stakes are small, when lawyers are beyond their reach, or when the disputants have close, personal relationships, they may decide to negotiate or mediate. When disputants know the law, when the stakes are high, when lawyers are close at hand, or when the relationship between the parties is remote, they may choose arbitration or adjudication. People use the law when they know what it permits and prohibits, when they understand what sanctions and remedies are available, and when they both

[26]Barbara A. Curran, *The Legal Needs of the Public: The Final Report of a National Survey* (Chicago: American Bar Foundation, 1977), p. 135. Curran's data refer to "problems" rather than "disputes" and therefore may underestimate the proportion of persons going to an attorney once they become involved in a dispute.
[27]Miller and Sarat, supra, note 2, p. 537.
[28]Herbert Jacob, *Debtors in Court* (Chicago: Rand McNally, 1969), p. 119.

understand and have the resources to use the procedures that must be followed to transform their claims into legal disputes.

Because knowledge of the law and possession of the resources required for its use are unevenly distributed in the United States, use of the law is also unequal. It is well established that wealthier persons are more likely to invoke the law in their affairs than poorer ones.[29] This results from a combination of factors: the wealthy have more problems that explicitly involve the law, they have better knowledge of the law, they are more skilled at framing grievances in legal terms, and they are offered greater benefits by the law. In Curran's study, as shown in Figure 3.2, wills were the problem that most frequently brought people to lawyers. Those mostly involve problems of the rich because the poor have little property to bequeath. Likewise, corporations, whether large or small, are much more likely to use lawyers than are individuals. In part, that is the result of the need to execute certain legal documents to create and run a corporation, but it is also a consequence of businesses being accustomed to using specialists, and lawyers are the specialists if there is legal trouble.

EXPERIENCE AND DISPUTING

Another important distinction that may affect the choice of disputing forum is between those Galanter labels as **one-shotters** and **repeat players.**[30] Repeat players frequently, and sometimes continuously, participate in disputes, while one-shotters are only occasionally involved. The difference is epitomized by the contrast between docile tenants who during their entire lifetime may never confront their landlord about a problem and executives of a property management firm who routinely go to court to evict problematic tenants.

Recurrent use of legal procedures provides important advantages to the repeat players. They are likely to be more familiar with both the law and the courts that deal with their cases, and their attorneys are likely to be more specialized. Repeat players are better able to adapt their mode of operations or business style to the vagaries of the law. For instance, debtors who have had their wages seized several times learn how to disguise their place of employment; lenders learn how to take advantage of ways the law helps creditors collect bad debts. Repeat players often can absorb occasional losses more readily, a fact that enables them to develop a long-term dispute-processing strategy that one-shotters cannot match. For one-shotters, each dispute is likely to be a matter of great urgency; it may mean loss of their home, depletion of their savings, or a substantial reduction in other assets. Repeat players can more readily absorb defeats because they are not catastrophes; a lost case is only one of a continuous stream, most of which are won. While repeat players normally are large organizations with seemingly limitless resources, one-shotters usually are individuals with minimal resources. Organizations generally have greater resources than individuals, and they are often re-

---

[29]Curran, supra, note 26, pp. 188–189; Leon H. Hayhew, "Institutions of Representation: Civil Justice and the Public," *Law & Society Review* 9 (1975), pp. 424–425; Leon H. Mayhew and Albert J. Reiss, Jr., "The Social Organization of Legal Contacts," *American Sociological Review* 34 (1969), pp. 311–313.
[30]Marc Galanter, "Why the Haves Come Out Ahead: Speculations on the Limits of Legal Change," *Law & Society Review* 9 (1974), pp. 95 ff.

peat players rather than one-shotters. It is not always easy to discern whether someone's advantage in a legal process comes from experience or affluence, but there can be
no doubt that the combination favors some people. However, while experience, expertise, and economic resources often go together, it would be a mistake to think that
they always give one party in a dispute an advantage over the other. Sometimes both
parties are relatively wealthy and experienced, as we shall see in our discussion of commercial cases.

Even when disputes involve repeat players, it is not clear they will always prefer invocation of the law to less formal means of dispute processing. Stewart Macaulay has argued, for example, that most businesses exhibit little concern for the details of contract
law. His studies of corporate dealings, particularly in the automobile industry, indicate
that while business people routinely draw up contracts for their business arrangements,
they place little reliance on them if the deal goes sour. Macaulay writes that business
people use contract law as a tactic to obtain a negotiated settlement, but that heroic efforts are often made to avoid litigation. According to his findings, the use of the law in
business is subtle:

> At least among many business people in the United States, an intelligent threat to
> sue for breach of contract by one who wants to maintain a relationship will be
> made only tacitly or very indirectly. Even a letter from a lawyer may be deemed a
> declaration of war, and so business people may do all the negotiating although they
> may speak from scripts written by lawyers. Yet the very vocabulary used by these
> nonlawyers may signal that matters have moved a step further toward litigation,
> and thus constitute an intelligent threat.[31]

SUMMARY

The choice of forum for processing disputes is both subtle and complex. Many persons
with grievances never invoke the law because they abandon their claims without taking
them to a dispute-processing arena. In other instances, the grievance does not become a
dispute because the claim is satisfied by the other party. Even when a claim becomes a
dispute, the role of the law varies. If disputants use negotiation or mediation, law often
remains in the background. When disputants resort to arbitration, law is usually invoked more explicitly. Whether a problem becomes a legal dispute depends on the disputants' knowledge of the law, their experience, their resources, and their calculation of
costs and benefits. Only when disputants bring their problems to court does the law play
an indisputably central role.

These complexities of the legal process become clearer when they are considered in
the context of concrete disputes. In the remainder of this chapter, we illustrate the ways
in which grievances migrate from one dispute-processing arena to another and how disputants use their resources in both the judicial and legislative arenas after they have decided to leave the more private arenas of negotiation, mediation, or arbitration.

[31]Stewart Macaulay, "Elegant Models, Empirical Pictures, and the Complexities of Contract," *Law & Society
Review 11* (1977), p. 520.

Disputes In and Out of Court

The parties involved in disputes span the social spectrum. Anyone may file for a divorce or be hit by an automobile. Even the poor may be involved in monetary disputes. They are sued for nonpayment of debts and rent; they may be victims of medical malpractice. Rich and poor quarrel among themselves and between one another, and some of these quarrels migrate from informal dispute-processing arenas to the courts. In this section, we examine a wide range of disputes. Most of the illustrations involve court actions because they are better documented than informal negotiation or mediation, but we need to remember that for every 1000 grievances, only 50 become lawsuits.[32] These cases also are more illustrative of large disputes, which are different in some ways from the ordinary ones that afflict the common person and are rarely researched in depth. Consequently, we keep an eye on the other forums and cases of dispute processing for the ways they affect what happens in court and in other formal legal institutions, and for their impact on common people as well as on the rich and powerful.

In most instances, aggrieved parties do not formally invoke the law, but use it informally to seek a private settlement of their dispute. They may go to the customer service desk of a store or to a Better Business Bureau with their complaint.[33] In such nonlegal forums, however, the complainant's legal position often affects the outcome, although other factors play a significant role. For instance, a purchase agreement often gives a car dealer the right to retain a deposit even if the customer decides not to buy the car. On the other hand, the dealer must consider that customers and their friends may take their future business to another dealer if the deposit is not returned. Because this relationship, like so many others, has the potential for continuity, the dealer may compromise by returning a portion of the deposit in the hope of retaining the customer's goodwill. In many business dealings, disputants reach a compromise in such a fashion, by direct negotiation, mediation, or arbitration, because both parties have a stake in continuing the supplier-consumer relationship. The law gives some parties a strong bargaining position they may partially surrender because of countervailing social or economic pressures; however, they generally remain better off than if they had not initially possessed the legal advantage.

No national statistics exist about the outcomes of court cases, but the best available estimates indicate that most cases involve relatively small amounts of money. This was the finding of the most comprehensive study yet conducted, which examined 1423 disputes in five locations scattered across the United States, and drawn from both federal and state trial courts.[34] In these cases, the median judgment was $4289; 38 percent of all cases surveyed brought judgments of less than $2500. When attorneys' fees are taken into account, the return was even smaller.[35] Indeed, 6 percent of the cases cost more to

---

[32]Miller and Sarat, supra, note 2, p. 544.

[33]Laura Nader (ed.), *No Access to Law: Alternatives to the American Judicial System* (New York: Academic, 1980); Marc Galanter, "Reading the Landscape of Disputes: What We Know and Don't Know (and Think We Know) About Our Allegedly Contentious and Litigious Society," *UCLA Law Review 31* (1983), pp. 1–71.

[34]Herbert M. Kritzer, *The Justice Broker: Lawyers and Ordinary Litigation* (New York: Oxford University Press, 1990), pp. 22–24.

litigate than was recovered in the judgment, meaning they resulted in a net loss to the "winner."

The advantages enjoyed by repeat players and litigants with substantial resources is supported in other research findings. In a study of foreclosure and eviction actions in Baltimore, Cleveland, and Milwaukee between 1965 and 1970, Wanner showed that individual defendants obtained a completely favorable outcome in only 8.8 percent of cases, while such plaintiffs as landlords, property management firms, and banks were completely successful in 71 percent of cases.[36] In summary debt actions, creditor plaintiffs won 13.5 times more often than debtor defendants.[37]

These findings provide important perspectives to the next stage of our examination of the disputing process. We first describe a set of disputes—divorces—that rarely involve large sums of money and in which vindication is frequently a goal. Divorce disputes also illustrate the mandatory use of the law, because the benefits of a divorce cannot be obtained without legal action. The second set of disputes we examine—consumer credit disputes—also typically involve ordinary people, but only as one party to the dispute, in the role of the customer or debtor. The other party in these disputes is often a large corporation with much greater wealth and litigation experience than the debtor.

After we examine these two kinds of disputes, which may touch the lives of every person, we look to more specialized uses of the law. We examine commercial litigation, which often involves huge corporations, large amounts of money, and very high stakes. The distinctions between one-shotters and repeat players and between winners and losers are more blurred here than in divorce and consumer credit disputes. Both sides often have experience in litigation and sufficient funds to finance a legal battle. Finally, we examine two situations in which the law has been explicitly used to advance policy and political objectives: the abortion and Watergate controversies. While even divorce disputes are encrusted with political overtones, if one looks beyond the immediate cases to their policy implications, abortion and Watergate illustrate explicitly political uses of legal arenas.

DIVORCE, CHILDREN, AND PROPERTY

When people seek a divorce, they want to get out of their legal marriage. The social ties that bind husband and wife together often have already been loosened by the couple's estrangment. The two may be living apart or as strangers under the same roof. They have often already made some financial arrangements between them. They seek a divorce decree to regularize their relationship; moreover, the divorce enables them to remarry.

Many divorces are more or less consensual. Many couples recognize that their marriage no longer is working. But disentangling their affairs is often a complicated process

---

[35]Ibid., p. 136.
[36]Craig Wanner, "The Public Ordering of Private Relations, Part II: Winning Civil Court Cases," *Law & Society Review* 9 (1975), p. 298. It is important to remember, however, that Wanner did not use as sophisticated a measure of winning or losing as Kritzer and his associates employed (see note 34). Wanner did not examine transaction costs and the net gain or loss from the court actions he studied.
[37]Ibid.

pockmarked with disputes. They must decide who owns what portion of their house, furniture, cars, bank accounts, pension funds, and other savings. They must also decide who will pay their debts to doctors, utilities, department stores, and credit card companies. How long, if at all, does one spouse provide support for the other, and at what level? If they have minor children, many more problems arise about where the children live, how the noncustodial parent has access to them, who makes important decisions such as where they go to school or college, what kinds of medical care are provided, or what religious education they receive. Children require financial support, and the couple must decide how much each will pay toward their support. All these decisions involve not only cold, hard cash but also deeply felt emotions. Moreover, they require trust that if future conditions change (and they almost always do), such as a much-reduced income resulting from unemployment or illness or substantially increased wealth resulting from promotions or a windfall, some reasonable accommodations will be made.

Thus, almost all elements of the couple's lives and those of their children are suddenly at stake. Even when the couple parts on friendly terms, they must negotiate the terms of their divorce, and those negotiations often are difficult, testing the limits of their relationship. When they part as enemies, as they sometimes do, obtaining an agreement or a settlement of these matters may be extremely difficult.

Some scholars have argued that divorce negotiations take place in "the shadow of the law,"[38] meaning that the many provisions imposed on divorce by statutes and court decisions influence the way uncoupling spouses negotiate. For instance, according to this model, knowledge about the conditions under which mothers obtain custody would influence a couple's decision involving whether the mother or father takes the children.

Jacob's research shows that while bargaining in the shadow of the law sometimes occurs, often it does not.[39] Many couples do not know much about the law. Moreover, their real concern is with themselves and their children, so they follow the social norms with which they are familiar in making decisions. Many presume that children will stay with the mother because in their social circles and experience, mothers care for children more often than fathers. They make financial arrangements that appear reasonable given their life circumstances. Having negotiated these issues—often in the informal setting of their kitchen table—they then take the results to an attorney to translate into a formal divorce decree, which can be submitted to a judge for approval.

When couples consult lawyers—and they almost always do sometime during the process—the law is likely to intrude more forcefully. On hearing the outcome of the negotiations, lawyers compare the terms with what they know is acceptable in their jurisdiction. If the property settlement or child support payments are out of line with what the law requires, lawyers must tell their clients the agreement will not pass muster, which leads to further negotiations to bring the terms into compliance with legal standards. In many instances, however, the legal standards are merely permissive and set guidelines. As long as the privately negotiated terms fall within the guidelines, they will be accepted in court.

[38]Mnookin and Kornhauser, supra, note 7.
[39]The following is based on the research reported by Jacob, supra, note 8.

Some couples use mediators to help them reach a settlement. They turn to a mediator—who may be a mental health professional or a lawyer—to assist them in negotiating. Many feel uncomfortable dealing directly with their estranged spouse. Many want to learn what alternatives are available. Typically, the mediator requires the couple to confront the financial realities that divorce imposes, to consider how they can continue parenting their children, and to adapt solutions familiar to the mediator to their own situation. At the end, the mediator drafts an agreement both spouses find acceptable and tells them to take it to an attorney for review and translation into a legal document that will be presented to a court. This process is more costly than private negotiations but less expensive than relying on lawyers to negotiate the entire agreement.

Despite the expense, other couples rely much more heavily on lawyers. The couple goes to them without an agreement; they may not be able to negotiate directly. They may not even be able to sit at the same table. In such cases, the husband's attorney negotiates with the wife's attorney, and the attorneys then try to convince their clients to accept the agreement they have reached. In such negotiations, the law plays a very large role because it provides the standards by which the attorneys decide what is reasonable and fair.

Very few divorce disputes go to trial. In most instances, trials are far too expensive for the issues involved. Moreover, few couples wish to bring their disputes into such a public arena. In addition, judges despise such cases because they involve obstinate disputants who should be able to settle their affairs privately, and rarely involve significant points of law. Thus, both attorneys and judges usually work hard to keep such cases out of court.

However, every divorce requires a brief court hearing. This occurs in a very brief ceremony during which the judge asks the complainant whether the agreement is voluntary and whether he or she is satisfied with it. The judge quickly scans the agreement to make sure all required provisions are present. The entire proceeding often takes less than ten minutes, after which the judge signs the proposed decree and it becomes an enforceable court order. Even when a real trial occurs, most of the issues of the divorce have been settled, and only one or two are contested in court. The remaining issues often involve child custody, because property can be compromised more easily than can relationships with children.

Note the progression from negotiation or mediation to adjudication. The transformation that takes place in settled divorce cases as they move to court is the translation of agreements from ordinary language into legalese. Divorces settled out of court almost always remain undisturbed by the judge who ratifies them. However, the requirement that a judge ratify the divorce serves to privilege legal requirements in divorce settlements. Attorneys and mediators rarely endorse arrangements that conflict with statutory provisions or court practices.

Divorce involves disputants who have been intimately related and who often have a future stake in their relationship because of their children. Most husbands and wives are one-shotters who are completely unfamiliar with the legal procedures they must follow. Their attorneys, of course, are repeat players, but as we have seen, they often play only a peripheral role in the negotiations. However, it would be incorrect to assume that because the disputants are spouses, they have equal resources. Traditionally husbands have enjoyed an advantage because they are usually more secure in their jobs, have the prospect of a steady income, and are often more accustomed to dealing with legal issues. In addition, most children continue to live with their mothers and usually represent a net financial burden to the mothers since fathers rarely pay adequate child support.

Although most of the dispute processing in divorces takes place outside courtrooms, divorce laws, and the standards they mandate, constitute an important form of social control. They increasingly seek to equalize the relative bargaining positions of men and women by imposing guidelines for child support and by defining property as belonging to the marriage rather than to a single spouse.[40] The law also subjects married partners to much more stringent controls than those who never married. Few standards exist for dividing property between roommates or lovers who separate after several years of living together. There is considerable debate among the general public and in legislatures about which standards are appropriate for protecting children and for treating ex-spouses equitably. The law, as it currently exists, reflects contemporary social standards that are shifting almost as rapidly as the social circumstances that confront people in a society in which most women work, in which many men and women are chronically underemployed or unemployed, and in which the roles of men and women as caregivers and breadwinners are rapidly changing.

DISPUTES ABOUT CONSUMER CREDIT

Disputes about debts usually involve parties with drastically unequal resources.[41] On one side stand lenders who are repeat players, wise in the ways of the law, and experienced in using the legal system. On the other are debtors who are one-shotters, often naive, inexperienced, and uninformed about the workings of the legal system.

Disputes about debts occur in every sector of American life. Almost every adult in the United States uses some form of consumer credit. Most obtain telephone service, electricity, and gas on credit, and they are billed at the end of the month for the amount they use. Almost all home buyers purchase their house on credit, as do those who buy cars, household appliances, and furniture. Many people also carry a credit card that permits them to charge purchases and be billed later. The overwhelming proportion of these transactions run their course without a dispute. Nevertheless, a large number of disputes occur when customers think they have been overcharged or when they fall behind in their payments.

---

[40]See Chapter 13 for a fuller discussion of these changes.
[41]On the more general phenomenon of consumer complaints and the courts, see Jack Ladinsky and Charles Susmilch, "Community Factors in the Brokerage of Consumer Product and Service Problems," Working Papers, Disputes Processing Research Program, University of Wisconsin, mimeographed (Madison, 1983); Arthur Best, *When Consumers Complain* (New York: Columbia University Press, 1981); Nader (ed.), supra, note 33; Kenneth McNeil, John R. Nevin, David M. Trubek, and Richard E. Miller, "Market Discrimination Against the Poor and the Impact of Consumer Disclosure Laws: The Used Car Industry," *Law & Society Review 13* (1979), pp. 695–721; H. Laurence Ross and Neil O. Littlefield, "Complaint as a Problem-Solving Mechanism," *Law & Society Review 12* (1978), pp. 199–216; and Arthur Best and Alan R. Andreasen, "Consumer Response to Unsatisfactory Purchases: A Survey of Perceiving Defects, Voicing Complaints, and Obtaining Redress," *Law & Society Review 11* (1977), pp. 701–742.

Although few consumers realize it, the credit agreements into which they enter are densely surrounded by legal provisions. In some instances, borrowers will be asked to provide a form of security for the loan. When it is a home they are purchasing, the lender usually takes a mortgage on the property. The mortgage's provisions allow the lender to seize the property if the borrower falls behind in the payment schedule; the lender then sells the house to satisfy the debt. If a lender obtains more from the sale than the borrower owed, it pays the balance back to the borrower. If the sale does not bring enough money (which is the more frequent situation), the borrower not only is deprived of the property, but may still owe the balance of the debt.

If no property is available to guarantee repayment, other kinds of security may be required. The lender may ask the borrower to find a relative or friend who will cosign the debt. If the borrower then fails to meet the payments, the cosigner becomes responsible. If a large item is to be bought, such as a car or household appliance, it may be sold on a conditional sales contract that in some ways is like a mortgage; it permits the creditor to repossess the item if the debtor fails to meet his or her obligations. In the simplest and perhaps most numerous cases, creditors depend on the debtors' income for assurance that the debt will be repaid. If it is not, they attempt to seize the debtor's income to satisfy the obligation.

Both the creditors' claims on their customers' property and the rights of debtors are woven into the contracts they sign and the law into which those contracts fit. A mortgage agreement is a complex document that describes in great detail the property being bought so that there can be no question later about its identity. The mortgage specifies the amount the creditor will lend and the interest rate the borrower is to pay. It also shows the debtor's payment schedule and establishes the actions that will take place if those payments are not made. The mortgage may even specify the conditions under which early payment is permitted and the consequences of such payment, indicating what portions of the early payment will be applied to interest and how much toward principal.

Most other consumer debt contracts are less intricate, but they do indicate the essentials of the transactions: the amount of the loan, the interest rate, the repayment schedule, and the consequences of paying early, late, or not at all. Although these arrangements may appear to be entirely a private matter between lenders and their customers, in reality they are embedded in many statutory provisions and judicial decisions. The interest rate, for example, is often regulated by state law to protect debtors against exorbitant rates, a regulation dating from medieval church prohibitions against usury, but frequently the target of consumer groups that wish to reduce the allowable interest and business groups that would like to increase it. Disclosure of the interest rate is required by federal statute. The contract between lender and borrower must also be deemed reasonable if it is to be enforceable through court action. Perhaps the most important legal provisions are those that make courts available to lenders and borrowers for handling disputes.

One source of the lenders' advantage in credit disputes is that they write the contracts to which the borrower agrees. While lenders may insert many alternative remedies in their contracts, borrowers often have little opportunity to negotiate those provisions. Because there are many more borrowers than lenders, lenders may reject someone who does not sign the standard agreement, because they know they will not lose substantial business. Borrowers, in contrast, often have only a handful of sources from which to obtain the needed funds. They must either agree to the proffered terms or do without the money they are seeking. This is especially true for consumer loans. Consequently, while borrowers may shop for alternatives in the cost of their loan or the sources of the product they are buying with borrowed funds, they rarely can shop for the conditions under which the money is lent. Each time consumers sign a credit slip, they agree to terms that have been written by attorneys for the creditor, shaped by a desire to optimize the creditor's legal advantages should a dispute arise.

It does not matter that most disputes between lenders and borrowers do not go to court, because court actions always lurk in the background of the negotiations that bind the two together. When creditors negotiate with their delinquent customers, the penalties that are activated only by formal court action may nevertheless be powerful counters in the negotiations. A creditor often reminds its delinquent debtor that his or her home or car is at risk if payment is not made. Creditors rely on debtors' perception that court action will be swift and sure should they fail to comply with the terms of their debt.

That perception is reinforced by the tactics some lenders use to collect overdue accounts. They often turn them over to debt collectors who employ quasi-legal maneuvers to collect the debt; this often involves harassing the debtor until the debt is paid. Such harassment may involve telephone calls late at night, calls to employers, personal confrontations, insults, and name calling.[42] In one extraordinary case a department store called a funeral parlor just after a debtor's wake had begun, to demand that the family pay her overdue debt.[43]

When negotiations between creditors and debtors fail, the remedies provided by law usually require some court action. Creditors may not simply seize whatever they can from their debtors to satisfy a debt, even when the contract provides for the forfeiture of specific property. A debtor's property, as well as that of creditors, is protected by a set of entitlements that can be abridged only after satisfying certain procedures in court. Debtors must be served with a summons and there must then be a hearing at which both sides may present evidence about the legitimacy of the claim. At the hearing, evidence may show that payment was made but not credited to the debtor's account, or that some other error was made by the lender. Only after a creditor has prevailed in the court action and obtained a judgment against the debtor may it seize the security the debtor pledged when he or she obtained the loan. In addition, if the creditor wishes to use the services of the court to help collect the loan, a further proceeding is usually required before the sheriff can be employed to seize and/or sell the property.

The circumstances surrounding delinquent debts are often complicated enough to justify these procedural safeguards. Disputes about debts are sometimes clouded by allegations of fraud or of the poor quality of the goods purchased; in addition, the debtor's circumstances have frequently changed. A study by Caplovitz[44] of debtors in three large cities in the 1970s illustrates the complexities of the situation.

---

[42]David Caplovitz, *Consumers in Trouble* (New York: Free Press, 1974), p. 182.
[43]Mike Royko, "Creditor Owes Overdue Apology," *Chicago Tribune*, 23 February 1984, p. 3.
[44]Caplovitz, supra, note 42.

TABLE 3.2   Major Categories of Reasons for Debt Default (Percent)

	First Reason	Second Reason	Third Reason	Total Reasons	Total Individuals
Debtor's mishaps and shortcomings					
Loss of income	43	18	10	24	48
Voluntary overextension	13	23	32	17	25
Involuntary overextension	5	12	7	7	11
Marital troubles	6	4	5	5	8
Debtor's third parties	8	4	6	6	9
Debtor irresponsibility	4	2	—	4	5
Creditor may be implicated					
Fraud, deception	14	13	15	14	19
Payment misunderstanding	7	3	—	6	8
Partial late payments	—	15	6	5	7
Item return to creditor	*	6	14	2	1
Harassment by creditor	—	1	6	1	1
All other	1	—	—	*	*
Total percent	101	101	100	101	145
N	1320	570	110	2000	1326

*Signifies less than one-half of 1 percent.

Source: David Caplovitz, *Consumers in Trouble* (New York: Free Press, 1974), p. 53.

Table 3.2 shows the reasons debtors gave for being behind in their debt payments. Although only three reasons for default are listed in the table, many more may exist. Sometimes debtors fail to repay only because of illness or because the item was returned. But in many cases, illness, marital problems, dissatisfaction with the product, and payment misunderstandings combine to produce default. The data in Table 3.2 for "first reason" also show that mishaps and shortcomings on the part of debtors account for the largest number of defaults (about 79 percent of the cases); however, a substantial proportion (21 percent) is caused by perceptions that the lender did something wrong.

Court processing of credit cases is not as evenhanded as the provisions of the law suggest. Given the circumstances reflected in Table 3.2, one might expect that most debtors would avail themselves of the court hearings mandated by the law, and sometimes, at least, would win their dispute with a creditor. That, however, is not the case.

When court action was initiated in the cases Caplovitz studied, most, but not all, debtors were notified. This varied by city: in Detroit, 84 percent received the summons; in Chicago, 71 percent reported doing so; but in New York, barely more than half (54 percent) received the notice.[45] Most of those who did not receive a summons nevertheless learned about the lawsuit, although a residual 10 percent were unaware of it until it was too late.[46] Even in the city where the largest number of debtors were notified, only one-fourth of all defendants appeared in court, and fewer still filed the necessary an-

[45]Ibid., p. 194.   [46]Ibid., p. 195.

swers to the creditor's complaint.[47] The result was that in all three cities, approximately 90 percent of the cases ended as default judgments in favor of the creditor; only a handful were decided in favor of the debtors.

It is clear that the repeat-player position of lenders and the one-shotter status of most debtors played an important part in the outcomes of these cases. Even when the debtors could afford to pay attorneys, the cases were usually not large enough to make it worthwhile to retain one. In addition, many lawyers know little about the laws that presumably protect consumers. Macaulay reports:

> We found that most lawyers in Wisconsin knew next to nothing about the Magnuson-Moss Warranty Act [which had just been passed amidst considerable fanfare]—many had never heard of it. . . . It was extremely difficult to find lawyers who knew much about any specific consumer protection law other than the Wisconsin Consumer Act [WCA], a law largely concerned with procedures for financing consumer transactions and collecting debts. A few lawyers were well informed about the WCA, but most knew only of "atrocity stories" about debtors who had used the statute to evade honest debts.[48]

As this example shows, debtors may not receive high-quality legal advice even when they are confident enough to seek it and solvent enough to pay for it.

By contrast, lenders are repeat players who frequently deal with delinquent debtors either because of the volume of their business or because they hire a collection agent, who is the repeat player par excellence. Not only do they use the courts repeatedly, but they also influence the legislature in the writing of relevant statutes. As Macaulay indicates, "Lawyers working for manufacturers, distributors, retailers, and financial institutions are likely to be present at the creation of any law that purports to aid the consumer."[49] Creditor repeat players possess other advantages, too. The decision involving the point at which to invoke the legal process is almost always made by lenders. As repeat players, they know when they have met the informal expectations of judges about reasonable treatment of debtors. Their decision is likely to be routine, based on a standard operating procedure they use in handling all their bad debts, rather than a procedure tailored to the debtor's particular circumstances. In addition, the summonses and other legal proceedings are not at all mysterious to lenders; they often hire attorneys who specialize in collections. Debtors, on the other hand, have grave difficulties deciphering the legalese of the summons or knowing what to do if they go to court on the appointed day. The creditor may even try to discourage the debtor who comes to court by seeking a postponement of the case on some excuse. Postponements present a real cost to the debtor, for whom going to court is usually quite inconvenient and threatening, while for the creditor it is, at best, a minor inconvenience, since the creditor (or its attorney) is frequently in court. Indeed, in some places in Wisconsin during the 1960s, it was not unusual for courts to reserve special days to accommodate the schedules of particular collection attorneys.[50] Such accommodations were never made for debtors. Consequently, it is not surprising to learn from Caplovitz that only a handful of debtors

[47]Ibid., p. 215.
[48]Stewart Macaulay, "Lawyers and Consumer Protection Laws," *Law & Society Review 14* (1979), p. 118.
[49]Ibid., p. 144.   [50]Jacob, supra, note 28, p. 100.

won favorable rulings from the courts. Courts handling such claims are largely collection courts, not tribunals that decide disputes after hearing evidence.

However, debtors are not always one-shotters.[51] Some persons have the misfortune of falling so hopelessly behind in their debts that not one but many creditors seek to seize their wages and personal property. Such debtors become wise in the ways of the formal and informal culture of the debt-collecting system. Many succeed in avoiding the clutches of the debt collector by moving to another city or assuming a new identity. Others find a legal remedy in personal bankruptcy, a legal process that wipes out most debts if the debtor can show that his or her current assets are less than current liabilities and if creditors cannot prove the debts were obtained through fraud on the debtor's part. Although a debtor may seek the protection of bankruptcy only once every seven years, and it reputedly devastates the debtor's credit rating, more than three-quarters of a million debtors resorted to this procedure in 1991.[52] Bankruptcy proceedings are relatively simple, although they do require the services of an attorney (consequently, the totally indigent debtor cannot use this method). Bankruptcy usually provides the protection that debtors seek. They often leave bankrupcty court with a more satisfactory outcome than they would find in small claims court or civil court, where creditors try to collect their debts.

The law and procedures employed in processing disputes between debtors and creditors constitute one of the pillars of the marketplace. Loans would be difficult to obtain if creditors did not have confidence that mechanisms exist for collecting them. At the same time, it is important that consumers have confidence they will not be cheated on the terms of their loans. All advanced economies depend on credit; the American economy particularly does so. In providing the rules and forums for processing disputes about credit, the law and courts are the instruments the State employs to facilitate the purchase of goods and services, but as we have seen, the law is not necessarily even-handed in pursuing this goal.

COMMERCIAL LITIGATION

Courts are not only an arena for contests between Davids and Goliaths. Some disputes involve only Goliaths, where repeat players are on both sides of the controversy and both bring considerable resources to their dispute. Such disputes often involve very large sums of money and may bring fortune or disaster to thousands of workers and investors. They involve firms such as International Business Machines (IBM), General Motors, American Telephone and Telegraph (AT&T), Apple Computer, and Westinghouse Electric Corporation.[53]

Although such cases involve giants, the disputes may not be even matches. On one side stands a giant firm; on the other is often a large company, but one with distinctly

---

[51]Ibid., pp. 48–73.

[52]U.S. Bureau of the Census, *Statistical Abstract of the United States: 1993*, 113th ed. (Washington, D.C. 1992,) p. 538.

[53]Note that much commercial litigation involves such large corporations. The average amount won is less than $5000. However, the blockbuster cases we discuss subsequently both received more publicity and have a greater legal, economic, and social impact.

fewer resources. Therefore, it is difficult to apply Galanter's observations about repeat players and one-shotters to this category of disputes, for although both sides may be repeat players, the larger firm often enjoys a significant advantage.

This is clearly evident in the many cases that match an automobile manufacturer against one of its franchised dealers.[54] The manufacturer is a giant compared to any dealer, yet the dealership is likely to be a respected and substantial member of its business circle and community. In many towns a car dealership is one of the largest locally owned businesses. During much of the twentieth century, car dealerships sold the product that best signified the status position of many Americans. When pitted against ordinary customers, car dealers are repeat players who know how to play the legal game to their advantage against debtors and dissatisfied customers. But their situation is reversed when they fight the manufacturer, on whom they depend for their supply of cars and parts. They have signed a franchise agreement that is likely to be disadvantageous to them, because it may force them to accept car models that are difficult to sell and may include conditions that could lead to cancellation of the franchise they need to stay in business. Car dealers are thus in almost the same position vis-à-vis manufacturers as are car buyers vis-à-vis the dealers. Like car buyers, dealers have little opportunity to negotiate the contracts they sign, and they face a much more experienced legal staff when engaged in a dispute with the manufacturer. While the manufacturer deals with hundreds of dealers on a continuing basis, dealers have only occasional problems. Dealers, of course, are important to manufacturers because without them they cannot easily sell their cars, but one franchise holder can often be replaced with another. However, for the dealers, retaining their franchise and avoiding burdensome conditions is not just a matter of convenience; it usually is a matter of economic survival.

Contract texts are full of cases reflecting the conflicts between these two parties. Because dealers are prominent locally, they have, in many instances, won significant legislative victories with the enactment of statutes that protect franchisees from abrupt and unreasonable termination. Nevertheless, most conflicts between dealers and manufacturers are probably won by the manufacturers, because their greater financial resources provide them a large bag of legal and economic tricks. Most such disputes, however, are negotiated rather than litigated. They often involve parties with long histories of association that will likely continue if the dispute does not involve termination. Even in termination disputes, manufacturers must consider the effect of the outcome on relations with other dealers, for dealers tend to be in contact with one another. However, the shadow of the law casts its influence in these negotiations as it does in others. Manufacturers usually prevail because they can bend the law to their advantage through their ability to draft the franchise agreements and their considerably greater economic power.

Some disputes involve somewhat more equally matched repeat players. Consider, for instance, the dispute between Apple Computer Inc. and Franklin Computer Corpo-

---

[54]Stewart Macaulay, *Law and the Balance of Power: The Automobile Manufacturers and Their Dealers* (New York: Russell Sage Foundation, 1966).

ration in the early 1980s, when Apple was a relatively small company.[55] Franklin had produced a microcomputer that was a clone of the popular Apple II and II+ but which sold at a considerably lower price and traded on Apple's reputation. Eventually, Apple sued Franklin for infringement of its copyright to a program embedded in a microchip that was an essential element of the Apple computer. If it had not been copied, there was a good chance that the Franklin computer would no longer be able to run all the programs developed for the Apple computer, thus considerably reducing its commercial appeal. The suit involved large stakes on both sides. For Apple, winning meant protecting its large investment against the encroachment of many potential competitors. Its economic health depended on maintaining the profit margin of its Apple II machines. For Franklin, losing the suit might mean immediate failure, because it was unlikely that it could sell a computer that was similar to the Apple computer but which could not use all its programs.

The dispute involved not only two relatively small companies, but also an important opportunity to maintain or expand the meaning of copyright law. Its outcome was of great interest to many computer manufacturers. Apple claimed that even though the computer program on the microchip was not a piece of literature, was not printed, and, indeed, could not be read without the use of special machines, it was nevertheless eligible for protection under copyright law, rather than patent law. Claiming copyright law protection was extremely important to Apple for two reasons. First, to be eligible for a patent, an invention must contribute substantially to technology. Simply performing a common procedure in another way (which is what most computer programs do) is not patentable. On the other hand, copyright law protects writings that need only be an original work to be protected against unauthorized copying. It might be difficult to qualify a computer program under patent law, but it is relatively simple to do so under copyright law. The second advantage of copyright law is that it provides for a much longer period of protection. However, copyright protection of a computer program on a microchip had never been tested in court, and no specific provision for copyright protection of computer programs on microchips had yet been enacted by Congress.

This was not the sort of dispute that was likely to be settled out of court. Neither side had a substantial advantage over the other. The two companies were both relatively small, although Apple was larger. The dispute involved issues with which neither party had much experience, nor could they hire attorneys who routinely handled such matters because the legal issues were novel. In addition, Apple and Franklin had no history of relationship to soften their conflict. They were competitors rather than suppliers or customers to each other. They therefore had no experience in dealing with each other and had little interest in each other's continued existence. Thus, the conflict inexorably moved to the courtroom.

Franklin won the first court skirmishes with a ruling that computer programs on a microchip were not protected by copyright law. The issue, however, was so important to both parties that an appeal was inevitable. A few months later, Apple won the appeal,

---

[55]Dennis Kneale and Erik Larson, "Franklin settles Apple's lawsuit over Copyright," *Wall Street Journal*, 5 January 1984, p. 10; *Infoworld*, 30 January 1984; Andrew J. Rodau, "Protecting Computer Software," *Temple Law Quarterly* 57 (Fall 1981), pp. 527–552.

but the amount of damages remained to be set, subject to further appeal. At this point, external circumstances pushed the dispute out of the courts and into the offices of the companies' lawyers. By the time Apple won the appeals court ruling, it was about to market its next model, the Macintosh. The technology employed in the Apple II was on the decline. Damages became less important to Apple than the principle of copyright protection won in the litigation. Prolonging the conflict would distract Apple from its effort to market its new product in competition with IBM personal computers; the conflict with Franklin had become peripheral. Consequently, rather than continue the dispute with further litigation, the two companies negotiated a settlement that required a $2 million payment to Apple by Franklin and a commitment by Franklin to stop using the Apple program. By this point, Franklin had written its own program, which allowed its machines to use Apple software, and it continued to sell its machines. However, the company emerged from the battle mortally wounded and filed for bankruptcy a few months later. Apple, on the other hand, became one of the world's largest suppliers of personal computers.

Apple's experience with Franklin and the courts illustrates how formal adjudicative procedures are employed when two relatively equally matched disputants confront each other. They resorted to the courts not only to resolve a dispute, but also to expand the meaning of statutory law. The case also illustrates an important characteristic of many disputes taken to court. It involved parties that did not have a stake in a continuing relationship through negotiation or arbitration that would have made settlement much more likely. Even in this instance, however, the parties did not fight to the bitter end. It would have been easy to extend the conflict through further litigation that might have lasted several more years. But in the fast-developing field of personal computer technology in the early 1980s, both parties realized that it was in their interest to cut their losses and negotiate a settlement on the basis of the interim court decision. However, the saga did not end with Apple's out-of-court victory. The dispute shifted to Congress, where manufacturers sought a firmer definition of their rights than would have been provided by a court interpretation. The outcome was the establishment of a new form of protection for computer chips that is valid for a shorter period than an ordinary copyright, but which avoids the hazards of patent laws.[56]

Whereas the dispute between Apple and Franklin largely centered in the courts, many commercial disputes involve significant negotiation and mediation efforts. This is apparent in the dispute Westinghouse Electric Corporation had with many electric utilities when it tried to renege on the price at which it had promised to sell them uranium.

In 1975, Westinghouse found itself in a terrible predicament.[57] As an inducement for utilities to buy its nuclear reactors, the company had included an offer of cheap fuel. For several years, Westinghouse contracted to sell uranium oxide (the fuel used in the reactors) to its utility customers at an average of $9.50 per pound, promising to deliver 80 million pounds of the fuel at that price. But in 1975, when Westinghouse had only 15 million pounds on hand, the price of uranium oxide rose to about $40 per pound.

[56]*Almanac 98th Congress, 2d Session 1984* (Washington, D.C.: Congressional Quarterly, 1985), pp. 254–256.
[57]James B. Stewart, *The Partners: Inside America's Most Powerful Law Firms* (New York: Simon & Schuster, 1983), pp. 153–200.

This meant that the firm would incur a loss as high as $2 billion if it carried out its contractual obligations to provide the fuel at less than one-fourth the current market price. Westinghouse then unilaterally cancelled its obligations by citing Section 2-615(a) of the Uniform Commercial Code, which excuses performance of a contract should a contingency arise, "the non-occurrence of which was a basic assumption on which the contract was made. . . ." Westinghouse claimed that the price increase (which it later discovered was the result of cartel price fixing) was such a contingency. The utilities, of course, disagreed, for if they allowed Westinghouse to renege on its contractual obligations to sell uranium cheaply, they would have to pay the much higher market price. Despite the high stakes this case did not go to trial. Rather, the judge assigned to the case brought the two sides together and urged them to find a compromise, acting as a mediator. Consequently, Westinghouse and the utilities negotiated a settlement. The application of Section 2-615(a) was never tested in this case.[58]

The Westinghouse case illustrates the importance of a calculation of costs and benefits, in addition to knowledge of the law, in deciding how to process a dispute. There can be no doubt that Westinghouse knew the law extremely well. Lawyers were involved both when the contracts were written and when they were broken. The law cast its shadow on the entire affair, but one can hardly claim that it determined its outcome. Judge and lawyers alike assiduously kept the matter from going to trial so the parties to the dispute could maintain more complete control over the outcome and avoid the unwanted consequences of a full-fledged victory by one side. Although the utilities needed to protect their right to cheap fuel to justify their decision to build nuclear power plants, they also had a common interest with Westinghouse in saving the company from bankruptcy. The utilities needed Westinghouse as a source for spare parts and as a participant in the bidding game for new power plants. Westinghouse needed to reduce its commitment to its customers, but also wanted to maintain enough goodwill to be able to continue to sell equipment to them. Thus, both parties forged a compromise around the law but not necessarily in strict accord with it.

In the commercial disputes we have discussed, the law and court procedures served to privilege common interests of significant market players. The outcome of neither the Apple-Franklin litigation nor that between Westinghouse and its utility customers was a winner-take-all. Apple benefited more than Franklin, but perhaps the real winner was the computer industry, which won protection for innovative products the law had not previously provided. That protection provided a powerful inducement for companies to invest in further innovation. In the Westinghouse litigation, the outcome imposed costs to both litigants in an effort to avoid damaging either mortally, since the survival of both was needed for the economical generation of electricity. Just as criminal law tries to constrain violence, commercial law often seeks to prevent the "law of the jungle" from prevailing in civil disputes.

---

[58]The judge who prodded Westinghouse and the utility companies to negotiate described some of his tactics in Hubert L. Will, Robert R. Herhige, Jr., and Alvin B. Rubin, *The Role of the Judge in the Settlement Process* (Washington, D.C.: Federal Judicial Center, 1977), pp. 10–11; see also Stewart, supra, note 57, pp. 167–169.

DISPUTES IN THE PUBLIC ARENA: ABORTION AND WATERGATE _____

The disputes discussed thus far have involved private parties. Many such disputes have policy implications, but they usually do not extend directly into the political arena. Some disputes, however, do have this dimension. Two that clearly demonstrate the overlap between legal disputes and political conflict are the issues of abortion and the Watergate affair.

ABORTION

There is scarcely a more private decision than whether a woman should bear a child.[59] Whether she has a constitutional right to abort the fetus has long been the object of public controversy. The availability of abortion, whether legal or clandestine, has given rise to innumerable grievances, claims, and disputes that have been taken to both private and public arenas. The public aspect has been most visible since the abortion issue flared into intense controversy after the Supreme Court's *Roe v. Wade* in 1973. But the private, less visible side of the controversy must not be neglected, because it involves the greatest proportion of all grievances and claims.

When a woman wants to have an abortion, she may be thwarted by the refusal of physicians or hospitals to perform one. This may lead to claims against the physicians and hospitals, between family members who have conflicting interests in the fetus, and between the woman (or the abortion provider) and public authorities who enforce legal norms. Many of those claims do not become disputes because the woman—whether seeking an abortion in the 1990s or a century earlier—finds an alternative provider. That may be either a different physician or hospital, or at great medical risk, a nonmedical person (the so-called back-alley abortionist) or herself. As long as no public official intervenes, no visible dispute arises. In many other cases, the woman may avoid the potential conflict by bearing the child and either rearing it or giving it up for adoption; in those instances no dispute arises because the claimant does not press her demands. However, if prosecution is threatened or if the woman seeks an open, legal abortion where the law makes that impossible, her grievance becomes a dispute in the legal arena. When negotiations fail to satisfy her demand (which is what happens in most instances because of legal prohibitions), her dispute quickly gravitates to the courts.

Abortion entered the public arena in the United States during the nineteenth century when it was prohibited in all states under criminal penalty. Those laws allowed an exception only when a medical doctor certified that an abortion was necessary to preserve the woman's life. This exception, however, permitted many abortions by physicians who were willing to certify that the standard was met; many abortions were also available by the use of home remedies at a time when medical practice did not promise much greater safety. By the mid-1950s, medical technology was making it easier to de-

---

[59]There are many books and articles arguing one side or the other of the abortion controversy. An excellent account of the events described below can be found in Barbara Hinkson Craig and David M. O'Brien, *Abortion and American Politics* (Chatham, N.J.: Chatham House, 1993). A broader analysis is Kristin Luker, *Abortion and the Politics of Motherhood* (Berkeley: University of California Press, 1984). An account of the early phases of the issue is Thomas C. Dienes, *Law, Politics, and Birth Control* (Urbana: University of Illinois Press, 1972).

tect malformed fetuses, and it was becoming clearer that certain circumstances, such as having taken the medicine called Thalidomide, would cause babies to have grotesquely malformed limbs and other deficiencies. At the same time, however, considerable controversy arose among physicians because it no longer was clear, with the improved medical technology available to them, that they could certify that most pregnancies they were asked to abort met the professional criteria of endangering the woman's life. Even in those states where abortions could be legally performed under specified conditions, those conditions were so onerous that fewer and fewer physicians and hospitals approved them. Consequently, women who sought abortions either had to travel abroad (an option the rich occasionally used) or risk an illegal abortion under unsanitary conditions (the only option available to the poor).[60] Consequently, thousands of women died or were injured. Many people came to see the prohibition of abortion as an unwarranted intrusion by the government into the private lives of women, and those prohibitions came under considerable legal and political attack.

Antiabortion laws affect a wide range of parties with quite different motivations and resources. Women wishing to end their pregnancy obviously have an intense interest in the laws; if they cannot abort their fetus, they have to bear the consequences for many years. The father may also have a considerable interest in the abortion, if the fetus is aborted, he won't have a child, and if the child is born, he has to help bear the expense of raising it. Physicians who are willing to perform abortions have a professional interest: they are concerned about the State's interference with their medical judgment. Physicians are more likely than pregnant women to be able to afford legal proceedings aimed at changing the law. Hospitals also have a keen interest in abortion, which are a source of potential business; like physicians, they have resources to carry out a long-range strategy for legal change. Finally, some people assert that the fetus has an interest because its life is at stake, although there is considerable controversy over the point at which a fetus becomes a legally recognized person. Since the 1950s medical and public perceptions of when a fetus became a person shifted, becoming progressively earlier during the pregnancy as advances in medical technology made it possible to preserve the life of increasingly premature fetuses. The different motivations and resources of the many interested parties have led to a wide array of actions on their part or on their behalf.

Women who were denied an abortion usually could not and did not bring the issue into the legal arena themselves. If they were poor, they could not afford a lawyer; if they had enough money, they could more easily obtain their abortion abroad. Moreover, all pregnant women had only a short time during which they could bring their dispute to court. The longer they carried the fetus, the less likely a court would permit an abortion, and after the child was born, the matter became moot. These women also worked under the handicap of severe emotional strain during their pregnancy. Therefore, many women who wanted an abortion decided either to continue the pregnancy or to obtain the abortion illegally. If they were to take their grievance to the courts or a legislature, they had to obtain outside assistance.

[60]Edwin M. Schur describes the conditions surrounding illegal abortions in *Crimes Without Victims* (Englewood Cliffs, N.J.: Prentice-Hall, 1965), pp. 25–35.

Feminist groups became concerned with the plight of some of these women, seeing abortion as an issue involving the right of women to control their bodies. In addition, many doctors allied themselves with these groups in working for a change in abortion laws because they could not perform abortions without the risk of arrest and prosecution. Although the criminal statutes prohibiting abortions were enforced only erratically before 1973, the risk of arrest was always present, and it prevented many physicians who were otherwise willing from performing abortions.

The effort to change abortion laws followed two routes. The first path led to state legislatures in attempts to amend or repeal antiabortion statutes. This involved mobilizing political support, getting the issue on the legislative agenda, and winning sufficient votes in the legislature. These efforts often proved futile. Abortion aroused the bitter opposition of the Catholic Church (other right-to-life groups were not organized before 1973), and in the 1960s feminist groups did not have the political clout to convince the predominantly male legislators that this issue was worth risking their careers. Invocation of the lawmaking process, therefore, often was not successful, although in a handful of states, including California and New York, feminist groups and physicians were able to weaken antiabortion statutes.[61]

Seeking change through the courts was the alternative strategy. This had the advantage of considerably lower visibility with less likelihood of arousing opposition. Moreover, judges, unlike legislators, were less likely to be sensitive to the electoral consequences of a decision that might be unpopular with some constituents. However, this campaign also faced some very serious obstacles.

One roadblock was the absence of well-financed organizations to coordinate a litigation campaign. The needs were quite different in the judicial than in the legislative arena. Whereas the legislative effort foundered on the absence of a groundswell of support and on the intense opposition by the Catholic Church, the judicial strategy required an organization that could choose good test cases and finance them through the appeals process. Many women wanting an abortion were poor; often they were the victims of rape. No well-established groups existed to which such women might turn for help. The cases that eventually brought the issue to the U.S. Supreme Court were financed on a shoestring budget.

Obtaining legal expertise was also crucial because a successful challenge of existing antiabortion statutes would require substantial legal research. One strategy involved seeking declaratory judgments about the statutes' constitutionality. Another was to find someone who would intentionally violate the law, face prosecution, and in the course of the criminal trial, raise the constitutional issues that might lead the courts to strike them down. Both tactics were attempted. The declaratory judgment approach permitted a remedy without someone violating the law, but it could succeed only if judges believed there was a real danger that the law would be enforced. A criminal prosecution offered such proof, but it was far riskier to the persons involved. Should they lose, they could face jail.

Test cases could be staged either by having committed opponents to antiabortion statutes intentionally violate the law by performing an abortion or by selecting appro-

[61]On California, cf. Luker, supra, note 59.

priate cases from a prosecutor's independent decision to charge someone with having performed an illegal abortion. The difficulty with the latter tactic was that many such prosecutions involved persons who would not make good material for a test case because they often lacked reputable credentials. A third alternative was seek a declaratory judgment using a pregnant woman who was willing to face the glare of publicity that might be associated with a successful test. Such a woman might be a rape victim or a married woman in a difficult personal situation that forced her to consider an abortion. However, without the help of a support group, such women normally did not have the knowledge of the law or legal procedures needed to test the constitutionality of antiabortion laws. Thus, the process of selecting the right person for the judicial challenge was a difficult one that depended, to a considerable degree, on luck.[62]

Getting a potential client together with a lawyer and into court is only one step in invoking the law to settle a dispute. Lawyers must also know how to use the law to their client's advantage. This presented particularly difficult problems in the campaign against the antiabortion laws. The Constitution makes no mention of abortion; it does not even specifically refer to a right to privacy. The strategy was to label antiabortion statutes as among those prohibited by the Constitution.

The principal hope centered on establishing a right to privacy. This was considerably advanced by an earlier case in which the litigants probably did not foresee its use in the abortion controversy. That case (*Griswold v. Connecticut*)[63] challenged Connecticut's right to prohibit the use of contraceptives. In deciding *Griswold* in 1965, Justice William 0. Douglas, writing for the majority of the Supreme Court, held that the right to privacy was inherent in the other rights expressly protected by the First, Third, Fourth, and Fifth Amendments to the Constitution. Each of these created a zone of privacy. In *Griswold*, the use of contraceptives was declared something that individual citizens should be free to decide for themselves. Five other justices agreed that such a right existed, although, as if often the case, they did not subscribe entirely to Justice Douglas's opinion. Thus, a constitutional doctrine was created that subsequently provided a rationale for striking down antiabortion statutes.

The Supreme Court's use of the *Griswold* doctrine to invalidate antiabortion statutes did not occur for another eight years, by which time President Nixon had not only replaced Chief Justice Earl Warren with Chief Justice Warren Burger, but had also appointed three other conservative justices (Harry Blackmun, Louis Powell, and William Rehnquist). The abortion decision involved cases from Texas and Georgia.[64] The Texas case involved a woman who had allegedly been raped; the case from Georgia concerned a woman whose husband threatened to leave her if she had another child and whose other children had already been taken away from her for alleged child abuse. Both stumbled into the hands of women attorneys interested in litigating the constitutionality of antiabortion laws.[65] This time it was not the liberal Justice Douglas but the more conservative Justice Blackmun who wrote the opinion of the Court. Like Douglas,

---

[62]For a description of how the plaintiffs were chosen in *Roe v. Wade*, see Marian Faux, Roe v. Wade: *The Untold Story of the Landmark Supreme Court Decision that Made Abortion Legal* (New York: Macmillan, 1988).
[63]*Griswold v. Connecticut*, 381 U.S. 471 (1965).
[64]*Roe v. Wade*, 410 U.S. 113 (1973); *Doe v. Bolton*, 410 U.S. 179 (1973). Faux, supra, note 62, p. 93.
[65]Faux, supra, note 62.

Blackmun based the Court's decision on a woman's right to privacy, which, he argued, outweighed any interest by the State during the early months of a pregnancy. Consequently, the Court held that the State could not regulate abortions during the first trimester of a pregnancy; it could, however, regulate them with increasing specificity during later months.

The Supreme Court's decision had immediate effects. It freed medical practitioners from the threat of criminal prosecution, and led to the opening of clinics specializing in abortions and to hospitals routinely performing the operation. But it also aroused bitter and vigorous opposition from the Catholic Church and a host of others who saw the decision as a violation of the fetus's right to life. These groups transformed individual disputes over abortion into a social conflict staged in the political arena because they were better situated for political action than had been the women's groups that originally sought repeal of antiabortion laws. Opponents of the Supreme Court's decision organized themselves into a "right-to-life" movement and turned to their state legislatures and Congress for remedial action. They were successful in both arenas. In Congress, they found their vehicle in the appropriations process by sponsoring amendments to appropriation bills that prohibited the use of federal funds for performing abortions.[66] Similar bills were introduced in state legislatures to prohibit the use of state funds. This strategy effectively kept the poor, who depended on welfare funds, from receiving legal abortions. In 1983, the abortion opponents even succeeded in prohibiting the use of health insurance fund of federal employees for abortions. Thus, abortions once more were barred for a large portion of the population, especially the poor. Only those who could pay their own medical bills could readily obtain one.

In addition, abortion opponents succeeded in getting state legislatures to enact increasingly restrictive laws, which did not entirely prohibit abortions but hedged legal abortions with procedures that would discourage many women. For instance, many such laws required minors to obtain permission either from one or both of their parents or go before a judge to do so; others required that women wait 24 hours to obtain an abortion after first appearing at a clinic; still others required abortions to be performed at full-fledged hospitals rather than at clinics. These state laws provided numerous opportunities for the Supreme Court to reconsider its *Roe* decision. As the Supreme Court became increasingly conservative in the 1980s, with justices explicitly opposed to *Roe* appointed by Presidents Reagan and Bush, these challenges led to a considerable weakening of a woman's ability to obtain a legal abortion. At the same time, opponents of abortion held many demonstrations in front of abortion clinics, which further restricted women's access to abortion.[67]

The abortion controversy illustrates some of the complex ways in which grievances become claims, which in turn may become disputes, court cases, and eventually lead to political conflict. Most persons who had potential claims because of the laws restricting abortions did not proceed to transform them into disputes, but dropped their claims for many reasons. Some found alternative ways to satisfy their claims, such as going abroad

[66]Craig and O'Brien, supra, note 59. Also see Roger H. Davidson, "Procedures and Politics in Congress," in Gilbert Y. Steiner (ed.), *The Abortion Dispute and the American System* (Washington, D.C.: The Brookings Institute, 1983), pp. 30–46.
[67]Craig and O'Brien, supra, note 59.

or obtaining an illegal abortion. Others decided that having an abortion was more trouble than having a baby. Many resigned to their fate because they did not see any way of pressing their claims successfully. Many probably did not know how to push their claims through the legal system. The probable failure of their efforts did not seem to justify the considerable expenditure of financial and emotional resources needed to pursue their claims.

The costs of pursuing such claims were high because informal means of processing the dispute were, for the most part, unavailable. The only way to change the law was to confront it directly. Although two alternative arenas existed, both presented formidable hurdles. One was the legislature, where the law might be repealed or altered; the other was the courts, where existing laws might be reinterpreted or declared unconstitutional. Both required far greater resources than ordinary claimants possessed. For either legislative or judicial pursuit of their claims, advocates of change in the antiabortion laws needed to mobilize support beyond their immediate circle of family and friends. Such support came from medical groups whose self-interest coincided with that of women seeking abortions and from feminist groups who enlarged the interests of individual women to a concern about the career potentials of women and the role of motherhood. After these advocates succeeded, right-to-life forces mobilized in the same fashion.

Thus, the abortion controversy shows how private claims may be transformed into public issues. The court cases always involved individual parties, but those individuals represented an entire class of potential claimants who remained almost invisible in the formal litigation. The legislative struggle, on the other hand, brought the group interests of the claimants to the surface.

WATERGATE

The abortion controversy began with private claims and was transformed into a public controversy. Affairs of state sometimes go directly to the courts, but they also go through complex transformations that are well illustrated by the example of Watergate.[68]

Watergate was a dispute in which the participants never made a serious attempt to reconcile their differences. It was also a dispute that continually shifted between the political and legal arenas. It illustrates how the law molded what was essentially a political dispute, and how the dispute was transformed from a political to a legal one. It began with a break-in that was originally classified as an ordinary burglary and ended with the unprecedented resignation of the president. It was a dispute that continually moved across the boundaries of the legal and political arenas, and, in the process, was continually redefined.

Richard Nixon was elected president in November 1968, by a slight margin in the popular vote after a hard-fought campaign against Hubert Humphrey. As he ap-

[68]Shelves of books have been written about the Watergate affair, by both participants and observers. The basic chronology of events essential to unraveling the complicated web of events is best presented in *Watergate: Chronology of a Crisis* (Washington, D.C.: Congressional Quarterly, 1975), and *The End of a Presidency* (New York: New York Times, 1974). Both also present the text of important documents. The chronology of the court case that eventually was decided by the Supreme Court as *United States v. Nixon*, 417 U.S. 683 (1974) is well presented in Leon Friedman (ed.), United States v. Nixon: *The President Before the Supreme Court* (New York: Chelsea House, 1974).

proached reelection in 1972, it appeared that he might face another tough contest. Although he ultimately won in a landslide against George McGovern (winning the electoral votes of 49 states), he and his campaign aides did not take victory for granted. They were determined to leave no stone unturned to assure Nixon's reelection, and it was this determination that proved to be his undoing.

The Nixon administration, more than most presidencies, had been troubled with leaks of what it considered confidential information. The most spectacular leak was that of the so-called Pentagon Papers relating to the war in Vietnam. The administration first attempted to halt the publication of the documents by court action and then proceeded to prosecute those whom it believed responsible for leaking them to the press. It authorized a number of clandestine operations to track and stop those leaks. These people proposed, in February 1972, to wiretap the Democratic National Committee (DNC) headquarters at the Watergate Apartments in Washington, D.C., to obtain campaign information. After two failed attempts, the operatives succeeded in breaking into the DNC offices and photographing documents as well as planting wiretaps. No one was apprehended during this first burglary, but during a second break-in in June 1972, the police arrested five men. Telephone numbers found on the burglars were identified as White House numbers and suggested a connection between the break-in and the Nixon administration. From that moment, associates of those arrested were in touch with White House aides to the president. However, there was no evidence that the president was involved in planning the burglary, even though he knew of its connection with his reelection committee as early as six days after the burglars were apprehended.

Four versions of the Watergate affair unfolded more or less simultaneously in a complex web. Each version focused on different elements of the incident; three involved transformations into legal disputes while one was a transformation into the political arena. It is important to remember that the whole affair involved the attempt to gain power—to win the office of President of the United States. It was, in its essence, a dispute over political power.

The earliest version involved a transformation of the dispute into a criminal matter. The break-in was treated as a burglary. Those arrested at the DNC and those implicated in its planning were charged with burglary and tried for that offense. The Nixon administration made every effort to maintain this definition of the dispute. However, within a week of the incident, President Nixon ordered his aides to invoke national security in an effort to prevent the FBI from uncovering the links between the break-in and his reelection campaign. The pretext given was that closer investigation would reveal secret details of the Bay of Pigs invasion of Cuba in 1961. The president and his aides often referred to the incident disparagingly as a mere "third-rate burglary." In this version, the questions to be addressed were whether the men who were arrested had broken into the DNC office with the intent to commit the crime of burglary. Over the course of several months, this narrow definition of Watergate slowly changed, but only to the extent that an alleged conspiracy to commit such a crime dragged more persons into the original charge, and another crime, the obstruction of justice was added to the charges. The matter, however, remained one of criminal law. It involved the U.S. Attorney for the District of Columbia as the prosecutor and seemingly private individuals as suspects. Either party could have sought to settle the charges through negotiation of a plea bargain, and, indeed, there were strong pressures for them to do so because that would result in guilty pleas, thus ending the investigation. The suspects had the benefit of advice from defense lawyers from the time of their arrest and, therefore, possessed knowledge of the law and how it might be applied to them.

A second version of the Watergate story evolved on the heels of the first. To investigate the possible criminal violations in the affair, President Nixon had been forced by public opinion and leaders of Congress to appoint a special prosecutor, Archibald Cox. After it was accidentally revealed that Nixon had tape recorded all conversations in the Oval Office, Cox sought to obtain recordings of those conversations between the president and his advisers in the Oval Office relating to the Watergate incident. Nixon refused, arguing that "the President is not subject to compulsory process from the courts."[69] Nixon lost that case and gave the special prosecutor the documents that had been requested. Several months later, Cox's successor, Leon Jaworski, subpoenaed additional tape recordings in connection with his prosecution of John Mitchell, Nixon's former attorney general and campaign chief, for obstruction of justice. The president once again refused, on the grounds that the tapes involved "executive privilege," a constitutional doctrine that protected the confidential conversations between a president and his advisers from outside scrutiny so they could be frank and optimally useful to the president. At this point, Watergate was transformed into a constitutional dispute over the extent of presidental power. The question became whether the president could refuse to provide a grand jury with documents that might prove wrongdoing by the president or his aides. This was the issue decided by a unanimous decision of the Supreme Court on July 24, 1974,[70] in which the Court held that the president must deliver the subpoenaed tapes. Those tapes revealed for the first time that Nixon had known of the coverup almost from the beginning and had played a leading role in constructing it. Within two weeks, he found himself forced to resign the presidency or face almost certain removal from office through the impeachment process.

A third version of the Watergate affair transformed it into the legal proceedings required for impeachment of the president. Impeachment involves the voting of charges by the House of Representatives and a trial before the full Senate; conviction is by vote of the Senate. Calls for Nixon's impeachment began to arise in 1973, but they were not seriously considered until Spiro Agnew resigned as vice-president after pleading no contest to tax evasion charges in October 1973. Nixon's political opponents had not wanted to see Agnew as president. But with Agnew replaced by the relatively uncontroversial Gerald Ford, a long-time Michigan congressman, impeachment became an attractive alternative, and on October 23, two weeks after Agnew's resignation, eight impeachment resolutions were referred to the House Judiciary Committee for its consideration. According to Article 2, Section 2, of the Constitution, removal of a president through impeachment can take place only upon conviction of "Treason, Bribery, or other high Crimes and Misdemeanors." The House Judiciary Committee struggled to find a precise meaning for those words. It finally voted to approve three articles of impeachment involving charges of obstructing justice, violating the constitu-

[69]Friedman, supra, note 68, p. 3.   [70]United States v. Nixon, 417 U.S. 683 (1974).

tional rights of citizens by misusing the FBI and the Internal Revenue Service for surveillance of political opponents, and failing to execute faithfully the law by refusing to obey subpoenas issued by the committee.

Each of these three legal versions of Watergate involved different elements of the incident. The most constrained was the burglary charge. The Supreme Court case involved matters of fundamental constitutional doctrine, but touched only a peripheral element of the Watergate affair—the involvement of John Mitchell in its planning and coverup. The impeachment proceedings were the broadest legal version, for they involved not only the affair itself but also charges of abuse of presidential power. It focused entirely on President Nixon rather than on the many subordinates who had been involved in the other legal proceedings.

A fourth version of Watergate unfolded in the political arena and was intertwined with the three legal versions, namely, the set of charges which were developed before the Select Senate Committee that investigated the Watergate affair under the chairmanship of Senator Sam Ervin of North Carolina. This was the broadest ranging inquiry of the four; it followed whatever clues developed during the investigation. Its unfolding did not follow a logical or chronological sequence. Rather, whenever a witness made some revelation, succeeding investigations ensued. Many of the materials for the legal versions were uncovered by the Senate inquiry. For instance, it was during the Ervin hearings that the country learned that Oval Office conversations had been routinely tape recorded. The hearings were thus much wider ranging than the legal proceedings. Their purpose was not to convict, but to convince. They undermined President Nixon's political base of support, and his standing in public opinion polls declined precipitously.

This fourth version overlapped the legal versions, but had quite different emphases. It was more partisan, with the Democrats playing a much more prominent role than in any of the court cases, even though they had been the victims of the burglary that was the focus of the first set of criminal charges. It was more publicity oriented, with hearings that were televised daily; for an entire summer, they virtually replaced afternoon soap operas. These hearings provided a public forum for former administration officials to confess or deny misdeeds. If there was a court, it was the court of public opinion. The function of the hearings (if not their official goal) was to generate enough controversy to have President Nixon removed or his power effectively shackled. The resolution of the dispute came with the president's resignation from office.

Watergate illustrates how a single incident may spawn several disputes, some of which may migrate into the political arena. At first, the only aggrieved party was the DNC, whose offices had been burglarized. But because the burglary was committed to influence an election campaign, and because the president became personally involved in covering up its connection to the White House, Congress, as the representative of the entire nation, became an aggrieved party. There were numerous occasions at which informal dispute-processing channels might have settled the issue. Had President Nixon immediately disavowed the burglary and promised prosecution of all involved (including his former attorney general), it is unlikely the affair would have gone further than criminal trials against those involved. As in the case of Vice-President Agnew, plea bargaining negotiations might well have settled those cases without a public trial.

However, the failure to use such alternatives allowed the dispute to mushroom. Every participant was well endowed with resources and legal expertise. Once the president's prestige became involved, the stakes become so high that the principals were willing to commit whatever resources seemed necessary to pursue their claims.

Watergate also illustrates how disputes become transformed as they migrate from one dispute-processing arena to another. None of the four versions represented the whole truth. Each version of the Watergate events carefully reconstructed the facts to suit the particular forum in which it was presented. Each used the law as a strategic weapon, and the participants constructed a version of the events to fit their purposes. Both law and politics thus played central roles in the dispute.

Are Americans Overly Contentious?

Many observers in recent years have decried what they perceive to be an overenthusiasm among Americans to dispute and litigate. Former Chief Justice Warren Burger spoke extensively about a litigation crisis, while others complained about "hyperlexis," an alleged tendency among Americans to turn to law at every opportunity. The media continuously report instances of what appears to be a rush to dispute, as when lawyers hurry to the scene of major disasters to help survivors and the families of the dead make negligence claims, when children sue their parents for a "divorce," or when consumers file huge claims against manufacturers for allegedly defective products. Such stories are packed with human interest and are easy to find. There is no news in incidents where people decide against making a claim or where they settle a nascent dispute over a cup of coffee; moreover, such incidents can be uncovered only with an enormous amount of effort.

As a consequence, many Americans believe that the United States is an overly litigious society. For instance, in a 1986 Louis Harris Poll, 69 percent thought it was too easy for people to sue for damages, and in a Roper poll at the same time, 66 percent thought the number of personal injury suits was too high.[71] However, comparisons with earlier periods and with other countries do not provide strong support for such a conclusion.

First, we have no data on the total number of disputes in the United States or any other country and therefore do not know how most disputes are processed. We have no way of counting disputes or tracking them until they come to an institution such as a court or an arbitration board. Consequently, we do not know whether Americans engage in disputes more or less frequently now than in the past, or more or less often than people in other countries. All we can do is speak about court cases, and they are only the visible tip of an iceberg that may be very deep or relatively shallow.

Evidence about court cases over American history is also spotty because courts have not published reliable counts on their activities and because courts in the United States are scattered among many federal, state, and local jurisdictions. However, the few studies that have carefully culled archival materials appear to indicate that litiga-

[71]Data from Roper Center.

tion rates were higher during most of the nineteenth century than during the twentieth century.[72]. Other studies indicate that in recent years, the rate of court filings has increased, but not dramatically.[73]

When we attempt to compare the litigation rate in the United States with that of other countries, the difficulties multiply because court structures and statistical procedures vary considerably. Marc Galanter has made the most careful cross-national assessment and finds the U.S. litigation rate high, but not the highest among the countries he examined. His estimate was that in 1980, the civil case rate in the United States was 44 per 1000 inhabitants, while in New Zealand it was 53, in Ontario, Canada, it was 47, in Denmark and in England and Wales it was 41, and in West Germany it was 23.[74] By many accounts, Japan has a quite low litigation rate; by Galanter's estimate, it was one-fourth of the U.S. rate.[75]

Explaining such variations over time and across countries has so far eluded scholars. To do so, one would first have to obtain far better data about the true level of litigation rates and understand how other disputing forums operate in these contexts. For instance, the low Japanese litigation rate has been explained both as the product of unique cultural traits and as the result of institutional arrangements that impede litigation.[76] At present, we do not know how much either factor contributes.

Conclusion

At the beginning of this chapter, we discussed the ways in which disputes migrate from one disputing process to another and the changes that take place during those migrations. As we have seen from the examples of disputes, important consequences flow from the availability of resources, the involvement of third parties, the degree of participant control, the role of legal norms, the degree of formality, and the varying use of facts. It is these elements, and not simply what happened that generated the dispute, that determine who wins and who loses, and what winning and losing mean.

Four sets of disputes have been discussed in this chapter. We began with disputes that involved ordinary people with marital problems. Next, we described the range of experiences confronting consumers having difficulties with their creditors. Third, we examined several commercial disputes. The fourth set involved two disputes in which the boundaries between law and politics had almost completely dissolved—the abortion controversy and the Watergate affair. These disputes illustrate characteristics of

---

[72]Wayne V. McIntosh, "Private Use of a Public Forum: A Long- Range View of the Dispute Processing Role of the Courts," *American Political Science Review 77* (1983), pp. 990–1010; Wayne V. McIntosh, *The Appeal of Civil Law: A Political-Social Analysis of Litigation* (Urbana: University of Illinois Press, 1990).

[73]Galanter, supra, note 33.

[74]Ibid., p. 52. Note that the years for these countries varied from 1970 in Canada to 1980 in the United States.

[75]Marc Galanter, "Adjudication, Litigation, and Related Phenomena," in Leon Lipson and Stanton Wheeler (eds.), *Law and the Social Sciences* (New York: Russell Sage Foundation 1986), pp. 194–95.

[76]Setsuo Miyazawa, "Taking Kawashima Seriously: A Review of Japanese Research on Japanese Legal Consciousness and Disputing Behavior," *Law & Society Review 21* (1987), pp. 219–242.

dispute processing in the legal arena that are central to understanding the relationship of law to politics.

The first two sets of disputes demonstrated the advantage enjoyed by repeat players and those with substantial resources as compared to one-shotters and disputants with few resources. This advantage is perhaps shown most clearly when cases go to court, but it is also often significant in out-of-court negotiation and mediation. We saw that husbands often have an advantage over wives in negotiating divorce settlements because— even though both parties are one-shotters —men have greater economic resources. In creditor-debtor disputes, inequalities of resources combine with differences in experience to advantage lenders. Such disputes are often between creditors who are repeat players and debtors who are one-shotters; the repeat players frequently win because they know better how to use the law.

The disputes also illustrate that the law itself is by no means neutral, but rather reflects values that happen to dominate a society at a particular time. Those values may be relics of an earlier period or a reflection of recent political victories. The more complex the laws, the more they favor frequent users of the courts. It is for this reason that people struggle over the substance of new and revised laws.

These examples also show the importance of social position and economic resources in settling disputes in and around the legal arena. Social position here refers to whether parties are one-shot users of the legal system or repeat players. One-shotters suffer from inexperience and naivete. Repeat players can manipulate the legal process to their advantage by deciding when to initiate court action, choosing their legal arena and sometimes even their courtroom, and knowing when it is wise to withdraw temporarily. Economic resources can buy legal expertise and thus permit one party to impose legal disadvantages on others. The economic strength of creditors over debtors means that their disputes are fought on legal grounds selected by creditors, who write the contracts.

The social and economic motivations of the parties in these disputes are also apparent. Partisan politics were entirely absent in most of them even when, as in the case of the Apple-Franklin litigation, important policy issues were at stake. Disputes arising from divorces are generated by myriad social stresses that are only remotely connected to the political arena. Although these disputes involve many people, the disputants are in no position to organize politically. Disputes between creditors and debtors are principally the product of economic stresses. Even the disputes between economic giants are more the product of economic conditions than of political circumstance.

However, other disputes typically migrate between the political and legal arenas. Both the abortion controversy and the Watergate affair illustrate the overlap between the two areas. Even when such a dispute was in court, one could not confidently assert that it was simply a legal issue, as the litigation concerning President Nixon surely was not. Nor could one argue that legislation —although it might reflect partisan divisions as in the abortion controversy—concerned only politics. Such disputes weld law and politics so closely together that they become almost indistinguishable.

The examples in this chapter have, however, neglected one very important set of disputes that occupies a large portion of legal system: the processing of allegations that crimes have been committed. Criminal cases have many special characteristics, and we turn to these disputes in the next chapter.

KEY WORDS

grievance	adjudication
claim	dispute processing
exit	dispute resolution
negotiation	one-shotter
mediation	repeat player
arbitration	

FOR FURTHER STUDY . . .

For a fuller discussion of the paths taken by grievances toward litigation, see Richard E. Miller and Austin Sarat, "Grievances, Claims, and Disputes: Assessing the Adversary Culture," *Law* and *Society Review* 15 (1980–81), pp. 525–566, and Lynn Mather and Barbara Yngvesson, "Language, Audience, and the Transformation of Disputes," Ibid. pp. 775–882. David M. Engel explores these processes as they take place in a small midwestern community in two articles: "Legal Pluralism in an American Community: Perspectives on a Civil Trial Court," *American Bar Foundation Research Journal 1980* (1980) pp. 425–454; and "Cases, Conflict, and Accommodation: Patterns of Legal Interaction in a Small Community," Ibid. *1983* (1983), pp. 803–874.

You may uncover the relationships between disputing and law in your own experience by studying how disputes are processed within organizations to which you belong. Examine, for instance, disputes that arise within campus organizations. Compare the law on the books in bylaws, organization constitutions, and formal rules and regulations with the living law reflected in the rules and procedures that people actually apply. Examine whether dispute processing varies when friends and acquaintances, not strangers, are involved. How do the resources of those concerned affect the outcomes? Do you find support for the conceptualization presented in this chapter? If not, why do you think that is the case?

4

USING THE LAW TO PROMOTE
PUBLIC ORDER AND SAFETY

People do not use law only when they have disputes. They also employ it to protect themselves against crime and criminals. Indeed, for the media, the law's use to promote public order and safety is its most salient characteristic. News programs and newspapers inundate their audiences with information about lawbreaking. Most news coverage focuses on the unlawful incident itself rather than on the ways in which the law has been invoked to set things right.

At first glance, decisions to invoke the criminal law appear to be distinctly different from the decisions to invoke the civil law discussed in Chapter 3. There are, in fact, many differences. Whereas most civil disputes involve two parties—a complainant (plaintiff) and a defendant—criminal cases normally involve three distinct parties: a victim, an alleged offender, and state officials, such as the police and prosecutor. Crimes are considered to be offenses against the State, which represents the public at large. Thus, even though crimes cause injuries that might be compensated by a monetary payment, monetary compensation plays a decidedly secondary role in American criminal proceedings. In place of monetary compensation, the prosecution of crime is primarily motivated by an official's sense of duty and by bureaucratic routine, sometimes prodded by a victim's desire for retribution.

Criminal incidents are distinctly more in the public sphere than most civil disputes. This may be seen in the prominent role of the police, for the police symbolize the public character of criminal proceedings. Whereas most civil disputes are purely private quarrels played out on a public stage, criminal incidents are inherently public and engage the attention of public officials. Criminal prosecution in the United States is almost never a private matter; it is pursued only when the police and the public prosecutor decide to act. Criminal proceedings are more public than private in still another way: in criminal proceedings, public officials use the legal system to promote their version of public order. Law is used to distinguish between permissible and deviant behavior and to punish many, but not all, forms of deviance. Consequently, politics intrudes more prominently into the provision of public order than in the areas of the legal system explored in previous chapters. Indeed, criminal law is generally considered to be public rather than private law, for it deals with matters that most people admit have public dimensions.

At the same time, this public dimension suggests a fundamental similarity to civil disputes, for as we have seen the law is also used in civil disputes to establish order. Just as the law defines what behavior may lead to judicially imposed penalties in civil disputes, it defines both what constitutes criminal behavior and what penalties may be imposed for such acts. An additional similarity to civil disputes lies in the impact of resources on the outcome of criminal proceedings. Differences in the resources and experience victims, criminals, and state officials bring to criminal proceedings have a distinct bearing on how the criminal law is invoked. Decisions to invoke the criminal law also have private aspects, especially for victims.

These considerations can best be unraveled if we employ the framework used in Chapter 3 to explore both the submerged, privatized segments of the criminal justice process and its explicitly public elements. Our analysis is made simpler if we examine separately the situations of victims, offenders, and public officials.

Victims and Their Decisions to Invoke the Criminal Law

When something happens that appears to be against the criminal law, it is often up to the victim to decide whether to invoke the law. That decision is affected by victims' understanding of what constitutes a crime and by their estimate of the utility of reporting it. In many instances, victims find ways other than police involvement to redress their grievance. In 1990, for instance, about three-fifths of all incidents that public authorities might have regarded as victimizations were not reported to the police, although some kinds of incidents, such as automobile thefts, were reported much more frequently, while petty thefts were reported less frequently.[1] When victims were asked by the national crime survey why they did not report such incidents, they cited many reasons. In almost one-fourth of all unreported incidents, the victims reported that they themselves had recovered what was stolen; in another 15 percent, the victims said they had taken the matter to officials other than the police. Prominent among the other reasons for not reporting the incidents to the police was the victim's estimate that the "police would not want to be bothered" or that it was a "private or personal matter."[2] For instance, when incidents involve a family member, many victims feel it is inappropriate to call the police; likewise, if the offense appears trivial, such as the theft of a ball, many are reluctant to report it. Those responses, in part, reflect variations in what the law defines as a crime and what ordinary people consider criminal. Many women, for instance,

---

[1] Timothy J. Flanagan and Kathleen Maguire, *Sourcebook of Criminal Justice Statistics, 1991* Washington, D.C.: U.S. Department of Justice, Bureau of Justice Statistics, 1992), p. 266.
[2] Ibid., p. 268.

have been reluctant to report being slapped by their husband as an assault, or unwanted fondling of their breasts by a date as sexual assault, even though statutes define them as crimes. As with civil disputes, close social relationships inhibit invocation of the law. An abused wife may choose to retaliate by locking her husband out of the house, and the victim of a date assault may refuse future social encounters.

Victims also take into account the likelihood that public authorities can or will take effective action. When it appears that the police are unlikely to catch the thief or retrieve the stolen property, many people simply don't bother reporting the incident unless they need a police report to obtain compensation from their insurance company. The survey responses suggest that victims weigh the appropriateness of reporting an incident and the amount of effort involved in reporting it to the police against the probability that corrective action will be taken.

The perceived severity of crimes varies greatly. One indication of these variations comes from responses to a 1977 survey in which 60,000 respondents were asked to rank a series of incidents.[3] The crime ranked most serious involved neither murder nor rape but a bomb planted in a public building that exploded and killed twenty people. This was considered twice as serious as a fatal stabbing, almost 2.5 times more serious than rape, and 72 times more serious than taking bets on the numbers.[4] Such disparities in the perceived seriousness of offenses contribute to variations in the likelihood that the law will be invoked. The family of a bombing victim is very likely to demand prosecution, while the probability that someone who witnesses or participates in a numbers operation will call the police is almost zero. In general, the more serious the offense, the more likely it will be reported.[5] Moreover, it is striking that many of the offenses not considered serious by the public are so-called victimless crimes, such as illegal betting and prostitution, in which the presumed victim is often a willing participant. Such offenses represent offenses against public mores and values that are not universally shared; the absence of a concrete, identifiable victim makes such crimes appear trivial to many people.

These data help explain why many incidents considered criminal according to legal criteria nevertheless do not lead to invocation of the criminal law. Victims instead respond in other ways. Many decide to forget the incident, as they do when confronted with civil disputes involving landlords or merchants. They simply accept whatever loss or injury occurred and proceed with their lives. Other victims exit, leaving the neighborhood or city to move to a new environment which they hope will be safer. Still others pursue justice through private channels, wreaking revenge by invoking peer pressure, retaliating with equal violence, or withholding favors and assistance to the offender.

As with civil disputes, in criminal matters willingness to invoke the law depends, in part, on the prior relationship between the parties. Even when people know they

[3] The Severity of Crime (Washington, D.C.: U.S. Department of Justice, Bureau of Justice Statistics, 1984), pp. 2–3.
[4] Ibid.
[5] Albert J. Reiss, Jr., Studies in Crime and Law Enforcement in Major Metropolitan Areas: A Report to the President's Commission of Law Enforcement and the Administration of Criminal Justice (Washington, D.C.: Government Printing Office, 1967), Section II, p. 67.

have been victimized by a crime, they invoke the law more readily when a stranger is involved than when the offender is someone they know and with whom they may have a close, continuing relationship. Invoking the law often threatens to alienate the offender permanently. It may be difficult to terminate the relationship, or the offender may be in a position to exercise power or influence over the victim in future transactions. These are among the reasons that many instances of domestic violence are not reported to the police. The victim—often a child or wife—commonly fears that the offender will make their life more miserable. For these and many other reasons, private responses often replace invocation of the law when criminal incidents involve acquaintances. The 1990 National Crime Survey indicates that such circumstances frequently arise; almost two-fifths of all violent incidents reported in the survey involved acquaintances of the victims.[6] There is reason to believe the proportion is even higher, because victims were reluctant to reveal such acts of violence to Census Bureau interviewers. In addition, the survey does not include homicides or the many incidents that involve schoolchildren under the age of twelve, both of which often involve assailants known to the victims. Moreover, a substantial number of property crimes in which the offender is apprehended also involve acquaintances of the victim. That may explain why almost 35 percent of the respondents indicated they failed to report an automobile theft because they considered it a private matter. There are thus many private reasons for victims to refuse to invoke the criminal law.

Other social circumstances also promote or impede invocation of the law by victims. Many victims respond to suggestions from friends, acquaintances, or bystanders. This was strongly suggested by a study by Greenberg, Barry, and Westcott, who staged petty thefts in an office and then varied the degree of peer pressure to call the police. When bystanders urged victims to call the police, they were much more likely to do so than if those persons suggested they forget the incident.[7] Because in real-life situations peers often suggest that invoking the law will be troublesome or useless, many victims fail to invoke the criminal law.

On the other hand, there are also private reasons for calling the criminal law into play. Some people are willing to sacrifice their relationship to the strain of the criminal process or to consider the relationship strong enough to withstand it. This may occur when someone refuses to return something they borrowed. The lender may report the item stolen and accuse the borrower. With the threat of jail hanging over them, some borrowers hastily return the property, after which complainants drop their charges. Police try to screen out such private uses of the law, but they do not always succeed. Examples of such uses can be observed in criminal courtrooms when a case is called only to be dismissed for want of prosecution, as the judge is given the whispered explanation that the "stolen" property has been returned and the complainant no longer has any interest in the case.[8] Since the police and courts do not consider small thefts to be serious crimes, they make no independent effort to prosecute despite the unwillingness of the

---

[6]Flanagan and Maguire, supra, note 1, p. 281.
[7]Martin S. Greenberg, Ruback R. Barry, and David R. Westcott, "Decision Making by Crime Victims: A Multi-Method Approach," *Law & Society Review 17* (1982), pp. 47–84. At the end of each experimental situation, the "victims" were told the nature of the experiment and paid a small bonus for participating in it.
[8]James Eisenstein and Herbert Jacob, *Felony Justice* (Boston: Little, Brown, 1977), p. 212.

victim to testify. Similar considerations may play a role in the invocation of the criminal law in domestic disputes. When a husband beats his wife, she may call the police to get him temporarily out of the house. Not only does that provide her a measure of safety, it may also help achieve a different kind of balance in their domestic relationship. She often does not pursue prosecution because sending her husband to jail may deprive her of financial support and permanently alienate him. Thus, in some domestic violence cases, the criminal law may be used to provide protection or to adjust the balance of power within the marriage rather than to punish unlawful behavior.

Some middle-class victims of burglary and automobile theft also use the criminal law for private purposes when they report their losses to the police. They know from experience that they stand little chance of retrieving their property, yet they call the police because they need a police report to obtain payment of their insurance claim.

The public purposes of the criminal law—to promote order and safety—are rarely the primary forces motivating victims to invoke it. Most victims want to be made whole again. Many also want society to punish their assailant, but they are not necessarily thinking about the larger social benefits of retribution. Punishment satisfies the personal needs of victims, and private punishment may suffice. Invocation of the criminal law to accomplish some policy aim is also rare. Thus, although criminal law is public law, its invocation by victims often reflects private motives.

The resources people can command also play a role in their willingness to invoke the criminal process. Middle-class families may be more likely to take their domestic problems to a therapist than to the police. Arguments among friends, if they culminate in violence, may lead to private restitution (such as paying the hospital bill) if the assailant has sufficient funds. For the middle class, fights are more likely to occur in private spaces rather than quasi-public places such as bars, with the result being that the police are less likely to be called into the fray. Even theft in the form of embezzlement is often handled quietly and privately, with a job dismissal, rather than with the more public and embarrassing act of invoking the criminal law. Many have argued that the law is invoked much less frequently in alleged instances of white-collar crime than for crimes committed by blue-collar offenders.[9]

The distinction seen in civil disputes between one-shotters and repeat players appears to be less important in the criminal sphere, at least among victims. Indeed, there is little public recognition of the fact that approximately 25 percent of all victims suffer multiple victimizations.[10] There is some indication that people who live in high crime neighborhoods are particularly likely to attempt to leave the area of the incidents.[11] It is not known whether they invoke the law before exiting, but their characteristics suggest that they do not. Victims of multiple offenses are often particularly hapless individuals. They may wander through dangerous parts of the city at very late hours, or may fail to

[9]See, for instance, Susan P. Shapiro, "The Road Not Taken: The Elusive Path to Criminal Prosecution for White Collar Offenders," *Law & Society Review* 19 (1985), pp. 179–218.
[10]Robert J. Lehnen and Albert Reiss, "Response Effects in the National Crime Survey," *Victimology* 3 (1978), p. 115; Edward A. Ziegenhagen, "The Recidivist Victim of Violent Crime," *Victimology* 1 (1976), pp. 538–550.
[11]Wesley G. Skogan and Michael B. Maxfield, *Coping with Crime: Individual and Neighborhood Reactions* (Beverly Hills, Calif.: Sage, 1981), pp. 241–255.

lock their cars or houses. Some feel it is unlikely that such people would be vigorous invokers of the criminal law. The overwhelming proportion of crime victims, however, are one-shotters or at least consider themselves to be so. No special advantage seems to adhere to the repeat players among victims.

Thus, only some of the factors involved in invocation of civil law are equally important to the invocation of criminal law by victims. The desire to redress a grievance motivates individuals to invoke the criminal law as it does in civil disputes. The relationship of the victim to the offender is also crucial, as is the social context. Victims are much more likely to invoke the criminal process against strangers than against acquaintances and when victims receive peer group support for doing so. Resource differences also have an impact, because those with greater resources are more likely to use private sanctions in dealing with the incident. However, the distinction between one-shotters and repeat players has little significance for explaining the law-invoking activities of victims of crime.

Public Authorities and Invocation of the Criminal Law

Victims are not the only parties who invoke the criminal law. Public authorities, such as the police and prosecutors, sometimes take independent action.[12] They are motivated by substantially different forces than are private victims, for bureaucratic routines and political considerations loom large in their decisions.

Organizational considerations govern some of the law enforcement activities of police and prosecutors. For both, effective law enforcement is a primary goal. Police typically judge themselves by the increase or decrease in the crime rate and the number of arrests they make. An arrest for a major crime, for example, is an important event in the life of a police officer. Likewise, prosecutors typically evaluate themselves by the number or proportion of convictions they obtain.

As we see in Chapter 6, social circumstances play a large part in police decisions to make an arrest rather than to handle incidents less formally. Not only the social milieu of police work, but also the respect that police officers may win from those they encounter, affects their likelihood to respond to a problem by making an arrest.

For certain crimes, police officers' and prosecutors' decisions to invoke the law reflect policy decisions because victims typically do not complain about them; the police must rely on their own initiative and be **proactive** in bringing offenders to court. This is most evident for so-called victimless crimes, offenses in which the victims participate in the perpetration of the offense. Thus, a prostitute's customer is as much a part of the crime of prostitution as the prostitute, the crap game player is as much a part of the gambling offense as the game operator, and a drug user is as much an offender as a drug seller. These "victims" do not report such crimes because they usually do not consider themselves victims, and if they do, they fear exposure and their own culpability. Conse-

---

[12]Our principal discussion of the police will be deferred until Chapter 6, where we examine their role as gate-keepers to the criminal justice system. It is essential to examine them here briefly, however, because they serve as stand-ins for victims in many cases.

quently, the police themselves must invoke the law if it is to be applied to such situations. Whether they do so often depends on departmental policy and departmental allocation of resources. Those factors, in turn, often depend on political pressure for action. Communities that tolerate prostitution, gambling, or drug use usually have police departments that do not commit resources to the suppression of such crimes.

Certain other crimes also depend on police or prosecutor action to invoke the law. Offenses such as muggings are difficult to stop because they usually occur when no police are around. Therefore, police officers sometimes act as decoy victims to catch the perpetrators of such crimes. Likewise, many thieves are not caught until they land in the net of a police "sting" in which the police have, for example, opened a fencing operation and videotaped their customers. Such operations are the product of decisions by public authorities to allocate resources to particular problems.

Public authorities not only take the initiative in pursuing some crimes but also play a central role in defining what constitutes a crime.[13] Criminal behavior sometimes exists as much in the eye of the beholder as in the action of the perpetrator. For instance, the distinction between manslaughter and justifiable homicide is very subjective. The police typically hesitate to classify a street shooting as justifiable homicide except when the shot has been fired by a police officer. They rarely treat police shootings as criminal offenses. Another instance of the subjectivity of the definition of crime may be found in the classification of shady business practices as fraud or simply questionable. The violator often tries to stay just within the boundaries of the law. The deceit and trickery inherent in fraud depends very much on the context of the behavior and the perceptions of the victim. The same is true of violations of moral codes, such as pornography. While most people think they can recognize pornography when they see it, defining it in concrete terms has bedeviled such sophisticated analysts as Supreme Court justices. A police officer's or prosecutor's determination that some book, video, or picture is pornographic often does not coincide with the judgment of the seller or an art critic.

Recognizing the importance of social definitions of crime alerts us to the subjectivity of many criminal prohibitions and the ways in which societies use the criminal code to enforce dominant values. The criminal law in the United States has been employed in this fashion throughout the nation's history. One example is the blue laws that imposed criminal sanctions against shopkeepers who violated the Christian Sabbath; another is the attempt to impose sobriety on the nation through the Eighteenth Amendment to the Constitution, which prohibited the manufacture and sale of alcoholic beverages. Still another is the use of criminal law to punish gay men and lesbians for their relationships. Such use of the criminal law stems from public and political objectives rather than the private forces that motivate most victims to invoke the law against their assailants. We explore such political motivations to invoke the criminal law more fully in Chapter 6.

[13]See particularly Richard Quinney, *The Social Reality of Crime* (Boston: Little, Brown, 1970); and Harold Pepinsky, *Crime and Conflict* (New York: Academic, 1976).

Offenders as Targets of the Legal Process

The third party involved in the invocation of the criminal law is the offender. There would be no crime without offenders and their illegal acts. In some cases, no doubt exists that an act was criminal from the victim's viewpoint. In many such instances, the offender also recognizes the act as criminal. Consequently, we need to examine the circumstances that lead people to commit acts they know may invoke the criminal law against them.

Many persons believe such behavior demonstrates the failure of the criminal law to deter the offensive activity. According to them, the invocation of the law is too slow, too uncertain, or too mild to prevent such action. Criminal justice in the United States is indeed sometimes slow and often uncertain. It is common for more than six months to elapse in cases of serious offenses before an alleged offender is brought to trial or the case is otherwise disposed;[14] in some places, it may take as long as nine months.[15] On the other hand, many persons charged with minor offenses plead guilty or are tried almost as soon as they are charged.[16]

The **uncertainty** of justice is much more widespread than its **delay**. The police make arrests in only a small proportion of all reported incidents; this is particularly true of property crimes, where many do not even enter the police records because the victims do not report them. Even when they are reported, many remain unsolved. It is not unusual to read of a burglary ring being caught only after it has committed dozens of break-ins. Much uncertainty about the outcome of a case exists even after an arrest for a serious offense. The best evidence we possess indicates that fewer than 3 of every 5 persons arrested for a felony are convicted, and fewer than 2 of every 5 go to prison.[17] Because the arrest rate for many offenses is well under 50 percent, offenders may calculate that their chances of being punished are minuscule.

On the other hand, the penalties assessed against criminals who are arrested, tried, and convicted are quite harsh in the United States. Forty-four percent of those incarcerated in the study cited above received terms of more than one year,[18] and sentences in excess of five years are quite common. For instance, half of all prison sentences for murder in 1988 were longer than 21 years; for robbery, half were longer than 7 years; for burglary, half were longer than 4 years.[19] Such sentences are longer than they would be in almost any other industrialized country.

It is extraordinarily difficult to estimate the effect on potential offenders of the mixture of delay, uncertainty, and **severity** that exists in the United States. We do not know whether a different mix of these factors might lead people to refrain from committing criminal acts. Part of our uncertainty stems from the complex blend of motives that leads people to commit offenses. The belief that the law deters offenders is based

---

[14]Flanagan and Maguire, supra, note 1, p. 546.   [15]Eisenstein and Jacob, supra, note 8, p. 233.

[16]Malcolm M. Feeley, *The Process Is the Punishment: Handling Cases in a Lower Criminal Court* (New York: Russell Sage Foundation, 1979).

[17]Flanagan and Maguire, supra, note 1, p. 546; the data come from eight states across the country.

[18]Supra, note 1, p. 545.   [19]Supra, note 1, p. 545.

on an assumption that offenders behave rationally and respond to changes in risks and costs.[20] This is the assumption underlying a large body of research that applies economic principles to the study of crime and law enforcement. Those studies have fueled the controversy over whether the death penalty deters murder. The balance of opinion doubts the validity of such analyses because only some offenders are the **rational calculators** assumed by the economic model. To understand how criminal law affects behavior, we need to examine the variety of motivations that may lead to criminal acts.[21]

Some criminal acts are purposive and result from rational calculation. They are intended to produce a material profit to the offender. For instance, most burglars break into houses to acquire property that they then sell for money to buy food, clothing, entertainment, or drugs. Criminologists do not agree on the number of offenders motivated by profit. Because many such offenders are not arrested or punished for each offense they commit, the risk of apprehension and conviction may appear to be relatively slight even though potential punishments are harsh. Hence, even for such crimes the deterrent effect of increasing penalties without raising the likelihood of apprehension and conviction remains in doubt.

A further complication lies in the fact that not all rationally calculating or purposive offenders believe their acts to be criminal. Some commit crimes for political purposes. They break the law without admitting that it is legitimate or binding on them. For instance, the draft card burners during the Vietnam War era knew Congress had enacted a law making such an action criminal, but they denied the validity of that law. Those protestors burned their draft cards to voice their objections to American involvement in Vietnam. Similarly, terrorists may rob banks, kidnap officials, or commit random acts of violence believing that such actions are legitimate ways to protest perceived oppression by a government to which they pledge no allegiance. They see their deeds as political protests against illegitimate regimes; many analysts consider such **political crimes** to be a distinct category of offenses. Neither swift, certain, nor harsh punishment is likely to deter such offenders.

An entirely different situation is presented by those who break the law for **expressive** rather than purposive reasons. They are driven by a variety of internalized, psychological forces not clearly related to material profit. For instance, autobiographical accounts by criminals sometimes refer to the thrill felt when a crime is committed. One thief reported, "Whenever I start stealing, boy, I dig a hell of a charge out of it. I dig a fantastic charge!"[22] The thrill may be related to the danger involved or to the feeling that one is outwitting the police. Because danger contributes to the thrill, protective measures do not deter such offenders. These considerations may explain the sharp rise in bank robberies in the 1970s despite elaborate security precautions and the high incidence of arrest and imprisonment of bank robbers.[23] The best security devices do not

[20]Franklin E. Zimring and Gordon J. Hawkins, *Deterrence* (Chicago: University of Chicago Press, 1973); Jack P. Gibbs, *Crime, Punishment, and Deterrence* (New York: Elsevier, 1975); Alfred Blumstein, Jacqueline Cohen, Susan E. Martin, and Michael H. Tonry (eds.), *Research on Sentencing: The Search of Reform,* 2 vols. (Washington, D.C.: National Academy Press, 1983).

[21]The following typology is quite similar to that used by William Chambliss in *Crime and the Legal Process* (New York: McGraw-Hill, 1969), pp. 368–370.

[22]Bruce Jackson, *Outside the Law: A Thief's Primer* (New Brunswick, N.J.: Transaction, 1972), p. 76.

[23]*Bank Robbery* (Washington, D.C.: U.S. Department of Justice, Bureau of Justice Statistics, 1984).

deter crime if robbers are oblivious to the risk of apprehension or if increasing the risk makes robbery more rather than less attractive.

Similarly, our increasing knowledge of rapists and other sex offenders indicates that they are often driven by deeply rooted antagonisms that have no relationship to their victims. By their attacks, they express a general rage against women; their particular victims simply happened to be available. For instance, it appears that Christopher Wilder, once at the top of the FBI's list of most-wanted fugitives, was such a person. He was apparently wealthy and able to purchase whatever sexual favors he wanted. He had also been convicted of a number of sexual assaults before beginning a cross-country spree in which he may have assaulted or murdered as many as eleven young women whom he met at shopping malls and enticed into his car.[24] The same expressive motivation might explain the brutal slayings by the so-called Hillside Strangler in Los Angeles. No instrumental motive was apparent in these cases.

Many other offenses are committed under the influence of alcohol or narcotics. Fifty-seven percent of all convicted prisoners in jails in 1989 reported they had been under the influence of alcohol or narcotics when they committed the offense for which they were convicted.[25] Alcohol abuse is particularly prevalent in assaults.[26] Thousands of assaults and many murders take place when the offender's drunkenness turns to blind rage. It is unclear why some people become aggressive while drunk, but the relationship between the commission of violent crimes and alcohol abuse is strong.

The several kinds of offenders we have discussed are made vivid by Conklin's description of robbers. On the one hand is the professional robber who "is committed to the crime of robbery because it is direct, fast, and often very profitable. Sophisticated planning, the neutralization of security measures near the target, and investigation of escape routes are important parts of the techniques of such offenders."[27] Such a professional is clearly a rational calculator. To a lesser degree, this may also be true of addicts who rob to support their habit. On the other hand, however, many robbers are opportunists rather than professionals. In contrast to the careful design of the professional, "robberies by opportunists often seem to happen in a random fashion. A vague idea of trying to get some money exists in the offender's mind, but the robbery sometimes 'just happens.'"[28] Alcoholic robbers are much like opportunists. In Conklin's words they "were drunk and simply decided to beat someone up. [They] . . . took the victim's money only as an afterthought." [29]

In all these examples, only those who break the law to change it have a public purpose in mind. The remainder run afoul of the law in the pursuit of their private interests or motives. Private rather than public considerations thus motivate most actions that may lead to the invocation of the criminal law. The fact that the law may severely punish offenders is likely to influence only those who are rational calculators.

[24]Rogers Worthington and James Coats, "Girl Tells of Wilder's Threats, Torture," *Chicago Tribune*, 15 April 1984, pp. A1.
[25]Flanagan and Maguire, supra, note 1, p. 629.   [26]Supra, note 1, p. 629.
[27]John E. Conklin, *Robbery and the Criminal Justice System* (Philadelphia: J.B. Lippincott, 1972), p. 64.
[28]Ibid., pp. 69–70.   [29]Ibid., p. 76.

Another important factor in understanding the actions of offenders is their relationships to their victims. As we have already seen, many acts that may be categorized as lawbreaking are committed against relatives or acquaintances. They are part of a continuous flow of interactions that one observer characterized as "the outcome of a dynamic interchange between an offender, victim, and, in many cases, bystanders."[30] Their meaning can be understood only in the context of those relationships, just as a contract dispute can best be understood in the context of the prior and potential future dealings between the two disputants.

It is no accident that so many crimes are committed against acquaintances and relatives, because the opportunity is greatest in the context of such relationships. There are different social constraints about expressing anger against friends or relatives than toward strangers, and those expressions sometimes turn to violence. Likewise, the borrowing that occurs between acquaintances may serve as the foundation for criminal charges if the relationship sours and the borrowed goods have not been returned. Those offenses are often not intended as criminal acts, but as we have seen, they can assume such a dimension.

Even when crimes are committed against strangers, the victim may play a role in the offense. With many such offenses, the crime is almost invited by acts of gross carelessness such as leaving keys in car ignitions, leaving homes unlocked, and walking in dangerous neighborhoods late at night. Offenders often prey upon such opportunities.[31] The same is true for the casual relationship which some victims strike up in bars with their assailants.

Resources also seem to be important in provoking criminal activity. Those with the poorest opportunities for legitimate occupations appear more likely to be involved in crime.[32] This is by no means a simple relationship but is nonetheless prominent. The reported crime rate is usually the greatest in neighborhoods where youth unemployment is highest. In part, this is because police know they can find likely suspects in such neighborhoods; policing may be harsher there than in middle-class sections of a city. But more than police bias produces such results. The relative scarcity of legitimate work makes illegal opportunities appear more attractive in these settings. Thus, resources play a significant role in the invocation of the criminal law, but with an opposite effect than in civil cases. Whereas the rich are most likely to invoke the civil law, it is the poor who are most likely to commit noticeable criminal acts.

Both one-shotters and repeat players can be found among criminal offenders. Repeat offenders are those most frequently featured in the media; they account for a very large proportion of all crimes but they do not constitute the majority of offenders. Most offenders appear to be **occasional** rather than **career criminals**. Many offenders—both

---

[30]David F. Luckenbill, "Criminal Homicide as a Situated Transaction," *Social Problems* 25 (1977), p. 185.

[31]A sophisticated analysis of the role of opportunity in engendering crime can be found in a series of articles by Lawrence E. Cohen and his associates. See Lawrence E. Cohen and Marcus Felson, "Social Change and Crime Rate Trends: A Routine Activity Approach," *American Sociological Review* 44 (1979), pp. 588–608; Lawrence E. Cohen, Marcus Felson, and Kenneth C. Land, "Property Crime Rates in the United States," *American Journal of Sociology* 86 (1980), pp. 90–118; and Lawrence E. Cohen and David Cantor, "The Determinants of Larceny," *Journal of Research in Crime & Delinquency* (1980), pp. 140–159.

[32]Richard A. Cloward and Lloyd E. Ohlin, *Delinquency and Opportunity: A Theory of Delinquent* Gangs (New York: Free Press, 1960).

in and out of prison—commit few crimes during their lives. Moreover, many of these types of offenders have regular occupations. Many burglars, for instance, hold normal jobs and commit burglaries on the side, supplementing their regular incomes with the proceeds of their crimes. This is also true for many thieves and embezzlers who typically use their regular jobs to gain the access required for their crimes.[33] Indeed, in 1991, almost 55 percent of prison inmates in the United States had been employed full-time at the time of their arrest.[34] Such offenders are not destitute, although often they come from impoverished areas of the city and victimize their neighbors. In many instances, they cannot maintain the standard of living they desire from their regular income, so they "moonlight" as criminals. Some are also drug addicts seeking funds to meet the high cost of maintaining their habits. Such part-time criminals are not particularly skilled in their trade. Because their occasional contacts with the law do not provide them with a substantial advantage, they are more like the one-shotters in civil disputes than repeat players.

Even career criminals who do little but commit crimes have a low level of specialization. Research has shown that most engage in a wide variety of offenses,[35] many of which do not require a high level of skill; most offenders do not specialize enough to become skilled. Thus, the vast majority of criminal offenders are amateurish one-shotters rather than skilled repeat players.

The Experiences of Other Countries

Crime is more an everyday occurrence in the United States than in other industrialized countries. Although crime statistics are not entirely reliable, because they are collected in different ways in various countries, all signs point to the United States as having among the highest rate for violent crimes. In early 1980s, the latest years for which such comparative data are available, only Thailand exceeded the U.S.'s homicide rate of 10.5 per 100,000 population; the rate for Canada was 2.1, for Germany, 1.2, for France and Japan, 1.0, and for England, 0.8.[36] Reported rapes in the United States stood at 36 per 100,000, a number approached only by Chile, with 34.2. Reported robberies in the United States ranked second with 240.9 per 100,000, which was outpaced only by Chile with 403.4 per 100,000.[37]

Why that is so remains a puzzle. There are many theories but no firm proof. One theory is that the degree of heterogeneity in the United States fosters a higher crime rate. That is sometimes no more than a polite way of pointing to the persistence of

---

[33]Harold R. Holzman, "The Serious Habitual Property Offender as Moonlighter: An Empirical Study of Labor Force Participation Among Robbers and Burglars," *Journal of Criminal Law & Criminology* 73 (1982), p. 1778.
[34]Allen Beck et al., *Survey of State Prison Inmates, 1991* (Washington, D.C.: U.S. Department of Justice, Bureau of Justice Statistics, 1993), p. 3.
[35]Holzman, supra, note 33; Joan Petersilia, Peter W. Greenwood, and Marvin Lavin, *Criminal Careers of Habitual Felons* (Washington, D.C.: U.S. Department of Justice, National Institute of Law Enforcement and Criminal Justice, 1978).
[36]Carol H. Kalish, "International Crime Rates," *Special Report* (Washington, D.C.: U.S. Department of Justice, Bureau of Justice Statistics, 1988), p. 5.
[37]Ibid. pp. 5–6.

racism that leads to discrimination against African Americans, Hispanics, and Asians in many spheres of life, particularly in the job market and in housing opportunities. Very high proportions of these minorities find themselves impoverished and living in the least desirable neighborhoods and circumstances. However, large numbers of these minorities are not involved in crime. Moreover, some other countries with distinct minorities, such as Great Britain and Spain, suffer from organized political violence that is rare in the United States. In England, bombings by the Irish Republican Army were much feared in the 1980s and the early 1990s, while in Spain such violence emanated from Basque nationalists. Analysts tend to think of such incidents as terrorism rather than crime, but that may be a false distinction.

Another theory links crime to income disparities, and it is true that the United States has a larger gap between rich and poor than other industrialized countries. However, we have already seen that much crime is not instrumental in character; it is not an attempt to clamber up the income scale. Moreover, most of the poor do not commit crimes.

A third theory links violent crime with the easy access to handguns that is quite unique to the United States. In no other industrialized country can one obtain handguns so easily. It is true that many criminals use handguns when they commit their offense. However, an even larger number of law-abiding citizens possess guns and the defensive potential of those weapons seems to deter very few crimes. Moreover, the most frequent crimes are thefts that do not involve handguns.

Another theory popular with some politicians is the inefficiency and leniency of the criminal justice system. As we have noted, many persons arrested for serious crimes are not convicted and even if convicted are not sent to prison. However, the United States incarcerates a larger proportion of its population than any other industrialized nation. In 1989, 398 persons per 100,000 population were in prison or jail in the United States; England had 93, France 82, and West Germany 78.[38] However, there is no compelling evidence that nations with lower crime rates enjoy more efficient criminal justice procedures.

Finally, some point to the "culture of violence" that appears so prevalent in the United States. The United States is still captivated by the myth of the Wild West, which embraces and celebrates violence as the instrument of the courageous pioneer. More immediately, Americans are barraged by violence on their television screens and in their movie theaters. However, very few of those exposed to violence emulate it. Moreover, many of the same television shows Americans see are later exported to other countries, with no discernible deleterious effect.

Thus, we are left with a puzzle for which there is no easy answer. Some combination of all these factors may well play a substantial role in the high rate of crime in the United States. However, it is very difficult to demonstrate the effect of each or all of these factors in the face of the many other differences that exist from country to country.

---

[38]Warren Young and Mark Brown, "Cross-National Comparisons of Imprisonment," in Michael Tonry (ed.), *Crime and Justice: A Review of Research 17* (Chicago: University of Chicago Press, 1993), p. 15.

Conclusion

The public purposes of the criminal law are unquestioned. No one doubts the necessity of maintaining public order and safety for the general welfare of all citizens. This is one of the fundamental duties of government. Yet we have seen in this chapter that private motives play the dominant role in private invocation of the criminal law. Victims and offenders alike more often respond to private imperatives than to perceptions of public duty, although in some cases private and public considerations overlap and intermingle.

However, a public function for criminal law remains, as seen in our brief discussion of the role of police and prosecutors, which we pursue in greater depth in the following chapters as we examine the bureaucratic and political pressures that motivate these public authorities. We must also explore the role that perceptions of public welfare play when legislators consider adopting criminal laws, a subject we examine in Chapter 11.

Key Words

proactive
uncertainty [of criminal justice]
delay [of criminal justice]
severity [of criminal justice]
rational calculator

political crime
expressive [crimes]
occasional [criminals]
career criminal

For further study . . .

A good read as well as a fascinating account of the ways in which the United States has dealt with crime and criminals throughout its history is Lawrence M. Friedman's *Crime and Punishment in American History* (New York: Basic Books, 1993). A particularly thoughtful analysis of crime and the fear of crime is by Wesley G. Skogan, *Disorder and Decline: Crime and the Spiral of Decay in American Neighborhoods* (New York: Free Press, 1990). The best compendium of statistics of many phases of the criminal justice system is the annual publication of the *Sourcebook of Criminal Justice Statistics* by the U.S. Department of Justice, Bureau of Justice Statistics.

To see for yourself how perceptions of victims affect the invocation of the criminal justice system, conduct a small survey of friends and relatives about incidents in which they considered themselves victimized, what they did about them, and why they pursued that course of action. Be sure to distinguish between offenders who were acquaintances and those who were strangers.

III

THE MIDDLE RING: GATEKEEPERS

F ew people think of the police, lawyers, and interest groups in the same instant. Each has quite distinctive characteristics and a seemingly separate place (if any at all) in the legal system. However, as we saw in Chapter 1, they share the important role of gatekeeper to legal processes and institutions. They have substantial influence in determining who uses their services, in what ways, and with what results.

In the following three chapters, we examine each of these institutions to see how they perform their gatekeeping function and why they help some disputants use the legal system, while excluding others. The social characteristics of the gatekeepers constitute one part of the story; their location in the political arena is another. Each exercises considerable discretion, but the guideposts that usher some disputes into the courts, legislatures, or executive agencies and steer others away are distinctive. We begin with the police, then move to lawyers, and, finally, examine interest groups.

5

THE POLICE

The police are perhaps the most visible agents of modern government. For some people, they symbolize safety and order; to others they represent nuisance enforcers of traffic rules, to be evaded if possible but respected when encountered. Viewed as part of the judicial process, police appear to control access to criminal justice. But to still others, the police embody brute force and repression that is to be feared and resisted. These multiple images of the police symbolize the many roles police play. We focus on two: as gatekeepers to the criminal justice process and as agents for the State to enforce social control.

The Police as Agents of Social Control

The police are the internal security forces of the modern state. Public safety is a prerequisite for stable government. The founders of the Constitution recognized this when they wrote in the preamble that they were establishing the Union in order ". . . to insure domestic Tranquility," a condition free from commotion, violence, or threats to one's property.

Formal police agencies were established early in the nineteenth century in American cities. However, they were not the uniformed, trained forces that we know today. Rather, they were patronage employees of the mayor, whose job it was to keep cities reasonably safe; however, they also had to help their patron retain power at the polls. When a mayor lost an election, most of the police force was replaced by his successor's patronage employees.[1] These police forces, however, were not large. As late as 1880, New York City, with 1.2 million people, had only 2,500 police officers, and towns like Kalamazoo, Michigan and Keokuk, Iowa, with populations just over 10,000, had only a

---

[1]Lawrence M. Friedman, *Crime and Punishment in American History* (New York: Basic Books, 1993), pp. 67–71.

handful.[2] Requiring uniforms and imposing quasi-military discipline was a reform adopted late in the nineteenth century to bring the police under control and make them more effective.[3]

Assuring domestic tranquility has never been an easy task. Nineteenth-century cities were dangerous places like their twentieth century counterparts. They were inhabited by many footloose men. In addition, immigrants from rural backwaters of many European countries filled the cities with people unaccustomed both to American customs and to living in large places. The clamor of peddlers selling their wares, the cries of mothers disciplining their children, the drinking outside bars may have seemed natural to many of the newcomers, but they signified danger to older residents of the cities. One of the first tasks of the newly militarized police in the late nineteenth century was to control these "dangerous classes." Cities employed police to squelch strikes, limit public drunkenness, and prevent the rowdiness of the ghettos from spreading to "better" neighborhoods. As Friedman concludes, "Nineteenth-century criminal justice was not, in short, blindfolded Justice. It was very definitely the servant of power, the protector of privilege."[4]

So, too, in the late twentieth century. As agents of social control, the police enforce the norms dominant in the cities they serve. For most of the twentieth century, this meant treating African Americans as if they were ipso facto suspicious characters, to be stopped and interrogated whenever they appeared outside their own neighborhoods. For much of the twentieth century, it meant looking with suspicion on allegations of rape and refusing to take seriously most charges of domestic violence. This was the result both of the kind of personnel recruited for the job of policing as well as the laws the police were to enforce.

Until recently, police officers were almost entirely male; the only women on the force were secretaries and clerical personnel. It was also almost entirely a white force until the 1960s. The white men who became police officers often came from Irish or Italian families, a reflection of the power of Irish and Italian communities in city politics until the end of World War II. Many of these men harbored the prejudices of their neighbors—suspicion of African Americans and other racial minorities and macho values that assumed the subordination of women. Thus, social control meant keeping such people "in their place" and privileging men when they quarrelled with women. It also meant treating youths with ambivalence. Some youthful criminality was overlooked as part of the growing up process, but it was more readily tolerated among middle-class and working-class youths than among the poor.

The substantive content of social control is defined not only by the prejudices of individual police officers but also by the laws and policies adopted by the cities and states in which they work. Thus, for instance, rape was always a criminal offense, but courts routinely permitted defendants to question the reputation of the victim at trial. This sent a signal to the police that rape allegations were normally not to be taken seriously, particularly when the victim knew the alleged offender. Most cities outlawed public drunkenness and one of the principal activities of the police until the 1970s was picking up drunks from the streets and taking them to jail to get sober.

[2]Ibid., p. 149.   [3]Ibid., pp. 148–155.
[4]Ibid., p. 106.

The contents of criminal laws are the product of the legislative process. Those decisions have enormous consequences for setting priorities for local policing decisions. State legislatures and, to a lesser extent, Congress decide which activities shall be labeled criminal and what penalties may be applied.

Most criminal law in the United States is state law; although many similarities exist, the details of the criminal code differ in each state. In addition, there is a second layer of criminal law contained in federal legislation; the same acts may be punishable under both state and federal law.

Each year, legislatures decide on additions, amendments, and deletions to the criminal code. For instance, when a spate of incidents became publicized in the 1980s in which spurned lovers and husbands stalked their girlfriends or spouses, a number of state legislatures created a new crime, "stalking," which made it possible for police to arrest persons who repeatedly followed and threatened others.[5] Similarly, when armed robbers began brazenly seizing cars from motorists stopped at traffic lights, some state legislatures defined "carnapping" as criminal and attached severe penalties to it.[6] Such additions to the criminal code, however, are relatively rare. Much more common are small changes in the definition of a crime or alterations in the penalties judges may impose. Rarer still are deletions, such as the decriminalization of public drunkenness.

The criminal code, as it emerges from legislation and court interpretations, is the authority on which police rely for their actions. In the first instance, the criminal code determines which acts the police *may* refer to the criminal courts. This authorization is very important, for it sets limits to police power. The police may intervene only where the criminal code authorizes it; without this authorization, the police are subject to lawsuits for making unlawful arrests. However, the criminal law is only the first guide to police action; it prohibits many more acts than the police can monitor. Therefore, police must choose where to focus their attention among many alleged crimes. For instance, both burglary and assault are criminal. Yet most police departments respond to calls involving assault much more rapidly than those reporting burglaries, since assaults involve injuries to people while burglaries concern only the loss of property. Moreover, it is much easier to catch those accused of assault because the victim has seen them and perhaps knows them, while burglars typically work unseen among strangers. These considerations are typical of police departments. They choose priorities according to what seems most valued by their community. As James Q. Wilson suggested, this leads to quite distinctive styles of policing. Some police departments emphasize **order maintenance** and engage in much informal sanctioning of street offenders; others are **legalistic** and write tickets and make arrests whenever the occasion arises; a third style discerned by Wilson is **service-oriented,** in which departments reflect the demands of their community for efficient service and swift response to calls by the public.[7] Consequently,

[5]Patricia Davis, "New Stalking Law Flushing Crime into the Open in Va.," *Washington Post,* 24 January 24 1993, p. B1; Ibid., September 17, 1993, p. A20.

[6]Joseph F. Sullivan, Florida Anti-Carjacking Plan Features Stiff Jail Sentences," *New York Times,* 25 November 1992, p. B6; "Cathy Trost, Carjacking Spreads to Nation's Suburbs" *Wall Street Journal,* 30 September 1992, p. B1.

[7]James Q. Wilson, *Varieties of Police Behavior: The Management of Law and Order in Eight Communities* (Cambridge, Mass.: Harvard University Press, 1968).

many segments of the criminal code are infrequently used and are only symbolic rebukes of unwanted behavior. Moreover, enforcement of many sections of the criminal code varies from city to city. Police departments choose their priorities and allow individual police officers to exercise discretion about which acts necessitate a police response and which violators to haul into court.

Policy preferences, thus, create much more variation in police practices than do differences in criminal codes. Each city has its own set of preferences about what is important for maintaining tranquility. While burglary prevention may rank high in a bedroom suburb, gang violence is likely to be more important to a central city. Traffic control scarcely counts in many small towns; maintaining the smooth flow of rush-hour traffic on expressways, however, is vital to big cities. These preferences display themselves particularly vividly with respect to such crimes as prostitution, pornography, and gambling. Some cities tolerate prostitution, although it is against the law, as long as it remains confined to a distinct (so-called red light) neighborhood. Others instruct their police to arrest prostitutes wherever they find them. Some permit "adult" bookstores to flourish; others pursue them relentlessly. In most cities, gambling of some sorts—such as church bingo games—is openly permitted, while corner crap game players and numbers runners are arrested on sight.

Public order does not only involve suppressing crime. Equally important (although most people take it for granted) is the maintenance of order on the streets so that traffic flows smoothly through the city. This is essential for people to get to their workplaces and for businesses to receive deliveries. Traffic control presses hard on police time and resources. Keeping expressways clear, managing the flow of cars, trucks, and buses through business districts, and rationing on-street parking is important for cities both because the movement of people and goods is vital for city commerce and because enforcement of traffic regulations brings substantial revenues to city treasuries. It requires a great deal of patrol time because each traffic ticket written takes as long as ten minutes and ties up the patrol car.

Traffic enforcement competes with crime control. While the radio rush-hour traffic reports tell harried commuters the efficiency of police traffic management, the evening television news features the murder and mayhem police have been unable to prevent. Police who are writing speeding tickets cannot be dispatched to respond to a burglary call or a murder scene.

It is a matter of considerable importance to city officials that they set police priorities in a manner their constituents will approve or at least support. In practice, this means local pressures determine how police departments allocate their officers between traffic and crime fighting, which neighborhoods receive the heaviest patrolling, which kinds of crimes receive priority attention, when police may shoot at suspects, and what procedures shall be followed in citizen-officer confrontations. While these are problems debated across the nation, they are addressed entirely by locally devised solutions. The police chief of Inglewood, California, put it succinctly in comparing his priorities with those of Los Angeles:

> . . . we don't have enough police officers, and neither does Chief Davis, to bust every pot smoker around, so the whole matter shakes down to a sense of priorities,

a discretionary decision. With LAPD maybe it's pot, but with us the priority is providing the best protection for Inglewood residents.[8]

The Police as Gatekeepers

By imposing social control according to the policy preferences of their city governments, the police bring some offenders to the criminal justice process while keeping others clear of entanglement with the criminal courts. In the United States, as elsewhere, the criminal justice process cannot be initiated without help from the police. When people think they have been victimized by a criminal act, they can enlist the force of the State to obtain justice only by obtaining cooperation from the police. It is the police who decide whether a crime appears to have been committed and whether a particular person is to be considered the suspected wrongdoer. Unless the police make those decisions, it is unlikely that any criminal sanction will result from the incident. Standing astride the portals to the criminal justice process, the police exercise enormous discretion in deciding what acts will be considered by the criminal courts for potential punishment.

Both the degree of discretion exercised by the police and some of the difficulties they face in combatting crime are displayed by our knowledge of the extensiveness of crime in the United States. Statistics that purport to indicate how much crime occurs in fact show only how much crime the police do not know about, either because they choose to ignore it or because citizens choose not to report criminal incidents to them. Two different enumerations exist, but neither provides a complete or accurate count of the number of crimes.[9]

COUNTING CRIME

One count of crime depends on police records and is known as the FBI **Uniform Crime Reports.** The FBI collects from all police agencies the number of **offenses known to the police.** Local police departments complete the data forms and send them to Washington for compilation. On the basis of these accounts, the FBI calculates crime rates for every sizeable city.

The resulting count of crimes suffers from many limitations. The crime count to which people pay most attention is that of "index" crimes, which consists of serious violent crimes (such as homicides, assaults, and robberies) and serious property offenses (such as burglaries, larceny theft, and car thefts). However, not all crimes considered serious are included; most notably, the FBI does not count drug offenses as part of the crime rate. They are reported separately.

[8]Bill Hazlett, "Police Rock Concerts: A Question of Priorities," *Los Angeles Times,* 12 May 1975, II 6 quoted in Michael K. Brown, *Working the Street: Police Discretion and the Dilemmas of Reform* (New York: Russell Sage Foundation, 1981), p. 64.
[9]Herbert Jacob, *The Frustration of Policy: Responses to Crime by American Cities* (Boston: Little, Brown, 1984), pp. 39–46.

In addition, the crime count reported in the Uniform Crime Reports suffers from two other serious faults. One is that this crime count depends primarily on citizens calling offenses to the attention of the police. The police themselves witness relatively few crimes, since most offenders go to considerable lengths to hide their transgressions from the police. Most burglaries occur at night; many fights occur inside private spaces. Even street violence usually occurs when the police are not in the vicinity. Crimes not called into the police are not recorded in these counts.[10] Almost half of all rape victims do not call the police because they fear the shame they will be put to by police who will inquire into the exact circumstances of the incident. About half of all household burglary victims and three-fourths of household theft victims do not report the crime.[11] So many victims fail to call the police because there is often little the police can do for them. The police rarely recover stolen property; often the only reason to report a burglary is to secure a police report for insurance reimbursement. Many victims are also distrustful of the police. In addition, many white-collar crimes go undetected and not reported in the Uniform Crime Reports.

The second principal defect of the Uniform Crime Reports is that they are not uniform. Some police departments have been known to doctor their numbers in order to show lower crime rates for their cities;[12] In 1983, when Mayor Harold Washington took office in Chicago, he ordered the police to stop reducing the crime rate by "unfounding" reports of crime; this resulted in an immediate upsurge of the crime statistics for Chicago, but did not reflect any change in the actual amount of crime.[13] In addition, police departments vary in their attentiveness to accurate recording of crime reports; the Bureau of Justice Statistic's *Sourcebook of Criminal Justice Statistics* for 1992 noted that arson was not included in their index of crime "due to the incompleteness of arson reporting by the police in 1979–91."[14]

An alternative count of crime comes from the **National Crime Survey** conducted by the Census Bureau. This is an elaborate survey that annually asks special samples of Americans about criminal victimizations that have occurred to them or their households during the preceding six months. These surveys uncover more crime than the police reports, because respondents report incidents to census surveyors who come to their house even though they neglected to call the police when the incident occurred. In fact, these surveys indicate that two-thirds of all crimes are never reported to the police and, therefore, are not included in the Uniform Crime Reports.[15] However, serious inaccuracies of a different kind mar the survey numbers. The count revealed by the surveys excludes homicides, since the surveys use victims as respondents. Nor do they in-

[10]Kathleen Maguire and Timothy J. Flanagan, eds. *Sourcebook of Criminal Justice Statistics, 1990* (Washington, D.C.:, U.S. Department of Justice, Bureau of Justice Statistics, 1991). no. 26 p. 26b.
[11]Ibid.
[12]David Seidman and Michael Couzens, "Getting the Crime Rate Down: Political Pressure and Crime Reporting," *Law & Society Review* 8 (1974), pp. 457–518; Marvin E. Wolfgang, "Uniform Crime Reports: A Critical Appraisal," *University of Pennsylvania Law Review* 109 (1963), pp. 708–738.
[13]Philip Watley, "Chicago Crime Data Hit," *Chicago Tribune*, 28 April 1983, Sec. 2, p. 1.
[14]Kathleen Maguire, Anne L. Pastore, and Timothy J. Flanagan, *Sourcebook of Criminal Justice Statistics, 1992* (Washington, D.C.: U.S. Department of Justice, Bureau of Justice Statistics, 1993), p. 358.
[15]Marianne W. Zawitz et al., *Highlights from 20 Years of Surveying Crime Victims* (Washington, D.C.: U.S. Department of Justice, Bureau of Justice Statistics, 1993), p. 3.

clude so-called victimless crimes where the "victim" often willingly participates, such as narcotics use, public drunkenness, and gambling. The surveys underreport other crimes because a single informant is asked about what happened to everyone in a household and many informants do not know all the events that have occurred to other household members; for instance, many children do not tell their parents of having their lunch money stolen at school. Still other incidents are not reported because of memory lapses by respondents, since the surveys take place several months after the incidents occurred. Finally, an entire class of victims—business enterprises—are not surveyed because it is difficult to identify the person who could provide reliable information for complex organizations. Nevertheless, the census numbers are more complete than the Uniform Crime Reports. They are also more reliable, because the data collection is much more closely supervised and it does not depend on the vagaries of administrative practice in thousands of separate agencies.

Figure 5.1 shows the results of the two kinds of crime rates; it displays only the rates for violent crimes because those two are most comparable. Several features of these data are noteworthy. The gap between the two lines indicates the vast amount of underreporting in the Uniform Crime Reports. If we compared property crimes, the gap would be still larger, since people report even fewer such crimes to the police. Second, victimizations seem to have fallen slightly between 1976 and 1991, while offenses known to

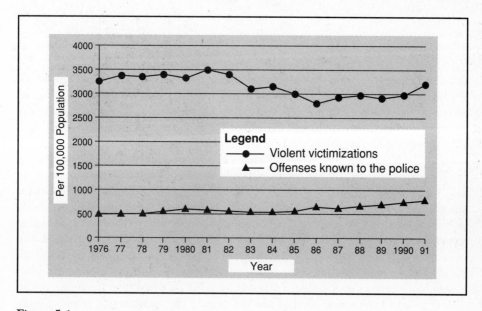

Figure 5.1
Violent Crimes according to Victimization Survey and FBI Uniform Crime Report's Offenses Known to the Police.
Source: Kathleen Maguire, Ann L. Pastore, and Timothy J. Flanagan, (eds) *Sourcebook of Criminal Justice Statistics, 1992* (Washington, D.C.: U.S. Department of Justice, Bureau of Justice Statistics, 1993), pp. 145, 357.

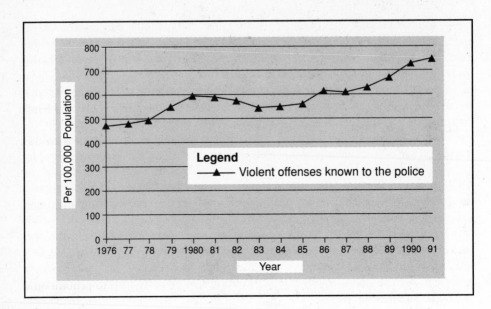

Figure 5.2
Violent Crimes Known to the Police, 1976–1991

the police have risen somewhat, although not as much as one might expect given the rhetoric about increasing crime. If we magnify the portion of the figure showing the Uniform Crime Reports crime rate as in Figure 5.2, we see that the violent crime rate appeared to rise considerably over this interval. This helps explain the common belief that violent crime exploded in the 1980s. However, measured by the more complete count of the National Crime Survey (Figure 5.1), violent crime did not increase steeply.

The gap between the two counts not only shows the incompleteness of the Uniform Crime Report crime rates but also reflects the large number of criminal incidents the police fail to bring to the courts. Because people do not inform the police, only 30 percent of all thefts, 41 percent of all household crimes, and 50 percent of all violent crimes were recorded by the police in 1992.[16] The cases the police bring into the criminal justice system are clearly only a small part of all potential cases. Moreover, the impact of this screening has different impacts on different segments of a community. Most household burglaries and violent crimes unrecorded by the police victimize African American and low-income families and individuals; the victimization rates for those with high incomes or who are white are much lower.[17]

[16]Ibid., p. 31.   [17]Ibid., pp. 18–9.

ORGANIZING TO COMBAT CRIME

Either of the crime statistics justifies considerable efforts to combat crime. Whether these data show a marked or small increase, public concern about crime has steadily spotlighted the political stage since Richard Nixon was elected in 1972. By 1994, polls showed more of the public was concerned about crime than any other public problem.[18] Moreover, the vast majority of the nation perceived large cities such as New York, Miami, and Washington to be unsafe to visit or live in.[19] When asked about their own neighborhoods in 1992, 56 percent of respondents in a nationwide survey reported being afraid to walk alone at night.[20]

Although fear of crime is measured on a national scale and presidents and governors often talk about the crime problem, the police are very much a local institution. Unlike police in most countries, American police are not centralized under the aegis of the federal government. There are national police agencies, such as the FBI and the Immigration and Naturalization Service (INS), but they constitute only a tiny portion of all police in the United States. Nor are police functions concentrated at the state level, although states have small police forces to patrol rural highways and to perform other specialized duties. Instead, most police departments are responsible only to the most local units of government: cities and counties. Each city possesses its own police force, which has no organizational ties to police departments in neighboring communities and is not responsible to a higher police authority at the state or national level. Counties also have police forces organized in a sheriff's department; in urban areas, such county police play only a minor law enforcement role, but in rural areas they are the primary police force. This organizational structure produced 17,358 police and sheriff's departments in 1992.[21]

The autonomy of police departments means there is no national or state official responsible for planning police services or supervising law enforcement policy. No national or even statewide strategy exists for combatting crime. Likewise, no superior agency routinely supervises or even audits the work of local police departments. How well or poorly they perform is almost entirely the business of local officials.

The **local character of policing** in the United States is reflected in police expenditures and staffing. Of the almost $31.8 billion spent on police protection in 1990, 72.3 percent was consumed by local police agencies, and city police accounted for three-fourths of that amount.[22] The federal government spent only 12.5 percent and state governments only 16.3 percent of that $31.8 billion. The same story is told by the employment of police officers. In 1990, the United States employed 800,000 police officers, 58 percent of whom worked for city police agencies and another 19 percent for

[18]"Washington Wire" *Wall Street Journal*, 21 January 1994, p. A1; Richard L. Berke, "Crime is Becoming Nation's Top Fear," *New York Times*, 23 January 1994, p. A1.
[19]Maguire, Pastore, and Flanagan, supra, note 14, p. 184.
[20]Ibid., p. 189.
[21]Brian A. Reaves, "Census of State and Local Law Enforcement Agencies, 1992," *Bulletin* (Washington, D.C.: U.S. Department of Justice, Bureau of Justice Statistics, 1993), p. 4.
[22]Maguire, Pastore, and Flanagan, supra, note 14, p. 2.

counties, mostly policing sparsely inhabited rural areas. The remaining 23 percent wore the uniforms of the state police or worked under the aegis of the various federal agencies such as the FBI, INS, or the Drug Enforcement Agency (DEA).[23]

Budgetary and personnel statistics, however, do not tell the entire story of the decentralization of police power in the United States. The funds that pay city and county police come overwhelmingly from local taxes, such as property and sales taxes, for which local officials must take responsibility. Less than 2 percent of the more than $23 billion that cities and counties spent on policing in 1990 came from other sources.[24] Although grants from the federal government sometimes have helped fund innovative police programs or made possible the purchase of high-tech equipment, city police know their bread is buttered by the city council and that local taxpayers bear the burden. Moreover, police expenditures loom large in city budgets; in most cities, they are by far the largest single expenditure item, exceeding spending for streets, sanitation, and, in many cases, all other municipal services.

Consequently, what police do and how they do it is determined by city officials who have to answer to their local constituents in frequent city elections. It is no coincidence that police chiefs generally serve at the pleasure of the mayor and normally are replaced when a new mayor takes office.[25] It is also no coincidence that charges of inadequate policing play a substantial role in many municipal elections, as challengers assert the police should do more to combat crime and incumbents claim credit for improvements in police performance.[26] Locally elected officials have reason to be concerned when, as reported by a 1989 Gallup poll, 58 percent of large city dwellers indicated they had "not very much" or "no" confidence in the ability of the police to protect them from violent crime; 49 percent of the suburbanites responded in the same way.[27]

The role of the federal government and its police agencies is marginal. Each large city has an FBI office, a contingent of Drug Enforcement Agency (DEA) agents, and Immigration and Naturalization Service (INS) officers. However, these and other smaller federal agencies account for little of the policing that occurs, and they have no authority to order city police to alter their own priorities or to coordinate the activities of city police with their own. Since the race riots of the mid-1960s, it has been common for presidents to issue a national agenda for combatting crime. However, such presidential statements have little consequence for what happens on the street; federal agencies can do little to alter the local pressures that guide city policing.

THE STRUCTURE OF CITY POLICE DEPARTMENTS

Reflecting their roots in the police agencies of the early twentieth century, police departments in the 1990s are militaristically organized bureaucracies. All officers except detectives and undercover agents wear uniforms. Their ranks run from patrol officer to sergeant, through lieutenant and captain to commander. It is rare for a civilian to head a police department. Reflecting this military culture, police departments place much

---

[23]Ibid., p. 23.

[24]Ibid., p. 2.

[25]Jacob, supra, note 9, pp. 96–100.

[26]Jacob, supra, note 9, pp. 18–24.

[27]Maguire and Flanagan, supra, note 10, p. 266.

emphasis on the uniform; the failure to wear one's cap or unpressed trousers quickly earns a reprimand.

Policing is no longer exclusively a white man's occupation. By 1990, 7 percent of the officers in the largest cities were women, 17 percent were African American and 10 percent were Hispanic. In three cities—Detroit, Washington, D.C., and Atlanta—the majority of police officers were African American, and in El Paso, Texas, the majority were Hispanic.[28]

The appointment of police officers is also no longer based on patronage in most communities. Officers are hired after a competitive examination. However, the skill level of entering patrol officers remains low. Most police departments require no more than a high school diploma, although an increasing number of applicants also have some college education. The particular skills required for policing are taught during a probationary period of employment. That is when rookies learn how to handle firearms, manage threatening confrontations, complete the required paperwork, and deal with citizen requests and complaints. The amount of time police departments devote to such training programs varies greatly. Some run as short as six weeks; others provide more than six months. Almost all formal training programs, however, culminate in a period of apprenticeship, when rookies work with experienced patrol officers on the beat, learning the real life and work of being a police officer.[29] Because police departments in each city are independent of others, there is no career ladder by which officers may work their way from small towns to large cities because in moving, they lose their seniority and often forfeit their benefits. The pay of officers is solidly working-class. The average beginning salaries in 1992 ranged from $22,791 in the smallest cities to $29,411 in the largest; the maximum salary in the smallest cities was $30,366, while in the largest it was $38,405.[30]

Police departments in large cities have become massive operations. In 1992, New York had more than 27,000 police officers, while Chicago had over 12,000. Among the 25 largest cities, the ratio of officers to population ranged from 7.2:1000 in Washington, D.C., to 1.3:1000 in Indianapolis; only Indianapolis and El Paso had fewer than 1000 police officers.[31]

Organizing these large forces for effective intervention has been a continuing problem. The officers' distinctive clothing, their rotating work shifts, the dangers they face, and their frequent confrontations with civilians set them apart from their communities. These characteristics of police work create a distinctive culture among police officers.

In part, the culture is based on intense social relations with other police officers. Many tend to live in particular areas of the city in close proximity to each other. The rotating shifts they work make it difficult to maintain a normal social schedule. In addition, relationships with civilians are often strained by the peculiar combination of au-

---

[28]Maguire, Pastore, and Flanagan, supra, note 14, pp. 46–48.
[29]Michael J. Rich, Robert L. Lineberry, and Herbert Jacob, "Police Policies and Urban Crime," in Herbert Jacob and Robert L. Lineberry (eds.), *Governmental Responses to Crime* (Washington, D.C.: U.S. Department of Justice, National Institute of Justice, 1982), pp. 75–79.
[30]Maguire, Pastore, and Flanagan, supra, note 14, p. 62.
[31]Ibid., p. 48. The ratios are calculated on the basis of 1990 census data.

thority and disdain police encounter. One police officer interviewed by Jerome Skolnick described this situation with a personal anecdote:

> Several months after I joined the force, my wife and I used to be socially active with a crowd of young people, mostly married, who gave a lot of parties where there was drinking and dancing, and we enjoyed it. I've never forgotten, though, an incident that happened on one Fourth of July party. Everybody had been drinking, there was a lot of talking, people were feeling boisterous, and some kid there— he must have been twenty or twenty-two—threw a firecracker that hit my wife in the leg and burned her. I didn't know exactly what to do—punch the guy in the nose, bawl him out, just forget it. Anyway, I couldn't let it pass, so I walked over to him and told him he ought to be careful. He began to rise up at me, and when he did, somebody yelled, "Better watch out, he's a cop." I saw everybody standing there, and I could feel they were all against me and for the kid, even though he had thrown the firecracker at my wife. I went over to the host and said it was probably better if my wife and I left because a fight would put a damper on the party. Actually, I'd hoped he would ask the kid to leave, since the kid had thrown the firecracker. But he didn't, so we left. After that incident, my wife and I stopped going around with that crowd and decided that if we were going to go to parties where there was to be drinking and boisterousness, we weren't going to be the only police people there.[32]

Strained relations with civilians are also the result of the contacts police officers have with civilians during their shifts. Unlike other public officials, most contacts between the police and members of the public show civilians at their worst. Many civilians are belligerent when stopped by a police officer for a traffic offense. Others are openly disrespectful. Many are viewed by the police as "punks" who are trying to show off. It is not unusual for a drunk to vomit in the officer's patrol car. The accumulation of such contacts leads the police to develop an "us versus them" attitude toward civilians, where the police are "good" and the civilians they encounter during their work are "bad."[33]

Officers often work with a partner for a long period of time and get to know that other officer extremely well, since they may share eight hours a day in a car cruising through their patrol area. They become very protective of each other. They need to be able to depend on their partner and other officers in times of crisis; they need their complete confidence. One result is that officers tend to cover for each other's misdeeds. It is a way of showing solidarity and accumulating chits that can be called in during a time of need.[34]

The character of police work makes it difficult for supervisors to exercise close control over the ways in which officers perform their duties. Police work is extremely dispersed. Officers perform their duties alone or in pairs as they patrol. Unlike most other workers, they work out of sight of their immediate supervisor. When the police respond to a call for service or when they notice a suspicious event, they must make an immedi-

---

[32]Jerome H. Skolnick, *Justice Without Trial: Law Enforcement in Democratic Society*, 3d ed. (New York: Macmillan, 1994), pp. 49–50.
[33]Jonathan Rubenstein, *City Police* (New York: Ballantine, 1973).
[34]Ibid., particularly pp. 32–68.

ate assessment of the appropriate course of action. They cannot deliberate among themselves or check with their supervisor about what they should do; even hesitation may have disastrous consequences. When their supervisor arrives or when they report on their actions, their initial response has often already conclusively framed the event in an almost irreversible manner.[35]

However, since 1950, three major technological innovations have substantially affected the manner in which patrol officers perform their gatekeeping function; two of them increased their responsiveness to central control. These innovations placed officers in patrol cars, provided them with radio-telephones, and supplied them with portable computers.

Equipping police with patrol cars fundamentally altered police work. The mobility provided by police cruisers allowed officers to patrol much larger areas. The police, however, paid a heavy price for their mobility. The use of patrol cars removed most officers from walking street beats where they were highly visible and could become acquainted with neighborhood residents. They were much less visible in cars and got to know fewer residents or business people in their area. Because they were directed to trouble spots, their interactions predominantly involved interventions in threatening situations. Patrol cars effectively removed them from the normal routines of the communities in which they worked; an even larger proportion of the contact officers had with civilians was with the seamy side of life.

Radio communications were a necessary corollary to patrol cars since the greater mobility cars provided could be used to best advantage if officers could be quickly directed to citizens calling for help. The establishment of radio communication systems placed officers on a much shorter leash than they enjoyed on foot patrol. When they walked their beats, officers checked in through call boxes on a predetermined schedule. Between calls, they were entirely on their own. Radio communications, however, permitted supervisors to remain in constant touch with patrol officers, check on their whereabouts, and direct them to calls for assistance. In addition, radio communications could produce a record of officers' communications with headquarters and between themselves, for superiors and outsiders to use when investigations of alleged misconduct took place.

The most recent innovation has been equipping patrol cars with portable computers that provide instant access to information stored in computers at headquarters. Consequently, officers can rapidly check whether a car they have stopped has been reported as stolen or whether a person they are questioning is being sought by some other police agency. In some instances, it no longer is necessary to bring a suspect to headquarters because the computer check can provide information that allows the officer to release the person, such as the absence of outstanding warrants or that the car has not been stolen.

Radio communication and on-board computers have reduced officers' discretion in carrying out their tasks. On foot patrol, they alone decided when and how to intervene; they had a decisive role in choosing which portions of the criminal code to enforce at any particular time. Their sergeant could check on them intermittently by meeting

---

[35]Brown, supra, note 8, pp. 96–131.

them at an appointed place during their beat, but the sergeant usually was not present when they made an arrest. Consequently, training in standard operating procedures and the use of policy directives were the most important tools for controlling the use of police discretion. With patrol cars controlled by radio communications, superior officers can be in touch with their patrol officers at all times. They no longer need to rely entirely on training and policy directives; they choose where the patrol cars go. The communications room decides on the priority of calls and can decide to privilege certain areas and types of calls over others. A report of a drunk in a high-rent district is likely to receive quicker attention than such a call from a run-down area. In addition, supervisors can now require patrol officers to get in touch with superiors before taking extraordinary action; radio communications also allow supervisors to go to trouble spots to watch over the actions of their patrol officers. Computers increase the flow of information to the patrolling officers, although the information to be provided is determined by headquarters personnel. Thus, technology has moved at least some discretionary decisions from the street to headquarters.

Even with new technologies, however, much discretion remains with beat officers. This was well illustrated by the Rodney King incident in Los Angeles.[36] The beat officers made an independent decision to engage in a high-speed chase; they began beating King before their supervisors arrived. In that case, as their subsequent trial demonstrated, the supervisors shared the prejudices of their patrol officers and did not prevent King's beating. Thus, the criteria the police use to push offenders into the criminal justice process or to keep them out continues to reflect the personal preferences of police officers as well as policy decisions by police superiors.

Conclusion

Most scholars of crime conclude that crime is the product of forces over which the police have little control. Macrosocial forces that breed crime—poverty, poor housing, poor education, and unemployment—are far from the purview of the police. The areas in which those conditions are most concentrated are those with the highest crime rates. No matter how stringently police enforce the law, the pool of potential criminals appears bottomless in these areas. When one person is arrested, another takes his or her place, since the opportunities for crime are more abundant and attractive in those neighborhoods than are opportunities for legitimate employment. In addition, drug addiction generates a large amount of criminal activity, which simple suppression does not appear to halt. A stark example appeared in a newspaper story about Hempstead, New York, a suburb of New York City. The report noted that a six-month effort by the police had led to the arrest of 104 low-level drug dealers. It concluded: ". . . over the weekend, *for a few hours at least*, the street corners were 'virtually free of crime.'"[37] The police, in short, walk a treadmill; much activity often produces little forward motion.

[36]Jerome H. Skolnick and James J. Fyfe, *Above the Law: Police and the Excessive Use of Force* (New York: Free Press, 1993), pp. 1–22.
[37]John T. McQuiston, "For a Few Hours, a Village Sees Victory in War on Drugs," *New York Times*, 8 December 1992, p. B12, emphasis added.

The task of imposing social control is not simply a mission of the "good guys" keeping the "bad guys" in check. The definitions of "good" and "bad" are often controversial. The police represent dominant social mores of a community. The mayors, aldermen, and legislators decide what acts shall be declared criminal and which shall be enforced in each neighborhood. In many high-crime areas, there is a feeling among residents that police are merely occupying forces who have little understanding of life in those places and who are not very good at distinguishing between truly dangerous persons who ought to be apprehended and harmless yet quirky people who are quite visible but should be left alone. Thus, the gatekeeping activities of the police are often at the center of political controversy.

KEY WORDS

order maintenance
legalistic
service-oriented
offenses known to the police

Uniform Crime Reports
National Crime Survey
local character of policing

FOR FURTHER STUDY . . .

Many insights into policing are provided by Donald Black, *The Manners and Customs of the Police* (New York: Longman, 1980) and Michael K. Brown, *Working the Street: Police Discretion and the Dilemmas of Reform* (New York: Russell Sage Foundation, 1981). The conditions under which police abuse their discretion are examined by Jerome H. Skolnick and James J. Fyfe, *Above the Law: Police and the Excessive Use of Force* (New York: Free Press, 1993). To study the intertwining of policing and local politics, see Herbert Jacob, *The Frustration of Policy: Responses to Crime by American Cities* (Boston: Little, Brown, 1984) and Stuart A. Scheingold, *The Politics of Street Crime: Criminal Process and Cultural Obsession* (Philadelphia: Temple University Press, 1991).

For a glimpse of policing in the community in which you live ask your instructor if it is possible to ride in a police car for one evening. If you do that, keep notes on what kinds of activities the police officers observe, where they intervene, and how they use their discretion. A different kind of picture of policing may be obtained by charting the incidence of crime as reported in the Uniform Crime Report for one or two communities that you know well; then interview a police official and a city council member or mayor of each about the trends shown in those data. What kinds of explanations do they give for the changes you have detected?

6

LAWYERS

The law, as we have seen, is pervasive. It intrudes into almost every element of contemporary American life. One easily falls victim to it. Almost as easily, one may use it as a tool to advance a myriad of personal and public goals.

Although in theory the legal system is equally available to everyone, in practice access to the law is rationed. To use the law, one must understand its provisions, master its institutions, and pay the fees and costs that accompany its invocation. Those costs involve not only direct expenses, such as filing fees and attorneys' retainers, but also "opportunity" costs, that is, those missed opportunities that might have been pursued had one not been preoccupied with a legal action. For most people, lawyers hold the keys that open or close the gates of the legal system. Without using their special training, one cannot be sure the law will provide a remedy for one's problem. Even if laypersons can identify the remedy, most do not know how to manipulate the legal process to obtain it. Therefore, a person who has a problem that might be solved by the law must usually find a lawyer.

Attorneys consequently serve as buffers between ordinary citizens and legal institutions. They interpret the law for clients, explaining their opportunities and obligations under the law. In these circumstances, the lawyer simply tells the client what the law says. For example, this may involve discovering which expenses qualify as income tax deductions or which type of building the local zoning ordinance permits on a vacant lot the client wants to buy. Lawyers have the technical expertise to find such information and understand the legal jargon in which it is usually written.

In many situations, however, lawyers perform a service much more valuable than simply giving information. They often help clients manipulate their own situation so they qualify for whatever benefit the law provides. One example is the work of tax lawyers who help clients arrange their financial affairs to take maximum advantage of the tax code. They may, for instance, advise clients to employ their children rather than simply giving them an allowance while attending college. Or they may advise a client to incorporate, rather than establish a partnership, to avoid problems should one

118

of the business principals die. Many firms routinely consult attorneys for advice on drafting supply or sales contracts in a way that avoids disputes yet maximizes their chances of winning any disputes that might nevertheless arise.

Providing information and advice are the principal tasks of lawyers. They spend most of their time in their offices doing this kind of work. Many never work outside their offices except to go to the law library or meet with a client.

However, lawyers are most visible when they represent clients before one of the institutions of the legal system. Lawyers are the most prominent advocates in the United States. They play that role conspicuously in courtrooms, where they monopolize representation of clients. Although people may represent themselves in court, if they want another representative, it must be a lawyer. Attorneys bring powerful tools to this task. They have been trained in the intricacies of courtroom procedure. The courtroom, as we shall see, requires use of a special terminology; ordinary language will usually not suffice. To get into court, one must fill out special forms that also require mastery of the law's language. In addition, lawyers who are frequently in court know the informal practices that govern the pace of the court's work. Because most laypersons are lost in the world of the courtroom, they almost always hire an attorney to represent them.

Lawyers play almost as prominent a role in helping people navigate their way through the mazes of government agencies that often offer the remedies people are pursuing. Of course, many government agencies design their procedures so that no lawyer is required; one can certainly buy stamps or get a driver's license without a lawyer. On the other hand, if someone applies for a disability benefit from Social Security, it may be helpful to have a lawyer assist in completing the forms. If the Social Security Administration denies the benefit or later withdraws it, an attorney is almost always helpful. This is true for many of the same reasons that people find attorneys essential in the courtroom. Lawyers understand the technical language of administrative regulations better than most laypersons. They also know the informal practices of agencies. In some instances, lawyers are also acquainted with agency officials and may even have been formerly employed in the agency. Ideally, bureaucratic decisions are untainted by personal relationships, but in practice, personal acquaintances can often ease one's way through the bureaucratic maze.

Lawyers also play a prominent role in the administrative process and other lobbying. They are particularly useful to clients when policy is developed by a formal process where procedural correctness may be important. Lawyers, however, play a subsidiary role in informal policy development and in legislative lobbying, because the free-flowing political process attracts many other kinds of lobbyists (such as former legislators) who have at least as much expertise as do lawyers.[1]

The three tasks lawyers perform—**providing information, giving advice,** and **representing clients** in court, before administrative agencies, and occasionally before legislative bodies—constitute their gatekeeping functions. The manner in which attorneys perform those tasks and their actual availability to the general public depend on struc-

[1]Robert L. Nelson and John P. Heinz, "Lawyers and the Structure of Influence in Washington," *Law & Society Review 22* (1988) pp. 237–300; John P. Heinz, Edward O. Laumann, Robert L. Nelson, and Robert H. Salisbury, *The Hollow Core: Private Interests in National Policy Making* (Cambridge: Harvard University Press, 1993).

tural characteristics of the legal profession. It is, therefore, to these structural characteristics that we now turn.

The Structure of the Bar

The legal profession in the United States is enormous, having grown from 450,000 in 1978 to 750,000 in 1991.[2] In raw numbers, as well as on a per capita basis, the United States has more lawyers than any other nation.[3] These attorneys work in a variety of settings and bring to their tasks quite different resources. Some are socially prominent; many are obscure. Some have been educated at prestigious law schools; others are the product of many years of part-time enrollment at night schools. Some work in large firms; others work alone. Some consider themselves specialists in a narrow field of the law; others try to deal with whatever cases come to them. Some handle the affairs of a few large corporations over many years; others represent individuals on a one-time basis. All are regulated.

THE EDUCATION OF LAWYERS

Almost all lawyers in the United States are the product of formal training in law school,[4] a postgraduate institution that usually admits only those with a college degree. This fact itself restricts the profession of law to those who can afford seven years of education beyond high school. An undergraduate degree at a state university might cost $40,000: In addition, one must calculate the wages a student might have earned had he or she not gone to college. If one estimates those earnings modestly at $15,000 per year, the total "cost" of the college degree is $100,000. To this must be added at least another $75,000 of law school expenses and forgone earnings: Thus, a law degree from a state university will cost at least $175,000 (in 1993 dollars), and much more if the student attends a private university. For those who cannot afford such an expense, the only option is to obtain a less expensive college degree and then attend law school part-time. While costing less, such a program takes longer and provides fewer opportunities to embark on a successful legal career.

The curricula of all law schools are very similar.[5] Whether one goes to Harvard or to John Marshall, a first-year student is immersed in such subjects as contracts, torts, property, and civil procedure. Only in the second and third years do students enjoy some choice in course selection, with larger schools offering a broader range of courses in highly specialized areas of the law. Yet Abel writes, ". . . even at Yale, reputed for its

---

[2]Edward Frost and Margaret Cronin Fisk, "The Profession after 15 years," *National Law Journal*, 9 August 1993, p. 40.

[3]Marc Galanter, "Adjudication, Litigation, and Related Phenomena," in Leon Lipson and Stanton Wheeler (eds.), *Law and the Social Sciences* (New York: Russell Sage Foundation, 1986), pp. 151–256.

[4]In general see Robert B. Stevens, *Law School: Legal Education in America from the 1850s to the 1980s* (Chapel Hill: University of North Carolina Press, 1983); and Frances K. Zemans and Victor G. Rosenblum, *The Making of a Public Profession* (Chicago: American Bar Foundation, 1981), pp. 5–12.

[5]Richard L. Abel, *American Lawyers* (New York: Oxford University Press, 1989).

innovation, 75 to 90 percent of student time was devoted to traditional subjects."[6] The standardization of law curricula results from several factors. One is the limited variety of law texts; many differ only in subtle details rather than in basic approach. Thus, many students across the nation read similar materials in their quest for legal expertise. Another reason is that almost all law school graduates must pass a bar examination to qualify for practice. These examinations are largely standardized throughout the country. If a law school wants its graduates to pass those examinations, it must offer standard courses. In addition, most law graduates take a bar review course before attempting to take the bar examination; a handful of commercial firms offer these courses, and they also emphasize legal basics.

However, despite this uniform base, significant differences distinguish various law schools. Some are much more selective in their admission requirements and thus recruit a much more academically talented group of students. These selective schools also tend to teach more abstract legal principles rather than specific facts of local practice; they orient themselves more to national rather than local law. The faculty of such schools often serve as consultants to large corporations and are involved in cases of national significance. It is not unusual for them to represent clients before the Supreme Court. This is rarely the case with less prestigious law schools whose faculties have small private practices: They are more likely to be concerned with property tax abatements than with constitutional law principles. While many of the graduates of every law school eventually practice in a small office and serve individual clients, the prestigious law schools expect many of their graduates to work for large firms servicing the corporate sector. Students who desire a career in a large law firm are much more likely to find such a position if they graduate from Harvard, Stanford, or Michigan than if they graduate from John Marshall, Williamette, or Suffolk. In addition, prestigious law schools often are expensive and prefer academically distinguished graduates from well-known (and often equally expensive) undergraduate colleges. Consequently, a large proportion of their students come from well-to-do families that often have connections useful to a law career. Thus, although one can discern important similarities in the curricula of law schools, fundamental differences exist in the final product. The graduates of a few high-prestige schools tend to corner the market for high-paying jobs in large law firms. The graduates of the average law schools capture a few of those positions, but most work in regional or local law practices. Low-prestige law schools mostly graduate lawyers who serve individual clients and small neighborhood businesses.

THE SETTINGS OF LEGAL PRACTICE

The stereotype of a lawyer pictures a man working in a small office near the courthouse. This image is incorrect on several counts.

One error is thinking of the law as an exclusively male profession. While this was true for most of the twentieth century, it is no longer the case. In 1991, the *National Law Journal* reported that almost one-fourth of all lawyers were women; only 12 years earlier, the proportion was only 5–8 percent.[7] Women, however, have not yet pene-

---

[6]Ibid., p. 214.   [7]*National Law Journal*, supra, note 2, p. 40.

trated all segments of the legal profession to an equal degree. In 1991, only 11 percent of the partners in large law firms were women.[8] By 1991, the count of female judges had risen from a previously minuscule number, but the bench remains predominantly male.[9] Even with sex discrimination being clearly illegal, women who choose to have both a family and a career have had a difficult time reaching the upper echelons of the legal world. This is in part because law firms often expect workaholic behavior from their associates; evening and weekend work is the norm, not the exception. Moreover, most large firms employ attorneys as associates for only a limited number of years before either promoting them to partner status or letting them go. Consequently, the young lawyer has only a brief period in which to win promotion to partnership. Both these practices make it very difficult for a woman who attempts to combine family and professional obligations to rise to the top of such firms.

Another error in the stereotype of the lawyer is the image of an attorney working alone in a small office. Many lawyers now pursue their profession in large bureaucratic organizations. They operate in several different settings that have a very significant impact on the manner by which attorneys perform their gatekeeping role; those settings affect the services lawyers offer and the rewards they may receive.

The apex of the legal profession is the large **law firm.** They are a relatively recent phenomenon, originating in New York. In the 1960s, there were 38 large firms in the United States, 21 of which were in New York;[10] large law firms were at that time referred to as Wall Street firms, so named because they were located on Wall Street in New York City and served the financial and corporate world centered there. However, such firms are now found in most metropolitan areas, and many have become national and, in some cases, international. Their size mushroomed in the 1980s; before that a large law firm was one with more than 100 lawyers all working in one suite of offices. By 1988, Galanter and Palay report that 149 firms exceeded the size of the largest firm 20 years earlier.[11] While in the 1960s the largest firms were in New York, by 1993, some of the largest ones were also in Chicago and Los Angeles, and all of the largest firms had acquired branch offices in other cities. The nation's largest law firm in 1993 was Baker and McKenzie, with 1662 attorneys scattered over 50 offices in the United States and abroad.[12] Another typical case is the Chicago firm of Sidley & Austin, which in 1991 had 700 attorneys with offices in Washington, Los Angeles, New York, London, Singapore, and Tokyo; its Washington office alone had 119 lawyers.[13] In 1993, the size of the largest 250 law firms in the nation ranged from the 1662 attorneys of Baker and McKenzie to 131 at Kansas City's Morrison and Becker; the median firm had 218 lawyers.[14]

[8]*National Law Journal,* supra, note 2, p. 40.
[9]Sheldon Goldman," Bush's Judicial Legacy: The Final Imprint," *Judicature* 76 (April-May 1993), pp. 282–297.
[10]Marc Galanter and Thomas Palay, *Tournament of Lawyers: The Transformation of the Big Law Firm* (Chicago: University of Chicago Press, 1991), p. 22.
[11]Ibid., p. 46.
[12]"Annual Survey of the Nation's Largest Firms" *National Law Journal,* 27 September 1993, p. S5.
[13]Ibid.   [14]Ibid., pp. S5, S19, S26.

Work in a large firm is distinctive in several ways.[15] First, such firms operate with a clear hierarchy. Newly hired lawyers are called **associates.** They serve in that capacity for seven to ten years; they are then either promoted to junior partnership or told to find work elsewhere. In Baker & McKenzie in 1993, for instance, 626 of its attorneys were partners and 1009 were associates.[16] Associates earn a salary (which may be supplemented by a bonus), while equity partners generally share in the profits of the firm.[17] Associates' beginning salaries are quite substantial; many of the largest firms in 1993 offered salaries of more than $70,000 to starting associates.[18] Partners earned several times that amount. The high salaries of associates reflects their importance to the law firm; they do much of the detail work under the supervision of partners and put in incredibly long hours. As law firms grew between 1960 and 1990, they increasingly leveraged the work of their associates, with more and more associates working for each partner.

In large firms, clear differences also exist between various levels of partners. **Salaried partners** receive salaries substantially larger than associates but do not share in the firm's profits. Junior **equity partners** earn the smallest share of the profits, while senior equity partners earn a larger share. Senior partners also have more responsibility for running the firm; they decide whom the firm should hire and promote and which clients to accept. They also decide the schedule of fees. The more senior a lawyer, the greater the freedom he or she enjoys in practicing the law. Senior partners have close relationships with clients and choose their own work. Junior employees often perform whatever tasks a senior partner assigns.

The structure of large firms promotes specialization. Many have departments that concentrate on particular areas of the law. One department typically handles most of the litigation undertaken by the firm; whenever a matter requires a court appearance, a lawyer from that department will go to court (sometimes accompanied by some other specialist). Other departments may specialize in such fields as probate law, tax law, mergers, antitrust suits, or a particular field of government regulation. Some firms are like department stores, offering expertise in many fields of law; others are specialized boutiques, offering only one or two kinds of legal practice. In both situations, the clients obtain highly expert assistance. Their lawyers not only have developed a deep understanding of the law in their field, but also are likely to have made personal contacts with key government decision makers in their areas. The most prominent of such attorneys shuttle between high-level government positions and periods of work in their law firms.

Some large firms enjoy long-term relationships with their clients; corporate clients hire them on an annual fee called a retainer and rely on the law firm to handle numerous matters over many years. In this situation, law firms become intimate partners in the operations of many of their clients. However, during the 1980s business corpora-

[15]Galanter and Palay, supra, note 10; Robert L. Nelson, "Ideology, Scholarship, and Sociolegal Change: Lessons from Galanter and the 'Litigation Crisis,'" *Law & Society Review* 25 (1988), pp. 677–693; John A. Flood, "Anatomy of Lawyering: An Ethnography of a Corporate Law Firm," Unpublished Ph.D. Dissertation, Northwestern University, 1987; Erwin O. Smigel, *The Wall Street Lawyer: Professional Organization Man?* (New York: Free Press, 1964).
[16]*National Law Journal*, supra, note 12, p. S5.
[17]There are, however, some salaried partners in many firms.
[18]*National Law Journal*, supra, note 12, p. S5.

tions increasingly relied on **in-house legal departments** in order to control the cost of legal services.[19] In addition, corporations used the greater expertise of their law departments to obtain outside legal services in a more cost-conscious manner.

The cost of legal services provided by large firms dictates that their clients be wealthy. Most, in fact, are giant corporations rather than individuals. Consequently, the legal services available to corporate America are quite different than those offered to individuals. The lawyers working in large firms bring prestige and status to whatever task their corporate client assigns them. They often have social and business contacts with high-level government officials. They enjoy access to the latest information technology, which brings the most recent judicial decisions and administrative rulings to their computer consoles. Perhaps most important, they can harness large numbers of associates and experienced partners to assemble a merger bid or a bankruptcy petition over a weekend as well as to sustain behemoth litigation projects that may last several years.

At the opposite end of the continuum of legal practice is the **solo practitioner,** who provides a wide array of legal services to individuals and small businesses.[20] While they constitute a dwindling proportion of the legal profession in the 1990s, their absolute numbers had not declined much since the 1960s. These lawyers operate in small offices, where they often share a receptionist and secretary with other attorneys. Such lawyers rarely specialize; instead they take whatever cases come into their offices. They are the jacks-of-all-trades of the legal profession. The diversity of cases they handle makes it difficult for them to bring a high degree of expertise to their work. Moreover, they less frequently have close contacts with the officials who decide some of their cases. Such lawyers are as likely to go to court as they are to offer advice in their office. They typically have a large number of clients, each of whom pays a small fee. Clients come to solo practitioners with single problems, and such attorneys rarely develop enduring relationships with their clients. Most of their clients are neither wealthy nor prestigious. The income solo practitioners earn is often quite marginal.

Between the two extremes of the large law firm and the solo practitioner are many other kinds of legal practice. At the higher end of the status scale are the many lawyers who work in medium-sized firms that resemble departments of a large firm, concentrating on one area of the law and working for corporations. Another set of lawyers works in government offices[21] or in the legal departments of business enterprises. Such lawyers are more like bureaucrats than independent professionals. Their work environment is similar to that of the large firm lawyer, and they are likely to be highly specialized, but they serve only a single client. They do not command the income of large firm partners, and their prestige largely depends on the status of their employer.

---

[19]*National Law Journal,* supra, note 2, p. 41.
[20]Jerome E. Carlin, *Lawyers on Their Own: A Study of Individual Practitioners in Chicago* (New Brunswick, N.J.: Rutgers University Press, 1962).
[21]James Eisenstein, *Counsel for the United States: U.S. Attorneys in the Political and Legal Systems* (Baltimore: Johns Hopkins University Press, 1978); Suzanne Weaver, *Decision to Prosecute: Organization and Public Policy in the Antitrust Division* (Cambridge, Mass.: MIT Press, 1977); Victor S. Navasky, *Kennedy Justice* (New York: Atheneum, 1971).

The prestige ranking of lawyers puts partners in large law firms serving corporate clients at the top, and solo practitioners who serve individual clients at the bottom.[22] Lawyers handling divorces and criminal accusations stand near the bottom of the status ladder, for many lawyers find those kinds of cases and clientele distasteful. Sharing the bottom of the status scale are lawyers who collect debts for small businesses. Only slightly higher are attorneys who handle the grievances of individuals arising from automobile accidents and other mishaps.

Thus, lawyers serving individuals generally have low status within the legal profession and bring only modest resources to their work. That severely affects the quality of legal representation they can offer their clients. While there are some outstanding criminal and personal injury lawyers, clients with these kinds of problems typically receive much less expert representation than do corporations represented by large law firms.

THE SPECIALIZATION OF LAWYERS

As we have seen, lawyers have varying opportunities to specialize in different work settings. Attorneys in large firms are much more likely to specialize than those working alone in small offices. However, the term *specialization* carries an ambiguous meaning in the legal world. It is instructive to compare it to specialization in the medical profession. Medical specialists, such as pediatricians, psychiatrists, obstetricians, or surgeons, acquire their skills through additional training at the beginning of their careers and become "board-certified" after passing a rigorous examination. Thereafter, they restrict their practice to their specialty and advertise themselves accordingly. Thus, a pregnant woman looking in a telephone book for obstetricians will find a list of them, each of whom has completed the specialized training and passed the required examination. She will not unwittingly stumble into the waiting room of a psychiatrist.

Lawyers specialize in a different way than physicians. Almost all lawyers complete their formal legal training without acquiring any specialized knowledge or skills. In most areas of law, there are no opportunities for concentrated advanced training and certification. Attorneys drift into specializations as the result of particular clients who come to them or, if they are in law firms, the assignment of particular cases. As a result, some attorneys become highly skilled in certain tasks and limit their practice to such cases. In a few instances, they will indicate this in their telephone book listing. However, there is no parallel to board certification, and the potential client has no guarantee that even an attorney who advertises a specialty is a bona fide expert. Moreover, in most instances, lawyers do not indicate their specialty. Someone thinking about divorce can easily stumble into the office of a lawyer who in fact knows little about divorce but is quite skilled in bankruptcy petitions; a person in trouble with the police may unwittingly go to a lawyer much more skilled in personal injury cases. Unlike most physicians, who would refuse to treat a patient who has a problem with which they are not familiar, lawyers are much more likely to take any case that walks through their office door.

[22]John P. Heinz and Edward O. Laumann, *Chicago Lawyers: The Social Structure of the Bar* (New York: Russell Sage Foundation, 1982).

There is, however, a high degree of specialization by type of client. Attorneys in large cities seem to cluster into several sets that have very little overlap in clientele. Heinz and Laumann[23] characterize them in two hemispheres: one provides services to corporations (and government), while the other works with individual clients. In Chicago, for example, the corporate hemisphere includes the large corporate law practices that handle antitrust, patent, business tax, securities, general corporate, banking, and commercial cases. It also consists of general corporate practices that handle business litigation, business real estate, personal injury defense (representing insurance companies), regulatory practices that handle public utilities' regulation, patent law, and labor cases (for either management or the union). Government lawyers who concentrate on criminal prosecution and municipal cases also belong to the corporate hemisphere. In the personal service hemisphere are lawyers who mostly have individual clients and who handle a vast array of cases, including real estate transactions, personal taxes, general litigation, criminal defense, family law and divorce, personal injury (for plaintiffs), and probate of wills.[24] This kind of clustering means that corporate clients are very unlikely to seek services from attorneys serving individuals. And it is doubtful that individuals will stumble into corporate law offices; when they do, the law firm refers them to an individual practitioner. Thus, the advantages gained in large law firms by subject matter specialization and by their informational resources redound entirely to corporate clients rather than to individuals.

Opportunities for informal specialization in the corporate sector are much greater than this list of practices suggests. Large firms themselves develop a reputation for concentrating on particular problems. Thus, for many years Kirkland & Ellis, in Chicago, was known as a leading antitrust firm; it was unlikely that a corporation with international trade problems would go to that firm. Such a firm's lawyers not only became specialists in antitrust cases, they also often became experts in particular industries because of the continuing problems of those industries. For example, an attorney in the New York law firm of Cravath Swaine & Moore working on the government's antitrust suit against IBM might have spent a quarter of his or her career on that case before it was finally settled after more than 13 years of litigation; during that time he or she would inevitably have learned a great deal about the computer industry. Moreover, because quite different skills are required in negotiating a contract than in arguing a case before a court, such firms also channel lawyers into departments specializing in one or the other area.

In the personal service hemisphere of the legal profession, fewer opportunities for specialization exist. Some lawyers handle mostly one or another kind of case, such as divorce, personal injury, or criminal defense, but even these lawyers rarely handle such cases exclusively. For instance, in Chicago, almost two-thirds of a sample of lawyers who handled divorces in 1990 did so only occasionally or infrequently.[25] Unless they fortuitously develop a reputation for a particular kind of case and begin to attract only one kind of clientele, they cannot afford to specialize. Moreover, when such attorneys do specialize, they are usually self-taught, rather than learning by supervised apprentice-

[23]Ibid.   [24]Ibid., pp. 439–440.
[25]Herbert Jacob, "Legal Services for Personal Troubles," typescript, Northwestern University, 1992.

ship; the result is much more haphazard than in the large law firm. One exception is criminal defense lawyers who begin their private practice after having worked for the prosecutor's office or the public defender; they begin with a reputation for criminal work. With that exception, lawyers who serve individual clients usually do not offer them the fruits of specialization.

Rural areas constitute an important exception in the contrast between lawyers serving corporations and individual clients.[26] In rural areas the legal profession is much less stratified: Few large corporations exist there; country lawyers serve primarily small companies and individuals. Such businesses often do not generate enough legal business to sustain specialized practices. Consequently, lawyers in small towns often have a general practice that includes both businesses and individuals. Neither obtain the rarified legal services large law firms offer to national corporations. However, ordinary individuals in small towns stand a better chance of getting the best legal help available since reputations in such a context are much more widely disseminated and even the best lawyers take some individual clients.

THE REGULATION OF LAWYERS

All practicing attorneys are subject to regulation. In order to practice law, an attorney must obtain a license; in most states the state supreme court or some other arm of the judiciary serves as the licensing authority. Fledgling attorneys must overcome two hurdles to obtain their license. The first is demonstrating their knowledge of the law. In most states they do so by passing a written examination; in a few they automatically qualify for the license if they graduate from an approved law school in the state. The second hurdle is a character examination. The applicant must demonstrate good character, which in most cases simply means the absence of a criminal record. Applicants must provide information about their past and a list of references. The licensing authority then considers that evidence—commendatory or derogatory—and makes its decision. Because the licensing authority is often the state's highest court, the decision is, in practice, beyond appeal. When applicants pass both hurdles, they receive a license to practice law, but only in the state in which the examination was taken. When a lawyer wishes to practice somewhere else, he or she must apply anew. Lawyers in good standing and with several years of experience can usually obtain a license from additional states without further examination. However, some states use the examination to restrict competition and may require even experienced attorneys from another state to take the examination to receive a license.[27]

The initial licensing procedure for attorneys assures the general public that those who advertise their services as lawyers meet minimum standards. However, many states do not require substantial continuing education, nor do they certify specialties. The fact that a person has an attorney's license is not a strong guarantee of competence.

---

[26]Donald D. Landon, *Country Lawyers: The Impact of Context on Professional Practice* (New York: Praeger, 1990).
[27]Abel, supra, note 5, p. 124.

The licensing of lawyers also was intended to restrict entry into the legal profession to protect the lawyers' income limiting the supply of legal providers. Viewed from that perspective, the licensing process has been a failure. By the early 1990s, law schools were producing a substantial surplus of lawyers, so that two-thirds of the 1992 graduating class of lawyers had not secured full-time legal positions six months after graduation.[28]

Another failed effort by the legal profession to maintain their income was rules restricting legal advertising. These were declared unconstitutional violations of freedom of speech by the Supreme Court in 1977.[29] Advertising by attorneys now is common on television, in telephone directories, and on billboards. Television, however, is very expensive and reaches a large audience that has no interest in legal services; hence it tends to be limited to cable stations and late night broadcasts. Telephone directory ads are the most common. None of these efforts, however, have resulted in price competition for legal services. Attorneys negotiate fees with clients on an individual basis, and information about costs has remained private.

State licensing authorities also regulate the behavior of lawyers in a very loose manner.[30] Every state has a code of professional ethics to which attorneys are supposed to adhere. This code details the lawyers' obligations to clients and to the courts. In addition to mandating elementary honesty, the code establishes standards about fee sharing, confidentiality of information obtained from clients, and conflicts of interests. Attorneys may be reprimanded or even have their license revoked for a major breach of these regulations. Every state has special agencies for investigating alleged violations of the ethical code and recommending appropriate punishment to the state's highest court. In practice, very few lawyers are punished for anything except convictions for serious criminal offenses or tax evasion, either of which almost always results in revocation of the attorney's professional license. Complaints from former clients rarely lead to formal sanctions, except where the clients can demonstrate that their attorneys defrauded them of funds.[31] Until 1993, no state professional code prohibited sexual liaisons with particularly vulnerable clients whom the attorney was representing, such as in a divorce. New York was the first state to adopt such a standard, which was drafted by that state's first woman chief justice.[32]

Implications for Gatekeeping

The characteristics of the legal profession that we have described have important consequences for the way in which lawyers perform their gatekeeping function. They dictate that quite different types and levels of service are provided for different users of the law.

Corporations, we have seen, are repeat players, and generally receive the best legal service in the United States. Many have their own legal departments for routine work.

[28]*National Law Journal*, supra, note 2, p. 40.   [29]*Bates v. State Bar of Arizona*, (1977) 433 U.S. 350.
[30]Erick H. Steele and Raymond T. Nimmer, "Lawyer, Clients, and Professional Regulation," *American Bar Foundation Research Journal* (1976), pp. 917–1019.
[31]Abel, supra, note 5, pp. 143–157.   [32]*New York Times*, 5 September 1993, p. E5.

Lawyers in these departments develop a high level of expertise in the services their corporate employer regularly needs. For instance, they become intimately familiar with the intricacies of the supply and sales contracts for their corporation's products and the standard legal matters that arise in employee relations. Because they repeatedly perform the same legal tasks, such lawyers become specialists. The corporation's routine bureaucratic procedures help assure that each matter will find its way to an attorney capable of handling it.

Another advantage corporations enjoy comes from their relationships with the large, specialized law firms to which they turn when facing unusual legal problems. This is what Westinghouse did when confronted by the huge damage suit over its cancellation of the contracted delivery of nuclear fuel (see Chapter 3). Such law firms may spend millions of dollars in behalf of their client; they are likely to assign whole teams of lawyers to one case. Examine, for instance, the situation of the Manville Corporation when it was sued by those exposed to asbestos that it had manufactured for many years. The company faced more than 15,000 damage suits; in addition, 14,000 school districts sought $1.4 billion in a nationwide class action suit.[33] Dozens of lawyers were thrown into the fray. Some did nothing but take **depositions** from potential witnesses; depositions are question and answer periods during which witnesses testify outside the courtroom but under oath, in the presence of attorneys for both sides, and they take place weeks or months before a trial begins. They serve to provide as much information as can be gathered before the trial. Other attorneys searched for relevant documents and indexed them on a computer for easy retrieval. Those attorneys eventually decided that the firm should seek protection under the bankruptcy statute, and this led to lengthy negotiations with committees of lawyers representing plaintiffs in the damage suits. Many of the lawyers worked only on this case for years.

Such a concentration of effort by high-priced lawyers optimizes the lawyer's gatekeeping services for the clients. First, it provides clients with the best possible information about their legal remedies and liabilities. Attorneys in such cases have almost unlimited access to computerized information services and are able to search exhaustively for relevant statutes, regulations, and court decisions; their own expertise to tap large data bases also permits them to discover similar situations that might have arisen elsewhere and the manner in which those cases were disposed. Consequently, lawyers for large corporations in such cases are almost never surprised during negotiations by their opponent's legal assertions and almost always know the full range of legal possibilities.

Representation of corporate clients in court and before regulatory agencies also draws on the specialized talents of large law firms. These trials are conducted by lawyers who have experience in complicated proceedings. They will have personally interviewed almost all their witnesses and prepared them for their testimony; such rehearsals involve many hours of mock direct examination and cross-examination to enable the witnesses to withstand whatever questions the opposition might ask. They will also have at their disposal depositions taken from the opposition's witnesses so they can pounce on inconsistencies. When the matter involves a hearing before a regulatory agency, rather than a trial, similar preparations are made. The attorneys making the

---

[33]Tamar Lewin, "New Asbestos Property Suits," *New York Times*, 13 November 1984, p. D2.

presentation are likely to have had substantial prior experience with the agency, knowing the quirks of its personnel and the procedural requirements it imposes.

Finally, large law firms may provide creative and innovative solutions for their clients' problems.[34] Many corporations take a long view when they retain a large law firm. They are interested not only in immediate results, but also in the creation of a favorable overall legal climate for their endeavors. This often requires the development of novel legal doctrines or quite different applications of conventional remedies. The extension of the copyright law to computer programs encoded in microchips by Apple Computer Corporation described in Chapter 3 is an example of a legal innovation a large law firm helped to provide. Another example is the Manville bankruptcy petition, which was startling because the corporation was highly profitable at the time it sought the protection of the bankruptcy court. No similar action had ever been taken by a large business, because the stigma of bankruptcy was believed to be so damaging. But the Manville attorneys believed bankruptcy was the only way the company could protect itself against unlimited claims. Of course, other creditors, such as suppliers, were also affected by the bankruptcy petition. Nevertheless, the company's lawyers were correct in believing that freezing the business debts under bankruptcy laws would permit the company to continue to operate. Similarly, large law firms often develop new ways of helping corporations obtain financing or reduce their tax exposure. The large firm may also assist its client in structuring operations to take advantage of existing law. For instance, it may advise a corporate client to shift its headquarters to a state with more accommodating security or banking laws or to change its bylaws to reduce the company's vulnerability to an unfriendly takeover.

In all these functions, large law firms try to act as friendly gatekeepers to the legal system. They do as much as they can to open the gates and assure their clients' advantageous use of the legal arena. When it seems that the gates might be closed by an overburdened agency or by the lack of an appropriate legal remedy, these firms often have the creative talent and sufficient resources to invent an alternative. For all these reasons, corporations receive excellent legal services from their attorneys.

The situation is different for individuals who are one-shotters and who are served by solo practitioners. Unless they are wealthy, individual clients ordinarily do not have a longstanding relationship with a lawyer. They go to a lawyer only occasionally: when they buy a house, want a divorce, or need a will. They may also require legal services if they are involved in an accident, a dispute over a debt, or a tax problem. Such individuals may consult different attorneys each time they have one of these problems, and each lawyer is likely to have little or no special expertise in the matter at hand. Individuals choose attorneys on the basis of social acquaintance, geographic accessibility, and the experience of friends and neighbors; they may know little about the attorney's professional reputation or areas of competence. The attorney they choose may know little about their lives except for the details of the current problem.

Perhaps the biggest contrast to the position of the large corporation is in the resources solo practitioners can commit to an individual's case. In most instances, rela-

---

[34]Michael J. Powell, "Professional Innovation: Corporate Lawyers and Private Law Making," *Law & Social Inquiry*, 18 (1993) pp. 423–452.

tively small amounts of money are at stake—usually less than $5000. Because it would be wasteful to invest large sums in such cases, attorneys for individual clients rarely have access to computerized information bases search for legal precedents. They likewise cannot spend endless hours taking depositions and accumulating thousands of documents.

The same attorney who interviews the client and manages the office will appear in court, negotiate with the opposing attorney, or go to the government agency controlling the matter. The lawyer may have considerable experience in some of these arenas but less in others. Moreover, such attorneys go into legal confrontations with relatively little preparation. They are likely to have scant information about the decision makers. Their witnesses often are examined and cross-examined without preparation. No records of prior depositions are available because none were taken. Consequently, much more is left to chance and luck. Lawyers for individuals rarely know how well their witnesses will perform; they are much more frequently surprised by testimony from the opposition, with little time to counterattack.

Finally, lawyers for individuals have few resources to develop novel remedies or steer their clients' affairs in directions that will optimize their use of existing law. There simply is not enough money in the cases of most individual clients for such work. Of course many routine cases do not need such services, but they are not available even when they would help.

Consequently, attorneys for ordinary individuals perform the gatekeeping function differently than do large law firms with corporate clients. Attorneys for individuals are much less facilitative about their clients' use of the law. Although they normally hold the gates open, they occasionally slam them shut.

Special arrangements sometimes cushion these effects. One such arrangement is the **contingent fee,** an arrangement whereby an attorney is paid a percentage of any damages that are collected. Lawyers typically charge contingent fees in tort cases, such as personal injury cases arising from automobile accidents, defective products, and medical malpractice. For example, when a plaintiff is awarded $10,000 in damages, the attorney receives between one-fourth and one-third of the amount, in this example between $2500 and $3333. Lawyers justify contingent fees by pointing to the risk lawyers assume: if the case is lost, the lawyer receives nothing. An important side effect is that this arrangement results in very large fees when attorneys win substantial damage awards for their clients. When there is the potential for a large damage award and large fees as, for instance, in medical malpractice cases, attorneys are sometimes willing to invest considerable sums of money to hire investigators, medical specialists, and social workers to buttress their client's case. In these situations individual clients may sometimes receive legal services that are comparable to those provided corporations. However, the risk lies entirely with the attorney, and the lawyer's financial success depends on guessing correctly which cases are winners and which are losers. To make a living, attorneys must be cautious about which cases they take avoiding those in which the probability of victory is questionable. Otherwise, they will lose much time and money in fruitless causes. Consequently, clients with risky cases have difficulty obtaining a lawyer. Only those who are able to pay a regular retainer are not shut out of the legal system.

This kind of gatekeeping may be interpreted in two quite different ways. One view is that attorneys help both clients and the courts by rejecting cases with a low probability of success. They help clients because they provide realistic assessments of success and persuade clients to give up hopeless causes; they help courts by keeping such cases from wasting the courts' time. Another view, however, is less charitable. Note that the attorneys who make assessments are sometimes not particularly expert in such cases. They may be wrong in their assessment; or they may be reflecting their own lack of skill; another attorney might be successful with the case. Many individual clients do not have enough information to shop for the most skillful attorney. Thus, this second view points to a bias that may make the legal process less responsive to individual needs than to corporate demands in the United States.

Another means of providing access to the legal system is via institutionalized legal assistance from public or private agencies.[35] One set of such agencies provides legal help to the poor. In most instances, the services involve only routine matters, and many shun appearances in court because of the cost involved. However, even when they provide only limited services, such agencies usually have much experience in handling their cases. In a few instances, the services extend much further. Sometimes **legal aid offices** are willing and able to pursue a change in the law that helps not only their current client but also an entire class of clients whom they ordinarily serve. Before the Reagan administration cut the budget of legal assistance programs in 1981, such programs financed by federal grants were sometimes able to provide services comparable to those that corporate clients received from large law firms. Since the budget cuts, however, services of this sort have become a rare exception in the provision of legal assistance to the poor.

Lawyers sometimes provide legal services pro bono publico (for the public good) to persons who cannot afford to pay. Some bar associations have suggested that all lawyers should take such no-fee or low-fee cases, but many cannot afford to do so or work in situations where it is impractical. No accurate count of **pro bono** services exists, but they are often important in providing access to the legal system for those who otherwise would be excluded.

The gatekeeping roles of lawyers working between the two extremes of the legal world—the large law firm and the solo practitioner—have some qualities of both settings. At one end of the scale, attorneys working in middle-sized firms and serving middle-sized businesses provide some of the same services as do large law firms working for giant corporations. They are likely to have the same relationships with their clients and provide similar information about legal services. They often offer a level of expertise comparable to that delivered by large law firms. On the other hand, they do not enjoy the same level of resources as do attorneys working in large firms, for their clients usually allow them fewer expenses. The stakes are often so much smaller that only limited expenditures are practical.

Attorneys working in the legal department of a corporation or government agency are more like those in legal aid offices. They provide routine services in routine matters.

[35]Robert G. Meadow and Carrie Menkel-Meadow "Personalized or Bureaucratized Justice in Legal Services: Resolving Sociological Ambivalence in the Delivery of Legal Aid for the Poor" *Law and Human Behavior,* 9 (1985) pp. 397–414.

They are likely to be restricted by bureaucratic rules that limit informational searches, travel, and unusual efforts on behalf of their employer. They bring much expertise to their routine operations but may enjoy few opportunities for creative legal thinking. Consequently, their clients may not benefit from innovative applications of existing law or the invention of new legal remedies.

Finally, lawyers who work for individuals but who limit their practice to one type of case provide some of the services offered by the large law firm to their clients. A handful of such attorneys have national or regional reputations for handling criminal matters, matrimonial cases, or personal injury claims. Such attorneys command very large fees, deliver a high level of effort, and provide great skill in pursuit of their cases. Those attorneys do not, however, typify the legal services available to most individual clients in the United States. Only the fortunate few benefit from their performance.

SUMMARY

When we presented the paradigm of the legal arena in Chapter 1, we asserted that social, economic, and political factors may affect the work of gatekeepers. The significance of social and economic factors is apparent from our description of the work of the legal profession.

As we have seen, the services lawyers provide are relative to the wealth of clients and their organizational status. Corporations receive more extensive services than most individuals for several reasons. Most important, they can afford to hire expensive attorneys and have them spend large amounts of money preparing their case; in response to these needs, some lawyers have organized themselves into large law firms in order to meet the complex needs of corporate clients. In addition, large corporations almost always have in-house attorneys who handle routine legal tasks on a continuing basis and who can identify appropriate outside counsel when needed. The in-house counsel know the reputations of the available law firms and can evaluate their personnel and their past performance. Thus, corporations have reliable information to assist them in choosing outside counsel.

Both in-house and outside counsel work hard to open the gates of the legal system to their corporate clients. These attorneys have corralled sufficient money, staff, information, and specialized skills to exploit all possibilities the legal system might offer their clients. They can choose the timing of potential lawsuits and select the most advantageous jurisdiction. Even more important is their skill in drafting contracts in the most advantageous manner and their ability to avoid litigation by skilled negotiation of disputes.

The situation of individuals who seek legal services is different. Even wealthy individuals may not be as well served as corporations, because the legal profession has not organized itself in a special way to serve that clientele, as they have for corporate clients. The wealthy do, of course, obtain more expensive lawyers, who sometimes are more skilled than those serving middle- or low-income clients. However, nothing like the large law firm exists to meet the needs of any but the wealthiest clients. Middle- and low-income clients are least well served. They do not have sufficient information to find attorneys most suited to their needs. The result is that individual clients rarely obtain inventive solutions to their legal problems. Their attorneys are much more likely to close the gates of the legal system because there is too little profit in a case and because they may not know other ways to obtain a remedy for their clients' grievances.

There are important exceptions to these conclusions. One exception is that differences in legal services are, as we have noted, somewhat smaller in small towns than in large cities. Small towns have no large law firms. Their businesses, often also relatively small, are served by some of the same lawyers who represent individual clients. Another exception is a public agency or pro bono attorney that takes up the cause of low-income clients. Such occasions open the legal system to clients who would otherwise remain excluded and provides them remedies instead of turning them away empty-handed.

Politics, on the other hand, plays a minor role in the gatekeeping services of attorneys. It has virtually no effect on the work of private attorneys. The situation is somewhat different for those attorneys who work for public agencies that must be responsive to policies developed by the legislatures that fund them and the elected officials who appoint them. The impact of political forces on the agencies was forcefully demonstrated during the Reagan and Bush administrations when the federal program for providing legal services for the poor was consistently battered by draconian budget cuts and hostile administrative appointments. They were spared only by the equally partisan actions of Congress, which appropriated larger sums than had been requested and which mandated their continued existence. The hostility of the Reagan and Bush administrations to these legal services stemmed from their perception that these offices had been used by political liberals to force government agencies to provide better services to the poor.

Public attorneys constitute only a tiny proportion of all lawyers working in the United States. In addition, some attorneys are motivated to work for public causes to promote careers in politics or win judgeships that require approval from politicians. For the most part, however, the gatekeeping functions lawyers provide are predominantly affected by private sector forces—the wealth and organizational structure of their clients and the complexity of their problems.

Three Examples of Gatekeeping

The varying ways in which attorneys perform gatekeeping roles will become more evident as we examine three quite different examples of actual cases. The first involved what was at the time one of the largest and most successful corporations in the United States; it paid top-level attorneys' fee and received top-level services. By contrast, in the second example, individual plaintiffs who sought damages for injuries suffered in automobile accidents received legal services ranging from the superb to the indifferent and, in many instances, were effectively closed out of the legal system. Finally, we consider a group of poor coal miners who also received top-level service thanks to the pro bono efforts of a very large Washington, D.C., law firm and the incentives of a contingency fee.

IBM AND ANTITRUST LITIGATION

International Business Machines (IBM) was, until the mid-1980s, the dominant firm in the computer field.[36] It built its position through the development of mainframe computers used by governments and large corporations for data processing and number crunching of all sorts. However, it was not without competitors. Some developed larger and faster computers; other companies sought to capture some of the market for peripheral equipment, such as high-speed printers and tape and disk drives for information storage. To compete successfully, however, these firms had to design their equipment so it could be connected to IBM machines. Some competitors complained that IBM was stifling competition.

The federal government began investigating alleged violations of the antitrust laws by IBM in the mid-1960s. It examined charges that IBM was monopolizing the computer market by frequently changing its technical specifications so that independent companies could not keep their products compatible with IBM equipment, and by leasing and pricing practices that drove competitors out of the market. The results of the investigation were revealed on the last business day of the Johnson administration, January 17, 1969, when Attorney General Ramsey Clark signed a complaint alleging that IBM practices constituted a monopoly and seeking a breakup of the corporation. This was not the only legal problem IBM faced, for competing firms such as Control Data Corporation (CDC), Greyhound Computer Leasing Corporation, Memorex Corporation, California Computer Products Inc. (Calcomp), and Telex Corporation had filed their own private antitrust suits.

IBM's outside law firm was one of the nation's most prestigious, Cravath Swaine & Moore, located in New York City. Among its partners was Roswell Gilpatric, deputy secretary of defense in the Kennedy administration. IBM's own general counsel, Nicholas Katzenbach, had been attorney general of the United States in the early years of the Johnson administration.

The value of employing a first-rate law firm and providing it with almost unlimited resources quickly became evident. As with all large and complex suits, each party sought to examine numerous documents from the other side to find evidence to buttress its case. CDC, being one of the first to file an antitrust suit against IBM, was also among the first to engage in this **discovery** procedure. It sought truckloads of data from IBM, and IBM in turn asked for documents from CDC. But there was a big difference in the way each side handled their requests. Cravath Swaine's lawyers read every file they gave CDC to make sure it was not privileged (i.e., not subject to the discovery proceeding) and so they would know about any potentially damaging information in the document. CDC apparently did not take the same precaution. Consequently, when the IBM lawyers began reading CDC's documents, they discovered CDC was trying to join a multinational group of firms to fix prices, divide markets, and drive IBM out of the computer business. This discovery led IBM to file a countersuit against CDC, which forced CDC to settle its case against IBM.

---

[36]This narrative is based largely on James B. Stewart, *The Partners: Inside America's Most Powerful Law Firms* (New York: Simon & Schuster, 1983).

Cravath Swaine was not equally successful in all its efforts. It lost the trial in the Telex case. Yet that loss (subsequently overturned on appeal) simply led the firm to exert greater efforts. It established a field office with several dozen lawyers in White Plains, New York, where IBM had its headquarters. In the course of defending the corporation against the federal government's antitrust charges, Cravath Swaine lawyers took more than a thousand depositions from witnesses. It not only defended the corporation against the government suit in New York federal district court but also handled the Telex case in Oklahoma; the trials of other cases, such as those instituted by Memorex and Calcomp in Los Angeles and by Transamerica in San Francisco, were supervised by the White Plains team of Cravath Swaine but were actually handled by large firms in those cities who worked in tandem with Cravath Swaine.

The government case against IBM began to be heard in New York in November 1976, almost seven years after it had been filed. It dragged on for six more years. The discovery of documents by the government from IBM encompassed more than 700 million files. IBM's legal fees may have exceeded $150 million during the entire period; it was reported to have paid Cravath Swaine alone more than $15 million a year for legal fees. To what result? IBM and Cravath Swaine won or favorably settled all the cases filed by competitors. The government case dragged on through the Nixon, Ford, and Carter administrations. Finally, the Reagan administration, with its much friendlier stance toward big business, dismissed the case in December 1982. After paying for thousands of hours of legal work, IBM found itself free to pursue its business without fear of immediate legal problems.

There is, however, an ironic ending to this story. The computer market changed abruptly in the 1980s, with the emergence of small but increasingly powerful personal computers. Through a series of business mistakes, IBM lost its dominant position in the computer market and by the 1990s was only one of many players manufacturing computers.

PERSONAL INJURY PLAINTIFFS

Few litigants can afford to spend $150 million to pursue a case, and few cases are worth that sum. Ordinary individual clients do not go to Cravath Swaine & Moore. The resulting differences will become quite apparent as we examine the travails of some clients who seek compensation in personal injury suits arising from automobile accidents.[37]

The plaintiffs in such cases are usually individuals whose cars are hit or who are injured. The other drivers are technically the defendants, but in fact their insurance companies have to pay the judgment and, therefore, often handle the defense of their cases. Insurance companies normally want to settle quickly and for as little as possible. They may seek out the injured parties, sometimes when they are still in the hospital, and try to persuade them to sign a release from all further claims in return for a modest amount,

[37]H. Laurence Ross, *Settled Out of Court: The Social Process of Insurance Claims Adjustment* (Chicago: Aldine, 1970); Douglas E. Rosenthal, *Lawyer and Client: Who's in Charge?* (New York: Russell Sage Foundation, 1974).

such as payment of the hospital charges. Such an agreement, however, will preclude later claims should future treatment be needed. In almost all cases, those injured in automobile accidents will do better if they wait and hire an attorney. In the most comprehensive study of such suits, Ross found that claimants with attorneys obtained 1.5 times more from insurance companies than unrepresented claimants.[38] In addition, the compensation increased with each level of representation by attorneys: claimants received more when they went to a small law firm, even if it did not specialize in such suits, than if they went to a solo practitioner; they received still more if they went to a specialist. Such claimants received almost 12 times more than those who settled without an attorney. Of course, part of the difference is explained by the degree of injury of each claimant. Those with trivial injuries or damages were much more likely to settle without an attorney than those with extremely serious problems. The larger the potential claim, the more likely it was that the injured person found a relatively specialized attorney.

Relationships between clients and attorneys in such cases are often less than amicable. Clients are under enormous pressure to pay their bills, but they also want to maximize any judgment they might win. Their lawyers, on the other hand, know that the insurance company's offer may be improved by delay or by going to trial, but a trial requires much more preparation and considerable cost. If the attorney recommends acceptance of an early offer, the client may be disappointed by the size of the settlement. If their attorneys wait for a larger offer, clients often feel neglected. As Rosenthal explained in his study of attorney-client relationship:

> The single source of pressure upon the lawyer most likely to affect adversely the client's interest . . . is the strain of prolonged litigation and the economics of case preparation. Simply put, a quick settlement is often in the lawyer's financial interest, while waiting the insurer out is often in the client's financial interest. . . . Two competing pressures affect the lawyer's motivation to terminate the case: on the one hand, the sooner he settles, the less effort expended pursuing the claim; on the other hand, given the reluctance of most insurers to make generous early settlements the longer he holds out the greater the recovery he can anticipate.[39]

In addition, communication between clients and their attorneys may be poor because the lawyers are reluctant to discuss all possible options with their clients. Attorneys sometimes keep information to themselves because they presume clients know little about the law; attorneys also believe that possessing information allows them to retain control over the case. Thus, as Rosenthal describes such cases, lawyers handling personal injury claims often are less than candid about what is happening. Understandably, they may be reluctant to admit they might have more cases than they can handle quickly. They may be uncomfortable telling their clients that waiting could yield a greater profit (sometimes at the client's expense). They may also resent being badgered by their clients because the clients are laypeople. Rosenthal found that on the average, clients who actively pushed their cases both were more satisfied and obtained better

---

[38]Ross, supra, note 37, p. 193.   [39]Rosenthal, supra, note 37, p. 96.

judgments than those who passively accepted their attorneys' actions.[40] However, active participation in litigation and negotiation is not the norm for individual clients.

Thus, personal injury victims may find the legal system inhospitable to their claims. They may have difficulty finding the right attorney even though the choice of attorney will have a substantial impact on the handling of their claim. They may engage lawyers whose interests do not entirely coincide with their own. They may encounter attorneys who are eager to maintain control over their cases and to defend their professional turf. Most personal injury victims do receive compensation, but not without paying a large portion of it to their attorney and not without waiting much longer than they originally anticipated.

THE BUFFALO CREEK DISASTER

Some individual clients fare better in legal proceedings than do ordinary personal injury plaintiffs. This was true of the survivors of the Buffalo Creek flood.[41] In February 1972, a terrible flood swept through a little hollow in West Virginia in which 16 communities were located. A dam built by the Buffalo Creek Mining Company to hold water used to wash coal burst after severe winter rains. A wave of water 20 to 30 feet high swept through the valley early one Saturday morning. More than 125 residents were killed, and the communities were almost entirely destroyed.

Although the mining company and its corporate parent, the Pittston Company of New York, did not accept responsibility, they quickly established a claims office. The company tried to discourage survivors from using the legal system by telling them that all claims would be treated equally; Pittston would not pay more to those who retained an attorney.

The survivors, however, had heard of a Washington, D.C., law firm, Arnold & Porter, which had won a multimillion dollar suit for disabled miners. They asked the firm to represent them even though they could not afford the costs of the suit. The law firm agreed to do so partly on a pro bono and partly on a contingent fee basis. Before a settlement was reached, the law firm had risked more than $500,000 in expenses in the hope of winning a large claim.

Gerald Stern, the lead attorney for Arnold & Porter in the Buffalo Creek case, used many of the resources ordinarily enjoyed by only large corporate clients. He and his staff thoroughly researched West Virginia and federal law to establish a basis for bringing suit against Pittston in the federal courts. They believed the federal courts would probably be more sympathetic to the miners than West Virginia courts and that Pittston could pay greater damages than Buffalo Creek Mining. To file in federal court against Pittston, however, required proof that the Buffalo Creek Mining Company was only a division of Pittston, rather than an autonomous subsidiary. Stern's legal research and examination of company records established Pittston's tight control over Buffalo Creek

---

[40]Ibid., p. 57.
[41]This account is based largely on Gerald M. Stern, *The Buffalo Creek Disaster* (New York: Vintage, 1976). See also Kai T. Erickson, *Everything in Its Path* (New York: Simon & Schuster, 1976); and Goldine C. Gleser, Bonnie L. Gren, and Carolyn Winget, *Prolonged Psychological Effects of Disaster: A Study of Buffalo Creek* (New York: Academic, 1981).

Mining and provided the basis for suing Pittston directly. Next, Stern and his associates researched the records of the federal judges to determine the arguments to which the judges might be most responsive. This research was not fruitful because the case was eventually assigned to a recently appointed judge who had decided too few cases to be accurately analyzed. Ultimately, however, this judge made key rulings in favor of the survivors.

Perhaps the most important contribution of Stern and his associates was their decision to seek damages for psychic impairment. Arnold & Porter retained the renowned psychiatrist Jay Lifton, who identified the symptoms displayed by Buffalo Creek survivors as similar to the syndrome found among the survivors of the atomic bombings of Hiroshima and Nagasaki and the Nazi death camps. The Buffalo Creek survivors, having witnessed at close hand the death of many relatives and friends, felt guilty that they too had not perished; they were nervous, suffered sleepless nights, and could not remain indoors when they heard rain pounding on the tin roofs of their dwellings. By identifying and documenting the mental suffering of its clients in this way, Arnold & Porter was able to establish a much larger damage claim than would otherwise have been possible. Without such a claim, the law would have permitted the survivors to sue only for the humble homes and furnishings they lost, for $100,000 for each wage earner, and for $10,000 for any other person who had perished.

Finally, Stern was able to collect sufficient information, from the documents obtained through discovery motions and from depositions, to show that Pittston had probably acted in reckless disregard of established rules of safety by constructing the dam that broke and two others downstream that had also ruptured. He found company documents indicating that company officials had been aware of problems with the dam. Pittston files established that the officials had corresponded about these problems, and depositions demonstrated that they had talked about them.

More than three years after the disaster, Stern was able to negotiate a settlement with Pittston on behalf of the survivors. They agreed to a payment of $13.5 million, providing a much larger payment to most of the plaintiffs than was available before Arnold & Porter entered the case. This recovery was obtained, however, only after Porter & Arnold invested 40,000 staff-hours. In return for their effort and their gamble, Arnold & Porter earned a contingent fee of nearly $3 million.

Conclusion

The Buffalo Creek survivors were lucky. They stumbled onto a very large, wealthy, and experienced law firm that was willing to risk a huge sum of money. Without Arnold & Porter's services, many of the survivors would have been closed out of the legal system. Others would have been confined to suing in state courts for property damages alone. It is unlikely a local attorney would have brought claims for psychic impairment to the West Virginia courts, nor could large claims have been paid by the Buffalo Mining Company.

In ordinary circumstances, there can be little doubt that clients like IBM receive much better legal services than personal injury clients. This is true for many reasons.

IBM possessed the resources to invest huge sums in legal assistance and they had a large enough stake in the outcome to justify the expenditure. It received the best that money could buy. In its cases, attorneys were extremely helpful gatekeepers to the legal system. They consistently helped their client get the most from the system, opening the gates wide and directing their client to the right portion of the system. Nor did IBM's lawyers hold their client at arm's length. They collaborated closely with the corporation in planning its defense against the several antitrust charges the company faced. One difference between IBM and individual clients is that IBM had its own excellent attorneys to monitor the work of those from Cravath Swaine & Moore. By contrast, individual clients must deal with their attorneys as laypeople. The individual attorneys handling personal injury claims often close the gates of the legal system to their clients, or keep them in the dark and make settlements that are more in the interest of the attorney than the client.

Individuals with potential legal problems who do not employ lawyers have an even greater disadvantage. They have no one who will open the gates of the legal system for them. They often forgo legal claims because they do not know how to pursue them, or they pursue their claims through informal negotiations without the help of an attorney and without the information about their legal rights that might help them obtain a better settlement even without formal litigation.

As we have seen, these disparities in the provision of services are not the result of political factors to any considerable degree. Politics plays only a subordinate role in the provision of legal services and the conditions under which they are provided. These disparities derive instead from inequalities in the social and economic arenas which provide unequal resources to different elements of the population that may be involved in legal proceedings. Although most litigation in the United States (in terms of absolute numbers) involves individuals with little money to invest in legal assistance, some of the most important policy-making cases involve wealthy clients who know how to use the legal system to their advantage. These clients have not only forged the legal profession in their own interest but also use it to their own advantage.

KEY WORDS

providing information	in-house legal department
giving advice	solo practitioner
representing clients	deposition
law firm	contingent fee
associate	legal aid office
salaried partner	pro bono publico
equity partner	discovery

FOR FURTHER STUDY . . .

Robert L. Nelson's Partners with *Power: Social Transformation of the Large Law Firm* (Berkeley: University of California Press, 1988) provides an excellent description of the ways in which large law firms operate. The best description of the legal profession as a whole remains John P. Heinz and Edward O. Laumann, *Chicago Lawyers: The Social Structure of the Bar* (New York: Russell Sage Foundation, 1982).

Donald Landon's, *Country Lawyers* (New York: Praeger, 1990) provides a parallel analysis of small town law practice. The best coverage of developments in the legal profession may be found in the *National Law Journal,* a weekly newspaper that devotes itself exclusively to news about lawyers and legal affairs.

One of the ways in which you can explore the ways in which lawyers work is to speak to relatives and friends who have recently used an attorney. Ask your informants how they chose their lawyer, what services their lawyer performed for them, what the attorney's fee was, and how satisfied they were at the end of the case. You might then also try to interview their lawyers to learn how they view cases like your informant's and the kinds of problems they perceived in their handling of such cases and clients.

7

INTEREST GROUPS

Like the other gatekeepers of the legal system, interest groups do not have an unsullied reputation. They are derisively known as "pressure" groups, "special" interest groups, and lobbies; each of those names suggests an element of illegitimacy, as if interest groups undermined the true character of democracy and representative government. This issue dates back at least to James Madison's *Federalist Paper #10,* in which he warned against the evils of factions. However, many contemporary political scientists have a quite different view of interest groups. They appreciate them for the services interest groups perform, mediating between citizens and government institutions.

Interest groups help bring peoples' concerns to government institutions. Individuals have many concerns that spill over to the public arena. They are simultaneously workers, consumers, investors, hobbyists; they find their identity in their ethnic backgrounds, gender, age cohort, religious beliefs, and geographic location. These and many more interests become salient for individuals at various times during their lives. Formal representative institutions, such as elected legislators, cannot reflect these interests well because each representative has tens of thousands constituents, each of whom has multiple interests.

In order to promote their interests, many people join groups that represent particular concerns. For example, one may belong to an ethnic group reflecting the fact that one is an African American, an Italian American, a Latino, or a Polish American. At the same time, one may belong to the International Brotherhood of Electrical Workers or the American Nursing Association reflecting the job one has. In addition, one may belong to the National Rifle Association, or the American Philatelist Association, or other groups that reflect one's hobbies. One's wallet may also hold a membership card of the local Parent-Teacher's Association, the local taxpayers' association, and the American Automobile Association. As a consumer, one may belong to Consumer's Union and the Citizens Utility Board. All of these groups articulate interests that at one time or another are important to their members.

Ever since Alexis de Tocqueville's observations about the ubiquity of groups in American life, observers of American politics have also noted it. It is a feature of American life that still impresses foreign observers. For instance, I was surprised by a Polish guest's amazement at the variety of community groups that marched down the street in a recent Fourth of July parade; the existence of so many groups is taken for granted by most Americans.

Not all groups participate in the political or legal process on a regular basis. However, there is a vast number which specialize in political representation, most of which organized in the past 30 years.[1] There are currently more than 2000 professional and trade associations based in Washington, D.C., in addition to many corporations and other associations that also maintain offices there.[2] Many interest groups also have offices in state capitals.[3]

The principal political activity of these groups is providing access for their members to government decision makers. The groups use a variety of techniques for this purpose. Many contribute to election campaigns through political action committees (PACs); there were more than 4100 PACs in 1990.[4] They mobilize members to contact their legislators and are responsible for much of the mail that reaches government offices addressing the formulation and implementation of policies. They provide information to decision makers, and their data often constitute a significant basis for policy decisions. They help their members understand and conform to government policies and assist members with individual concerns in contacting the appropriate officials.

Although numerous, interest groups by no means reflect all segments of American society. The affluent, well-educated, and powerful are better represented by such groups than the poor, ill-educated, and powerless. However, there are groups whose focus is representing the concerns of those with few other resources, such as the American Civil Liberties Union (ACLU), the American Coalition for Citizens with Disabilities, the Community Nutrition Institute, and the Children's Defense Fund.

Interest groups do not have the same monopoly over access to legislatures and administrative agencies as lawyers and police do in the courts. As noted earlier, almost no criminal prosecution can occur without initial action by the police. Similarly, very few people can use the courts for their disputes without hiring an attorney. However, individuals and corporations that wish to contact a government official can do so on their own. Legislators are very sensitive to constituent requests. Many of their staff do nothing but respond to letters from constituents writing about a particular issue or seeking information or assistance with a problem. The same is true for many administrative agencies. Their procedures are often designed to make it possible for individuals to contact them directly. One does not need an interest group to obtain veteran's benefits, a student loan, or information about the Peace Corps.

[1]Jack L. Walker, "The Origins and Maintenance of Interest Groups in America," *American Political Science Review* 77 (1983), p. 395.
[2]Jeffrey M. Berry, *The Interest Group Society* (Boston: Little, Brown, 1984), p. 20.
[3]Clive S. Thomas and Ronald J. Hrebenar, "Interest Groups in the States," in Virginia Gray, Herbert Jacob, and Robert B. Albritton (eds.), *Politics in the American States*, 5th ed. (Glenview, Ill: Scott, Foresman, 1990), p. 129.
[4]Harold W. Stanley and Richard G. Niemi, *Vital Statistics on American Politics* (Washington, D.C.: Congressional Quarterly Press, 1992), p. 175.

However, interest groups provide a different kind of access. Their size and strength lend added weight to their requests and information. Their representatives develop special relationships with legislators, administrative officials, and judges. They not only concern themselves with immediate crises but also articulate long-range concerns and plans. They sometimes offer public officials alliances that may help those officials achieve their own goals. Individuals rarely have the resources to conduct concerted campaigns to alter the law in their favor; that, however, is the special strength of interest groups.

Interest groups operate differently in each of the core institutions. We begin by examining them in the contexts with which most Americans identify them: in—legislative and administrative arenas—before turning to their activities before courts.

Interest Groups in Legislatures

"Lobbies" and "lobbyists" got their names from the fact that they congregated in the antechambers of legislatures during debates. Interest group representatives literally stand there in order to hear what lawmakers are saying and observe how they are voting. Sometimes they participate in last-minute deal making, suggesting compromises or urging protection of their interests. Interest groups focus on the details of policy formulation and draftings. Because particular phraseology produces benefits and costs for their members, it is there that interest groups focus their attention.

This is illustrated by the manner in which the Clean Air Act of 1990 became law.[5] The bill as proposed by President Bush in 1989 was more than 300 pages long.[6] It was replete with complicated, technical details on how to reduce sulphur-dioxide emissions, encourage the use of alternative fuels, regulate toxic chemicals, reduce smog by reducing emissions from automobiles, and cut acid rain by encouraging use of cleaner fuels by electric utilities. As Senator Max Baucus of Montana, chair of the Environmental Protection Subcommittee of the Senate Environment and Public Works Committee ruefully noted, "I forgot, and probably Senator Mitchell [the majority leader] forgot, just how complicated it all is, substantively and politically. It takes longer for senators to understand the legislation than we thought."[7] The substantive complexity arose from understanding difficult scientific testimony and complex economic analyses; the political complexity resulted from conflicting interests between regions. For example, southern California would need to pay the costs of emission controls in order to reduce smog, while others, such as Iowa, would benefit from the sale of corn for producing ethanol. Environmentalists, chemical manufacturers, automobile makers, coal mine operators, their employees, and business and civic organizations in the towns in which they operated were just a few of the many groups that focused their attention on this bill.

Some of the most intensive negotiating centered on the reduction of acid rain, which required cutting the use of high-sulphur coal. Not only were the fortunes of par-

---

[5]The following is based on Richard E. Cohen, *Washington At Work: Back Rooms and Clean Air* (New York: Macmillan, 1992).
[6]Ibid., p. 61.   [7]Ibid., p. 83.

ticular coal companies at stake but so were the jobs of many coal miners. Those in West Virginia, Pennsylvania, and southern Illinois, where high-sulphur coal was mined, stood to lose the most, while the winners would be in western states that produced low-sulphur coal. Lobbyists for these interests worked furiously with their senators to win the most favorable treatment possible. The result was a complicated plan for establishing certificates utilities could earn for using low-sulphur coal. These certificates could be sold to plants using dirtier fuel. However, the plan drew heated opposition from the National Wildlife Federation, even while it was supported by another environmental group, the National Clean Air Coalition.[8]

The negotiations took place largely behind the closed doors of committee rooms. Therefore, interest groups depended on members of Congress who sat on the committees to represent their concerns. As Cohen reports, "Groups that had made campaign contributions often had a better chance of eliciting sympathy inside congressional offices. . . . The steelworkers—whose political action committee contributed $897,675 to congressional candidates in 1989–90—had better lobbying access to many congressional offices than did environmental lawyers."[9]

Such lobbying is not uncommon. It brings interest group representatives to committee hearings to testify and to legislator's offices to persuade and cajole. They stimulate mail to legislators and contribute to their election coffers. These activities occur not only in Congress but also in state legislatures and city councils. In the states, for instance, teachers' interests are often reflected in the technical requirements of state legislation about teacher certification and curricula. At the local level, some of the most heated lobbying occurs with respect to building codes that affect which materials can be used in new construction and which trade unions will find their employment opportunities enhanced or reduced.

The details of much, perhaps even most, legislation are the product of lobbying by interest groups. In this way, some of those who later use the law or find it imposed on them gain a substantial advantage in the legal process. If they are present at the law's creation, they will find few surprises when it is implemented. On the other hand, those who remain unrepresented by groups often discover the law has been written either with no concern for their interests or crafted specifically to limit their opportunities.

An important caveat to the apparent influence of interest groups in the legislative process must be noted. Activity does not equal influence, and for many groups on one side of an issue, there are others on the opposing side. For every winner there are also losers. Groups may be effective in gaining access and yet fail to convince lawmakers to adopt their suggestions, for legislators must face the electorate, which may defeat them if they cast unpopular votes. The representative from Carbondale, Illinois, may have little choice but to side with supporters of high-sulphur coal. However, other legislators, such as those from rural areas that have neither smog nor coal mines, may have a "free" vote on the question of low-sulphur or high-sulphur coal; they may be persuaded to ally themselves with one side or the other.

[8]Ibid., pp. 100–103.   [9]Ibid., p. 103.

Interest Groups in the Administrative Process

Interest groups have some of the same objectives when they focus on the administrative process as when they lobby legislatures: they want to influence the making of law. The law in this instance is in the form of administrative regulations. Legislatures often delegate "rule making" to administrative agencies because the details of many policies are too complex for legislatures to handle. Groups that succeeded in the legislature therefore need to press forward in the administrative process to cement their victory; groups that failed in the legislative process have a second chance when administrative agencies consider the issuance of regulations to implement a law.[10]

The influence of interest groups in the administrative process rests on somewhat different foundations. Administrators are further removed from the electoral process; PAC contributions often produce less response from them. However, administrators may be influenced by two other techniques that are much less common to legislatures.

One lobbying technique used with administrative agencies is to build close links between an agency and its clientele. Many agencies depend on their users to provide political support at budget hearings, when pushing for new legislation, or when facing external attack. The classic case is the role of farmers in supporting the Department of Agriculture and its programs. The department used its extension agents to build a strong corps of supporters in rural areas. Those supporters organized their own interest group, the Farm Bureau Federation, which through the years has continued to lend political strength to the department. Other departments have a similar relationship with their clientele: the Veterans Administration with veterans' groups, the Department of Defense with defense contractors, the Social Security Administration with senior citizen groups, highway departments with motor clubs, and schools with parent-teacher organizations. The relationships between agencies and client groups are not always harmonious, but agencies are often the object of strong lobbying from such groups.

A second technique used by lobbies to gain influence in administrative agencies is to provide employment for agency administrators when they leave government service. This revolving door involves administrators who are not career civil servants. From their government position they go to positions in private industry or with interest groups and sometimes return to government after several years.[11] When they leave public service, they bring to their new employer valuable knowledge of an agency's inner workings and many personal contacts. Examples include such high-profile lobbyists as Robert K. Gray, secretary of the cabinet in the Eisenhower administration who then went to the public relations firm of Hill and Knowlton before forming his own firm; Charls E. Walker, deputy secretary of the Treasury Department during the Nixon administration before founding his consulting firm of Charls E. Walker Associates; Stuart Eizenstat, President Carter's chief domestic advisor who later became a lobbyist for

---

[10]For the growth and significance of rule making, see Theodore J. Lowi, *The End of Liberalism* (New York: W.W. Norton, 1969).

[11]The most rigorous analysis of this phenomenon is by John P. Heinz, Edward O. Laumann, Robert L. Nelson, and Robert H. Salisbury, *The Hollow Core: Private Interests in National Policy Making* (Cambridge: Harvard University Press, 1993), pp. 105–155.

high-technology companies.[12] An example of an official who moved in the other direction—from lobbyist to administrator—is William Sullivan, Jr., who was appointed associate administrator of the Environmental Protection Agency in the Reagan administration after he had led the Steel Communities Coalition, an industry group that sought to relax pollution control standards.[13]

As with legislatures, interest groups seek an insider's role in administrative agencies to influence the formulation and implementation of policy. Again, the meat of the legal issues lies in the small print of the regulations and the details of the implementation. When most effective, lobbyists are able to suggest ways to follow the letter of an unfavorable law that don't really harm their clients. They may do this by suggesting exceptions for situations, by obtaining delayed deadlines, and by advocating weak inspections.

As with legislators, the presence of lobbyists does not automatically translate into favorable action. Much depends on the context of the situation, such as the degree of opposition or the basic inclinations of the agency leadership. For instance, Republican administrations, such as those of Ronald Reagan and George Bush, are hospitable to the interests of business because the business community is its core constituency. In a Democratic administration, such as that of Bill Clinton, the same lobbyists may engage in identical activities as under Republicans but with indifferent success, because Democratic administrations historically have been less responsive to ideas from the business community.

The most successful lobbying does not necessarily occur on highly visible, controversial issues. Rather, success must be gauged by the routine activities of administrative agencies and their impact on interest group members. A recent study of Washington lobbying summarized this caveat by saying, "For many groups, including the most privileged and powerful corporate actors in this society, interest representation involves a game of running to stand still."[14]

Interest Groups in Courts

Lobbying before courts is substantially different from that in the legislative or administrative process. Interest group representatives do not congregate in courthouse lobbies. There is no revolving door by which judges become interest group representatives or interest group representatives become judges. Judges do not attempt to win the favor of clientele groups. However, interest groups play an important role as a gatekeeper to the courts; for some types of cases, they are as important as in the legislative and administrative processes.

The interest groups' methods employ to influence courts parallel those they use before legislatures and administrative agencies but take a different form. Interest groups

[12]On Gray and Walker, see Berry, supra, note 2, pp. 133–134; on Eizenstat, Jeffrey H. Birnbaum, *The Lobbyists* (New York: Random House, 1992), p. 19.
[13]Kenneth Janda, Jeffrey M. Berry, and Jerry Goldman, *The Challenge of Democracy*, 2d ed. (Boston: Houghton Mifflin, 1989), p. 530.
[14]Heinz, Laumann, Nelson, and Salisbury, supra, note 11, p. 5.

seek a voice in the selection of decision makers, influence their agendas, and provide information that might form the basis of a favorable decision.

Interest groups' activities differ substantially in trial and appellate courts. In trial courts, they are important in making it possible for clients to sue. They participate directly in the litigation. In appellate courts, they are more active in seeking to influence the selection of judges; in addition, they may take a leading role in appealing a case or intervene indirectly by providing additional information to judges through **amicus curiae** briefs. However, in neither arena do interest group representatives approach judges or other decision makers in the courtroom to persuade them to decide a case in their favor. Such **ex-parte** approaches constitute serious violations of judicial ethics and could lead to a judge's dismissal and the revocation of an attorney's license. They also might lead to a reconsideration of the decision. Thus, what is normal and widely accepted behavior in the legislative and administrative contexts is interpreted as corrupt in the judicial arena.

INTEREST GROUPS IN TRIAL COURTS

Most litigation begins either by the police and prosecutor filing a criminal charge or by a plaintiff initiating a civil case. Thus, the *initiation* of most litigation typically occurs without interest group intervention. However, the defense of a few criminal cases and the initiation of some very important civil cases may involve interest groups in a significant way.

As we have already noted, most defendants in criminal cases are represented either by their own attorneys or by public defenders or other attorneys provided by the State. However, in a few cases an interest group provides the defense. For instance, demonstrators arrested while protesting at abortion clinics are routinely defended by antiabortion interest groups. What distinguishes most such cases is that the alleged crime is viewed as a political act by an interest group that provides counsel for the defendant as part of its campaign to advance its policy position.

More frequently, interest groups use civil litigation to pursue their policy goals. They do so by initiating **test cases.** The occasion for a test case usually arises when a group has failed to persuade a legislative body to pass a law favorable to its interests or has been unable to obtain administrative implementation of some statute in a manner to its liking. A test case may involve such diverse matters as the delivery of services, the regulation of an industry, the danger posed by a consumer product, or harm being done to the environment. The interest groups involved include such organizations as the National Association for the Advancement of Colored People (NAACP) Legal Defense Fund, the Natural Resource Defense Council, the American Civil Liberties Union, the Food Resources Action Center, the National Association for Retarded Citizens, and the Legal Services Corporation. The results have sometimes drastically affected public policy.

A dramatic example of such litigation may be found in the efforts of advocates for improved opportunities for physically disadvantaged children.[15] Beginning in the

---

[15]The account of the litigation of the rights of physically disadvantaged children is based on R. Shep Melnick, *Between the Lines: Interpreting Welfare Rights* (Washington, D.C.: The Brookings Institute, 1994), pp. 144–179.

1970s, lawyers from four civil rights organizations—the National Legal Aid and Defenders Association, the Center for Law and Social Policy, the Harvard Center for Law and Education—and the Pennsylvania Association for Retarded Children, began litigation to assure equal educational opportunities for physically and mentally disadvantaged children. That litigation produced enough citizen concern and pressure to persuade Congress to adopt the Education for All Handicapped Children Act of 1975.[16] After Congress enacted the law, the groups initiated further litigation to ensure delivery of educational services to these children. As a result of the litigation, school districts extended the school year for such children, dealt with their disciplinary problems in a more sensitive manner, and provided them with services such as specialized therapies.[17]

Several characteristics mark such intervention by interest groups. First, the groups often do not intervene in only a single case but rather develop a stream of litigation over many years. This is required because the implementation of many policies lies with state agencies; forcing agencies in many states to comply with judicially developed standards often necessitates litigation in many jurisdictions. Second, the litigation is part of a broader strategy of action, rather than an attempt to obtain a remedy for a single grievance, as is typical of most civil cases. Third, groups carefully select their clients to provide the best chance of obtaining a favorable ruling. They do not seek to intervene in all instances where persons are deprived of a benefit or have a grievance. One of the attorneys responsible for choosing cases to challenge welfare regulations put it this way:

> . . . the locale, court, regulation and plaintiff were carefully selected. Litigation strategy and tactics were the determinants and . . . [we] rendered a fairly comprehensive service in such cases. That strategy represents the erosion theory of litigation: the worst example of a practice or rule, the gross or excessive form, so to speak, in the most highly suspect social setting was chosen as the subject of challenge.[18]

In describing the case selection in one instance, Melnick concludes:

> Legal Services attorneys searched for a case that would shock the conscience of judges by pitting a sympathetic client against malicious state officials. They found such a client in Mrs. Sylvester Smith, a hard-working, widowed black woman with four children.[19]

Such interest group intervention leads to a quite distinctive kind of gatekeeping. Cases reach the court not because of the determination of an aggrieved party or because of the lure of a remedy in a particular case. Interest group attorneys choose test cases such as these for the likelihood that they will advance their policy goals. This represents a calculated strategy that balances the groups' need to ration their resources with the need to satisfy their membership. In some instances, groups can be selective about their cases because their membership has an ideological commitment to a cause rather than a material stake in the outcome. In the cases described above, the beneficiaries were usually severely disadvantaged people with few resources, but the members of groups that

---

[16]Pub. L. No. 94-142.   [17]Melnick, supra, note 15, pp. 164-168.
[18]Lee Albert, "Choosing the Test Case in Welfare Litigation: A Plea for Planning," *Clearinghouse Review 1* (November 1968), pp. 4-6, 28, as quoted in Melnick, supra, note 15, p. 78.
[19]Melnick, supra, note 15, p. 85.

funded their cases were ideologically committed to alter the policies being attacked. Thus, the failure to service every person with a plausible grievance caused few repercussions to the groups; they pointed to their policy successes and argued that in the long run, they had greater success in improving the lot of the disadvantaged than if they had pursued every possible case. Thus, test cases produce access for a cause but not for all persons with similar grievances.

The consequences for the courts and policy-making process are substantial. These cases bring to trial courts social issues that rarely surface in ordinary litigation. The judges who hear these cases spend most of their time deciding cases involving automobile accidents, commercial disputes, criminal charges, and the like. Suddenly they find on their docket a case challenging a state or federal agency. They are likely to approach these cases quite differently than legislators or administrators. Rather than seeing the issue as part of a policy stream they confront on a daily basis, judges deal with these test cases as a unique part of their docket. Consequently, interest groups that bring such cases find themselves in a uniquely influential position because they can bend the agenda of the courts to their own purposes in a way they could rarely affect the agendas of legislatures or administrative agencies.

It is worth noting that many such cases do not reach an appellate court, or if they do, go only to the intermediate appellate court (such as, the Court of Appeals in the federal system) rather than to the Supreme Court. If an interest group wins its case at trial, the appeal rests with the government agency, which often does not find a suitable ground for challenging the decision or does not wish to elevate it to regional or national application, the result if an appellate court affirmed the trial court's decision. In addition, many such cases do not go to trial at all, but are settled by the interest group and agency involved with a **consent decree.** Such a decree, crafted as a compromise between the litigants, is signed by the judge and often involves further monitoring and supervision by the court. However, the consent decree does not set a precedent and, therefore, does not have the same impact on other cases as a trial or appellate court decision. Yet, for the interest groups involved consent decrees often save scarce resources, satisfy their immediate grievance, and pressure other agencies involved in similar issues to conform lest they become the next target of litigation.

The groups we have examined thus far represented mostly disadvantaged persons, and the groups themselves are relatively weak. However, as several scholars of interest group litigation have observed, other interest groups also use the courts to advance their interests. In her study of a federal district court in Minnesota, excluding litigation by legal service groups (representing the disadvantaged), Olson found that occupational and for-profit groups made up more than half the groups in cases involving group representation.[20] Some of these cases involved corporations seeking favorable rulings, labor unions representing clients in personal grievances, trade or business groups, and associations of townships.[21] Olson points out that these cases indicate groups use trial courts in a wide variety of circumstances. Whether they litigate appears to depend more on a

[20]Susan M. Olson, "Interest Group Litigation in Federal District Court: Beyond the Political Disadvantage Theory," *Journal of Politics* 52 (1990), pp. 874–875.
[21]Ibid., p. 871.

comparison of their political and legal resources to those of their opponents than on the absolute level of their resources. Thus, groups with substantial resources that possess greater legal skills than political clout when compared to their opponents are as likely to use the courts as are groups with minimal resources in both arenas. Moreover, these groups may also use the courts to nail down victories in other arenas by urging courts to confirm legislation and administrative regulations which the groups won in those arenas.

Much remains to be learned about the scope and impact of interest group litigation in trial courts. For instance, it is not clear that groups are more successful than individual litigants in litigation that challenges the government or in such areas as employment discrimination, the environment, religion, and the death penalty. When Epstein and Rowland sought to test the success of group intervention in such cases, they found that groups won and lost virtually the same proportion of cases as other litigants.[22] However, we have learned that groups are successful in providing access to the courts for those whose day in court might otherwise be denied.

INTEREST GROUPS IN APPELLATE COURTS

Interest group activity is more varied and more apparent in appellate courts. Groups employ three strategies in appellate courts: influencing the selection of judges, sponsoring test cases, and filing amicus curiae briefs.

While a few interest groups overtly intrude into the process of selecting trial judges, either by making campaign contributions in jurisdictions that elect their judges or in behind-the-scenes lobbying where judges are appointed, their activity is much more apparent at the state and national supreme court levels. When a supreme court appointment becomes available to a governor or president, a wide variety of groups advance their favorites. Some are ethnic groups who seek representation on the court. Others are concerned with the candidates' views on such matters as abortion, the death penalty, election reform, free speech, government intervention in religious programs, educational reform, and the like. Groups work behind the scenes to advance their candidates. Occasionally, they succeed in obtaining the appointment of a lawyer closely associated with their cause. For example, Thurgood Marshall, had been Director and principal strategist for the NAACP Legal Defense Fund for many years before his appointment to the U.S. Court of Appeals and the U.S. Supreme Court. Similarly, Ruth Bader Ginsburg had worked with the ACLU before her judicial appointments. Groups also seek to block appointments of those whom they oppose. When the nomination requires legislative confirmation (as U.S. Supreme Court justices do), interest groups surface during confirmation hearings to record their approval or opposition. In the case of the failed nomination of Robert H. Bork to the U.S. Supreme Court in 1987, a coalition of civil rights groups generated a tidal wave of mail and other contacts with sena-

[22]Lee Epstein and C. K. Rowland, "Debunking the Myth of Interest Group Invincibility in the Courts," *American Political Science Review* 85 (1991), pp. 205–217.

tors to persuade them to reject the nomination.[23] Indeed, that experience spawned the term to "bork" a nomination—that is, to weaken it by organized group opposition. Almost every vacancy on the Supreme Court generates group activity; with one exception, groups are much less vigilante about other appellate judgeships. The exception is the American Bar Association and state bar groups. Bar associations have had substantial success obtaining access to the judicial selection process. They routinely evaluate judicial candidates, claiming to have unique capabilities to rate their qualifications for a judgeship.[24]

A second avenue for group influence in appellate courts lies, as it does in the trial courts, in the sponsorship of test cases. Some of the test cases that interest groups sponsor at trial make their way to appellate courts. In addition, these groups support some cases that private parties initiated in trial courts but cannot afford to appeal. It is unknown how frequently this strategy is used in courts other than the Supreme Court. However, since many of the sponsored cases that reach the Supreme Court were also sponsored at their earlier appellate hearings, it is evident that some groups use this instrument before lower appellate courts. It is clear from studies of group sponsorship of Supreme Court cases that lobbies which sponsor cases for the so-called underdogs are by no means alone in bringing test cases. Looking at the 1987 term of the Supreme Court, Epstein found groups that represented commercial interests, and such legal groups as the American Bar Assocation and the Pacific Legal Foundation also sponsored a substantial number of cases.[25]

The widespread participation of interest groups in appellate litigation is more apparent when we examine their use of amicus briefs. To file such a brief, a group usually requires the approval of one of the parties to the case or of the court. This requirement, however, does not constitute a serious obstacle and, as we shall see, many groups file amicus briefs, which serve many functions. For interest groups, they provide a highly visible way to present policy preferences to the courts. Their primary audience is the court to which the brief is addressed, but such briefs are also sometimes cited by the media, thus providing arguments to the general discourse. Another audience is the group's members. Filing the brief is evidence of group activity on their behalf, and it is routinely noted in newsletters and other information provided to members and supporters. Amicus briefs also provide additional information to the courts. They typically indicate the range of people concerned about the matter, provide information about the potential consequences of decisions, and propose legal theories to support a favorable outcome. As groups often have greater resources than the original litigants, the added information provided by the briefs may be substantial.

The number of such briefs in Supreme Court cases increased markedly in the 1970s and 1980s. Existing research has uncovered only three amicus briefs in noncommercial

[23]Contrasting views of the Bork nomination are presented in Ethan Bronner, *Battle for Justice: How the Bork Nomination Shook America* (New York: W.W. Norton, 1989) and William Eaton, *Judge Bork and the Confirmation Game* (Washington, D.C.: Washington Legal Foundation, 1987).
[24]Although outdated in its details, the influence of the bar is described well in Joel B. Grossman, *Lawyers and Judges: The ABA and the Politics of Judicial Selection* (New York: Wiley, 1965).
[25]Lee Epstein, "Interest Groups," in John B. Gates and Charles A. Johnson (eds.), *The American Courts: A Critical Assessment* (Washington: Congressional Quarterly Press, 1991), p. 355.

cases before 1940; however, between 1953 and 1966, interest group submissions of amicus briefs increased to about one-fourth of all noncommercial cases. In the 1970s, such activity involved more than 50 percent of all such cases, and by 1988, it increased to 80 percent.[26] In addition, amicus briefs are filed in commercial cases. These numbers somewhat exaggerate interest group participation since a very large number of briefs come from the office of the Solicitor General of the United States, whose activities and influence we examine in Chapter 10. However, even excluding such government amicus briefs, it is apparent that interest group participation in the Supreme Court's consideration of cases has become quite common. Some interest group lawyers litigate so frequently in particular kinds of cases and represent their causes so well that they win the respect of the justices. For many years, a brief on a First Amendment separation of church and state case signed by Leo Pfeffer of the American Jewish Congress was almost certain to win careful reading by some of the justices; the same was true of a brief on racial discrimination signed by Jack Greenberg of the NAACP Legal Defense Fund.

Interest group participation has also become common in some state supreme courts, although its frequency varies from state to state. For example, in 1985, 76 percent of the cases before the California Supreme Court had at least one amicus brief. In New Jersey, however, the use of amicus briefs peaked in 1990 at 40 percent of the cases; in Kansas, it reached only 30 percent that year; in Tennessee never more than 5 percent of the cases had an amicus brief.[27] We do not know why such variations exist, but they indicate that interest group use of amicus briefs varies dramatically across the United States; it is much less common in state court litigation than in U.S. Supreme Court cases.

Interest groups often work together on such briefs. Collaboration shares costs, presents a united front to the court, and builds alliances that may be useful in other cases or in other arenas. Sometimes collaborators work on a common brief and cosign it; in other cases, they write separate briefs that support each other. For instance, O'Connor and Epstein show that in women's rights cases between 1969 and 1980, the National Organization for Women (NOW) supported the ACLU in almost 80 percent of the cases in which it participated.[28] The degree of mutual support was almost as high between the ACLU and the Center for Constitutional Rights (CCR). However, not all feminist organizations supported each other so frequently. Examining the mutual support between the relatively radical CCR and the relatively conservative Women's Equity Action League, O'Connor and Epstein found they supported each other in only about 10 percent of the cases in which they participated.[29] Occasionally, a case is so prominent and raises so many issues that an avalanche of amicus briefs descends on the Supreme Court. One such case was *Bowen v. Kendrick*.[30] It involved an ACLU-sponsored challenge to the Adolescent Family Life Act, which provided federal funds to re-

---

[26]Epstein in Gates and Johnson, supra, note 25, p. 351.
[27]Lee Epstein, "Exploring the Participation of Organized Interests in State Court Litigation," *Political Research Quarterly*, (1994 forthcoming).
[28]Karen O'Connor and Lee Epstein, "Beyond Legislative Lobbying: Women's Rights Groups and the Supreme Court," *Judicature* 67 (1983), p. 140.
[29]Ibid.
[30]108 S.Ct. 2562 (1988); see Epstein in Gates and Johnson, supra, note 25.

ligious programs for research and programs to prevent premarital adolescent sexual relations. Eight briefs were filed by groups urging the Court to strike down the law as an unconstitutional involvement by the government in religion. One of those briefs, written
by the National Coalition for Public Education and Religious Liberty, was signed by 29
other organizations, including such diverse groups as the Central Conference of American Rabbis, the Missouri Baptist Christian Life Commission, the National Association
of Catholic Laity, and the Society for the Scientific Study of Sex.[31] Amicus filing
reached a highwater mark in *Webster v. Reproductive Health Services*,[32] a 1989 case involving a crucial challenge to the standards established in the *Roe v. Wade* abortion
case, with 78 separate amicus briefs in which more than 400 groups participated.[33]

Both sponsorship of test cases and submission of amicus briefs are widely used to attempt to influence the Supreme Court. In the 1987 term of the Supreme Court, 65 percent of cases on the docket were sponsored by groups and 80 percent attracted amicus
briefs.[34] Thus, interest group activity has become an integral part of the Supreme
Court's decisional process.

Case sponsorship and the filing of amicus briefs have several consequences. They
provide a wide array of groups an opportunity to voice their concerns to appellate
courts. Obversely, the courts need not depend only on the litigants for information
about the significance of cases nor about alternative legal strategies for addressing the
issues raised.

By voicing their concerns, groups particularly affect the agendas of appellate courts.
They do so in two ways. First, they have some discernible influence in persuading courts
to accept cases for review. When the Supreme Court is considering whether to accept a
case for full consideration, cases for which amicus briefs have been filed are 40 percent
to 50 percent more likely to be accepted than those in which no amicus brief was
filed.[35] The second way they raise important issues lies in the arguments presented in
the briefs. Groups who intervene often have somewhat different concerns than the
original litigants; the groups are much more likely to raise broad policy issues and to
highlight legal ramifications buried within the cases. One reflection of such influence is
the mention of a brief in the court's decision. For example, Epstein indicates that for
the 1987 term of the Supreme Court, an amicus brief was cited in the decision in approximately one-third of the cases in which such a brief had been filed.[36]

Evidence also exists that interest groups succeed in influencing the Supreme Court.
Unlike the experience in trial courts discussed earlier, in some types of litigation, cases
supported by interest groups seem to have more success than those without such support. For instance, in cases alleging discrimination, those sponsored by groups won 80
percent of the time, while litigants with similar claims but without group support won
only 63 percent of their cases. Similarly, litigants defending claims of discrimination

[31]Epstein, in Gates and Johnson, supra, note 25, p. 347.
[32]U.S. 490 (1989).
[33]Epstein, in Gates and Johnson, supra, note 25, pp. 336 and 349.
[34]Epstein in Gates and Johnson, supra, note 25, p. 358.
[35]Gregory A. Caldeira and John R. Wright, "Interest Groups and Agenda-Setting in the Supreme Court of
the United States," *American Political Science Review 82*, (1988), p. 1122.
[36]Epstein, in Gates and Johnson, supra, note 25, p. 361.

won their cases 50 percent of the time when sponsored by groups but only 22 percent of the time when not.[37] Other research focusing on the Legal Services Program's advocacy of cases indicates that that group also had considerable success.[38]

However, this evidence does not show that interest groups persuade the Court to adopt positions it would otherwise decline to support. In many instances, group success is a result of careful selection of cases by the groups. Given limited resources, few groups are likely to support hopeless causes. Before deciding to accept a case, most groups consider the likelihood of success. This does not imply that they accept only guaranteed winners, but rather that they consider the weight of legal precedent in their favor, the strength of the legal arguments they might make, and the ideological bent of the judges they will face.

Conclusion

It is evident that interest groups are significant gatekeepers for the core institutions of the legal system. Accounting for their activities is essential to understanding the legislative process and the ways in which laws come to be implemented by administrative agencies. They are also active before courts but use quite different instruments—the test case and amicus curiae briefs—to present their concerns. As a consequence, interest groups mold the courts' agendas in ways somewhat similar to those by which the media, political parties, and elections influence the legislatures' and administrative agencies' agendas. However, interest group activity should not be confused with influence or success. Interest groups sometimes win and sometimes lose. Why they do so will become clearer as we examine the legal process more fully.

KEY WORDS

amicus curiae	test cases
ex parte	consent decree

FOR FURTHER STUDY . . .

The classic work on interest groups is David B. Truman, *The Governmental Process* (New York: Knopf, 1951); it includes a chapter on courts that remains fundamentally correct even though the details are outdated. Current research on interest group activity of courts is well summarized by Lee Epstein, "Courts and Interest Groups," in John B. Gates and Charles A. Johnson (eds.), *The American Courts* (Washington, D.C.: CQ Press, 1991).

---

[37]Ibid.

[38]Susan E. Lawrence, "Legal Services before the Supreme Court," *Judicature* 72 (1989), pp. 266–273.

IV

CORE INSTITUTIONS: THE COURTS

Courts breathe the very essence of the law. They apply, interpret, and, sometimes, make law. For good reasons, most people consider courts to be the core of the legal system.

Courts are very complicated organizations. Like most elements of government in the United States, courts are strewn over the political landscape in a seemingly haphazard fashion. State courts are almost entirely independent of federal courts. Higher courts, such as the state courts of appeal and state supreme courts, have only limited power over trial courts. Unlike most organizations, courts do not recruit their own staff, have little control over their budgets, and can scarcely regulate the flow of cases.

The organization of courts is portrayed in Figure IV.1 as a series of boxes connected. We connect these boxes by thin, dotted lines to indicate that the flow of authority top to bottom is quite tenuous. Each court within each box (there are tens of thousands in the trial court boxes, and dozens in the appellate court boxes) is fairly autonomous. They all must follow the law and have more or less the same procedures, but each varies in local detail.

This peculiar organizational structure reflects a feature of American courts that becomes clear in the following chapters: the degree to which they are embedded in their own political arenas. The trial courts of Manhattan are very much New York City institutions, reflecting the peculiar habits, preferences, accents, pace, and problems of New York lawyers and citizens. The U.S. Supreme Court is very much a Washington institution, tied closely to the highest levels of the government. The rarefied atmosphere of its chambers would be out of place in state capitals like Springfield, Illinois, or Austin, Texas, where state supreme courts sit and work in a climate that is a political hemisphere away from Washington.

As we shall see, the disconnected character of courts in the United States has important implications for how various segments of the population manage to use the courts. Repeat players can take advantage of the many-tiered structure in ways that one-shotters cannot. And because there are so many "highest" courts (one for each

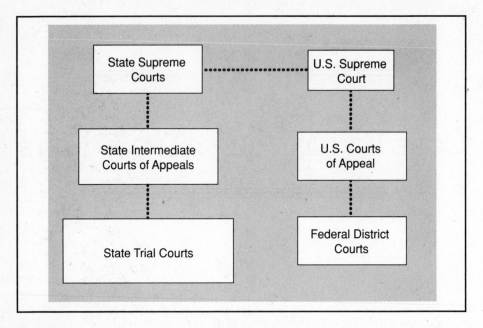

Figure 4.1
Courts in the United States

state and one for the nation), judicial policy often lurches forward (or backward) with the awkwardness of a neophyte ice skater rather than the grace of an Olympic competitor.

Each level of courts operates with different rules and under different circumstances. We examine each of them in the following three chapters.

8

TRIAL COURTS

Trial courts are both the most dramatic arenas of the legal system and the most banal. Here, the sensational stories of lurid crimes unfold and the intrigues of commercial plunder are laid bare. But trial courts are also the places where ordinary crimes and petty grievances seek resolution in a mass production process that rarely attracts even cursory attention from anyone except those immediately involved.

Trial court proceedings are enormously varied and yet they share common characteristics. We first examine those commonalities before delving into the variations used to handle distinctive sets of cases.

Common Elements of Trial Courts

THE TRANSFORMATION OF DISPUTES

Disputes or allegations of lawbreaking constitute the issues that come to trial courts. They are rooted in incidents involving people with conflicting claims. Often the incident has been the object of prior negotiation, mediation, or arbitration attempts, as in many marital disputes, personal injury claims, consumer complaints, and commercial disputes. However, when people bring a dispute to court, it may be transformed in significant ways.[1] The story of the dispute told to the court is a reconstruction of the incident as it actually occurred. It is usually the truth, but it is almost never the whole truth. This is not because the participants lie, but because conflicting versions of the incident seem to be equally true to each side of the dispute. One witness may remember seeing a blue car used in a robbery while another may remember it as gray. While the driver of one car remembers driving at the speed limit, a witness may assert that the driver was

---

[1]Lynn Mather and Barbara Yngvesson, "Language, Audience, and the Transformation of Disputes," *Law & Society Review* 15 (1980–1981), pp. 775–822.

speeding. Each side asserts the version of the story they believe to be true, which is often the version most favorable to their cause.

Another element in this transformation is that lawyers guide their clients to mold their stories to fit the legal parameters of their case. If the law provides damages only when the plaintiff was blameless, the plaintiff's attorney will not dwell on his client's possible contributory negligence; that is for the defense attorney to discover. The plaintiff's story will instead focus exclusively on the defendant's negligence. Thus, a plaintiff injured in a rear end automobile collision is likely to claim that he or she took all reasonable precautions, while the defense is likely to claim that the plaintiff slammed on the brakes unexpectedly. However, plaintiffs telling the story of their misfortune to friends might confess to being worried that morning about their children or having left the house distracted by an argument with their spouse. Little or none of this information is pertinent to the lawsuit, and it will not be raised in court.

The stories told to judges and juries are highly stylized versions of the actual incidents. Lawyers are specialized storytellers. They know which parts of an incident to emphasize and which to subordinate. They do not even want to hear all the details of their client's tale because they consider them irrelevant. The apocryphal divorce lawyer tells clients that they may recite their tale of woe but reminds them that the clock is running at $150 per hour.

These special characteristics of a court case are highlighted by the following descriptions of a divorcing couple's marital problems as recorded by David Engel, a legal anthropologist who studied the work of trial courts in a small Illinois town. The husband, who was the plaintiff in the divorce action, originally wrote to the local judge, saying he wanted a divorce. Without benefit of legal counsel, he expressed his problem in the following way:

> We have had happy times and we have had bad times together. There is no argument about any settlement on property or money. No argument about custody of our [children]. . . . Everything stays as it is except we want a divorce. The reason is we don't have any love left for each other. We just argue and fight. We think this is best for all concerned mostly our children. I John Smith will still help make payments on the home and property. And also keep food and clothes for all the family. Everything will stay the same except we won't be husband and wife anymore.

His wife also wrote the judge; her letter revealed more about their problems:

> To the Judge From Mary Smith I do want a divorce. I am in love with some one else. And I would rather not name him in Order to save him. He don't know this right now. But I don't love John any more I haven't for a long time. And we have tryed for 5 years . . . there are Other things. We have had to Call the Police out here to settle are Fights. . . .
> He has Wittness to all this. Thank you. Mary Smith.

After the husband consulted an attorney, the story changed, and the legal document seeking the divorce described their situation somewhat differently. The formal complaint filed in court read as follows:

> Now Comes the Plaintiff, John Smith, complaining of the Defendant, Mary Smith, and alleges as follows:

1. That he is a resident of the County of Sander and for more than one year last past prior to the commmencement of this action has been an actual bona fide and continuous resident of the State of Illinois.

2. That the parties hereto were legally married on————, at Jonesburg, Brown County, Illinois, and thereafter lived together as husband and wife until the commencement of this action.

3. That————children have been born as a result of said marriage, namely,. . . [names, and ages of children] . . . that no children have been adopted by the parties hereto.

4. That during the time the parties hereto lived together as husband and wife, the Plaintiff conducted himself as a kind dutiful and affectionate husband, and gave her no just cause for complaint.

5. That the Defendant has been guilty of extreme and repeated mental cruelty as defined by the Statutes of the State of Illinois relating to divorce, without cause or provocation on the part of the Plaintiff, thereby making the plaintiff nervous and upset and affecting his health.[2]

The informal letters the Smiths had written to the judge differ from the formal petition for a divorce on many dimensions. The informal letters reveal much more about the actual cause of the marital breakdown. There were arguments, fights, and a lover. All of that is swept under the legal category "extreme and repeated mental cruelty" in the formal petition. On the other hand, the court papers carefully lay out the court's jurisdiction by specifying the residency of the Smiths and their legal marriage; it also names the children and makes clear that no adopted children are involved. Finally, the petition also alleges that only Mary Smith was at fault in the marriage because that was a requirement of Illinois law at the time; none of the mutual problems described in the Smiths' letters appear in the formal court story of the breakdown of their marriage, because if both spouses were at fault, the court might not have granted a divorce to either.[3]

THE APPLICATION OF LAW

Incidents like the Smiths' marital problems are transformed in court because decisions about them are made with reference to procedural and substantive law. All trial courts follow the law's prescribed procedures and apply the law's remedies to the factual situations attorneys present to the court. Unlike many private negotiations or mediation, courts rely more on law and less on social custom.

Application of the law gives trial courts a large element of predictability. The law is written down and available to all to read. It may not always mean what it appears to say and the law sometimes changes, but it is considerably more precise than many customs that usually are unwritten. Nevertheless, the law may be interpreted quite differently by various individuals.

[2]David Engel, "Legal Pluralism in an American Community: Perspectives on a Civil Trial Court," *American Bar Foundation Research Journal 1890* (1980), pp. 434–435.
[3]Such a situation involved what was called the recrimination doctrine in divorce law. This doctrine has now been eliminated in every state.

The dominance of legal norms in trial courts means that lawyers play a controlling role. No one but attorneys may represent litigants and only in a few courts (mostly small claims courts) do litigants routinely present their own cases. Moreover, lay judges are rare; almost all judges have legal training. Even lay judges are committed to deciding cases on the basis of the law, although they may understand it imperfectly.

The use of the law in trial courts limits what can be accomplished in court. A dispute can be "fixed" only to the extent that the remedies provided by law are pertinent. For example, if the law authorizes damages but not a return to the situation as it existed before a breach of contract, only damages can be obtained. Where the law provides for a maximum sentence of fifteen years, a judge cannot impose one for thirty years. If the law prohibits a trial court from considering a matter—as American law prohibits federal courts from considering disputes involving foreign policy matters—trial courts must throw the dispute out of court. In contrast, negotiation, mediation, and arbitration are not so bound by the law and may produce more inventive and more effective remedies.

However, unlike other dispute-processing arenas, trial courts *impose* their judgments. A trial court's decision is usually a win-or-lose situation rather than a mutually satisfying compromise. Moreover, such decisions are imposed by a third party—the judge—who is not chosen by the disputants but is a servant of the State. Disputants thus surrender control over their problem to a stranger whose decision will be binding. They have much less say in the way their dispute will be handled in court than in other dispute-processing arenas. If they win, they can use the power of the government to satisfy their claim. If they lose, they are obliged to abide by the judge's decision, barring a reversal of the decision on appeal.

SPECIAL PROCEDURES

Trial courts are also marked by their special procedures. They are principally concerned with determining the factual circumstances of the incidents brought before them. Consequently, many trial court procedures focus on fact finding. Rules of evidence—which differ somewhat between criminal and civil complaints—guide the presentation of facts. Only those with firsthand exposure to the situation or with certified expertise may provide information, which is elicited under oath. Witnesses typically present evidence in person under one attorney's questioning by **direct examination.** This evidence may then be tested by **cross-examination** from the opposing attorney and by comparison with other evidence introduced at the trial.

Formal rules also mold the judgment process. Judgment is rendered either by the judge alone or in conjunction with a **jury** that almost always consists entirely of laypersons. When juries participate, judges provide them with intricate instructions on how to arrive at a decision (for instance, the number of votes required), the manner in which they must weigh the evidence, and the verdicts they may reach. Similar considerations bind judges, but because they have legal training, the rules are not formally announced at each trial. Legal scholars often emphasize that both judges and juries exercise much discretion in reaching their judgments. This observation is accurate, but the amount of discretion they enjoy is not as great as that available to decision makers in less formal settings, such as when police officers decide whether to make an arrest.

THE PUBLIC CHARACTER OF TRIAL COURTS _____

Litigants often bring their private troubles to trial courts, but courtroom disputes do not remain private. Trial courts are the public's concern because public facilities and the public's law are used to achieve a resolution. In recent years, the public nature of trial courts has been highlighted by the introduction of television cameras. It has become common in some communities to watch excerpts of court proceedings on the local news each evening. Television's intrusion into the courtroom has vastly increased the public nature of the proceedings. Before, only a handful of spectators observed the events in a courtroom; with television coverage, one's trial might appear in the neighbors' living rooms.

Criminal Proceedings

The most common distinction between different kinds of trial courts is between criminal and civil proceedings. Crimes are entirely a public matter even though a private complainant usually launches the proceedings with a call to the police. Civil cases, by contrast, often involve private disputes that the parties could not settle out of court. Those convicted of a crime stand to lose their freedom and risk being labeled a "convict," which often threatens their employment; in civil proceedings, the usual outcome is simply paying damages. For these and other reasons, criminal and civil proceedings are quite different even though they may use the same courtroom and take place before the same judge.

WHAT CRIMINAL COURTS ARE SUPPOSED TO DO _____

The principal task of criminal courts is to separate the guilty from the innocent and to impose appropriate penalties on those found guilty. Identifying guilt is no easy task. It involves two separate decisions. The first is a determination of what happened in a particular incident: who did what to whom. The relevant details are often fuzzy in the witnesses' minds, and the varying perspectives of witnesses, defendant, complainant, and the police may make a determination of the "truth" difficult. Second, the court must determine whether the actions attributed to the defendant violated the criminal code. If a person took a television set but had the permission of the owner, it is not theft. If a person took clothing from a store but has a receipt for its purchase, it is not shoplifting.

Viewed more broadly, the task of the criminal courts is to impose **social control** and order in accordance with legal prescriptions. The courts do not decide what kinds of conduct are treated as deviant or criminal, but they are supposed to make certain that when criminal acts occur and the perpetrator is caught, he or she is punished. Punishing the guilty is to have two effects. One is to deter the guilty person from committing crimes in the future, called **special deterrence.** In many cases, imprisonment will incapacitate the convict for some period of time, but imprisonment is also intended to protect the community in the future by convincing the perpetrator that crime does not pay. In addition, such punishment is supposed to make it clear that the community expects lawful behavior and those who commit criminal acts will be punished. This is called **general deterrence.** Thus, the spectacle of the public trial has purposes far beyond any entertainment value; it should attract widespread public attention so its lesson will be learned.

Social control is not the criminal court's only function. Criminal courts are obligated to decide cases fairly. Rich and poor, men and women, minorities and whites, those with good reputations and those with tarnished ones should be treated alike. The duty to deal fairly with those accused is immensely important for assuring that court judgments are perceived as legitimate by the community. The capacity of criminal courts to punish is enormous; it represents the raw power of the State against the individual and is widely feared. Perceptions that criminal courts impose sanctions unfairly may severely undermine the legitimacy of the political system; courts that are a model of propriety have the opposite effect.

THE WORKLOAD OF CRIMINAL COURTS

Crime is a booming business in much of the United States. Even though the police are selective in enforcing the law, they make an enormous number of arrests, all of which must be processed. In 1991, the FBI estimated the police made 10.7 million arrests. Almost 3 million of those arrests took place in the 53 cities that have at least a quarter million population, but 3.6 million arrests occurred in suburban areas.[4] In Manhattan in 1987, there were almost 40,000 arrests resulting in a felony or misdemeanor court case; in Seattle, 6365; in Portland, Oregon, 6638.[5] Caseloads are heavy in smaller cities, too. Denver, for instance, had 3210 criminal cases handled by thirteen judges who also took care of many other matters. The six judges of the judicial district south of Denver (Littleton) handled 2004 criminal cases in addition to their other responsibilities; the district to the north of Denver (Brighton), with its two criminal court judges, handled 1417 cases.[6]

Caseload comparisons per judge are difficult to make because different locales use their judges in different ways. In some, particular judges work full time on criminal cases; in others, judges rotate from minor to major criminal cases and then to civil cases; in still others, judges handle the entire spectrum, from big criminal cases to traffic offenses. This variation is illustrated by all three Colorado jurisdictions described above; it is clear that each of those judges carries a heavy caseload.

Consequently, even though patrol officers screen out the most inconsequential cases by not making an arrest, a key characteristic of criminal court processes is the way they winnow cases for full treatment. In 1987, of every 100 felony arrests, approximately 56 led to a conviction and only 2 of those convictions were the result of a full

[4]Kathleen Maguire, Ann L. Pastore, and Timothy Flanagan, *Sourcebook of Criminal Justice Statistics, 1992,* (Washington, D.C.: U.S. Department of Justice, Bureau of Justice Statistics, 1993), p. 422.
[5]Barbara Boland, Catherine H. Conly, Paul Mahanna, Lynn Warner, and Ronald Sones, *The Prosecution of Felony Arrests, 1987* (Washington, D.C.: U.S. Department of Justice, Bureau of Justice Statistics, 1990), pp. 20–23.
[6]The number of cases come from Boland et al, supra, note 5, pp. 24–25; the data for the number of judges come from Boland et al, supra, note 5, pp. 127, 136, and 142.

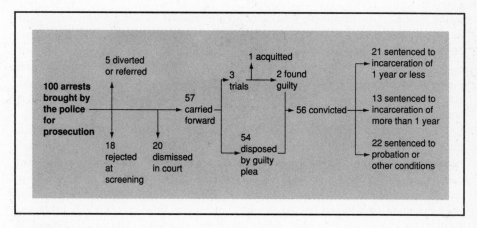

Figure 8.1
The Disposition of Felony Cases
Source: Barbara Boland, Catherine H. Conly, Paul Mahanna, Lynn Warner, and
Ronald Sones, *The Prosecution of Felony Arrests, 1987* (Washington, D.C.: U.S. De-
partment of Justice, Bureau of Justice Statistics, 1990), p. 3

trial; the other 54 resulted from **guilty pleas.** Forty-three percent of the felony arrests
did not even lead to an appearance in felony court: they were disposed of through early
rejection at the police station, dismissal, misdemeanor conviction, or diversion to a
nonjudicial agency (such as a drug or alcohol abuse program).[7] These statistics are
shown in a flow chart in Figure 8.1. Each of the major paths on the flow chart involves
different procedures and opportunities for various court personnel to exercise their influence and authority.

The first decision point occurs at the station house, where the patrol officer brings
the arrested person and writes a report alleging either a minor crime (**misdemeanor**) or
a major crime (**felony**). The distinction usually hinges on the maximum prison term the
law permits: misdemeanors normally provide for less than one year's imprisonment
while felonies permit more. In most instances, prisoners serve misdemeanor sentences
at the local jail but felons are sent to the state penitentiary.

Judges have no voice in the decision to hold a prisoner for either a misdemeanor or
a felony. That decision is made in the first instance by the patrol officer or a supervisor
and in many places is reviewed subsequently by an attorney from the prosecutor's office.
The decisions of these officials hinge on their evaluation of the seriousness of the offense and their judgment of the evidence collected by the police. Felony charges not
only require more grievous offenses but also demand better evidence, because they are
both hard to prove and more likely to be vigorously contested by the defendant.

The prosecutor who screens arrests also may decline to pursue any criminal charge
at all. In most jurisdictions, such a discharge results in the immediate release of the ar-

[7]Boland et al, supra, note 5, p. 3.

rested person. These **dismissals** may occur because alleged behavior does not rise to the level of a misdemeanor or because the evidence is so weak the prosecutor does not feel a conviction could be obtained. Sometimes extenuating circumstances justify a dismissal, such as when the victim started a fight or when the alleged offender is especially old or young or has never previously been in trouble. Sometimes such dismissals also involve a referral to a social service agency, but in many instances they entail no further official action.

Those held on misdemeanor charges may appear before the judge almost immediately, although they often are held overnight in the police station. When they appear before the judge, they are informed of the charges and may plead guilty or innocent. Some (particularly if they do not have an attorney) plead guilty at this stage and are sentenced immediately. Of those, most receive suspended sentences or probation; many must pay a fine. Others may have their case continued to the next court date (a week or month later) at which time they either plead guilty or have their case dismissed. In most cities, very few choose to go to trial;[8] to do so is to risk a substantially harsher punishment if convicted. While some guilty pleas are spontaneous, many are the result of brief negotiations around a **going rate** that is well known by courthouse insiders.[9] The going rate is the usual and expected treatment accorded to particular offenses; it facilitates bargaining between the regular participants in the courtroom workgroup.

In the words of several authors,[10] the mere fact of being arrested and held for several hours, overnight, or several days constitutes a punishment. The police deliberately treat those whom they arrest in degrading ways that emphasize police authority and the powerlessness of the prisoner, such as photographing and fingerprinting the prisoner, calling them by their first names, and removing their shoe laces and belts before locking the prisoner in a cell with several other (possibly dangerous) persons. People who are arrested receive little information about when their hearing will occur or what might happen to them. Most do not have the money to call an attorney and do not see one until they are thrust into a courtroom. No one in the station house or courtroom treats them with respect. Thus, even when defendants leave court with no more than a sentence of probation or a small fine, many have already been punished. A distinct minority of those convicted (usually fewer than 30 percent) serve additional jail time for their misdemeanors.[11] However, in 1991 even this small percentage amounted to 186,000 men and 21,000 women in the United States serving time in jail after conviction for a crime.[12]

Courts devote little time and few resources to processing misdemeanors. In some cities, the police herd groups of a dozen misdemeanor offenders before the judge and

[8]But see the apparent exception of Philadelphia and possibly Boston: Stephen J. Schulhofer, "No Job Too Small: Justice Without Bargaining in the Lower Criminal Courts," *American Bar Foundation Research Journal* 1985 (1985), pp. 519–600.

[9]Malcolm M. Feeley, *The Process Is the Punishment: Handling Cases in a Lower Criminal Court* (New York: Russell Sage Foundation, 1979).

[10]Ibid.; John Paul Ryan, "Adjudication and Sentencing in a Misdemeanor Court: The Outcome is the Punishment," *Law & Society Review 15*, (1980–1981), pp. 79–108.

[11]Schulhofer, supra, note 8, p. 623.

[12]Timothy J. Flanagan and Kathleen Maguire, *Sourcebook of Criminal Justice Statistics, 1991* (Washington, D.C.: U.S. Department of Justice, Bureau of Justice Statistics, 1992), p. 623.

they are processed as a group.[13] Those pleading guilty win immediate release, while those insisting on their innocence are held for a trial later in the day or on another day. Prosecutors normally have little time to prepare misdemeanor trials; they are likely to glance at the police report as the defendant is called to the bench and if there is a trial, the arresting officer is the principal witness. Often no other witnesses testify and little additional evidence is heard. Most defendants are too poor to hire lawyers and rely on a **public defender** or a **court-appointed attorney** for counsel; these attorneys have equally little time for preparation. In addition, where misdemeanors go to specialized court-rooms, the staff is composed of the least experienced personnel in the criminal justice system. Misdemeanor court is the first assignment for a rookie prosecutor, a novice de-fender, and a newly appointed judge; it becomes the permanent assignment for those who cannot be fired but should not be promoted. Everyone in the courtroom treats these cases as routine matters that require little attention. Even when trials occur, they usually take less than 15 minutes and rarely involve a jury.[14]

The treatment of arrests that do not justify felony charges and those that from the outset are considered misdemeanors epitomizes the social control function of the crimi-nal justice system. Viewed individually, the offenses do not involve large sums of money or serious harm. However, because they are so numerous, they constitute a serious threat to an orderly and safe life. It is essential that such behavior not go unrestrained. Yet the legal system does not have the resources to consider each misdemeanor in any depth. It relies principally on the police who make such arrests and the prosecutors who supervise them to winnow the likely innocent defendants as well as the clearly inconse-quential acts. Those remaining are then handled in an expeditious manner that scarcely qualifies as a fact-finding, adversarial procedure.

Felonies receive quite different treatment. These crimes involve large sums of money, serious injuries, and the potential for long prison sentences. The criminal courts focus most of their efforts on such cases.

Within 48 hours of arrest, felony defendants are brought before a judge (albeit a low level judge) who informs them of the charges being pressed and sets the conditions for their release.[15] Both because the legal system considers defendants innocent until proven guilty and because of the protections of the **Eighth Amendment,** which pro-hibits excessive bail, many defendants win immediate release pending the outcome of their case. However, the courts condition a defendant's release on his or her promise to reappear for all hearings in the case. To reinforce that promise, defendants often must put up a large amount of money **(bail),** which they forfeit if they do not appear as or-dered; it may be in the form of cash or property. In most instances, however, defendants buy bail from a bond company located near the courthouse; for no more than 10 per-cent of the face amount, the bond company guarantees the payment if the defendant defaults. Thus, $10,000 bonds generally require the payment of only $1000 or less.

[13]Schulhofer, supra, note 8, p. 555.

[14]The best sources of information on misdemeanor processing are: Feeley, supra, note 9; Schulhofer, supra, note 8; Ryan, supra, note 10; and Douglas W. Maynard, "Structure of Discourse in Misdemeanor Plea Bar-gaining," *Law & Society Review* 18 (1984), pp. 75–104.

[15]Roy B. Flemming, *Punishment before Trial: An Organizational Perspective of Felony Bail Processes* (New York: Longman, 1982)

However, since most defendants are poor, many cannot afford a bail bond. To avoid fill-ing jails with trustworthy defendants who cannot meet ordinary bail requirements, many courts allow for **release on recognizance (ROR);** this involves only a promise to appear and is provided to defendants who have strong roots in the community and seem likely to make all required court appearances.

Many felony defendants neither make bond nor are provided release on their own recognizance and, therefore, must await their trial in jail. In 1990, in the 75 largest counties of the United States, more than half of all defendants who had previously been convicted of a violent felony were detained pending trial; one-fifth of those with no prior conviction of any kind were also denied pretrial release.[16] Most of those with prior convictions who won their pretrial freedom did so with bail bonds rather than release on recognizance; however, the majority of those without prior convictions were freed under ROR programs.

After bail has been set, the case proceeds to a **preliminary hearing** (or **examina-tion**) at which time the prosecutor must present sufficient evidence for a judge to rule that there is **probable cause** the defendant violated the law as charged. Ordinarily, the defendant is represented by a lawyer at the hearing and the lawyer may present evi-dence on behalf of the defendant. However, most attorneys at this stage have had little time to prepare a defense and most consider it foolish to tip their hand at this early stage. Defense attorneys, therefore, generally restrict themselves to cross-examining the prosecution's witnesses in an effort to get a ruling of no probable cause and their client released, but few such rulings occur at this stage. Prosecutors may also move to dismiss cases at the preliminary hearing because their witness fails to appear, seems to be unreli-able, or some other evidentiary problem becomes apparent.

This stage's outcome varies greatly from one city to another, as shown in Table 8.1. For example, in Baltimore and Detroit, most cases moved forward to the next stage; in

Table 8.1   Outcome of Probable Cause Proceedings by City

	Baltimore[a]	*Chicago[b]*	*Detroit[c]*
Dismissed	21.0%	63.4%	5.1%
Findings of innocence or no probable cause	4.0	10.8	14.2
Findings of guilt	7.9	4.5	0
Guilty pleas	.3	8.6	0
Sent to grand jury but not indicted	4.0	0	N.A.
Indicted by grand jury or information	62.6	12.7	80.5
	99.8%	100%	99.8%

a. Based on weighted file sample: $N = 1,577$

b. Based on weighted preliminary hearing observation samples: $N = 982$

c. Based on preliminary examination observation sample: $N = 350$

Source: James Eisenstein and Herbert Jacob, *Felony Justice: An Organizational Analysis of Criminal Courts* (Boston: Little, Brown, 1977) p. 191. Reprinted by permission of the authors.

[16]Maguire, et al, supra, note 4, p. 533.

Chicago, however, preliminary hearings were used to screen out the majority of cases by motions to dismiss. The handful of guilty pleas or findings of guilt reflect the fact that the preliminary hearing court is also a misdemeanor court and a few defendants were permitted to plead guilty to a lesser charge or were found guilty of such a lesser charge as the result of an agreement to reduce the charges and hold an immediate trial.

If the judge decides probable cause exists (or with the preliminary hearing waived), the prosecutor then decides which felony charges to bring against the defendant. In some places, such as Detroit, the prosecutor is solely responsible for this function and returns the charges in the form of an **information.** In others, the prosecutor must go before a **grand jury,** which consists of two dozen or so ordinary citizens who hear the evidence presented by the prosecutor and vote an **indictment;** defendants have no right to appear before the grand jury to contest the accusation. Although theoretically grand juries can reject a prosecutor's recommendation, they rarely do so and the presentation of a case before the grand jury is usually little more than a formality.[17] After an indictment or information is returned, the defendant once again appears in court to hear the formal charges, permit a judge to review the amount of bail, and schedule a trial date.

The trial date is typically delayed once or twice, and most defendants plead guilty in the interim; it is estimated that 90 percent of all felony defendants plead guilty (see Figure 8.1). That statistic poses two questions: Why, in a legal system that celebrates the adversarial process and public trial, do so many defendants plead guilty? And why do the remaining few opt for the public trial?

Guilty pleas are rooted in several fundamental characteristics of criminal courts. First is the heavy caseload most courts face. Given the resources courts receive, little more than glancing attention can be provided to the typical case. Judges in large city felony courtrooms confront daily dockets of well over two dozen cases. Trials usually require at least a full day and often run longer. Consequently, the only way in which courts can process their caseload is either to dismiss a large portion of it even after pruning the least important cases or to promote a large number of guilty pleas.

Second is that the entire workgroup in the courthouse feels the weight of the caseload, and all have an incentive to process cases expeditiously. Prosecutors are assigned more cases than they can prepare for trial. They often do not work on a case until the afternoon before the trial, do not interview witnesses until just before the trial begins, and depend almost entirely on the report written by the police many weeks earlier when they arrested the defendant. Yet the public holds the prosecutor responsible for processing cases and obtaining convictions. Since too many acquittals or the release of defendants because they could not be given a speedy trial is a sure prescription for defeat at the next election, the prosecutor's office usually is quite willing to promote guilty pleas.

The defense is in an even more precarious position. Public defenders or court-assigned counsel represent the vast majority of felony defendants who are too poor to hire attorneys. These defense counsel are usually not well paid; they often have fewer resources than prosecutors and are just as overworked. Typically, they have little contact

---

[17]Janet A. Gilboy, "Prosecutor's Discretionary Use of the Grand Jury to Initiate or to Reinitiate Prosecution," *American Bar Foundation Research Journal 1984* (1984), pp. 1–82.

with their clients until just before the trial, and the defence constructed relies almost entirely on police reports and their clients' version of the events. While they attack gaps in the prosecutor's case and identify inconsistencies in the testimony of prosecution witnesses, they have little time to prepare a more vigorous defense. Moreover, most defendants are factually guilty of some criminal act although it may not be exactly the one charged. Most have a fear of spending a long time in prison. Hence, defense attorneys have a strong incentive to negotiate a guilty plea in exchange for a more lenient punishment than the defendant might otherwise receive.

The individual motivations of **courtroom workgroup** (or courthouse community) members become intensified through daily interaction.[18] Although adversarial in posture, they are forced to collaborate to manage their caseloads. Moreover, each wishes to minimize uncertainty and maintain control over the proceedings, a goal which cannot be readily achieved when trials are held because trials are full of surprises. Consequently, rather than contest with each other in the forum of a trial, prosecutors, defense attorneys, and judges normally collaborate to promote a large number of guilty pleas. Prosecutors offer to recommend a shorter sentence, dismiss multiple counts of an indictment, or reduce the charge to a less serious offense. Defense counsel, after pressing for the most favorable treatment, help prosecutors convince their client to accept the **plea bargain.** Judges usually approve the result to avoid trials.

The plea bargain leads to a surprisingly formal ritual in open court before the judge. Defendants are asked whether the guilty plea is voluntary, not forced, and the response must be affirmative for the plea to be accepted; defendants may not continue to maintain their innocence. The prosecutor then reads into the record the facts that support the guilty plea. Last, the judge accepts the plea and normally continues the case while the probation department prepares a sentencing report with its recommendation. That recommendation almost always mirrors the agreement that has been made between prosecuting and defense counsel. At the final hearing, the judge pronounces the sentence.

In most courts guilty pleas—often the result of explicit plea bargaining—are the normal way of processing a felony case. In those few jurisdictions that hold trials rather than depend on guilty pleas (such as Baltimore and Philadelphia), the trials are kept short and often are perfunctory. The result is the same as the plea bargain and the process is often called a **slow plea.**

Thus, guilty pleas are the product of a heavy caseload and interdependency between prosecutor, defense counsel, and judge. Why, then, do some trials occur? They take place for a number of reasons. Some trials involve notorious cases, which prosecutors wish to display through a public trial. They provide prosecutors an opportunity to exhibit their skills before a horde of reporters and cameras; at the same time, the trial avoids the risk of criticism for excessive leniency that might be perceived if they negotiated a plea with the defendant. Moreover, there is a widespread perception that plea bargaining cheats the public of its opportunity to learn the grisly details of the crime

[18]James Eisenstein and Herbert Jacob, *Felony Justice: An Organizational Analysis of Criminal Courts* (Boston: Little, Brown, 1977); James Eisenstein, Roy B. Flemming, and Peter Nardulli, *The Contours of Justice: Communities and Their Courts* (Boston: Little, Brown, 1987).

and observe the public punishment of its perpetrators. Thus, most notorious crimes go to trial.

Many more trials involve routine crimes, and those trials occur for different reasons. In some, the defendant has an extensive criminal record and probably will be sentenced to a long prison sentence even after a guilty plea. Having little or nothing to lose, the defendant may opt for a trial in the hope that through some quirk, an acquittal can be achieved. In other cases, negotiations break down because the prosecutor refuses to agree to the defense counsel's demands or is constrained by office guidelines about what kinds of deals are permissible. Still other trials occur because defendants truly believe themselves innocent or the defense counsel believes the prosecutor's case is too weak to sustain a guilty verdict. Since a sizeable number (as many as one-third) of trials do result in acquittals, such hopes are well grounded.

One further "cause" for staging trials lies in the expectations or norms of the courthouse community. In some locales, people simply expect most cases to be decided by trial rather than negotiation, and that expectation becomes a self-fulfilling prophecy. The high incidence of trials in Philadelphia, for instance, is explained by Shulhofer largely in these terms. In Pittsburgh, the other large metropolis of Pennsylvania, many fewer trials decide criminal cases.[19] Likewise, Eisenstein and Jacob found many more trials take place in Baltimore than in Chicago or Detroit.[20] It remains a mystery how such a legal culture comes into being.

Trials—whether before only a judge (so-called **bench trials**) or with a jury—involve much more uncertainty than plea negotiations. In negotiations, attorneys manage the flow of information, controlling what information about the crime and the defendant is revealed and how it is framed. Information spills out in narrative form and it is easy for prosecutors and defense counsel to put their spin on it. Moreover, in most instances the prosecutors and defense counsel know each other from previous negotiations and understand each other's style; there are few surprises and no loose cannon. Not so in trials. At trial, information is disclosed as the result of questioning witnesses and one can never entirely predict what they will say or how they will say it. Police officers are the most predictable witnesses, because they testify frequently and have been taught how to describe events. Ordinary people feel great stress on the witness stand, may respond in quirky ways to cross-examination, and may display mannerisms that belie their testimony. Moreover, it takes considerably greater skill and more thorough preparation to unfold the story of a crime through witness testimony than through informal conversation. As the burden of proof in criminal cases rests with the prosecution, prosecutors enter trials with justifiable trepidation.

Jury trials magnify the uncertainty. Jurors are strangers to the process; little is known about them and no relationships bind them to either prosecution or defense. Although considerable efforts sometimes go into attempts to fathom how jurors may react to testimony, few attorneys leave a jury trial with the confidence they have at the end of a bench trial or plea negotiations. That uncertainty affects both defense counsel and prosecutors. Thus, it is not surprising that jury trials are the exception.

---

[19]Schulhofer, supra, note 8.   [20]Eisenstein and Jacob, supra, note 18.

THE OUTCOME OF CRIMINAL PROCEEDINGS _____

Criminal proceedings have two goals. The first is to sift the guilty from the innocent; the second is to impose appropriate punishment on the guilty.

It is impossible to determine the courts' success in the first task, because we possess no independent indicators of innocence or guilt. The large number of dismissals may be interpreted alternatively as: (1) an index of the courts' commitment to protecting innocent people; (2) an indicator of the courts' conclusion that defendants are punished sufficiently by the stigma of arrest and the degrading rituals involved in preliminary processing; or (3) a token of the courts' ineptness by releasing guilty perpetrators without adequate punishment. All three interpretations involve threats to the legitimacy of the legal system. If the dismissals do reflect a vigorous protection of innocents, one must wonder why gatekeeping by the police is so inefficient that they arrest large numbers of innocent people. The second explanation also threatens judicial legitimacy since if an arrest imposes sufficient punishment, it ought not to be imposed on innocent people; if it is, many will find the justice system arbitrary and unfair. If dismissals are a form of rough justice for relatively minor crimes, critics will wonder whether the vast discretion by which prosecutors dispense such informal justice is fair, for there are no checks and no quality control over the issuance of dismissals; they remain invisible to outsiders. Finally, if the high rate of dismissals signifies judicial incompetence, those who yearn for the legal system to impose more effective social control will condemn the criminal justice system as a contributor to lawlessness. Thus, all of the interpretations of dismissals imply that the criminal justice system poses a danger to regime stability.

The second goal of the criminal justice system is to impose appropriate penalties on the guilty. A large range of authorized penalties exist. The most severe is the death penalty, which in 1992 was authorized in 36 states and by federal law for a limited number of crimes but is surrounded by numerous procedural complications. In the spring of 1992, 2558 prisoners were awaiting execution in U.S. prisons;[21] however, only about 250 prisoners each year receive the death sentence,[22] and although the pace of executions quickened in the 1980s, only 14 prisoners were executed in 1991.[23] Often as much as ten years elapse between the sentence and execution while appellate courts consider death sentence appeals.

Courts impose prison sentences of more than a year in about 28 percent of felony cases that result in convictions.[24] Given the large number of such cases across the country, this percentage produces a high incarceration rate when compared to other countries;[25] moreover, this rate more than doubled during the 1980s from 138 per 100,000 population in 1980 to 292 per 100,000 in 1990.[26] In 1990, almost 740,000 men and women were serving prison sentences in the United States.[27] In that same year, 28 per-

[21]Flanagan and Maguire, supra, note 12, p. 703.   [22]Flanagan and Maguire, supra, note 12, p. 707.
[23]Maguire et al, supra, note 4, p. 673.   [24]Boland et al, supra, note 5, p. 3.
[25]"Imprisonment in Four Countries," *Special Report*, (Washington, D.C.: U.S. Department of Justice, Bureau of Justice Statistics, February 1987), p. 2; Warren Young and Mark Brown, "Cross-national Comparisons of Imprisonment," in Michael Tonry (ed.), *Crime and Justice: A Review of Research 17* (Chicago: University of Chicago Press, 1993), p. 5.
[26]Flanagan and Maguire, supra, note 12, p. 636.   [27]Flanagan and Maguire, supra, note 12, p. 636.e

cent of those convicted of a felony received a sentence of less than one year,[28] with at least 28,000 persons serving felony sentences in local jails.[29] Thus, in the United States in 1990, more than three-quarters of a million persons were incarcerated as the result of a felony conviction.

The remaining 37 percent of those convicted of a felony receive probation or other sentences. **Probation** means the person promises to avoid further criminal acts for a specified period of time and must periodically report to a probation officer who checks on his or her status. First-time burglars charged with relatively small thefts often receive such a sentence. An alternative to probation is a **suspended sentence,** which is usually unsupervised; if the person is arrested during the period of suspension, the suspended sentence may be reinstated and the person sent to jail or prison. Youthful offenders are particularly likely to receive probation or suspended sentences. Another punishment is **community service,** in which the convict must devote a specified amount of time working without pay for local community organizations. Finally, some convicts are only assessed a monetary **fine.** Many of these penalties may be combined as, for example, when a period of incarceration is followed by community service.

Many problems exist with these sentences. Incarceration is expensive; a year in prison costs as much as a year of study at a university, but the taxpayer bears the entire cost. The length of imprisonment for a given offense varies substantially from state to state and even within states from one court to another. In one place, an armed robber serves a five year prison term; in another, it may be 10 or even 20. However, prisoners usually serve less than their full sentence because prisons award time off for good behavior to help control their inmates. In addition, judges sentence more people to prison than prisons have space to house. Consequently, penitentiaries release some prisoners before the end of their prison term in order to make room for new arrivals. Most important, however, is the low deterrent effect of imprisonment. **Recidivism,** as measured by the number of persons who are sent to prison a second time, is substantial. Twenty-eight percent of all admissions to federal and state prisons in 1990 were men and women who violated their parole. Many others commit new crimes after completing their parole period.[30]

The entire criminal justice enterprise enjoys, at best, mixed success in the United States. It does not perceptibly reduce crime, although it is impossible to know how much crime would exist if the system were less effective. A very large number of people are arrested and never convicted of a crime but informally punished by the process of going through arrest, booking, and investigation. Others go free later in the process as charges against them are dismissed (after they have borne additional transaction costs), because they are convicted but sentenced to the time they have already spent in jail awaiting disposition, or because they win acquittals. One must question whether the process from arrest to conviction produces a deterrent effect since the probability of punishment remains low.

On the other hand, the criminal justice process visibly toils to produce the appearance of fair treatment. Indigent defendants obtain defense lawyers at public expense; all

[28]Boland et al, supra, note 5, p. 3.   [29]Maguire et al, supra, note 4, p. 600.
[30]Flanagan and Maguire, supra, note 12, p. 638.

defendants may have their day in court. In court hearings, evidentiary rules favors the defense and the State remains obliged to meet the heavy evidentiary burden of proving guilt "beyond a reasonable doubt." Admittedly, these protections frustrate some police officers and segments of the general public who think that courts "coddle" criminals. But they are important in producing the perception that the courts deal fairly with ordinary citizens and that the process does not blindly produce convictions. If people perceive that the criminal justice process is fair, it may help reinforce the government's legitimacy of the regime as Tyler's research suggests.[31]

Three other characteristics of the criminal justice process are noteworthy. The first is the absence of political parties or interest groups. With very few exceptions, criminal justice in the United States is a nonpartisan process in which the usual participants of the political process remain absent. That lends the appearance of criminal justice being nonpolitical which it is in the narrow sense of not being partisan. However, since the ultimate purpose of criminal justice is the imposition of social control and the legitimation of the regime, it plays a key role in the political arena, albeit in a disguised fashion.

The second noteworthy characteristic is the absence of policy making in the process. Criminal court proceedings are driven by huge caseloads that demand disposition; consequently, judges mostly engage in routine processing rather than in the crafting of policy alternatives. Occasional cases present opportunities to formulate new policies, such as when a new crime or circumstance demands a response from the court, but that occurs very rarely. Policy also emerges silently from the flow of case dispositions, so that close observers will note it is the "policy" of a particular judge or court to impose heavy or lenient sentences or to tolerate poor lawyering or demand excellence in the disposition process. But that is a very different policy process than what is generally associated with the concept of policy making. Most notably, such policy emergence involves no explicit discussion of alternatives, nor does it invite public scrutiny and participation.

Finally, the criminal justice process leads to certain unintended and unanticipated consequences that create trouble. For example, minorities are treated much more harshly than whites. They are more likely to be held in jail without bail, more likely to be convicted, and more likely to receive long prison terms.[32] The consequences of such discrimination are serious. Many more African Americans than whites perceive the police as not treating people fairly and using excessive force;[33] jails and prisons house a disproportionate number of African Americans and Hispanics.[34] In Washington D.C. in 1992, two-fifths of all African-American men between the ages of 18 and 35 were "enmeshed" in the criminal justice system on any given day, and 70 percent of all African-American men had been arrested by their 35th birthday.[35] Because it is diffi-

[31]Tom R. Tyler, *Why People Obey the Law* (New Haven: Yale University Press, 1990). See also: Jean M. Landis and Lynne Goodstein, "When Is Justice Fair? An Integrated Approach to the Outcome Versus Procedure Debate," *American Bar Foundation Research Journal*, (1986) pp. 765–708; Tom R. Tyler, Jonathan D. Casper, and Bonnie Fisher, "Maintaining Allegiance toward Political Authorities: The Role of Prior Attitudes and the Use of Fair Procedures," *American Journal of Political Science 33* (1989) pp. 629–652.
[32]Coramae Richey Mann, *Unequal Justice: A Question of Color* Bloomington: Indiana University Press, 1993), pp. 166–210.
[33]Maguire et al, supra, note 4, p. 172.
[34]Maguire et al, supra, note 4, p. 613.
[35]Jason DeParle, "42% of Young Black Men in Capital's Justice System," *New York Times*, 18 April 1992, p. A1.

cult to obtain employment with a felony conviction on one's record, all the ordinary impediments minorities face in obtaining satisfactory jobs are increased by the manner in which the criminal justice process impinges on their lives.

A second unintended consequence of the way the criminal justice process works is that long delays between arrest and trial are typical in many American cities. This week's arrest often leads to a trial more than three months later; it is not unusual in complicated cases for trials to occur a year after an arrest. Such delays make convictions more difficult to obtain because witnesses forget or confuse events. They may reduce the deterrent effect of the trial and subsequent punishment, and erode public confidence that police, prosecutors, and judges are doing their job efficiently.

A third unintended consequence is that the widespread use of plea bargaining undermines public confidence in the fairness of courts and in knowing those convicted are punished appropriately. The secrecy of plea negotiations engenders distrust. The word "bargain" suggests that illegitimate considerations, such as favoritism or convenience, play a role in determining outcomes. Moreover, since plea bargains almost always result in the imposition of less than the maximum punishment, there is a widespread perception that courts coddle criminals. As we have seen, none of these allegations is true; there are legitimate reasons for processing cases by negotiation rather than trial, not the least of which is to save taxpayers the expense of many more trials. In comparison to most other industrialized countries, the United States punishes its criminals more harshly; nevertheless, much of the public thinks plea bargaining is improper both because it seems to subvert trials and because it appears to produce lenient results.

Civil Proceedings

Civil cases are very different from criminal charges. They involve different participants seeking different remedies and follow different procedures. Their diversity makes them much more complex.

GOALS OF CIVIL PROCEEDINGS

The most striking characteristic of civil proceedings is that they usually involve unresolved disputes. **Dispute resolution** is commonly thought to be the principal task of civil courts. Almost always, the dispute brought to court has already been the object of private negotiations and possibly even formal mediation and arbitration. Those prior attempts to resolve the dispute failed and now the parties are willing to have the court become involved in their disagreement. However, it is a mistake to think that a court's judgment resolves the dispute. In fact, many disputes linger, with one party or the other continuing the behavior that underlies the dispute, perhaps seeking either a revised resolution in another court (via an appeal) or another forum, such as seeking a new law from a legislature, or, more usually, by reopening the matter in private negotiations. Thus, disputes are not necessarily resolved by courts; the court's judgment may be just one step in an ongoing wrangle.

One reason cases are brought to court is that a disputant seeks remedies which courts alone can bestow or can provide better than other institutions. Among the remedies only courts can grant are divorces, bankruptcy, name changes, and the probate of wills. In the case of name changes and the probate of wills, the courts deliver what is essentially an administrative service. They record the transaction and provide an archive people can check if, for example, they are trying to find a person whose name might have been changed or are tracing a debt owed by someone who died. Divorce and bankruptcy are somewhat different because the remedies they provide involve an important change of status, which the state has strong reason to regulate. The courts' reordering of these familial and business relationships is a unique service.

Most cases come to court not because the remedy sought can be provided only by courts, but because courts do so with an authority lacking in other arrangements. Courts can force payment of judgments and can compel the losing parties to alter their behavior. Private agreements lack this element of duress.

Finally, a few disputants take their problem to court because they wish to obtain a new interpretation of the law or the acceptance of a new norm. They could, of course, seek a new statute from a legislature or an executive order from the president or governor, but for a variety of reasons they instead choose the judicial route. They may do so because they do not enjoy good relations with the executive in charge or do not have the necessary clout in the legislature. They may wish to avoid the publicity that legislative action usually entails while enjoying the obscurity of most court cases. Thus, disputants occasionally bring policy issues to civil courts.

In all of these activities of civil courts, however, there is a common thread that resembles what happens in criminal courts: Civil courts also play an important role in social control. When a court grants a divorce, it ensures that the property division and care of the children accord with the guidelines established by law. When a court accepts a petition for bankruptcy, it restrains creditors from harassing debtors and prohibits debtors from using their assets without the court's permission. When a court issues a judgment in a tort case, it does not simply designate a winner, it also reaffirms social and legal principles of liability, fault, and responsibility. When a court decides a contract is either valid or void, it affirms the principles that underlie the operation of the marketplace. In these and a myriad of other ways, courts produce a constant flow of decisions that control social and economic relationships according to publicly accepted norms in a fashion similar to the social control exerted by criminal courts.

Civil courts have another outcome similar to that of the criminal courts—their impact on the courts' legitimacy. While disputants certainly want to win their case, they are also concerned with the fairness of the proceedings. Unfair treatment erodes their support for courts and judges.[36] Research on the evaluation of several kinds of disputing processes shows that disputants prefer trials and arbitration to settlements because they feel they are taken more seriously; litigants perceive the relative formality of these proceedings as bestowing respectful treatment on them, and they have an opportunity to tell their story directly.[37] In contrast, settlements are often the product of attorney negotiations in which litigants do not participate; thus, disputants feel less in control and

---

[36]E. Allan Lind, Robert J. Maccoun, Patricia A. Ebener, William L.F. Felstiner, Deborah R. Hensler, Judith Resnik, and Tom Tyler, "In the Eye of the Beholder: Tort Litigants' Evaluations of Their Experiences in the Civil Justice System," *Law & Society Review* 24 (1990), pp. 953–996; Tom R. Tyler, supra, note 31.
[37]Lind et al, supra, note 37.

less valued. Litigants' expectations are also important. Outcomes that diverge from what they expect generates noticeable dissatisfaction.[38] For instance, unrealistic expectations about the burden of proof or about the remedies the court can provide helps generate dissatisfaction with courts and judges.

Such disappointments may have spillover effects. Litigants understand that the courts and the rules under which they operate are part of the government apparatus. When courts fail to meet litigants' expectations, they diminish the regime's claim to its citizens' allegiance. As with the criminal courts, we do not know just how much unfair treatment by courts people will tolerate before seeking a fundamental change in the regime that governs them. However, those that fail, such as the Communist regimes of Eastern Europe at the end of the 1980s, were clearly marked by judicial systems that failed to deliver the quality of civil justice their citizens desired.[39]

TYPES OF CIVIL LITIGATION

The conventional characterization of civil cases follows the contours of legal doctrine and legal education. **Torts** are disputes about injuries for which the claimant demands compensation. **Contract** disputes mostly concern commercial agreements, such as the sale of a commodity. **Property** involves disputes about the ownership and use of land and other kinds of property. **Domestic relations** deals primarily with marriage, divorce, and parent-child relationships. In addition, there are areas such as bankruptcy law, tax law, administrative regulation, labor law, and environmental law, all of which often provide for civil rather than criminal remedies.

The conventional categories, however, are not particularly helpful in understanding how the civil litigation process varies, they are blind to the stakes involved both for the litigants and for the polity. Thus, tort cases may involve both very small and very large claims; they may concern injuries in individual accidents or those incurred by thousands of people from a single catastrophic accident. Many claims involve several of the conventional categories. Bankruptcy affects labor contracts; domestic relations also involves property claims; contracts are pervasive in a free market economy but are quite different when they are between two commercial firms, between an employer and employees, or between unmarried domestic partners. While the conventional distinctions highlight doctrinal differences and the kinds of claims that might be privileged in court proceedings, they are insensitive to resource disparities that litigants bring to court and which mold the kinds of court actions litigants are able to pursue. These resources include not only financial backing, but also legal skills, personal or organizational status, and relationships with the court. Finally, the conventional categories do not provide information about the available remedies that motivate plaintiffs to go to court.

Consequently, we will focus on a different typology. One consideration for litigants is the relief the courts may provide, for if the courts cannot supply a useful remedy, dis-

[38]William M. O'Barr and John M. Conley, "Lay Expectations of the Civil Justice System," *Law & Society Review 22* (1988), pp. 137–161.
[39]Martin Krygier, "Marxism and the Rule of Law: Reflections after the Collapse of Communism," *Law & Social Inquiry 15* (1990), pp. 633–664.

putants will look elsewhere. A second consideration is the price a disputant must pay to obtain the remedy; litigants rich in resources have many more alternatives than those without them. Each of these considerations needs further exploration. We begin with resources.

RESOURCES.

Resources permit disputants to transform the raw opportunities provided by law and courts into desirable outcomes. Resources include money, legal skills, prior experience, personal status, organizational backing, and relationships with court personnel.

The most important resource is money. Money may buy time, legal skills, and information. Time is important because civil litigation often is a very lengthy process; today's accident may have a court hearing three years from now. In the meantime, doctor and hospital bills need to be paid, time lost from work remains uncompensated, and in many instances plaintiffs with little money find the damages so oppressive they cannot get on with their lives until the case is adjudicated. For the wealthy, these issues pose less of a problem. They have no difficulty paying their bills; the damages are likely to be relatively minor compared to their overall financial position. Consequently, they can endure delay and may even promote it to gain a tactical advantage in the law suit. In many instances, a large disparity exists between the wealth of the two parties in a suit. For example, most plaintiffs in automobile accident cases are ordinary people with average resources; their doctor bills and lost wages represent real threats to their well-being and cause them much worry and stress. The real defendants in such cases are insurance companies.[40] They sometimes are in no hurry to pay; time can be on their side.

Money also buys legal representation. Unlike the criminal process, few civil litigants receive free legal assistance, and those who do often obtain only minimal help because legal aid bureaus operate with very small budgets compared to the needs they are trying to meet.[41] For instance, in Chicago I found in the course of research on divorce that the Legal Assistance Foundation represented only women in divorce cases and provided them help only if their cases were uncomplicated. Poor men seeking divorce and those women or men with complicated cases had to proceed without legal assistance.

Some plaintiffs find attorneys on a **contingent fee** basis. As explained earlier, this means the attorney will be paid out of the damage award given to the plaintiff, if the plaintiff wins the case. If the plaintiff loses, the attorney receives nothing. This arrangement is not the equivalent of employing an attorney on a retainer, because the contingent fee constitutes a powerful incentive for the attorney to persuade the client to accept a settlement offer even if a trial might offer the hope for a substantially larger award. As Rosenthal[42] showed, going to trial not only exposes the attorney to a much greater risk but also requires a much greater investment of time and effort; therefore,

[40]Insurance companies are not named defendants in most of these cases; their policy holders are. However, the insurance companies control the defendants' legal actions, because it is they who pay the judgment. They often provide the attorney.
[41]Robert G. Meadow and Carrie Menkel-Meadow, "Personalized or Bureaucratized Justice in Legal Services: Resolving Sociological Ambivalence in the Delivery of Legal Aid for the Poor," *Law & Human Behavior* 9 (1985), pp. 397–414; Bruce Campbell and Susette Talarico, "Access to Legal Services: Examining Common Assumptions," *Judicature* 66 (1983), pp. 313–318.
[42]Douglas E. Rosenthal, *Lawyer and Client: Who's in Charge?* (New York: Russell Sage Foundation, 1974).

many such attorneys are likely to want to avoid trials unless the payoff to them is un-usually large.

Those with money can avoid these pitfalls. Wealthy clients and most corporate lit-igants hire attorneys on a **retainer,** paying for whatever services the attorney renders. Moreover, they are likely to hire more skilled and experienced attorneys than litigants with little money. In part, this is the result of the fact that the wealthy are likely to be involved in more court litigation[43] and therefore are more familiar with lawyers and their skills. Moreover, such litigants are more likely to employ lawyers on an ongoing basis to handle an entire range of personal matters in which they may be involved.

Money also buys information. This is particularly important in civil litigation, be-cause there is no equivalent of the police and public prosecutor to investigate com-plaints, compile a list of witnesses, and accumulate documentary evidence to be intro-duced in court. All of that needs to be done by the plaintiff and defendant at their own expense. The information gathering process is called **discovery** and typically includes **depositions,** which involve questioning potential witnesses under oath as well as sup-plying relevant documents. Depositions are expensive because they require a court re-porter to transcribe the entire process and an attorney to advise the witness; the request for documents may be quite simple, as in asking for doctor bills and medical reports, but in commercial litigation it may involve a search for tens of thousands of records and their subsequent examination. The prospect of a trial usually means the investment of thousands of dollars beyond the ordinary fees of an attorney. These costs (called **trans-action costs** by economists) constitute a powerful deterrent for many clients who other-wise take their case to trial.

We have noted that money buys legal skill. Legal skill is in itself a significant re-source for the potential litigant. The legal profession operates under the myth that any lawyer can handle any case; with very few exceptions, the license to practice law is a license to take any kind of case to court. The reality, however, is that some lawyers are more experienced and skilled than others in handling particular kinds of problems. As we saw in our examination of the legal profession, the bar is divided into two hemispheres. Lawyers handling business cases more often work in medium-sized to large firms than lawyers handling personal matters, and their practice may be more specialized. Thus, when an individual confronts a business in a legal dispute, the indi-vidual's lawyer may be a general practitioner who has only a cursory knowledge of the law in this matter while the business may be represented by a specialist who does nothing but deal with such cases. Moreover, wealthy individuals are more likely to find their way to specialists than are ordinary people because they have more contact with lawyers and are better able to judge their professional qualifications. We do not have any solid research showing the consequences of these different levels of skill, and it is clear that the unskilled lawyer does not always lose. However, particularly in pre-trial negotiations where the protective rituals of the courtroom are absent, lawyers with fewer skills are likely to be less effective because they lack the information and relevant experience.

---

[43]Barbara A. Curran, *The Legal Needs of the Public: The Final Report of a National Survey* (Chicago: American Bar Foundation, 1977).

Prior experience of litigants is another significant resource. As noted earlier, Galanter[44] has suggested the many ways in which experience provides an advantage to litigants. He contrasted **repeat players** with **one-shotters.** Repeat players have the equivalent of the home field advantage of a sports team. They know the peculiarities of the courtroom setting and are familiar with courtroom personnel. They are likely to know the "going rate" for their kind of case. One-shotters, on the other hand, are wandering in strange territory. They lack knowledge of informal customs and norms that repeat players possess; they must grope where repeat players confidently reach out. In many instances, the experiential disparity between repeat players and one-shotters is heightened by the fact that many repeat players are also wealthy while many one-shotters are not. Thus, all the advantages that wealth brings to the courtroom are increased by the additional benefits that accrue to repeat players, while the disadvantages suffered by those without financial resources are aggravated by the fact that they are often also one-shotters.

Personal status and organizational standing constitute an additional significant resource in civil litigation. Better-educated people are more likely to use civil courts than those with less education because they have access to more information.[45] Research indicates that minorities are less likely than whites to use the courts.[46] Moreover, litigants with high social standing are generally better able to control their attorneys, because there is little or no gap between their social standing and that of the lawyer. Organizations enjoy a distinct advantage in civil litigation because of their superior access to attorneys. Most either have in-house attorneys who specialize in the organization's ordinary litigation or have such lawyers on a retainer. Moreover, organizations are more likely to be able to evaluate litigation in a cold, calculating manner devoid of the emotional weight that it often carries for individuals. For example, accident injuries often leave terrible emotional scars on their victims; however, for insurance companies they constitute ordinary business. Similarly, sexual harassment charges are exceptionally stressful to both the victimized employee and the alleged perpetrator, but for a corporation's personnel or legal department they are just another problem among many that require routine attention.

REMEDIES.

While resources enable disputants to enter the legal process, remedies lure people into courtrooms. The promise to rectify a situation is undesirable for at least one party to the dispute. The most common remedy in civil actions is **compensation** for damages. Plaintiffs typically sue for a substantially larger amount than they realistically expect to win, but that gives them room to negotiate. A claim for compensation may simply be based on economic loss. However, it sometimes requires placing a monetary value on damages for which there is no real market value—such as the pain resulting from a back injury, the anguish caused by slander, or the disruption created by the failure to deliver goods. Moreover, in some circumstances, a plaintiff may seek not only compensation for actual

---

[44]Marc Galanter, "Why the 'Haves' Come Out Ahead: Speculations on the Limits of Legal Change," *Law & Society Review* 9 (1974), pp. 95–160.
[45]Curran, supra, note 44.   [46]Curran, supra, note 44.

damages but also **punitive damages** to punish the defendant for a particularly wilful, malicious, or outrageous action. For instance, in 1993, plaintiffs sought and received $105.2 million in punitive damages after suing General Motors over the injuries caused by an exploding gasoline tank on their pickup truck which was constructed in such a way that its tank punctured in a sideways collision; the jury believed that General Motors had wilfully neglected to correct the truck's design after it knew the placement of the gas tank was dangerous.[47] There is much controversy over the proper size of punitive damages and the conditions that justify them, but they are an important aspect of a small number of civil cases, sometimes offering a huge incentive to go to court. However, it is also important to keep such extraordinary judgments in perspective. The average outcome of ordinary cases in the late 1970s was about $5000; it was somewhat lower in state courts than in federal courts (where the bigger cases usually go).[48] Thus, in routine cases, courts deliver rather modest compensation for relatively minor injuries. The potential for bonanzas is real but limited.

Another large class of remedies in civil suits requires defendants to alter behavior or changes their status. **Temporary restraining orders** and **injunctions,** for instance, require defendants to stop doing what the plaintiff finds objectionable or to restore the situation to the conditions that prevailed before the dispute arose. For instance, an injunction may order striking teachers back to their classrooms or restrain a business from trying to purchase a competitor.

In a third type of remedy, courts may change the parties' status. The most common status change is a **divorce,** which ends the legal marriage, rearranges property and parental relationships of the couple, and permits each of them to marry someone else. In the business world, the equivalent of divorce is **bankruptcy,** which rearranges the relationships between the business and its creditors. Creditors may be forced to take only a fraction of what is owed them as full payment of the debt; some creditors may find their loans eliminated entirely, leaving them with no claim for future payment; employees may find the court changing their employment contracts.

A fourth remedy is a change in public policy. A few plaintiffs have more grandiose motives than the settlement of a personal dispute in taking their disputes to court. Technically, they may only be seeking compensation or a halt to some specific practice; in reality, they wish to force a change in public policy. They want old rules applied to new situations or the acceptance of new rules. They use litigation as an alternative to persuading the legislature to change the law or prevailing on an executive to handle their problem in an advantageous way. The legal vehicle they use is to obtain a new interpretation of the law from the courts or, in rare cases, a ruling that an existing law is unconstitutional. Such changes in public policy are produced mostly by appellate courts, and we discuss them in detail in that context. However, they must begin in a trial court and some of the characteristics of the policy case are already apparent at the trial level. Policy litigants are likely to enjoy interest group backing, which is quite unusual in ordinary cases; they are much more focused on the legal issues than many ordi-

[47]Paul Applebohm, "GM Is Held Liable Over Fuel Tanks in Pick-up Trucks," *New York Times*, 5 February 1993, p. A1.
[48]Herbert M. Kritzer, *The Justice Broker: Lawyers and Ordinary Litigation* (New York: Oxford University Press, 1990), p. 136.

nary cases, which concentrate more on factual claims; the litigants are more motivated by ideological considerations than by personal circumstances.

Thus, we may view civil litigation as the product of disputants with resources activating court-provided remedies. The ways in which resources combine with remedies may be clarified through a description of the litigation process itself as well as by examining some examples of court suits. We first turn to the litigation process.

THE LITIGATION PROCESS

As prosecutors drive criminal cases, plaintiffs guide civil litigation, but the defense may play a much more active role than in many criminal cases. The civil litigation process is marked by many choices of forum and procedure, which produce a large number of variations.

Few choices of forum exist in the criminal justice process; a case goes to the court that has jurisdiction and generally there is only one. Thus if a federal law has been broken, it goes to federal court; if a state law is broken, it goes to the state court in whose area the crime allegedly occurred. Many more choices exist for civil disputes. The disputants often live, work, and have offices in different jurisdictions, and plaintiffs may file their case in any of them as well as in the place where the incident occurred. Consequently, plaintiffs have a choice between several state courts and if the dispute involves citizens of several states and a claim in excess of $50,000, they may also choose a federal district court. These choices have important consequences. While the substantive law on which the claim will be considered is often the same, the procedures are not. Some courts are much more permissive than others in permitting discovery. Court dockets vary in size; in some courts the claim may be tried within months, while in others it will linger for years. The expertise of court personnel also varies. It is widely believed that federal judges are more knowledgeable and skilled than many state judges. Some locales may appear to be more hospitable to the claims of a particular plaintiff or defendant, as when a company that plays a dominant role in a city's economy becomes involved in a court case.[49] Finally, if the plaintiff contemplates a jury trial, the choice of court determines the composition of the jury pool. If plaintiffs wish to include minority jurors, they choose a court where many minorities live; if they wish to have working-class jurors, they choose a court in a working-class community. Defendants are not entirely at the mercy of the plaintiff's forum choice—they may ask for the case to be transferred to another jurisdiction, but the choice belongs in the first instance with the plaintiff.

Let us initially think of civil litigation as a linear process. Informal negotiations typically precede the filing of a case. When a dispute is taken to court by the plaintiff, the plaintiff's lawyer files a complaint with the court clerk alleging the defendant committed some act for which there is a legal remedy and asking that that remedy be supplied by the court. This complaint is then served on the defendant, who has a set period

---

[49] A good example is the litigation involving the R.H. Robbins pharmaceutical company; it is described in Richard B. Sobol, *Bending the Law: The Story of the Dalkon Shield Bankruptcy* (Chicago : University of Chicago Press, 1991).

of time (often ten days) to respond. The defendant's response may simply be a denial or it may contain a countercomplaint, which in turn must be served on the plaintiff for a response. When the exchange of complaints is completed, the case is ready for processing.

The next steps involve preparation for trial, even though few civil cases go to trial. Each side asks the other for discovery by requesting the court to issue subpoenas. Thus, each side's lawyers collect documents and take oral testimony not only from their own clients but also from the opposing party. In the meantime, the case is called in court every month or so for a status report.

When both attorneys report that the case is ready for trial, many courts require that a **settlement conference** be held, sometimes in the presence of a judge. Settlement conferences have several objectives. They seek to narrow differences between the two sides by identifying those facts and legal points that are not in dispute; those matters can then be presented to the court by **stipulation** rather than by testimony from unnecessary witnesses. In addition, settlement conferences permit renewed negotiations in the hope that a settlement will be reached now that both parties have collected all their information and are better able to assess their chances of winning. Many cases are settled at this stage.

However, some disputes go to trial, and trial procedure is quite different than in criminal cases. Jury trials are much more prevalent in civil cases than in the criminal process; in tort cases half or more of all trials typically involve a jury.[50] However, the size of the jury may be smaller than 12, and only a majority, not unanimity, is usually required for a verdict. Moreover, the burden of proof is not "beyond a reasonable doubt" as in criminal cases but usually only "the preponderance of the evidence." At the end of the trial, the judge or jury announces the judgment.

We know very little about the factors that lead some cases to go to trial rather than being settled. Several factors are self-evident. To go to trial, plaintiffs must have sufficient funds to pay their attorney or their claim must be potentially large enough to warrant the attorney risking a contingent fee. In divorce cases and a few others, parties generally insist on trials only in the most bitter disputes after strenuous efforts by attorneys and court officials to settle the case have failed; such trials often represent emotions gone amok. In addition, the larger the claim the more likely the case will go to trial, because the stakes are high enough to justify a large investment by lawyers—plaintiffs are unlikely to forego a large potential gain while defendants are unlikely to concede a substantial loss. Where one of the parties is a large organization, trials provide a way to protect bureaucratic decision makers from the personal responsibility of approving a large claim; after a trial, they can tell their superiors the court forced them to do so. Finally, claimants who are motivated by the desire for a policy change will almost always seek a trial because only by having a trial will they gain access to the appellate courts that can pronounce policy for a considerable section of the country.

The civil trial ends with a decision that either imposes a judgment against one of the parties or denies the plaintiff's request for a remedy. When juries make the decision,

---

[50]Brian Ostrom, David Rottman, and Roger Hanson, "What Are Tort Awards Really Like: The Untold Story from the State Courts," *Law & Policy 14* (1992), pp. 77–106.

they do so in the form dictated by the judge's instructions, which often consist of a se-ries of questions the jury must answer and which taken together constitute a decision for or against the plaintiff. Bench trials end with a decision from the judge in favor of one party or the other. Most cases end simply with such a decision; judges do not rou-tinely write lengthy opinions to justify their decisions and more rarely yet are such opin-ions published. The larger the stakes, the more likely it is that the judge's decision will be accompanied by a signed opinion that sets out the reasons for the outcome. How-ever, the verbatim record of the case is available to litigants if they pay for transcribing the court reporter's notes, and in that record, the judge's decisions on motions made to the court as well as other comments may provide clues to the basis of the decision.

This conception of civil litigation as a linear process however, oversimplifies the process. Negotiations and court proceedings are not neatly segregated into discrete stages. It is true that negotiations generally occur before a case is filed and just before the trial. However, they may also continue intermittently throughout the course of the case. Lawyers often go to court to seek a ruling on a disputed legal point or to force the production of evidence as part of their negotiation strategy. At the same time, negotia-tors often work under the shadow of what might happen if the case goes to trial. Thus, cases bounce between court and negotiations and sometimes negotiations and court ses-sions occur almost simultaneously.

The many possible combinations of resources with remedies in civil litigation can be seen best by considering concrete examples of remedies in cases with minimal re-sources and others with substantial resources. We begin by considering disputes in which the litigants seek a change of relationships. Divorces constitute one very large set of such cases where the disputants usually possess only modest resources. We contrast those cases with commercial bankruptcy, where very large sums of money are often at stake and the disputants are able to invest considerable resources into the dispute.

Divorce creates a new relationship between spouses.[51] It changes their legal obliga-tions to each other and to their children. Husbands may be obligated to support their former spouse (called **alimony** or **maintenance**),[52] but the obligations are specified in a court decree rather than in the loose verbal understandings common to ongoing mar-riages. The home, its furnishings, and all other property must be divided. In addition, divorce alters the relationships of parents to their children; in many cases, the divorce decree specifies the precise times that parents will spend with them, each parent's au-thority, and their precise financial obligations.

Few couples contest the divorce itself when their marriage fails, largely because current law does not permit it. All states have no-fault statutes, which under various conditions allow one spouse to end the marriage simply by declaring irreconcilable dif-ferences with the other. Rather, disputes center on finances (especially ownership of the family home, maintenance payments to the wife, and child support) and child cus-tody. In most cases, the lawyers involved are unlikely to be divorce specialists. The hus-

[51]Eleanor E. Maccoby and Robert H. Mnookin, *Dividing the Child* (Cambridge, Mass: Harvard University Press, 1992), chapter 1.
[52]Technically, maintenance is now gender neutral and women may be required to make payments to their former husbands. In practice, however, this almost never occurs. Almost all maintenance payments are from the former husband to his ex-spouse.

band and wife each usually hire their own attorney who charges an hourly fee but who requires a retainer constituting a large portion of the anticipated cost before taking the case. Because the fees come out of their joint assets, the couple has a shared interest in minimizing legal costs. This common interest together with the parties' remaining emotional ties often suffice to produce a negotiated settlement that is then presented to a judge in a formal hearing. The hearing itself is an empty ritual. In many instances, the court requires brief testimony to establish the breakdown of the marriage, but because divorce is available in every state without proving the other spouse is at fault, the testimony is only a formality to establish on the record that the requirements of the statute have been met. Judges then glance at the proposed decree to make sure all required elements are present. For instance, they confirm that every divorce involving children includes provisions for child support and custody. Having ascertained that the contents appear to meet required guidelines, they usually sign the decree without considering its contents in detail.

In many divorce courts, a dozen cases may be scheduled for a single morning, each allotted ten to fifteen minutes. One attorney told me that as a young lawyer he was advised by a more experienced colleague that he was doing something wrong if an uncontested divorce proceeding took more than seven minutes. This courtroom pace rivals that of misdemeanor courts. However, the atmosphere of divorce courts is quite different. Only the participants in the case being heard sit in the courtroom; everyone else waits outside. The parties are treated courteously even if hurriedly.

In rare instances, divorce negotiations fail. Such cases lead to full-blown trials but only on a limited number of issues, usually some part of the financial arrangement or the custody arrangements for their children. When that occurs, the ritual of the uncontested hearing is replaced by a formal trial before a judge (and sometimes a jury) with testimony from the husband, wife, friends, accountants, and, if custody is contested, mental health professionals who provide opinions about the children's welfare. In some cases, the children themselves are represented by a third attorney (generally called **guardian ad litem**) appointed by the court to look after their interests.

Several characteristics are important for our understanding of divorce cases. Usually, the parties come to court with fairly equal and modest resources. Only in a few cases is one spouse (usually the husband) much better endowed than the other; usually both can tap the couple's marital assets to pay for legal costs. Perhaps the one resource that is often unequal is time: if one spouse is impatient to remarry and wants the proceedings to come to a quick conclusion, he or she is at a decided disadvantage. A second significant characteristic is that both parties to a divorce know each other well, and if they have children, they have a basis for continuing their relationship, albeit in a different manner. Consequently, much of the process is directed toward altering current arrangements about money and children in such a way that the two can still cooperate in parenting their children. A third important characteristic is that in most instances, little money is involved and there are minimal rewards for heavy investment of time and effort by attorneys. Consequently, divorce cases are generally handled in a routine fashion resembling the manner in which prosecutors and defenders process common criminal cases.

Despite the fact that little money is involved, the stakes are high. What is involved is almost entirely psychological and emotional. In many divorces, one party feels wronged and seeks some form of vindication even though the law demands that questions of fault be laid aside. In addition, many fathers and mothers are unhappy about altering their parental roles and fight over the children. The State finds its stake with these emotional issues in what otherwise might be handled as privately as most other family matters. The State has an interest in seeing that emotions do not lead to settlements that severely disadvantage one party or the children. Moreover, the State has a strong interest in facilitating acceptable outcomes so that violence is avoided. It is no accident that when a shooting occurs in a courthouse, it often involves a divorce case. Thus, judges insist that the public norms of the divorce statute guide divorce settlements, and they impose them quite explicitly if issues go to trial.

Commercial bankruptcy also alters relationships, but the relationships are very different. Bankruptcy is a remedy available only in federal courts, which alters the obligations between debtors and their creditors. If debtors can show they are unable to pay their creditors and if no fraud is involved, the court may force the bankrupt petitioner to reorganize the business or liquidate it. In a reorganization, old debts are paid at a vastly reduced level—often only a few cents on the dollar—and the company's management may be replaced with a new team. If the company is liquidated, its business is closed, all its assets are sold, and creditors get whatever money they can from the proceeds. During the bankruptcy proceeding, which often takes years, the court protects the company against creditors, who cannot seize any of its assets or take any other measure to force payment.

The restructuring of relationships through bankruptcy can be as dramatic as in a divorce. For instance, when Continental Airlines sought bankruptcy in 1983, it won the court's permission to sever its union contracts.[53] Unilaterally, the company imposed new working conditions and wage scales, and the workers had no choice but to quit if they did not accept the new conditions. Similarly, the Johns Manville Company, a manufacturer of asbestos products, used bankruptcy to reorganize and protect itself from the almost limitless claims filed by victims of asbestos-related diseases.[54] Banks and other creditors find the assets securing their loans are suddenly frozen and unavailable for forcing repayment. Such creditors are forced either to renegotiate their loans at lower interest and longer payment terms or accept partial payments.

Bankruptcy proceedings take place before federal bankruptcy judges. On one side is the company that seeks the protection of the bankruptcy law; it is almost always represented by lawyers who specialize in bankruptcy law and who prepare the petition in great detail. On the other side are all the creditors, many of whom may also be substantial corporations represented by experienced attorneys, but some of whom may be individuals represented by solo practitioners unaccustomed to bankruptcy court. As in divorce, the parties rarely dispute the bankruptcy itself. Rather, they argue over the specific provisions of the bankruptcy: whether the company should be reorganized or liquidated, how much money will be available to creditors, and who among them should be paid first. As in divorce, most of these issues are settled by negotiations be-

---

[53]Anna Cifelli, "Management by Bankruptcy," *Fortune* 108 (October 1983), pp. 69–72; Arnold R. Weber, "Bankruptcy Ruling Changes Labor Relations Climate," *Dun's Business Month* 123 (April 1984), p. 83.
[54]Paul Brodeur, *Outrageous Misconduct: The Asbestos Industry on Trial* (New York: Pantheon, 1985).

cause almost everyone has an interest in a speedy resolution. However, some commercial bankruptcies are so complicated they linger in court for many years.

Moreover, like divorce, the restructuring of debt in commercial bankruptcies involves parties with ongoing relationships that may persist. Suppliers, workers, and lenders all are likely to have worked with the bankrupt company for a substantial period before the bankruptcy; many of them must continue their relationship in order to protect their interests. These past and ongoing relationships affect negotiations in fundamental ways. As in divorce, they often prevent total warfare between the parties because each has an interest in the others' survival.

However, commercial bankruptcies differ from divorces in that most of the parties have considerable resources, with some likely to be substantially richer than others. Suppliers to the bankrupt firm, for instance, are often much smaller than the bankrupt firm; they face the dilemma of calculating how much good money to throw after the bad debt. These cases almost always involve substantial attorneys fees because the issues are complicated corporate finance, and the creditors have to fight each other as well as the debtor to get their share of the payments. Thus, even creditors with substantial resources may find it difficult to resist an agreed settlement that is not very favorable to them simply because they do not wish to invest ever larger amounts of money to finance continuing litigation. Moreover, bankruptcy proceedings are routinely more complicated than divorce because they involve more than two parties. On one side is the bankrupt company; on the other is a horde of creditors with conflicting interests.

As in divorce cases, the State has a significant stake in the restructuring of commercial relationships through bankruptcy. One of the justifications for the bankruptcy remedy is to provide a second chance to failed ventures. It promotes the entrepreneurship needed to establish new enterprises, facilitates the ending of business ventures that have outlived their potential for profit, and provides an orderly way to manage the distribution of assets among many competing claimants. In all these ways, bankruptcy plays an important role in the maintenance of the marketplace.

A second type of remedy is compensation for damages. These comprise the bulk of civil court cases and range from very small claims to requests for millions of dollars. They may involve claims for broken contracts, disputes over the ownership of property, or injuries suffered from an accident or carelessness. We examine both relatively small claims and large ones in the context of injury claims (called **torts**). They differ from the restructuring of relationships in important ways.

Even cases involving claims for relatively small amounts of money may involve a repeat player as the defendant, because most situations involve insurance. However, damage suits resulting from accidents or carelessness often involve parties having little or no prior acquaintance, no future relationship, and quite unequal resources. These characteristics affect the manner in which trial courts handle these disputes.

Such cases are among the most common on civil court dockets. For instance, when someone claims damages as the result of an automobile accident, the claimant usually faces a repeat player—the other driver's insurance company. As with divorces, most such claims are negotiated because both sides find it advantageous to minimize their transaction costs. However, some claims go to trial either because the claim is too large for the insurance company's claim adjustor to approve it or because there is a genuine dispute over liability or the amount of damages.

The victim in such accidents often does not hire an attorney, but instead negotiates with the insurance company directly. If the victim does retain an attorney, it may be one who handles only occasional personal injury suits and who takes the case on a contingent fee. However, being represented by an attorney has been shown to be quite advantageous to victims,[55] for even attorneys who take only occasional personal injury cases are likely to be more knowledgeable than the ordinary victim. Attorneys know the importance of documentary evidence and can guide clients in the collection of receipts to substantiate damage claims. They understand rules governing liability, a subject that seems arcane to most victims. Attorneys are likely to know the going rate for accidents of various degrees of seriousness and can gauge the insurance company's payment offer. Moreover, retaining an attorney signals the insurance company that the victim is serious about pursuing the claim and might go to court over it.

Plaintiffs may be willing to take the case to trial when the expense of the trial will be paid out of the judgment. They may hope for sympathy from jurors. From the attorney's perspective, however, that increases the uncertainty of the outcome and their risk. Attorneys are often not eager to go to trial because they might lose everything, while a settlement would provide them a more modest but certain fee. The situation of insurance companies is quite different. Insurance companies are prototypical repeat players who can assign court cases to staff attorneys whose job is to litigate such cases. However, even under those circumstances, they risk considerable losses not only in covering the expenses of their legal department staff but also because they may be held liable for a much higher judgment than they offered in the settlement.

Tort trials hinge on factual issues, which involve fitting the details of the incident into the mold of the law. The first question concerns liability for the damages. The question of fault is often complex because both parties may have been careless. It is often settled by the police officer at the scene of the accident who decides to give a ticket to one or the other. Once liability has been determined (and it may be shared by both parties), the amount of damages must be determined. Damage to physical objects such as a car are simple; body shop estimates provide the relevant data. However, damages for injuries, pain and suffering, and lost wages are much more difficult to quantify. Where parties cannot agree on these matters, judges and juries provide authoritative answers by applying rules of the law to the circumstances of the accident.

Tort claims larger than the typical automobile accident are much more likely to reach the trial stage. This is true, for instance, of medical malpractice claims. Problems sometimes arise in medical treatment. Where the patient has not been cured or dies the physician or hospital might be at fault. The legal issues are not much different from those in automobile accident cases, but the facts are likely to be much more controversial. Diagnoses may be contested; aggressive versus conservative treatment may be debated; the defendant physician may claim that the failure to heal was due to other causes, such as the patient's resistance to treatment or some additional illness that complicated treatment.

[55]H. Laurence Ross, *Settled Out of Court: The Social Process of Insurance Claims Adjustment* (Chicago: Aldine, 1970).

Two major differences exist in the court outcomes of automobile accident and medical malpractice torts. The first is that plaintiffs win much more frequently suing over automobile accidents. Approximately two-thirds of the plaintiffs won automobile accident cases in a study of such litigation during 1989 in 27 different locations, but only 30 percent of the plaintiffs won in medical malpractice suits. However, when the plaintiff prevailed, the median judgments were twice as large for medical malpractice ($39,550) as for auto accidents ($19,157).[56]

Typically, tort cases bring together strangers with unequal resources. However, attorneys mitigate the effect of both factors. While it is true that no prior or future relationship exists between most tort plaintiffs and defendants, plaintiffs' attorneys often have continuing relationships with claims adjustors for the defendant insurance companies.[57] They are in a position comparable to that of the criminal defense attorney who must deal on a continuing basis with the prosecutor for a succession of clients. In tort cases, attorneys find themselves negotiating with a handful of insurance companies that dominate the market in their locale. They come to know their opponents in these companies and recognize that today's intransigence may result in more difficult negotiations in a future case. Thus, while the lack of relationship between the victim and perpetrator of the tort hinders negotiations, the mediating role of attorneys promotes it. However, attorneys do not necessarily overcome the inequality between many plaintiffs and defendants. Insurance company defendants almost always have greater resources than plaintiffs. They have more money and a more experienced staff; they know the court personnel and their idiosyncrasies; they can afford to be more patient. The ability of plaintiffs to hire attorneys on a contingent fee basis tends to lessen these inequalities but most often does not eliminate them. In these circumstances, trial courts operate more to the advantage of corporate defendants than individual plaintiffs. However, if plaintiffs can carry their case to trial and win a judgment, juries tend to give larger awards to individual plaintiffs suing corporations than when both parties are individuals.[58]

Cases brought to court to challenge a public policy constitute by far the smallest set of civil cases, even though they have the greatest visibility and immediate impact on the political arena. This is a use of the courts that is far more prominent in the United States than in most other countries. It has changed policy on such matters as the law on race relations,[59] the manner in which members of legislatures are elected,[60] the right of women to have an abortion,[61] the manner in which prisons are run,[62] the recitation of prayers in public schools,[63] and many other aspects of public life.

[56]Ostrom et al, supra, note 51.   [57]Ross, supra, note 55.
[58]Ostrom et al, supra, note 51.
[59]Richard Kluger, *Simple Justice* (New York: Vintage, 1975).
[60]*Baker v. Carr*, 369 U.S. 186 (1962).
[61]Marian Faux, *Roe v. Wade: The Untold Story of the Landmark Supreme Court Decision That Made Abortion Legal* (New York: Macmillan, 1988).
[62]William A. Taggart, "Redefining the Power of the Federal Judiciary: The Impact of Court-Ordered Prison Reform on State Expenditures for Corrections," *Law & Society Review* 23 (1989), pp. 241–272.
[63]Edward Keynes with Randall K. Miller, *The Court vs. Congress: Prayer, Busing, and Abortion* (Durham: Duke University Press, 1989).

Disputants without resources ordinarily cannot use the courts to challenge public policy because such cases require the investment of substantial resources. Such cases usually go to trial because settling them out of court would preclude an appeal to a higher court whose ruling would generally have a much greater impact on the agency administering the challenged policy. Further, these cases require an unusual amount of legal research to substantiate the illegality of the challenged policy; much time and money must be devoted to documenting the way the policy was adopted and its impact. They require the plaintiffs' willingness to withstand a great deal of public attention, including harassment from opponents. Plaintiffs must also have considerable patience, since it is likely that the policy will not be altered until an appeals court has given its decision; three to five years is not an unusual time span for such cases.

Interest group participation is one of the earmarks of such cases. Ordinary people may be the plaintiffs in seeking school desegregation or the liberalization of abortion policy, but ordinary people lack the resources to pursue their objective in the courts. Interest groups provide legal expertise and the funding necessary to carry the case through trial and to appeal. However, the groups themselves rarely act as the plaintiffs; rather, they recruit men and women who have been victims of the challenged policy. The victims' particular circumstances then become the basis for the policy challenge. This process is portrayed vividly by Marian Faux in her account of the manner in which Sarah Weddington and Linda Coffee recruited the plaintiffs in *Roe v. Wade*, the decision that legalized abortion in the United States.[64] They sought a pregnant woman whose circumstances would make her an appealing plaintiff and would not muddy the issues by extraneous issues (such as charges of immorality). They selected the plaintiff because her story—that she had been raped—met those specifications. The plaintiff could not finance such a case and did not have the legal expertise to carry it to a successful conclusion. Weddington and Coffee, however, were committed feminist lawyers who had connections with groups that supported a woman's right to choose whether to have an abortion.

The trial phase of policy-making cases has not been studied extensively. However, from the limited reports that exist,[65] it seems that successful efforts require much more care in laying out the legal basis for the claim than ordinary cases for compensation or restructuring of relationships; in ordinary cases, attorneys simply need to show that existing law applies to their clients' circumstances. However, in suits where plaintiffs challenge policies, they often ask the courts to interpret existing laws in new ways. To succeed, they must convince the courts that the old interpretation needs to be changed because it violates some other legal principle that should be given priority. Thus, the plaintiffs' attorneys in *Brown v. Board of Education*, the 1954 school desegregation case, had to convince courts that their prior interpretations of the Constitution permitting racial segregation in fact violated the provisions of the Fourteenth Amendment. Likewise, Weddington and Coffee had to convince the courts that laws criminalizing abortion were unconstitutional.

Such cases bring an entirely different set of disputes to trial courts. Policy disputes do not center on the claims of individual plaintiffs, although that is how they are framed

---

[64]Faux, supra, note 61.   [65]Faux, supra, note 61.

in the court case. Rather, plaintiffs implicitly or explicitly represent an entire class of persons with grievances; they bring to court a conflict that differs little from social conflicts that come to legislatures for resolution. Trial courts often reject these claims because they feel constrained to adhere to established interpretations of the law rather than to forge new ones. Some trial judges have little experience in working through the thickets of legal doctrines; such cases are rare in the trial courts, and a judge could spend an entire career on the bench without encountering one. Nor do trial judges have the support staff that their appellate counterparts enjoy to embark on that task.

Disputants seeking injunctive relief—seeking to stop an action that threatens them harm or the reinstatement of some prior condition—are also quite varied. Relatively few are ordinary people with ordinary troubles. Many are large businesses seeking to force the performance of a contract or to halt a competitor's action, and the stakes are often high. One example of such litigation involved the Paramount Communications takeover in late 1993. Two conglomerates sought to buy Paramount. When Paramount's board of directors favored one of them, the other went to court to obtain a court order prohibiting such favoritism. The Delaware courts, where the suit was filed, sided with the challenger, and the bidding subsequently escalated.[66] Many suits seeking policy change or court intervention in political affairs also request injunctive relief. One example of such a suit was the action taken by Chicago school officials in the fall of 1993 to stave off closing the schools due to a budgetary crisis. They went to the federal district court for a temporary restraining order halting the invocation of a state law that required a balanced budget.[67] This permitted schools to remain open while the legislature passed a new bill providing sufficient funds for the school system to operate.[68] Injunctive relief is a powerful remedy and one frequently sought by those who wish to influence public policy through litigation, for it places the courts squarely in the policy arena as they tell other agencies what they must or must not do.

Trial Judges

How trial courts impose social control and maintain their legitimacy rests largely on the shoulders of their judges. Conventional descriptions of trial courts sometimes make it appear that judges alone make trial court decisions. We have already noted that they are but one of many participants in the courtroom workgroup. Prosecutors, plaintiff's attorneys, defense attorneys, and court support staff also play important roles in molding trial court decisions. Nevertheless, judges wield substantial authority; they bear ultimate responsibility for their court's decisions. Who they are and how they reach their positions are important for understanding the work of trial courts.

Who becomes a judge depends, first, on who wants the job. In every locale, there is a distinct hierarchy of judicial positions. Federal district judges have more prestige than

---

[66]Edward P. Welch and Andrew J. Turezyn, "Courts Took Quick Action in Paramount," *National Law Journal* 16, 10 January 1994, p. 20.
[67]Penny Roberts, "Federal Judge Opens Schools Doors," *Chicago Tribune*, 14 September 1993, p. 1.
[68]Edward Walsh, "Illinois Officials Scramble to Stave off Another School Shutdown," *Washington Post*, 11 December 1993, p. A3.

state court judges, and those judges in state courts who handle more serious matters have more prestige than judges in minor trial courts. Not every lawyer wishes to become a judge. The most successful lawyers earn many times the salary of trial judges. Most of the work of trial judges is more routine than one might find in private practice, particularly in many big cities. Consequently, trial judges tend to come from the middle echelon of lawyers, for whom a judicial appointment is often very attractive. Judgeships pay good salaries often exceeding $75,000 (in 1993 dollars); the job has, as we shall see, a great deal of stability. Retirement and other fringe benefits are often generous. These are strong attractions for attorneys who work alone or in small firms where earning a living may be a continuous struggle.

Institutional factors are also important. In the United States being a judge is not a career young people can choose, working their way up the ladder as they may do in business. Rather, it first requires a commitment to a legal career, because almost all trial judges are lawyers. Some lawyers then become judges in midcareer, usually when they are in their 40s and have worked as an attorney for a decade or more. Moreover, trial judges must come from the state in which they serve; often they must come from the community they serve. Thus, lawyers who wish to become a judge in New York must work there; lawyers from other states will not be considered.

A second set of constraints arises from the many procedures used for selecting trial judges.[69] Who becomes a judge depends on whom one must know to get the position. Two broad categories of selection procedures, each with many variants, exist. In one, a chief executive makes the decision, although that choice may be constrained by a nominating process involving others. In the second, judges are chosen by elections, although the voters' choices may be constrained by the way in which the election is conducted.

No chief executive enjoys unfettered choice in selecting trial judges. The Constitution gives the president the power to nominate federal judges, but because appointment is contingent on confirmation by the Senate, in practice the president shares these appointment powers with senators. Senators make recommendations for filling judicial vacancies in their states. A custom known as **senatorial courtesy** dictates that if the senator belongs to the same political party as the president, the president must defer to the senator's choice. Even if the senator is of the opposite party, presidents often use judicial appointments to gain the senator's assistance with legislative matters. Consequently, most federal district judges—the judges who staff the federal trial courts—win appointment because of their connections with senators or other local party leaders. This means they must have been supporters of their senator, and often they will have worked in his or her election campaigns. It is rare for someone from an opposing party faction to win such an appointment. Once senators make their recommendation, the Justice Department investigates the candidate to determine whether anything in the candidate's background might embarrass the president or disqualify the nominee for a judgeship. The American Bar Association also evaluates and ranks the candidate as ei-

---

[69]Herbert Jacob, *Justice in America: Courts, Lawyers, and the Judicial Process*, 4th ed. (Boston: Little, Brown, 1984), pp. 113– 127; Philip L. Dubois, *From Bench to Ballot: Judicial Elections and the Quest for Accountability* (Austin: University of Texas Press, 1980), pp. 1–35.

ther qualified or unqualified. Barring complications, the name is sent to the Senate and in most instances receives only perfunctory examination by the Senate Judiciary Committee before winning confirmation by a vote on the floor of the Senate as a whole. Federal judges serve for life, unless they commit an offense that leads to impeachment by Congress.

The selection of the nation's more than 27,000 trial judges for state courts follows a bewildering array of procedures. As of 1992,[70] fourteen states appoint trial judges, but their choices are constrained differently than those of the president. Some governors have the power to choose without a constraint like senatorial courtesy. Political practice varies considerably in these states; in many, the governor uses such appointments to reward their campaign supporters; in others, they use the appointments to reward legislators for their support of the governor's legislative initiatives. In many of these states, however, a nominating commission proposes a list of candidates from which the governor must choose. However, the term of a trial judge at the state level is often as brief as four or six years, and therefore the appointment is not as desirable as a federal judgeship. Moreover, many gubernatorial appointments are made to fill vacancies only until the next election. The appointment merely gives the recipient the advantage of incumbency in the election; it does not assure long tenure.

In at least six states, governors appoint trial judges according to a so-called **merit plan.** Here, the governor's power of appointment is not only attenuated by having to make the appointment from a list prepared by a merit commission, but the candidate must also stand for approval in an election after having served a brief time as a judge. The politics of this appointment process is obscured by its several layers. However, as Watson and Downing have observed for Missouri, the merit system tends to give particular influence to the organized bar.[71] Lawyers who belong to the state bar association and sit on the nominating commission have exceptional influence, while others are excluded. Persons active in electoral politics are less likely to be chosen as judges by such merit plans. Instead, they may favor lawyers who have been active in the organizational politics of the legal profession.

In most[72] of the other states, those who wish to become judge must run in an election. Two types of elections are used. The first, election on a **partisan ballot** (used by eleven states in 1992), is in many ways like the elections used to fill other government offices. A person seeking to become a trial judge must first win his or her party's nomination. In some places, this is done by winning a primary election, in other places by winning the endorsement of a nominating convention. The nominee then competes for the right to hold office with the nominees of other parties in a general election. The second type of election, a **nonpartisan ballot,** was used by seventeen states in 1992. Candidates in these elections are not identified by party affiliation. To be placed on the ballot, a candidate needs only a petition signed by the requisite number of voters. The candidate with the largest number of votes wins the election. Both partisan and non-

---

[70]*The Book of the States 1992–1993* (Lexington, Ky.: Council of State Governments, 1992), pp. 216, 233–235.
[71]Richard Watson and Rondal G. Downing, *The Politics of the Bench and Bar: Judicial Selection Under the Missouri Nonpartisan Court Plan* (New York: Wiley, 1969).
[72]In two states, South Carolina and Virginia, legislatures select judges.

partisan judicial elections normally occur in obscurity.[73] Even when they coincide with presidential or congressional campaigns, such races rarely attract any notice above the din of the other election contests. When judicial elections occur at other times (for instance, in the spring when municipal elections may be held), voters tend to pay as little attention to them as to the other contests.

The electoral process generally favors incumbents and candidates who have name recognition as the result of prior public service or electioneering for other offices. Judges on partisan ballots are slightly affected by landslide results at the top of the ticket, but in recent elections, presidential victories have not been sufficient to elect local officials of the same party in areas generally not hospitable to them. For instance, President Reagan's landslide election in 1984 did not bring about the election of many local Republicans in areas that were not traditional party strongholds, and President Clinton's narrow election margin in 1992 carried few Democrats into office outside traditional areas of Democratic strength.

Despite the low visibility of judicial elections, they provide opportunities for eliminating judges who are deemed unsuitable by the electorate. This occurs in many different electoral contexts. In Texas, for instance, gay rights' advocates managed to defeat the bid of a Dallas trial judge for an appellate judgeship by publicizing his giving a light sentence to a convicted murderer; he had said publicly that he did so because the victims were homosexual.[74] However, such outcomes are rare. Elections involving trial judges rarely capture public attention; most sitting judges remain secure in their positions despite the formality of periodically facing the electorate.

Even though few judges lose elections, they remain sensitive to the possibility. With the help of their colleagues, they may seek to avoid controversial cases in the year before reelection and attend more closely to community sentiments. When judgeships are filled by appointment from chief executives, the courts are sometimes packed with persons reflecting the president's or governor's particular policy preferences on the grounds that their electoral mandate justifies placing men and women on the bench who agree with their policy views. For instance, Presidents Reagan and Bush appointed many lawyers who were known for their conservative views; before them, President Carter made a point of selecting many more women and minority group members to the federal bench than had any other president.[75] Thus, even appointive judges have links to popular policy preferences.

The collective portrait of the trial judges selected by these procedures has some distinctive characteristics.[76] The vast majority are white men. Fewer African Americans, Hispanics, and other minorities win judgeships than their proportion of the population would lead us to expect; that is caused in part by the low numbers of minorities in the legal profession and their lack of the kinds of political contacts needed to succeed in the quest for a trial judgeship. Women are underrepresented for some of the same reasons,

---

[73]Dubois, supra, note 69, pp. 36–62.

[74]"Gay Rights Groups Hail Defeat of Judge in Texas," *New York Times,* 4 December 1992, p. B8.

[75]Sheldon Goldman, "Bush's Judicial Legacy: The Final Imprint," *Judicature* 76 (April–May 1993), pp. 282–297.

[76]These are best described for the federal trial courts. See Goldman, supra, note 75; Henry, M.L. Jr., et al., *The Success of Women and Minorities in Achieving Judicial Office* (New York: Fund for Modern Courts, 1985).

although the number of women becoming trial judges has grown more rapidly than is the case for ethnic minorities. Most trial judgeships, regardless of the selection system, are filled by people with experience in electoral politics either as an elected official, as a failed candidate, or as a worker or contributor in another's campaigns.

Thus, the selection of judges creates important links between trial courts and the local political arena. Those links reinforce the ties courts have as government agencies. While this, the third branch, is constitutionally separate, it nevertheless remains a branch of the government tree, and its chief officials—the judges—often have affinity ties with officials in the other two branches. Those ties are particularly helpful to the courts when they go to legislative bodies for their budget. Like all other government agencies, trial courts need money to operate. They receive their funds from city councils, county boards, state legislatures, and Congress. In every instance, they must compete with other agencies for funds. Although court requests constitute only a tiny portion of the total budget of any government, they are often carefully scrutinized by lawmakers. The budgetary process provides occasions for lawmakers to voice their displeasure with judicial performance. Many local judges suffer from inadequate facilities and support personnel because they cannot convince county boards or state legislators to build new courtrooms or provide sufficient clerks. As with judicial elections, the budgetary process occurs in relative obscurity. However, while it provides legislators with leverage over trial courts, it does not open the judiciary to more generalized popular pressure.

Another potential link, but one that is unwanted by most judges, may be found in the procedures that exist for removal of judges. Because judicial independence is central to protecting the disinterestedness of courts, it is difficult to remove judges. Their terms of office are usually longer than those of other elected officials, and it is rare for them to be barred from seeking reelection or reappointment. They enjoy a tenure which is quite similar to that of civil servants and can be removed from office only for cause and after special procedures have been followed. Federal trial judges hold office "for life during good behavior" in the words of the Constitution (Article 3, Sec. 1) and may be removed only by **impeachment.** Impeachment requires first a vote in the House of Representatives to impeach (i.e., to charge) the judge with specific offenses and then a trial before the Senate in which a majority vote of the Senate is needed to remove the judge from office. Recently, both the impeachment proceedings in the House and the trial in the Senate have occurred before special committees, but a vote of each house remains necessary. It is a cumbersome procedure used only for the most serious offenses, and very few federal judges are removed by it. Moreover, Congress cannot punish judges by reducing their salaries while they hold office; it can only refuse to raise them.

State judges face more streamlined procedures when charged with abusing their office. While impeachment remains available in many States, most also have **disciplinary commissions** composed of other judges and sometimes lay people who hear charges and mete out punishment. These commissions often do less than remove errant judges; they may simply rebuke them. Unlike legislative bodies involved in impeachment proceedings, disciplinary commissions are outside the ordinary ebb and flow of partisan politics. In addition, many states provide that judges automatically lose their position if they are convicted of a felony.

Another means of removing judges in some states is the **recall election.** A specified percentage of voters must sign a recall petition before such an election is called. If the petition succeeds, the targeted judge runs against his or her record, with the electorate voting on whether the judge should be removed.

Despite the dizzying array of procedures used in the United States to select and remove judges, several common features help assure both the social control and legitimation functions that judges must perform. All of the selection procedures contain features that minimize the selection of mavericks. Would-be judges must often participate in political affairs before they can hope to win a judgeship; political apprenticeship serves to screen those who are not reliably committed to mainstream values. Even when judicial aspirants avoid political service, they always go through the socialization process involved in law school and a legal career. They are very likely to be well known to their fellow lawyers. Thus, it is unlikely that persons will be selected who do not adhere to most of the values that the regime relies on the judiciary to enforce.

Legitimation is served by judicial independence, for independence provides at least a veneer of disinterestedness; judicial independence assure litigants that the judge is not obligated to an interest involved in the litigation. Several features of the selection and removal process reinforce judicial independence. Terms are longer than for most other high officials and no term limits apply; consequently, trial judges do not have to worry about employment after their service on the bench. Tenure is also long; it is difficult to remove judges and, for the most part, judges need not look over their shoulders to see who might object to their decisions.

The price that is sometimes paid by these selection systems is in the quality of men and women who are recruited for trial judgeships. They do not come from the elite echelons of the legal profession, but perhaps they need not do so. The job of a trial judge is not as intellectually demanding as a position as leading partner of a large law firm. Nor is the pay as high. Moreover, it has proven very difficult to measure the quality of judges because judging is not simply a mechanical task for which one can give a test; it requires such qualities as concern, maturity, empathy, balance, judgment, and decisiveness, which display themselves over time but which are not easily quantified. Whether changes in selection would produce "better" judges thus remains an open and frequently debated question.

Conclusion

Trial courts play a significant role in governance. They are the principal means by which governments impose social control on their citizens. That is their foremost task. They do so in two quite different contexts. First, courts impose social control by enforcing the criminal law. Those who are found to violate the law pay with the punishment trial courts impose. The purpose is manifold: to deter others from violating the law, to incapacitate offenders, and to deter offenders from repeating their crime. Second, courts impose social control by enforcing legal norms in the settlement of disputes. While most disputes are settled out of court in private negotiations, the threat of court affects the terms of many settlements. Not only do the courts provide a forum in which disputes may be resolved peaceably, they also impose norms that have been adopted through the legislative process.

A second function of trial courts is to ensure that citizens are treated fairly by each other and by other government agencies. In imposing social control, courts bear a heavy responsibility to appear evenhanded in their actions. Americans expect to have an opportunity to voice their version of the events that led them to court; they demand that the judge have no personal interest in the outcome of the case; they expect that the rules of the court will be applied equally to both sides of the controversy; they expect to be treated respectfully. In short, they expect due process of the law. When courts fall short of these demands, they lose some of their legitimacy and may undermine the legitimacy of the government of which they are a part.

Explicit policy making is very much a tertiary role of trial courts. It is rare for trial courts to announce a new interpretation of the law; for the most part, they follow interpretations established by appellate courts. However, almost every case an appellate court uses to announce a new policy begins with trial court proceedings. Sometimes those cases are indistinguishable from other proceedings; that occurs most frequently in criminal cases which later blossom into celebrated policy cases because they exemplify a policy issue appellate attorneys or appellate courts themselves wish to address. Other cases, particularly those traversing the civil courts, begin with more attentiveness to legal issues and more involvement by interest groups than ordinary cases.

There is some controversy among scholars over when trial courts make policy in their routine administration of justice. A policy of sorts seems to emerge when a long string of cases reflects the same standard even though it is never articulated. For instance, court insiders often know it is the "policy" of a particular judge to give probation to youthful first offenders, while it is the "policy" of another judge to send them to jail. Mather[77] is the leading exponent of the view that policy emerges from such a flow of trial court decisions. I take a more cautious position. Policy that results from a flow of decisions is quite different from explicit policy announced by a public body such as a legislature or appellate court. Such emergent "policy" is produced by a different process than articulated policy: it rarely is the result of deliberations; it does not involve the participation of interest groups; it does not attract public attention. It is much more flexible than articulated policy because it is not cast in words (much less, in stone). Unlike Mather, I prefer to think of decisional tendencies of trial courts and reserve the term "policy making" for the work of some appellate courts.

This controversy is important for our view of what trial courts do. In Mather's view, policy making is an important function of trial courts; in mine, social control is the central function and policy making is tertiary. However, Mather and I do not differ on the political role of trial courts. The imposition of social control is fully as political as policy

[77]Lynn Mather, "Policy Making in State Trial Courts," in John B. Gates and Charles A. Johnson (eds.), *The American Courts: A Critical Assessment* (Washington, D.C.: Congressional Quarterly Press, 1990), pp. 119–58.

making. But it sets trial courts aside from appellate courts, as we see in the next chapters.

KEY WORDS

transformation of disputes	recidivism
direct examination	dispute resolution
cross-examination	torts
jury	contract
social control	property
special deterrence	domestic relations
general deterrence	contingent fee
guilty plea	retainer
misdemeanor	discovery
felony	deposition
dismissal	transaction costs
going rate	repeat player
public defender	one-shotter
court-appointed attorney	compensation
Eighth Amendment	punitive damages
bail	temporary restraining order
release on recognizance	injunction
preliminary hearing (or examination)	divorce
probable cause	bankruptcy
information	settlement conference
grand jury	stipulation
indictment	alimony/maintenance
courtroom workgroup	guardian ad litem
plea bargain	senatorial courtesy
slow plea	merit plan
bench trial	partisan ballot
probation	nonpartisan ballot
suspended sentence	impeachment
community service	disciplinary commission
fine	recall election

FOR FURTHER STUDY . . .

Criminal courts are described in a pair of studies that contrast big city and small town proceedings: James Eisenstein and Herbert Jacob, *Felony Justice* (Boston: Little, Brown, 1977) and James Eisenstein, Peter Nardulli, and Roy B. Flemming, *Contours of Justice* (Boston: Little, Brown, 1987). The best single book on civil proceedings is Herbert M. Kritzer, *The Justice Broker: Lawyers and Ordinary Litigation* (New York: Oxford University Press, 1990).

You may wish to observe criminal court in your community. Try to visit several different courtrooms presided over by different judges. While you are there, try to interview both assistant prosecutors and defense attorneys to see how proceedings in those courtrooms accord with the analysis of this chapter. Civil proceedings are more difficult to observe, since so much occurs behind the scenes. However, try to interview active litigators in your community to help you understand the many dimensions of these proceedings.

9

APPELLATE COURTS

For most litigants, the judicial process ends with the trial judgment. They accept it and go on with their lives or they seek to renegotiate the outcome in other forums. However, appeals have a special significance for the legal system. Appellate decisions provide the legal text to which lawyers look when researching the law because the raw language of statutes provides only a foundation for the living law that evolves through negotiation and litigation. Appellate court decisions tell lawyers what the law *really* means because they reveal how judges apply it. They also are the documents through which lawyers learned the law when they were students. Thus, appellate courts seem much more central to legal professionals than to the general public. They also have much greater influence on the development of law.

The Functions of Appellate Courts

Appeals courts are often called "higher courts" because to some degree they supervise the work of trial courts and make more authoritative rulings. The supervision takes three forms: they correct errors trial courts may have made, increase the uniformity of legal interpretation throughout the United States, and oversee the administration of the court system.

Error correction is a fundamental task of appellate courts. Even experienced trial judges make mistakes as they make snap decisions in the midst of trials. The errors most frequently involve incorrect admission or exclusion of evidence or details in the instructions given juries. Not all errors are worth correcting; appellate courts have crafted a **harmless error** rule by which they ignore mistakes they believe made no difference in the outcome of the trial. However, where appellate judges feel the errors are substantial, they may reverse the trial court decision; alternatively, they may return the case to the trial court for further hearings to clarify factual matters that are unclear on the record.

Error correction by appellate courts, however, is far less systematic than in many organizations. The appellate courts themselves do not seek out errors. Whereas manufacturers routinely sample products as they roll off the assembly line to check their quality and pathologists inspect tissue removed from patients in operations to determine whether it really was diseased, no similar quality control exists in the U.S. judicial process. If a litigant does not complain to an appeals court, the court will not examine the case or notice errors in it. As we shall see, there are many barriers that deter litigants from taking their case to an appeals court. Consequently, appellate courts catch only a fraction of the errors that occur in trials; we do not know how many uncorrected errors occur.[1]

The second supervisory function of appellate courts is to promote uniformity in deciding cases. A fundamental requirement of justice is that similar cases should have similar outcomes, regardless of the courtroom the litigants happened to use. In the United States, considerable variation exists in statutory provisions from one state to another; those differences are permitted as the expression of the preferences of state political coalitions as long as they do not violate some provision of the Constitution. However, variations in the rulings among federal trial courts applying federal statutes and among the trial courts within a single state are unfair. It should not matter whether a case is heard in the federal district court of Eastern Washington or Western Washington or in Cook County or DuPage County, Illinois. When litigants make appellate courts aware of such differences, appellate judges often impose a uniform standard on all trial courts in their jurisdiction. However, as with errors, appellate courts do not actively search for discrepancies, and relatively few cases seem to be appealed on the basis of diversity of rulings in lower courts.[2] Appeals courts address only those instances brought to their attention by litigants; all others remain untouched.

The third supervisory function performed by many (but not all) appellate courts focuses on the administration of trial courts. Some appellate courts have the authority to issue rules for trial courts that govern not only trial procedures but also budgetary and staff issues. Some appellate courts may transfer trial judges temporarily from one jurisdiction to another; some have authority to discipline trial judges for misconduct. Some can even reactivate former judges for temporary service.[3] Such administrative supervision often is carried out through a commission or council attached to an appellate court, and the appellate judges act as little more than a board of directors for the agency.

The first two functions have the greatest significance because they require appellate courts to issue authoritative interpretations of the law that bind the trial courts in their jurisdiction. As we noted, trial courts simply announce their judgments; they rarely issue opinions that supply the legal reasoning underling the decision, because

---

[1]Thomas Y. Davies, "Affirmed: A Study of Criminal Appeals and Decision-Making Norms in a California Court of Appeals," *American Bar Foundation Research Journal 1982* (1982), pp. 601–606; Francis A. Allen, "A Serendipitous Trek through the Citation Jungle: Criminal Justice in Courts of Review," *Iowa Law Review 70* (1985), pp. 311–342.

[2]J. Woodford Howard, Jr., *Courts of Appeals in the Federal Judicial System: A Study of the Second, Fifth, and District of Columbia Circuits* (Princeton: Princeton University Press, 1981), pp. 68–70; Stephen L. Wasby, *The Supreme Court in the Federal Judicial System*, 2d ed. (New York: Holt, Rinehart & Winston, 1984), pp. 34–35.

[3]Gary Taylor, "Have Gavel, Will Travel" *National Law Journal*, 26 April 1993, p. 1.

most trial decisions hinge on interpretations of facts rather than interpretations of the law. Moreover, many litigants are only interested in learning whether they won or lost; the reasons do not concern them particularly. By contrast, opinions that accompany decisions are a much more important product for appellate courts. Most appellate decisions simply reaffirm existing interpretations and rules, but even this reaffirmation provides important guidance to trial judges and attorneys. Occasionally, appellate courts explicitly develop novel interpretations that provide substantially new legal rights or obligations. These opinions become the law on which attorneys advise their clients. They govern subsequent trial court decisions and provide the basis for building new legal arguments for appealing future cases. The opinions also serve as the basis for future appellate decisions, becoming the **precedents** to which subsequent judges refer.

The quality of reasoning and literary finesse displayed in an appellate opinion determines its influence to a considerable degree. Some judges on appellate courts, such as Roger J. Traynor of the California Supreme Court and Learned Hand of the U.S. Court of Appeals for the Second Circuit, had extraordinary influence on the development of law in the United States, even though they did not sit on the U.S. Supreme Court, because of the high quality of their case opinions. On the other hand, justices of the Supreme Court may exert relatively little influence on the long-term development of the law despite their lofty position if their opinions are judged by the legal profession to be mediocre. This has been the fate of many decisions by Supreme Court justices, such as Chief Justice Warren Burger,[4] Justices Charles Whittaker and Sherman Minton, and Chief Justice Fred M. Vinson.[5]

Structural Characteristics of Appellate Courts

As with trial courts, a dual system of appeals courts operates in the United States. Every state has its own appellate courts. As of 1992, thirty-nine states had two tiers of such courts: intermediate appellate courts, which hear cases from trial courts, and a supreme court that mostly takes appeals from the intermediate courts. Oklahoma and Texas have two supreme courts; one to hear final appeals for criminal cases and the other, for civil cases.[6]

The federal government has its own appellate courts. The country is divided into twelve regions (called circuits), each of which has a court of appeals. These courts handle only cases that originate in the federal district courts of their region or in federal administrative agencies. However, the U.S. Supreme Court (which we examine in the next chapter) hears cases appealed both from this set of courts and from state supreme courts when the latter raise a federal question.

[4]Consider, for instance, the view of Vincent Blasi, who wrote of Burger: "The Chief Justice is a man of limited capacity and no discernible coherent philosophy," Vincent Blasi (ed.), *The Burger Court: The Counter-Revolution That Wasn't* (New Haven: Yale University Press, 1983), p. 211.
[5]This evaluation is the product of a poll taken of law school deans and other academics; see Henry J. Abraham, *Justices and Presidents: A Political History of Appointments to the Supreme Court,* 2d ed. (New York: Oxford University Press, 1985), p. 389.
[6]Kathleen Maguire, Ann L. Pastore, and Timothy J. Flanagan, *Sourcebook of Criminal Justice Statistics, 1992* (Washington, D.C.: U.S. Department of Justice, Bureau of Justice Statistics, 1993), pp. 80–81.

Another distinctive feature of appellate courts is that several judges hear each case. In some, all the judges on the court hear every case; in most, however, panels of three or more judges hear cases and it is rare for the entire bench to be involved in one case. To avoid the appearance of favoritism in the assignment of judges to particular cases, many appellate courts use a blind, random assignment procedure so that neither judges nor litigants can influence the composition of a panel for a particular case.

Each appellate court has a chief judge. In some courts, the chief is specially selected and serves for a long period of time. In the federal courts of appeal, the position automatically goes to the most senior judge (in years of service) who has not reached the age of 70; at the age of 70, the chief judge relinquishes that post but remains on the bench as long as he or she wishes. On many state supreme courts, the position rotates among all the members of the court with no judge serving as chief for a long period of time. The powers of a chief judge vary considerably. In some courts, the position is little more than an honorific; in others, the chief has real influence in assigning judges, managing the administration of trial courts, and setting internal procedures for the court. These details rarely come to the public's attention, but they are important for understanding who has influence in an appellate court's decisions.

Finally, appellate courts never employ juries. They are staffed only by legal professionals and possess no populist appendage. Their decisions are entirely the product of the judges and their staff.

What Appellate Courts Do

Every litigant has the right to one appeal. However, whether they exercise that right depends on the formal rules under which the court operates, the desire of litigants to appeal, and their ability to do so.

Several types of formal rules affect the court's docket. First are rules that govern the court's **jurisdiction.** They designate what kinds of cases the court may hear. For instance, such rules routinely specify the trial courts from which cases may be appealed to any particular appellate court. Thus, an unsuccessful litigant in a New Jersey state court cannot appeal to New York's appellate courts; only New Jersey appellate courts can hear those appeals. This is especially important for policy issues. Litigants need to choose their trial court carefully to reach the appeals court they wish to have hear their case. Likewise, only certain issues can be appealed. In general, only rulings on the law can be appealed; the veracity of evidence is not appealable. Someone appealing a criminal conviction does so on the basis of alleged mistakes made by the trial judge in interpreting the law (such as not admitting certain evidence); the appeal cannot be based on the judge's or jury's interpretation of the evidence. Moreover, a prosecutor can never appeal an acquittal, for that would violate the Fifth Amendment's prohibition against **double jeopardy** (trying someone twice for the same offense). In addition, guilty pleas can rarely be appealed.

Another set of rules specifies the procedure for appealing cases. Such rules routinely establish deadlines for filing an appeal, often 30 or 60 days after the trial court has entered its final judgment. The form of the appeal is also specified; normally it requires a **brief** indicating the errors the trial court is alleged to have made. In addition, copies of the trial judgment and transcript are usually required. In almost all instances, these must be prepared by an attorney admitted to practice before the appeals court.

Appeals are expensive, thus not every litigant can afford them. Those convicted of criminal offenses who cannot afford to hire their own attorney can turn to a public defender or similar state-paid attorney to bring their appeal; that is part of their right to due process of law. However, in civil cases public lawyers are rarely available to take appeals. Either the litigant foots the bill or the attorney agrees to take the case on a contingent fee basis; in rare cases, an interest group pays for the appeal. Otherwise, no appeal is filed.

Appeals often require the services of a new attorney. Appellate work is quite different than pretrial negotiations or trial litigation. It requires a greater knowledge of the law and an ability to write successful briefs. Like litigation specialists, lawyers specializing in appeals know the peculiarities of the courts in which they work, such as how to frame their appeals to optimize the likelihood of a favorable hearing. They can assess the likelihood of success and advise their client about the risks involved. If posttrial negotiations occur, they know the going rate at this stage and are likely to be acquainted with opposing counsel. All of this, of course, demands additional payments by the litigant.

More than the lack of money restrains litigants from appealing their case. In some instances, the losing party at trial did not really expect to win or became convinced that their case was weak. Satisfied with the fairness of the trial court's decision, they simply agree to abide by it. In other instances, the amount of time required for the appeal deters litigants, they want to get on with their affairs. In still other cases, the losing party decides to negotiate with the winning party, who may be eager to collect on the judgment without the further expense of an appeal; such posttrial negotiations are not uncommon in tort judgments.

The caseloads of courts of appeal have grown over the past several decades in almost every jurisdiction. In the federal courts of appeal, the caseload tripled between 1970 and 1987.[7] In state intermediate courts, filings on average more than doubled between 1974 and 1984,[8] but the growth moderated over the next five years.[9] Most state intermediate courts face dockets of several thousand cases, all of which require a decision; most state supreme courts have caseloads of over 1000 cases.[10]

Criminal appeals constitute about 20 percent of all appeals in federal courts of appeal[11] and probably a larger percentage of intermediate state courts of appeal. The stakes in criminal cases are high; moreover, many of the appellants are indigent and use a public attorney to argue their case; therefore, inadequate resources do not prevent their appeals. Nevertheless, most criminal cases are *not* appealed because the trial courts resolve them through a guilty plea that cannot normally be appealed.

[7]Donald R. Songer, "The Circuit Courts of Appeals," in John B. Gates and Charles A. Johnson (eds.), *The American Courts: A Critical Assessment* (Washington: Congressional Quarterly Press, 1991), p. 36.
[8]Thomas B. Marvell, "State Appellate Court Responses to Caseload Growth," *Judicature 72* (February–March 1989), p. 283.
[9]*State Court Caseload Statistics: Annual Report 1988* (Williamsburg, Vir.: National Center for State Courts, 1990), p. 38.
[10]Ibid., pp. 40–45.
[11]Songer, supra, note 7, p. 37; Howard, supra, note 2, p. 26.

Civil cases constitute the remainder of appellate courts' dockets. The cases range over the entire body of civil law: contracts, torts, divorces, environmental regulation, business regulation, taxes, and so on. However, the content of civil cases appealed has changed over the course of the twentieth century. In federal courts of appeal, cases involving private economic disputes, such as those over property, declined substantially, while those involving public regulation of the economy rose.[12] Similar changes occurred in the state supreme courts.[13] As we see below, the increase in public regulation cases has particular significance for our understanding of the political role of these courts. However, as with criminal cases, only a small fraction of all trial court decisions is appealed.

Once an appeals court rules, its decision is usually final as far as court action in that case is concerned. Only 2 percent of the court of appeals cases Howard studied in the 1960s were accepted by the Supreme Court, and only 1.3 percent were given a full review.[14] In 1986, that number had shrunk to 0.4 percent.[15] The proportions are similar for state appellate courts; litigants rarely take cases decided by an intermediate appellate court to their state supreme court.[16]

How Appellate Courts Work

Although appellate courts toil out of the public limelight, there is little mystery about how they process their cases. As we have noted, they are entirely passive about attracting cases. They process those cases that litigants happen to bring to them. These cases reach appellate courts with a notice (or petition) of appeal, a brief, and the record of the trial; these documents are filed by the party seeking the appeal (the **appellant**). The other party to the case (the **respondent**) generally answers with its own brief.

Cases undergo a new transformation at this stage of their judicial life. At trial, the dispute typically centers on facts and how the facts fit the law. On appeal, the dispute focuses on the law and its interpretation and application by the lower court. Consequently, briefs concentrate on legal arguments; they may not be used as a vehicle to make new factual assertions except to provide some general context for interpreting the law (as pioneered by Louis Brandeis with his briefs on working conditions in cases involving the constitutionality of laws regulating those conditions). Appellate courts have no facility for fact gathering and evidence testing like a trial; they take no testimony and conduct no examinations or cross-examinations. Thus, a case that begins as a

---

[12]Lawrence Baum, Sheldon Goldman, and Austin Sarat, "The Evolution of Litigation in the Federal Courts of Appeals, 1895–1975," *Law & Society Review* 16 (1981–1982), pp. 291–310.
[13]Robert A. Kagan, Bliss Cartwright, Lawrence M. Friedman, and Stanton Wheeler, "The Business of State Supreme Courts, 1870–1970," *Stanford Law Review* 30 (1977), pp. 121–156.
[14]Howard, supra, note 2.   [15]Songer, supra, note 7, p. 48.
[16]Robert A. Kagan, Bliss Cartwright, Lawrence M. Friedman, and Stanton Wheeler, "Courting Reversal: The Supervisory Role of State Supreme Courts," *Yale Law Journal* (1978), pp. 1211–1218; comparison tables of caseloads for intermediate appellate courts and supreme courts in *State Court Caseload Statistics*, supra, note 9, suggests that fewer than 10 percent of intermediate court decisions are appealed to state supreme courts in some states.

dispute over whether the defendant caused injury to the plaintiff becomes a dispute over interpretations of the law of liability in the appellate court.

Most appellate courts now employ staff attorneys to help screen the cases that come to them.[17] A large proportion of the appeals are routine. As noted, many come from persons convicted of a criminal offense who claim the trial judge made an error in handling their case. They usually challenge settled interpretations of law, which appeals judges often dismiss with little consideration. Many such cases are handled almost entirely by the staff, which identifies them, writes a brief memo for the judges, and submits that to the court for approval. Such cases are not argued before the judges; rather, the judges accept the proposed decision of the staff and issue it as their own.

The more difficult cases, which appear to have more merit because the trial judge's alleged error is more difficult to evaluate or because of the novelty of the legal issues raised by the briefs, go to a panel of judges or to the entire court if it does not routinely divide itself into panels. The judges read the briefs and schedule an **oral argument.** This is much shorter than a trial; usually it lasts less than an hour, during which time each side has the opportunity to present its case and the judges have a chance to ask questions of the lawyers. Following the reading of briefs, and oral argument if there is one, the judges vote whether to **affirm** or **reverse** the lower court's decision or to **remand** it to the trial court for further hearings. The issues are so complicated that the judges affirm on some points and reverse on others. In some instances (particularly for intermediate courts of appeal), the decision is simply announced, without a written opinion. However, in many cases, one judge from the panel writes a justification of the decision, which is called the **opinion of the court.** The parties involved receive the decision and opinion. Many (but not all) of the decisions are published in the official court reporter. When the appellate court decision is published, it becomes part of the general body of law, which other litigants may use in the future. If the appeals court affirms the lower court's decision, no further action need be taken, although the losing party may seek either a rehearing or appeal to a still higher court if there is one. If the appeals court reverses the lower court decision, and if that decision is not further appealed, the trial court often must schedule a new trial. However, in many instances, the litigants are weary and either let the appellate decision stand as final or negotiate a settlement on the basis of the appellate court's interpretation of the law. In criminal cases, a reversal of a conviction often ends the prosecution because the appellate decision may invalidate a key piece of evidence or because essential witnesses are no longer available for a retrial.

Appellate Courts and the Political Arena

Appellate courts, despite often being more obscure than trial courts, have many more connections with the political arena because they are often enmeshed in policy conflicts. But their ties to the political arena stem from more than the policy-making activities; they are also instruments of social control, and may play a more prominent role

---

[17]Davies, supra, note 1; Marvell, supra, note 8, pp. 286–287.

than trial courts in legitimating (or delegitimating) the regime. Moreover, like all government agencies, appellate courts are linked to politics through the process by which judges reach their posts.

POLICY MAKING BY APPELLATE COURTS

Because appellate courts focus on legal questions, they cannot escape policy questions. Their job is to approve or disapprove of the manner in which trial courts interpret the law. Given the facts uncovered in the trial, appellate courts face the task of deciding which alternative interpretations of existing law apply. The appellant offers one set of alternatives; the respondent, another. Both cite precedents by the same court or a higher court to support their interpretation. Both may elaborate theories of law that justify extending a precedent to cover the situation in their case. The choice of one precedent over another in a particular set of facts situation necessarily has policy implications because the decision, together with its accompanying opinion, becomes a guide to lawyers counselling clients and to other judges deciding similar cases. Often the interpretive extensions resulting from appellate decisions are small departures from existing law; sometimes, however, the appellate court announces a substantial change in the law that everyone recognizes as a new policy.

Intermediate appellate courts at both the state and federal levels engage in such overt policy making less frequently than do state supreme courts and the U.S. Supreme Court. That is due, in part, to the fact that these intermediate courts take all cases appealed to them in order to satisfy the requirement that each litigant has one opportunity to appeal a trial result. Consequently, intermediate courts process many cases in which there is not much doubt about the outcome. That leaves the judges less time to consider the legal and policy ramifications of cases involving more substantial interpretive questions. Moreover, a higher level of court peers over the shoulders of intermediate court judges; the most important new interpretations offered by intermediate court judges are likely to be reviewed by the state supreme court or the U.S. Supreme Court, and the new policy will be associated with the higher court rather than the intermediate tribunal.

State supreme courts are often the last judicial arbiter of a case. The U.S. Supreme Court accepts very few cases from the state court systems, and the state supreme courts' decisions often involve interpretations of state laws or state constitutions over which the U.S. Supreme Court has no jurisdiction. For instance, in recent years, some state supreme courts have been active in expanding the rights of criminal defendants based on guarantees in state constitutions, while the Supreme Court was narrowing those rights based on their interpretation of the U.S. Constitution.[18] In addition, in fields rarely addressed by the U.S. Supreme Court, such as tort law, state supreme courts have been active in developing new doctrines.[19]

---

[18]Craig F. Emmert and Carol Ann Traut, "A Quantitative Analysis of the New Judicial Federalism," Paper presented at the annual meeting of the American Political Science Association, San Francisco, August 1990; Craig F. Emmert, "Judicial Review in State Supreme Courts: Opportunity and Activism," Paper presented at the annual meeting of the Midwest Political Science Association, Chicago, April 1988.
[19]Bradley C. Canon and Lawrence Baum, "Patterns of Adoption of Tort Law Innovations: An Application of Diffusion Theory to Judicial Doctrines," *American Political Science Review* 75 (1981), pp. 975–987.

Sometimes state supreme courts venture into policy disputes because cases are filed by litigants in areas where legislatures and administrative agencies fail to provide statutory or administrative decisions. One example is the question of whether and under what circumstances a terminally ill or permanently unconscious patient may be allowed to die rather than be maintained on life support systems. Doctors and hospital administrators have been loathe to permit such practices, for fear of being prosecuted for murder or manslaughter or for civil damages in a wrongful death suit. Relatives of the patient, however, may wish to end their loved one's suffering; in many instances, patients leave instructions for doctors not to take heroic, intrusive efforts if the cause is hopeless. Since the *Karen Quinlan* decision in New Jersey in 1976, at least one-fourth of the state supreme courts have issued decisions that became their state's policy in such situations. In most states, legislatures failed to provide statutory guidance because they were deadlocked over the competing interests of patients, medical personnel, and religious convictions.[20] As Glick writes,

> In states in which the Catholic population is large and the church is especially powerful such as Massachusetts, New Jersey, and New York, living will laws generally have not been enacted. . . . However, the appellate courts in these states have served as important alternative sources of policy. While it might successfully oppose or limit legislation, the Catholic church and other groups cannot prevent individual citizens from putting an issue on the judicial agenda.[21]

Conflict between state supreme courts and state legislatures is most evident when the state courts exercise their power of **judicial review** and rule state laws unconstitutional under the provisions of their state's constitution. Between 1981 and 1985, state supreme courts decided 630 challenges to the constitutionality of state laws, based on the state constitution; in one-third of those cases, the courts held the law unconstitutional. In an additional 52 cases, where the challenge was on both state and federal grounds, the state constitutional provisions were used to invalidate the state law.[22] On average, such challenges occurred ten times a year for each state, with the result that twice a year a law was declared unconstitutional by each state's supreme court.[23] This occurred more frequently in southern states, partly because southern constitutions, being much longer and more detailed, present more opportunities for legislatures to run afoul of some constitutional provision. In many instances, state supreme courts placed themselves in direct conflict with the legislature on issues of current concern; more than half of the statutes they struck down had been adopted within the previous five years.[24] During the mid-1980s, a substantial number of the statutes declared unconstitutional involved legislative efforts to deal with what was perceived at that time to be a crisis in medical malpractice insurance. Thus, the supreme courts became enmeshed in one of the hottest political issues of the day.[25]

---

[20]Henry R. Glick, "The Right-to-Die: State Policymaking and the Elderly." *Journal of Aging Studies* 5 (1991), pp. 283–307.
[21]Henry R. Glick, *The Right to Die* (New York: Columbia University Press, 1992) p. 159.
[22]Craig F. Emmert and Carol Ann Traut, Supra, note 18.
[23]Craig F. Emmert, supra, note 18.   [24]Craig F. Emmert, supra, note 18.
[25]Craig F. Emmert, "Issues in State Supreme Court Judicial Review Cases," Paper presented at the annual meeting of the Southern Political Science Association, Atlanta, November 1988.

Intermediate appellate courts in the United States may also be significant participants in the political arena because of the characteristics of the judges who staff them. These characteristics become clear when we contrast the men and women who become appellate judges in the United States with those in countries such as Germany, France, and Italy, where ordinary appellate courts rarely intrude into policy making. As one of the leading scholars of comparative law has commented,

> A[nother] difference which further reduces the authority and creativity of decisions by higher courts in civil law countries is presented by the kind of judicial personnel prevailing in those courts. Continental judges usually are career judges who enter the judiciary at a very early age and are promoted to the higher courts largely on the basis of technical merits and seniority. . . . [I]n the common law counties [e.g., the United States] . . . a judicial nomination to a higher court position implies to a much larger extent the political choice of an emerging personality.[26]

Appellate judges in the United States are selected in the same manner as are trial judges. Some are elected; some win their position through a quasi-merit selection process; some are appointed.

As with federal district judges, nominations for judges in the courts of appeal are made by the president but the appointment must be confirmed by a majority vote of the Senate; the term is for life during "good behavior." Individual senators have less influence over the appointment of appellate judges than in the selection of trial judges because the appellate judges serve a jurisdiction larger than a single state. The greatest influence rests with officials in the Department of Justice and the White House who screen applicants and potential nominees. The process produces mostly men who have served on trial courts and who are in the middle of their career, since most trial judges do not get appointed until their late 30s or early 40s. However, the screening particularly during the Reagan and Bush administrations (1981–1993) focused not only on prior experience and indicators of legal expertise but also on ideological conformity with the Administration. Most of the appointees had substantial prior political experience (as was true for the Carter appointees as well). Typical Reagan and Bush appointees were Ilana Rovner, who had chaired the Illinois Finance Committee for Reagan–Bush in 1984, Morris Arnold, a former chairman of the Republican Party of Arkansas, and Paul Kelly, Jr., who had held many Republican party posts in New Mexico.[27] The Reagan and Bush administrations appointed judges with distinctly conservative viewpoints and politicos accustomed to thinking of disputes as policy questions. This also translated into the appointment of fewer women and minorities than by the previous Carter administration and a much higher proportion of millionaires.[28]

---

[26]Mauro Cappaletti, *The Judicial Process in Comparative Perspective* (Oxford: Clarendon, 1989), p. 51.
[27]Sheldon Goldman, "Bush's Judicial Legacy: The Final Imprint," *Judicature* 76 (1993), pp. 282–297.
[28]Sheldon Goldman, "Reagan's Judicial Appointments at Midterm: Shaping the Bench," *Judicature* 66 (1983), pp. 334–347; Sheldon Goldman, "Reagan's Second Term Judicial Appointments: The Battle at Midway," *Judicature* 70 (1987), pp. 324–339; Sheldon Goldman, "Reagan's Judicial Legacy: Completing the Puzzle and Summing Up," *Judicature* 72 (1989), pp. 318_330; Goldman, supra, note 27; Elaine Martin, "Gender and Judicial Selection: A Comparison of the Reagan and Carter Administrations," *Judicature* 71 (1987), pp. 136–142.

The ideological cast of the men and women appointed makes a difference. If one characterizes as liberal a vote for prisoner or defendant rights in criminal cases, a vote for women or minorities in discrimination cases, a vote for claimants in First Amendment cases, a vote for labor in labor-management disputes, a vote for welfare and disability claimants, or a vote for claimants (rather than defendants) in personal injury cases, the contrast in the voting record of judges appointed by different presidents is often sharp. Judges of the courts of appeal appointed by Democratic presidents consistently display more liberal voting records than those appointed by Republican presidents. The contrast is sharpest between Carter and Reagan/Bush appointees. According to one study, Carter's judges voted on the liberal side 95 percent of the time while the Reagan judges voted on the liberal side only 5 percent of the time;[29] in a later analysis using somewhat different calculations, Reagan appointees decided cases in a liberal manner least frequently, and Bush appointees were not far behind.[30]

Winners in the courts of appeal are likely to be the more privileged party to a dispute. Individuals who appeal their cases fare poorly; they win only 18 percent of appeals when the respondent is another individual, 16.6 percent when the respondent is a business, 10.2 percent when the respondent is a state or local government, and 12.5 percent when the respondent is a federal agency. When businesses appeal against individuals, the businesses win 25.2 percent of cases; when state or local governments appeal against individuals, the governments win 40.8 percent of cases; when a federal agency appeals against an individual, it wins 62 percent of cases.[31]

Two kinds of privilege operate to produce these results. One is the advantage resulting from access to greater resources. Individual appellants are likely to have the least amount of money, the least experience, the least expert lawyers, and the lowest tolerance for delay; they are most likely to be one-shotters. Businesses and government agencies usually have much greater resources and experience; they often are repeat players. The second kind of privilege involves the special position of government agencies. In administrative regulation cases, for instance, they enjoy a presumption of expertise that individuals and businesses do not. In criminal cases (which constitute a large proportion of those where individuals appeal against the government), the court is part of the order maintenance machinery of the State; the prior political and governmental experience of the judges sensitizes them to the consequences for social order that might follow from letting a criminal free on a legal technicality.

State intermediate court and supreme court judges are also the product of a politicized rather than career selection process. As with trial court judges, the so-called merit systems for selection became increasingly common in the 1980s; they involve lawyers and judges in the initial screening of candidates and require that the governor appoint someone from a list compiled by the nominating commission. The new judge then serves for one year before being put on the ballot and the electorate is asked whether

[29]Jon Gottschall, "Reagan's Appointments to the U.S. Courts of Appeals: The Continuation of a Judicial Revolution," *Judicature* 70 (1986), pp. 58–64.

[30]Robert Carp, Donald Songer, C. K. Rowland, Ronald Stidham, and Lisa Richey-Tracy, "The Voting Behavior of Judges Appointed by President Bush," *Judicature* 76 (1993), pp. 298–302.

[31]Donald R. Songer and Reginald S. Sheehan, "Who Wins on Appeal? Upperdogs and Underdogs in the United States Courts of Appeals," *American Journal of Political Science* 36 (1992), p. 241.

the judge should be retained. In most states, a majority vote determines the outcome. Comparing the characteristics of judges selected in this manner with normal elections indicates that this process produces the least diversity; otherwise, there is little difference in the outcome of the various selection processes. The so-called merit systems do not produce distinctly more meritorious judges.[32] In the 1980s, most appellate judges had some political experience before ascending the bench, but while previously appointed appellate judges had often served as a prosecutor, that position lost its distinctive role as a stepping stone to the judiciary.[33]

Most governors have a hand in the selection of state appellate judges; in some states they make the appointment alone, in others within the constraints imposed by nominating commissions; in many where elections are supposed to choose judges, governors make interim appointments that are usually ratified in subsequent elections.[34] As at the federal level, the governor's political values become stamped on the appellate bench. This is particularly well documented for California, where Ronald Reagan served as governor between the terms of two liberal Democrats, Edmund G. Brown, Sr. and Edmund G. Brown, Jr. The Reagan administration in Sacramento particularly favored candidates active in the business community; in the two Brown administrations, activity in political party organizations and candidate campaigns was much more important.[35]

Because state appellate courts handle a much larger proportion of routine appeals that often do not pose sharp decisional alternatives, the impact of ideology is somewhat muted there. Nevertheless, enough cases raise substantive issues in which judges have an opportunity to choose alternatives that one can sometimes see the difference between Democratic and Republican judges. For example, in California, panels of judges composed exclusively of Democrats voted quite differently in civil cases than those composed exclusively of Republicans. In criminal cases, (many of which do not involve plausible claims) the difference was much smaller but still discernible.[36]

However, this partisan effect is by no means limited to California. For instance, in Ohio during the 1970s and 1980s, control over the state supreme court oscillated between Republican and Democratic majorities. The result has been described in following terms:

> . . . the Democrats obtained a 4–3 and subsequently a 6–1 majority on the court. Under the leadership of Frank Celebrezze, a member of a politically powerful Cleveland family that personified the coming of age of ethnic politics in Ohio, the court as its chief proudly and publicly proclaimed, became a "people's court," concerned with "the little guy or gal." A long line of precedent pertaining, inter alia, to restrictions on suits against state and local governments and limitations on medical malpractice claims, and on the rights on tenants, consumers, workers injured

---

[32]Henry R. Glick and Craig F. Emmert, "Selection Systems and Judicial Characteristics: The Recruitment of State Supreme Court Judges," *Judicature* 70 (1987), pp. 228–235.
[33]Ibid.   [34]Ibid.
[35]Philip L. Dubois, "State Trial Court Appointments: Does the Governor Make a Difference?," *Judicature* 69 (1985), pp. 20–28.
[36]Philip L. Dubois, "The Illusion of Judicial Consensus Revisited: Partisan Conflict on an Intermediate Court of Appeals," *American Journal of Political Science* 32 (1988), pp. 946–967.

during the course of employment was reversed. Virtually overnight, the court became "prolabor and highly urban" in orientation.[37]

The switch to Republican control in 1986 did not alter the rulings of the court quite as radically, but partisanship on the court remained clear.

The 1986 election that swept Celebrezze from office, while not unique, was not commonplace. In that same year, Rose Bird, the Democratic Chief Justice of the California Supreme Court, and two fellow Supreme Court judges were ousted by California voters in a spectacular campaign centering on their rulings in death penalty cases.[38] Most of the time, however, state supreme court justices are safe from electoral defeat because they rarely face opposition, and when they do, they maintain their incumbency advantage since their races attract little media attention.

Elections and partisan differences in voting patterns on appellate courts are not the only ways in which these courts intersect with the political arena. Equally important is the impact of decisions that directly affect the agendas of state and national politics. Numerically, such decisions are few; they do not typify the work of intermediate appellate courts. However, their impact can be enormous.

In 1989, the Texas Supreme Court decided a case involving a claim that state aid to education violated the state constitution's pledge to provide education to all children in the state.[39] It ordered the state legislature to devise a new formula for distributing both state aid and the property tax support that finances Texas public schools. The effect would be to move money from rich districts to poor ones. After years of litigation and legislative attempts to satisfy the court's mandate, the court issued a June 1, 1993, deadline. However, every attempt to meet that deadline failed. No single issue has so monopolized the state's political agenda as the court's school finance decision.[40]

Such decisions, although exceptional, have the potential to become the driving force in the political arena for particular policy issues. One reason courts make such decisions is that the fierce partisanship aroused by such issues deadlocked the other branches of the government. Moreover, children who live in poor areas and attend substandard schools do not have much political clout. If they could, they might vote with their feet and move to wealthier areas with better schools or mobilize for legislative or administrative action. Their poverty, however, makes obtaining results from these arenas unlikely.

The neglect of such issues is not simply cold calculation by legislators and governors. They may feel that other issues are of greater importance for the citizens of their state, such as property tax relief for the elderly (some of whom are poor), a better business climate so that more people have jobs, or reform of the health care system so that more people receive adequate health care. Intermediate appellate courts do not need to

[37]G. Alan Tarr and Mary Cornelia Aldis Porter, *State Supreme Courts in State and Nation* (New Haven: Yale University Press, 1988), pp. 128–129.

[38]John H. Culver and John T. Wold, "Rose Bird and the Politics of Judicial Accountability in California," *Judicature 70* (1986), pp. 81–89; John T. Wold and John H. Culver, "The Defeat of the California Justices: The Campaign, the Electorate, and the Issue of Judicial Accountability," *Judicature 71* (1987), pp. 348–355.

[39]*Edgewood Indep. School Dist. v. Kirby*, 777 S.W.2d 391 (Tex. 1989).

[40]William Cellis 3d, "Texas Lawmakers Again Reject Plan to Equalize School Financing," *New York Times*, 4 December 1992, p. A26.

weigh these alternative demands. They are faced with a lawsuit alleging violations of a law or constitutional provision. If the judges decide a violation has occurred, they understand that their task requires a decision that orders a remedy regardless of the difficulties it may create for legislators or governors who seek reelection. Hence, courts may become loose cannon raising unwanted political issues at inconvenient times. In doing so, they have a substantial impact on the political arena.

An equally significant impact of intermediate appellate court decisions is the affirmation of the social control decisions made by trial courts. The vast majority of appellate court decisions affirm trial court decisions. These affirmances rarely receive attention in the media; they are "uninteresting" because they do not announce anything new. However, they transmit an important message to trial judges and the general public: that trial courts are doing the right thing. To be sure, almost no one hears about affirmances, but the absence both of reversals and of news that trial courts are making "bad" decisions helps maintain confidence in the operation of trial courts.

KEY WORDS

harmless error	oral argument
precedent	affirm
jurisdiction	reverse
double jeopardy	remand
brief	opinion of the court
appellant	judicial review
respondent	

FOR FURTHER STUDY . . .

The most thorough study of intermediate appellate courts remains J. Woodford Howard, Jr., *Courts of Appeals in the Federal Judicial System: A Study of the Second, Fifth and District of Columbia Circuits* (Princeton: Princeton University Press, 1981). G. Alan Tarr and Mary Cornelia Aldis Porter, *State Supreme Courts in State and Nation* (New Haven: Yale University Press, 1988) provides valuable insights into the political context in which state supreme courts work.

If an intermediate appellate court or state supreme court is located where you live, attend one of its public sessions; it can provide additional insight into the ways oral arguments are conducted. Also try to interview members of the local bar who practice before these courts for additional information about how the courts operate.

10

THE SUPREME COURT

The U.S. Supreme Court is an exceptional institution. No other court in the world enjoys its central position in the political arena; none has its prestige and power. While formally a court of "last resort," it spends little time correcting errors made in the judiciary. It is an institution bent on influencing policy. The words of Chief Justice Vinson spoke in 1946 remain true:

> The Supreme Court is not, and never has been primarily concerned with the correction of errors in lower court decisions. . . . If we took every case in which an interesting legal question is raised, or our *prima facie* impression is that the decision below is erroneous, we could not fulfill the Constitutional and statutory responsibilities placed upon the Court. To remain effective, the Supreme Court must continue to decide only those cases which present questions whose resolution will have immediate importance far beyond the particular facts and parties involved.[1]

Yet the Court is no ordinary political institution. It both is protected from partisan politics and reflects it. It is nested in a democratic regime, but its members enjoy life tenure. Located in a city overrun with journalists, it shuns publicity.

The scope of its policy-making activity since 1950 has been enormous. It sparked the Civil Rights movement with its 1954 decision that public schools could not be racially segregated (*Brown v. Board of Education*[2]). It ruled in 1963 (*Gideon v. Wainwright*[3]) that all defendants charged with serious offenses must be represented by counsel, a decision which stimulated the almost universal provision of counsel for indigent defendants in the United States. In 1966, the Court's decision in *Miranda v. Arizona*[4] revolutionized police practices; police now read Miranda warnings to all persons they take into custody. In 1973, the Supreme Court set off more than two decades of political turmoil with its decision in *Roe v. Wade*[5] legalizing most abortions. The following

---

[1]ct, Z (1949) Quoted in H. W. Perry, Jr., *Deciding to Decide: Agenda Setting in the United States Supreme Court* (Cambridge: Harvard University Press, 1992), p. 46.

[2]U.S. 483. [3]U.S. 335.

[4]U.S. 436. [5]U.S. 113.

214

year, the Court's decision in *Nixon v. U.S.*[6] ordered President Nixon to turn over to the Watergate prosecutor the tapes of his conversations in the Oval Office, which led to revelations that forced his resignation in the face of near-certain impeachment. In 1983, the Court declared the so-called legislative veto unconstitutional (*INS v. Chadha*[7]) requiring a substantial change in the ways Congress passes laws and shifting the balance of power toward the executive. These decisions, together with many others, have been an important part of the political agenda in the United States.

Much of the Supreme Court's policy role grows from its power of **judicial review.** Although not explicitly granted by the Constitution, since John Marshall's opinion in *Marbury v. Madison*[8] in 1803, the Court has presumed it had the authority to declare acts of Congress or the president void if they were contrary to a provision of the Constitution as interpreted by the Court. In fact, the Court exercises its power of judicial review much less frequently than presidents use the veto, but it brings many constitutional challenges to the Court. No Washington observer doubts that the Supreme Court is a major player in the nation's policy process.

This is a remarkable record for an institution that is dwarfed by those surrounding it in Washington. It is housed across from the Capitol in a building far smaller than those of any cabinet agency. The Court has only nine members, each assisted by two to four law clerks and one or two secretaries. The entire staff is smaller than those of some congressional committees. How the justices work, are chosen, and are perceived by others creates the Court's influence.

How the Court Works

THE COURT'S AGENDA

Like all other courts, the Supreme Court is formally a passive institution waiting for cases to arrive on its docket. However, we shall see that it manipulates its docket so effectively that it, in fact, chooses the cases it wants to hear.

The key to the Court's power lies in its control over its docket. In most years, litigants in almost 5000 cases appeal to the Court, half of whom are prisoners seeking a ruling that will set them free; they appeal to the Court as indigents (**in forma pauperis**) and do not pay the normal fees. Most of these cases are frivolous and fewer than 1 percent of those cases are reviewed by the Court,[9] although when they are, they permit the Court to address such important matters as the constitutionality of the death penalty. The other 2500 cases constitute a heavy workload for the Court; in fact, the Court gives a full hearing to fewer than 150 cases each year, while issuing a summary decision in approximately 350 others. Since 1925, the Court has enjoyed the power to reject most of these cases; since 1988, it has had almost complete control over its docket so that with few exceptions (such as the cases the Constitution specifies as original jurisdiction), the

---

[6]U.S. 683.   [7]U.S. 919.
[8]U.S. 137.
[9]Jeffrey A. Segal and Harold J. Spaeth, *The Supreme Court and the Attitudinal Model* (New York: Cambridge University Press, 1993), p. 181.

Court has a free hand in choosing which of the cases it wishes to decide. The process is one of granting a **writ of certiorari,** which formally is an order to the lower courts to send forward the record of the case. The appellants who seek review ask the Court to grant such a writ.

Much work goes into the winnowing process, as described by Perry in a careful analysis of the docket-building process.[10] Each petition is accompanied by a brief from the petitioner, limited to 30 pages but which may have appendices of many more, a response from the other party, and a response to the response. Much of that material must be read to decide whether the case is one of the charmed few to receive a full hearing; most of this preliminary reading is done by the justices' clerks. Since the 1970s, as many as six of the justices have pooled their case selection efforts and divide the task between their clerks, each of whom prepares a memorandum for all of these justices, outlining the issues in the case and recommending a grant or denial of the petition. The remaining justices have their own clerks read all of the petitions and prepare their memoranda individually.

Supreme Court clerks are recent law school graduates. The post is the most prestigious a young lawyer can obtain and it attracts the brightest graduates of the top law schools. Generally, they have served a clerkship at a court of appeals before being chosen to clerk for a Supreme Court justice. They typically begin their work during the summer and hold the position for one year. They must learn what criteria their justices use to select cases; after a few months, they develop a good feel for what kinds of cases are likely to warrant serious consideration. The most important lesson they learn is that the presumption is against granting certiorari, since fewer than 10 percent of the petitions will be granted. Therefore, when they believe a case is worth hearing, they must construct a strong argument in favor of doing so. When a case appears to have little merit, far less effort must be expended.

Rule 10 of the Supreme Court purports to provide some guidance to petitioners about which issues the Court will hear. It indicates, among other things, that the Court will be more likely to hear cases when conflicting decisions exist among lower courts, when lower courts have declared a federal statute unconstitutional, or when a court of appeals has issued a decision in an important but unsettled area of federal law. However, the wording of Rule 10 is intentionally vague and provides only slight clues for predicting which cases the Court will accept.

The justices personally review the memos prepared by the clerks and mark the cases they wish to have discussed in conference. The chief justice prepares an initial **discuss list,** which includes those cases he believes merit discussion and are likely to win support, and the other justices may add cases to the list. Cases not on the discuss list are automatically denied certiorari. At the Friday conference which occurs many weeks when the Court is in session, the afternoons are usually spent considering the discuss list, which typically will include 40 to 50 cases.[11] The chief justice begins the discussion with those cases he placed on the list. He indicates his reasons for thinking that the

---

[10]Perry, supra, note 1.
[11]Gregory A. Caldeira and John R. Wright, "The Discuss List: Agenda Building in the Supreme Court," *Law & Society Review* 24 (1990), pp. 807–836.

case should be granted certiorari, followed (in order of descending seniority) by each of the other justices. When a case has been placed on the discuss list by another justice, that justice begins the discussion, followed by the chief justice and on down the seniority order. There is very little give and take in this consideration; each justice speaks and votes, and then they move on to the next case.

Four votes are required to grant the petition; about one of three cases on the discuss list are actually granted certiorari.[12] The procedure used to consider these cases means that junior justices have little voice; by the time they speak, the issue is often already decided, and it is rare for a senior justice to respond to an argument proposed by one of the junior justices. Nor is there frequent discussion beforehand between justices about particular cases. Thus, what justices decide in their chambers, reading the memos prepared by their clerks and some of the materials contained in the petitions, usually determines whether the Court grants certiorari.[13]

Perry concludes that the justices consider a number of factors in deciding which cases to accept. Among these are the identity and reputation of the lower court that made the previous decision, the identity and reputation of the judge who wrote the opinion, and the vote by which it was decided. In addition, they consider whether the case involves a significant conflict between courts of appeal or state supreme courts; whether the solicitor general (who is the federal government's chief lawyer for appellate cases) supports granting certiorari; and whether a better case appears to be in the pipeline for considering the issues involved. In very few instances, an extremely egregious error by a lower court will merit Supreme Court review.[14]

Of all these factors, support by the **solicitor general** is the best single predictor. The solicitor general is the third-ranking official of the Justice Department, a presidential appointee who must be confirmed by the Senate and serves at the pleasure of the president. The solicitor general heads a fairly small office within the Justice Department that reviews all appellate litigation by federal agencies. All cases that go to the Supreme Court must be approved there; in addition, any **amicus briefs** submitted by the federal government to intervene in cases in which it is not a principal litigant must be approved by the solicitor general. The office is considered the administration's voice in the courts; the Supreme Court depends, in large part, on its guidance for determining which issues and cases are of sufficient importance to warrant its time. The Court depends on the office to winnow significant cases from frivolous appeals. When the solicitor general participates in a case, it is a strong signal to the Court that the issue is worth pursuing. The solicitor general's office is by far the most successful petitioner; between 75 and 90 percent of its certiorari petitions are granted.[15] By contrast, other types of petitioners obtain certiorari no more than 10 percent of the time.

Another set of relatively successful petitioners is a handful of interest groups that also carefully screen cases and closely watch the evolution of Court decisions. Justices occasionally send signals to these petitioners through footnotes, concurring opinions, or even dissents, indicating that they are ready to hear a case raising a particular issue if

---

[12]This proportion is based on Caldeira and Wright's estimate of 500 cases on the discuss list and 150 grants of certiorari. See Caldeira and Wright, supra, note 11.
[13]Perry, supra, note 1.   [14]Perry, supra, note 1, pp. 112–139.
[15]Perry, supra, note 1, pp. 112–139.

framed in the right way. Among the most successful groups in bringing cases during the 1960s and 1970s were the National Association for the Advancement of Colored People (NAACP) and the American Civil Liberties Union (ACLU). However, other groups have had much less success, so it would be wrong to conclude that interest groups in general have substantial influence on the Court's agenda-building decisions.

As a consequence of the Court's discretionary powers and its response to well-placed petitioners like the solicitor general and favored interest groups, its docket has changed markedly since the beginning of the New Deal in 1933. In the early 1930s, the Court's agenda was dominated by cases raising economic issues, such as wage and labor regulation, injury compensation, disputes over goods and services, and taxation. By the late 1940s, civil liberties issues began coming to the fore, and by the late 1960s, the majority of cases involved such issues instead of economic ones.[16] Thus, the Court has carved out a major role in the civil liberties policy arena while abandoning its former role on economic issues, even though the federal government's intervention in the economy vastly increased after 1933. In the face of New Deal reforms, after initially challenging the Roosevelt administration, the Court retreated from the economic policy arena, leaving it primarily in the hands of Congress and the president.

DECISION MAKING BY THE COURT

Once certiorari has been granted, two decisional routes exist. The first is to decide the case summarily without further briefs or oral argument. Sometimes these are companion cases to others that are argued fully, and the summary decision may merely refer to the central case. At other times, the summary opinions consist of a swift reminder of the standing law by reference to precedents. Such decisions, called per curiam, are usually very brief. The vote of the justices is indicated, but no opinion is attached. It is rare for a justice to issue a dissenting memo even though these decisions are not necessarily unanimous.

The most important route calls for additional briefs and oral argument on the questions the Court has decided to consider. Parties are given time to write the briefs, and oral argument is scheduled for several months after the certiorari petition has been accepted. In the meantime, additional briefs may come in from amicus curiae. As noted in Chapter 7, we have no evidence indicating how influential amicus briefs are, but they clearly signal to the Court the breadth of interest in a case, and they provide quite different perspectives on possible consequences of a Court decision.

The oral argument usually involves only the principals in the case. The Court generally grants an hour for each case, which is divided between the two parties. The lawyer for each party begins with a brief presentation of its argument, but most of the time is spent answering questions the justices pose. These questions often reveal the justices' concerns about a particular case, but justices use different strategies. Sometimes they seek to demonstrate weak points in arguments they oppose. At other times, they seek to buttress views they espouse. Thus, the oral argument is part of the interaction

---

[16]Richard L. Pacelle, Jr., *The Transformation of the Supreme Court's Agenda* (Boulder, Co: Westview, 1991), pp. 64, 138.

among the justices as much as it is a presentation of information by counsel for the parties. However, no analyses exist to clarify the circumstances under which justices employ alternative strategies.

On the Wednesday or Friday after oral argument, the justices discuss the case in conference. Again, there appears to be little give and take. Rather, the Court follows a procedure similar to that used in considering certiorari petitions. In conferences on argued cases, the chief justice always begins the discussions, which then proceed according to descending seniority. Justices not only give their view of the case but cast their vote at the same time. Once again, the most junior justices have little opportunity to persuade the others; by their turn to speak, it is often clear how the vote will turn out. These discussions are swift because the Court has little time to give them. The justices must decide as many as twelve argued cases at the Wednesday and Friday conferences, and other matters (notably petitions for certiorari) take up a substantial portion of the time. Consequently, most of the decision making occurs within the justices' individual chambers as the result of each justice's reading of the briefs and discussion with his or her clerks. There is apparently very little informal discussion between the justices over cases outside the conference.[17]

The conference produces a tentative vote on each case. The next step is to write an opinion that explains the rationale underlying the vote. The Court attempts to divide this work equally, but there is no rule requiring it and many circumstances, such as illness, newness on the Court, and individual work habits, lead some justices to write more opinions than others. The chief justice assigns the writing of the **majority opinion** if he is among the majority; otherwise, the senior justice in the majority makes the assignment. This is a very important strategic decision because the weight of the opinion depends not so much on the vote but on the clarity and logic of the supporting argument. Moreover, the conference vote is only tentative, and justices are free to change their vote upon reading the draft opinion. In a few cases, a draft opinion loses votes, and in exceptional circumstances, it may convert a majority into the minority. While Fred Vinson was chief justice (1946–1953), 86 percent of the time, conference votes were the same as those of the final decision and in 9 percent of cases, a majority vote was transformed into a minority during the opinion-writing stage;[18] similar results held for the later years of the Warren Court (1953–1965).[19] We have no such information yet for the Burger and Rehnquist Courts.

Majority vote governs the decision-making process. Normally it takes at least five votes to win, although if two justices are unable to vote, four votes suffice. A tie vote affirms the lower court's decision. The key question is, therefore, how justices form winning coalitions.

Party affiliation has little to do with how the justices vote. For instance, Justice White, a Democrat appointed by President Kennedy, was one of the reliable allies of

---

[17]For details on these conferences see Perry, *supra* note 1.

[18]Saul Brenner, "Fluidity on the Supreme Court: 1957–1967," *American Journal of Political Science* 26 (1982), pp. 388–390.

[19]Saul Brenner and Harold J. Spaeth, "Majority Opinion Assignments and the Maintenance of the Original Coalition on the Warren Court," *American Journal of Political Science* 32 (1988), pp. 72–81.

Chief Justices Rehnquis and Burger—both Republicans appointed by Republican presidents. On the other hand, Justice Brennan—appointed by Republican President Eisenhower—usually voted against the conservative justices more closely associated with Republican administrations.

Rather than party affiliation, ideological dimensions appear to be the most significant trait in understanding the justices' voting patterns. Two dimensions not closely associated with one another—economic liberalism and civil libertarian liberalism—provide the most powerful explanation for how the justices vote. There is a long record of research findings which shows that justices vote with a high degree of consistency along these two dimensions. The attitudes are operationalized so that, for instance, a liberal attitude may be displayed when a justice votes in favor of a criminal defendant over the prosecution or in favor of a labor union over management. Using votes from earlier years to predict how the same justices will vote in similar cases in later years, Segal and Spaeth[20] demonstrate a considerable degree of consistency, particularly as they break them down to specific issues, such as race discrimination, rather than examining only a global civil liberties category. For instance, they show that Justice Black supported the liberal position in 71 percent of the time in criminal cases, in 76 percent of in civil rights cases, and in 51 percent of judicial power cases during the Warren Court era. On the Rehnquist Court, Justices Brennan and Marshall exhibited comparable levels of support for liberal positions in criminal cases, while Chief Justice Rehnquist supported the liberal position only 17 percent of the time.[21] Moreover, they and many other researchers have shown that many justices vote in well-defined blocs. For instance, for the Court's 1986–1989 terms, Segal and Spaeth show terms, that in so-called "special opinions" (not opinions of the Court), Marshall joined Brennan's opinions 92 of the 113 times Brennan wrote such opinions, while Brennan joined Marshall 46 times in the 58 instances Marshall wrote such opinions. However, Marshall never joined a special opinion by Rehnquist and signed only 7 of Scalia's 116 special opinions.[22] Looking at Court (majority) opinions, it is clear that during the early years of the Rehnquist Court, Scalia, Rehnquist, Kennedy, and Powell formed a solid conservative bloc, which often gained a majority with the addition of either White or O'Connor. Marshall and Brennan formed a liberal coalition that was occasionally joined by Stevens, Blackmun, or O'Connor, but it was almost always in the minority.[23]

Unlike the experience of litigants before lower courts, differential resources seem to make little difference before the Supreme Court.[24] While poor individuals do worse than their opponents, so do businesses, while minorities generally fare better. Consonant with the success already noted for the solicitor general, the federal government is the most successful litigator before the Supreme Court. Much more important is the apparent ideological position of the parties.

---

[20]Segal and Spaeth, supra, note 9.   [21]Segal and Spaeth, supra, note 9, pp. 246–251.
[22]Segal and Spaeth, supra, note 9, pp. 246–251.   [23]Segal and Spaeth, supra, note 9, pp. 278–279.
[24]Reginald S. Sheehan, William Mishler, and Donald R. Songer, "Ideology, Status, and the Differential Success of Direct Parties Before the Supreme Court," *American Political Science Review* 86 (1992), pp. 464–471.

ANCILLARY PLAYERS IN THE DECISION PROCESS

Three sets of participants other than the justices have been thought by some to play an important role in the Court's decision-making process: the clerks, the attorneys who bring cases, and interest groups. Each operates from a very different position of strength and weakness.

The **justices' clerks** are in the most anomalous position. They are often young enough to be the justices' children or grandchildren; they are at the beginning of their careers while the justices for whom they work are at the pinnacle of theirs. The justices have a long set of political associations that brought them to their position; the clerks have rarely held more than a clerkship in a lower court. The clerks normally serve for a single year; the justices enjoy life tenure. A more unequal position could scarcely be imagined. Yet clerks play an important role in the Court's decision-making process. As already noted, they winnow the certiorari petitions; if they wished and made a secret concerted effort, they could probably keep an otherwise obscure case from catching the justices' attention. However, it is very unlikely they could or would engage in such an action, since each of them is hired by their individual justice and most form very strong bonds of loyalty to that justice. At the opinion-writing stage, most justices use their clerks for research, finding appropriate citations and researching those parts of the law the justice wants to discuss. Occasionally, the clerks' contributions are noteworthy, because they find something the justice has forgotten or overlooked. However, since the justices' knowledge is vastly superior to that of the clerks, they generally play the role of informed assistant. It is probably safe to say they play a smaller role than the staff of congressional committees or of individual members of Congress or junior staff in the White House.[25]

The lawyers who bring cases to the court are a mixed group. The most specialized are those in the solicitor general's office; they handle only appellate litigation and only for one client, the federal government. They participate in far more Supreme Court cases than any private lawyer. As already indicated, they have much greater success than any other set of attorneys in winning certiorari, for the Court views their office with special regard and respect; after all, they are the legal voice of the elected president. However, the justices do not automatically grant the solicitor general's requests or support the office's position on the merits of the cases. During the Reagan administration, for instance, when the solicitor general's office adopted extremely conservative positions, Justice Brennan supported its position only 46 percent of the time; on the relatively few occasions when the office took a liberal position, Brennan's support rose to 75 percent; when it adopted its more normal conservative position, Brennan supported it only 26 percent of the time. Justice Scalia (a conservative justice), supported the solicitor general 69 percent of the time; in the liberal briefs that spurred Brennan's support, Scalia's support dropped to 47 percent; however, on the normally conservative

[25]A more critical assessment of clerks is given by Bernard Schwartz, *A History of the Supreme Court* (New York: Oxford University Press, 1993), pp. 369–372.

briefs presented by Reagan's solicitor general, Scalia voted favorably 77 percent of the time.[26]

Thus, the solicitor general's influence is constrained by the political positions the justices have staked out. A solicitor general serving a conservative administration does better when working with a Court dominated by conservatives. Like all other attorneys, the solicitor general considers the likelihood of sustaining its position before the Court before asking for the Court's review. The solicitor general's real strength is that the office is the gatekeeper for all federal government cases that might go to the Court. If the office refuses to appeal a case, nothing can be done. Moreover, because it sits astride the entire case flow of federal agency litigation to the courts of appeal as well as the Supreme Court, the solicitor general's office is the quintessential repeat player. It knows what other cases might provide a vehicle for its legal argument. The solicitor general can do much to limit any damage the Court may do to the administration's legal position by restricting the flow of potentially damaging cases to the Court. The solicitor general's office may also systematically exploit the Court's receptiveness to its views and advance the administration's legal position. For instance, during Rex Lee's tenure in that position, he approved only one in six requests to file a certiorari petition on behalf of a government agency.[27] At the same time, Lee apparently focused on cases emanating from the Ninth Circuit Court of Appeals, which was dominated by liberal judges appointed by the administration of President Carter. More of those cases were reversed by the Supreme Court than of other courts of appeal.[28] Similarly, a comparison of the record of the solicitors general of the conservative Nixon and Ford administrations with that of the more liberal Carter administration show that Carter's solicitor general filed amicus briefs in favor of personal liberties claims (such as in free speech and obscenity cases) much more frequently than his predecessors.[29]

No other set of attorneys approaches the solicitor general's position vis-à-vis the Court. None handles as much litigation; none has the potential to control the flow of cases as does the solicitor general; none is as highly specialized or as consistently well-informed about the Court's preferences. Yet there are substantial differences among the other attorneys who appear before the Court. A small set of private attorneys from Washington, New York, and Chicago appear with some frequency before the Court. While not matching the solicitor general's office, they have substantial expertise in Supreme Court litigation. Many of these lawyers have previously worked for the Court as a clerk to one of the justices. They work in large firms that handle one or two Supreme Court cases almost every year. They advise many clients who are tempted to push their case to the Supreme Court but are dissuaded on the basis of these lawyers' expertise. Yet all of these lawyers together handle less than 20 percent of the cases appealed to the Court.[30]

[26]Segal and Spaeth, supra, note 9, p. 314.
[27]Gerald F. Uelmen, "The Influence of the Solicitor General Upon Supreme Court Disposition of Federal Circuit Court Decisions: A Closer Look at the Ninth Circuit Record," *Judicature* 69 (1986), p. 363.
[28]Ibid.
[29]Karen O'Connor, "The Amicus Curiae Role of the U.S. Solicitor General in Supreme Court Litigation," *Judicature* 66 (1983), p. 263.
[30]Kevin T. McGuire, "Lawyers and the U.S. Supreme Court: The Washington Community and Legal Elites," *American Journal of Political Science* 37 (1993), p. 368.

Most of the remaining attorneys who seek certiorari for their clients or appear before the Court in oral arguments are essentially one-timers. They may have considerable prestige in the city in which they work, but they do not carry a sufficient number of cases to the Court to be exceptionally knowledgeable about the Court's ways. They generally do not embarrass themselves before the Court, but neither do they exert a consistent influence on it.

Interest groups are the third group of ancillary players. Their activity before the Court has markedly increased since the 1930s. Interest groups intervene both at the certiorari stage, hoping to sway justices to accept a case, and when cases are briefed for subsequent oral argument. A large number of distinct organizations press their views on the Court. During the 1982 term, 455 distinct groups intervened at the certiorari stage and 987 did so as the Court was deciding on the merits of cases.[31] However, some groups participate much more than others; the most active group was state governments, who accounted for more than one-third of all amici appearances.[32]

As before legislatures, interest groups participate because they wish to convey information, and they do so in a variety of ways. The Court requires that they first submit a statement of interest, in which they indicate how the dispute in the case involves them, before they can submit an amicus brief. On the basis of that statement, the Court grants or denies permission to submit an amicus brief (although it almost never denies permission).[33] In the statement of interest, groups provide information about their membership and its concerns; in this way they signal the Court about some of the larger issues that the case involves. Since the Court favors hearing important questions, these statements tell the Court about the case's potential significance at the certiorari stage. Amicus briefs provide much additional information to the Court. They often differ from the litigants' briefs in the legal reasoning for supporting their favored result; thus, they provide the Court alternative ways for sustaining the group's position. The background circumstances of the conflict also are illuminated by many of the briefs with information about how many persons might be affected, what the prevailing practice in the law is, and what costs a change in legal policy might entail. The very number of such briefs also signals the Court about the breadth of interest in the outcome of a case, for some cases attract only one or two briefs while others attract dozens, with many additional groups cosigning some of the briefs. Amici briefs generally do not support only one side of a case; in approximately two-thirds of cases where amicus briefs were submitted on the merits, they came in supporting both sides of the case.[34]

However, interest group activity before the Supreme Court remains much more discreet than elsewhere in government. Lobbyists almost never cross the portals of the Supreme Court building. They never meet with the justices; indeed, they do not communicate with them except by way of the briefs. The justices have no campaign funds to which interest groups might contribute; the justices make few speeches, and when they do, they do not keep the honoraria. Occasionally, there is a hint of a justice's relationship with someone who might be considered a lobbyist, but it is immediately con-

[31]Gregory A. Caldeira and John R. Wright, "Amici Curiae Before the Supreme Court: Who Participates, When and How Much?," *Journal of Politics* 52 (1990), p. 793.
[32]Ibid., p. 794.   [33]Ibid., p. 786.
[34]Ibid., p. 801.

sidered scandalous rather than normal. This was how Justice Fortas's paid consultantship with a charitable foundation headed by a former client was widely perceived; it ultimately caused him to resign from the Court in 1969.[35] Moreover, the Supreme Court has none of the practice of revolving personnel between private industry and government positions that is typical of many executive agencies. The justices serve for life; they almost never accept another position after retirement. The clerks never return to the Court, except for a handful who win their own appointment as a justice decades later.

The Supreme Court and the Political Arena

There are many intersections between the Court and ordinary politics. Three are particularly important: the process that leads to the appointment of justices, the manner in which public opinion impinges on the Court, and the impact of Court decisions.

THE APPOINTMENT OF JUSTICES

Appointment to the Supreme Court is highly political. The president nominates, and the Senate confirms by a majority vote. Only nine positions exist, and rarely do more than two seats open during any presidential term. President Carter did not have the opportunity to select any justice; President Reagan had one appointment (Sandra Day O'Connor) during his first term and two (Antonin Scalia and Anthony M. Kennedy) during his second; President Bush also made two appointments (David H. Souter and Clarence Thomas). Two seats became vacant in President Clinton's first 15 months in office, leading to the appointment of Ruth Bader Ginsburg and Stephen G. Breyer.

Yet the manner in which presidents approach these appointments varies considerably. Some become quite personally involved in the selection, as was Lyndon B. Johnson; others, like Ronald Reagan, leave it almost entirely to their staff. Some, like Johnson, Reagan, and Bush, ensure that their staff pays close attention to the ideological bent of their appointees; others, like Harry S. Truman and John F. Kennedy, appoint personal friends.

The appointment process usually begins with notification to the White House of an impending vacancy by a retiring justice. Both the Justice Department and the White House Office of Legal Counsel begin generating lists of potential appointees. Although no one openly campaigns for the position, some do so quietly by mobilizing friends to recommend their names. There are no formal qualifications for the job; there is even no legal provision requiring that the appointee be a lawyer. However, the informal requirements are quite stringent and vary with the circumstances of each particular appointment. At the top of the list for many presidents is the requirement that the appointee reflect the president's general policy views. For Franklin Delano Roosevelt, this meant

---

[35]Laura Kalman, *Abe Fortas: A Biography* (New Haven: Yale University Press, 1990); Bruce Allen Murphy, *Fortas: The Rise and Ruin of a Supreme Court Justice* (New York: Morrow, 1988).

the appointee had to support his New Deal reforms on the Court, since the conservative majority on the Court at Roosevelt's election was busily blocking them. During the Truman, Eisenhower, and Kennedy administrations, there was less ideological conflict in Washington and less attention paid to appointees' policy positions. Thus, Truman appointed his friend Sherman Minton, who turned out to be a conservative on many issues, and Eisenhower appointed Earl Warren and William J. Brennan, both of whom became strongly liberal justices. However, since Richard Nixon's election in 1968, presidents have been careful to appoint justices whose general policy outlook is consonant with their own. Republicans blocked Abe Fortas's appointment as chief justice just before the 1968 election and forced him off the Court shortly after; this provided Nixon with the unusual opportunity to make four appointments during his first term, all of whom were judicial conservatives. Presidents Reagan and Bush continued that practice, while President Clinton used his first appointment to counter the trend by replacing the retiring conservative Byron R. White (a Kennedy appointee) with Ruth Bader Ginsburg.

The Senate has, on the whole, responded in kind. Senators also take also into account the likely policy preferences of the nominee.[36] When the president's party controls the Senate, ideological scrutiny of appointments has sometimes been superficial. However, when presidents present an ideologically well-defined nominee to a Senate dominated by the opposite party, opposition has often been fierce. This became clear with President Nixon's second appointment in 1969, Clement Haynsworth, Jr., a South Carolina court of appeals judge with distinctly conservative leanings. One commentator on that appointment describes the process as follows:

> In the confirmation debate, Haynsworth was charged with voting in two cases involving subsidiaries of companies in which he owned stock and with buying a company's stock between the decision and announcement of the decision in a case involving that company. Senators who had emphasized Fortas' ethical improprieties felt obligated to take these charges seriously. For many senators, however, the ethics charges masked opposition on ideological grounds. The NAACP and AFL-CIO opposed Haynsworth as insufficiently supportive of civil rights and labor litigants. Furthermore, the nomination debate occurred in the context of liberal-conservative tension over Representative Gerald Ford's proposal to impeach Supreme Court Justice William O. Douglas and the Nixon administration's efforts to slow southern school desegregation.[37]

When Haynsworth's nomination was defeated, Nixon nominated a still more conservative jurist, G. Harrold Carswell, who was also much less well qualified. That nomination also failed, and Nixon then selected the more moderate Harry G. Blackmun, who was a former associate of Chief Justice Warren Burger. At the time, the two were sometimes irreverently referred to as the "Minnesota twins."

A much more brutal battle occurred eighteen years later when President Reagan nominated Robert H. Bork. Bork was almost universally considered extremely compe-

---

[36]Donald R. Songer, "The Relevance of Policy Values for the Confirmation of Supreme Court Nominees," *Law & Society Review* 13 (1979), pp. 927–948.

[37]Susan M. Olson, "Clement Furman Haynsworth, Jr." in Kermit L. Hall (ed.), *The Oxford Companion to the Supreme Court of the United States* (New York: Oxford University Press, 1992), p. 368.

tent, but his past political history and the views he expressed in law review articles marked him as a presidential loyalist and an ardent conservative. He was solicitor general during the Nixon administration. When Nixon wished to dismiss Watergate prosecutor Archibald Cox in the midst of the Watergate investigations, Bork did his bidding after the attorney general and deputy attorney general resigned rather than obey. That action earned Bork enduring disdain among some Democrats. Mostly, however, Bork's nomination hearings turned on the conservative views he espoused in law review articles. Although he renounced some of them at the hearings, that action only increased distrust of him by some senators. In the end, his nomination failed.[38]

While policy views are in the long run the most important quality of Supreme Court nominees, presidents consider many other qualifications. At the least, the potential nominee must be free of scandal. To help assure that result, the FBI investigates each finalist before the president makes the nomination. It goes without saying that the nominee must be a lawyer, even though no such formal requirement exists. The nominee must generally be highly regarded in the legal profession; the public test of legal qualification is the rating granted to the nominee by the American Bar Association's Standing Committee on the Federal Judiciary. That committee privately investigates the qualifications of potential nominees and reports its rating to the president. As the largest national organization of lawyers, its evaluation signifies a widely regarded measure of legal competence. In addition, the nominee is expected to have some relevant prior experience. All but one (William H. Rehnquist) of those nominated by Presidents Nixon, Reagan, and Bush had previously served on an appellate court. But earlier nominees had come from academia (Felix Frankfurter), federal agencies (Rehnquist and Tom C. Clark), or prominent political careers (Hugo Black as senator from Alabama and Earl Warren as governor of California). Since the Supreme Court is unlike any other tribunal in its consideration of policy issues, both appellate judgeships and political experience are deemed relevant.

Presidents also use Supreme Court appointments to maintain coalitions and repay political debts. Minority groups, such as Jews and African Americans, have sought representation on the Court; many times there appeared to be a "Jewish seat" occupied in turn by Louis D. Brandeis, Felix Frankfurter, Arthur Goldberg, Abe Fortas, and Ruth Bader Ginsburg. President Johnson created an "African-American seat" held by Thurgood Marshall and Clarence Thomas. The first woman to be appointed, Sandra Day O'Connor, won plaudits for President Reagan from feminist groups, as did Ruth Bader Ginsburg for President Clinton. In addition, some presidents have considered geographical balance, making sure no single section of the country lacked someone on the Court. Age has been an important consideration for many presidents; presidents often shun potential nominees who are too old because they would not serve long enough on the Court. President Bush pushed that consideration to the opposite extreme with the appointment of Clarence Thomas at the age of 43, with the prospect of his serving for 25 years or more. Finally, political debts and associations play important roles in some appointments. Earl Warren probably owed his nomination to his role in the 1952 Re-

---

[38]The flavor of the Bork nomination struggle is well captured in Ethan Bronner, *Battle for Justice: How the Bork Nomination Shook America* (New York: W.W. Norton, 1989).

publican presidential nominating convention where he declined to block Dwight D. Eisenhower's nomination. Abe Fortas was a close political friend of President Lyndon Johnson.

Such concerns, together with the Senate's consideration of the nomination, assure that contemporary political issues play a role in the selection of justices. The process brings to the Court men and women who have been vetted for their political views and associations. Such justices also often have connections with the Washington community of policy makers with whom some of them maintain close contact. Justice Frankfurter, for instance, continued to entertain a large number of Washington notables and discuss current policy matters with them; he also gave intermittent advice to President Roosevelt.[39] Justice Fortas continued to be a behind-the-scenes advisor to President Johnson.[40] Similar, if less intense, associations between other justices and Washington notables have existed.

THE IMPACT OF COURT DECISIONS

Considerable controversy exists among scholars who have attempted to measure the impact of Supreme Court decisions. At one extreme are those who say it is almost self-evident that Court decisions such as *Brown*, *Miranda*, *Baker v. Carr*, and *Roe v. Wade* changed the landscape of American politics. The only question for these scholars is to determine how much influence the Court's decisions had and what paths the Court's influence take.[41] At the other extreme are scholars who have tried to isolate the impact of such Court decisions from prevailing social and political trends; their conclusion is that much of what happened after these Court decisions would have happened anyway. If the Court had not acted, Congress, the president, or the states eventually would have taken a similar policy path.[42]

Both camps agree that Court policies are rarely self-executing. They must be implemented by others, who may be the direct targets of the decision (the consumer population). Often, however, those directly addressed by judicial decisions depend on others to interpret them (the interpreting population) and on still other officials to enforce them (the implementing population).[43]

Interpreters of Court decisions are significant because the Court's decisions technically address only the direct litigants in the case before it. However, for the Court's decisions to be policy, they must affect all persons in similar circumstances. Lower court judges interpret the Court's broad edicts as they apply them to specific situations. In turn, lawyers advise clients based on the flow of lower court decisions generated by the Supreme Court's decision. Of course, the accuracy of the interpretation varies. The clearer the original Supreme Court decision, the less likely it is that the Court will have

[39]Bruce Allen Murphy, *The Brandeis Frankfurter Connection* (New York: Oxford University Press, 1982).
[40]Murphy, supra, note 35.
[41]Stephen L. Wasby, *The Impact of the United States Supreme Court: Some Perspectives* (Homewood, Ill.: Dorsey Press, 1970); Charles A. Johnson and Bradley C. Canon, *Judicial Policies: Implementation and Impact* (Washington, D.C.: Congressional Quarterly Press, 1984).
[42]Gerald N. Rosenberg, *The Hollow Hope: Can Courts Bring About Social Change?* (Chicago: University of Chicago Press, 1991).
[43]Johnson and Canon, supra, note 41.

to hear further cases on the matter to clarify its intent. However, clarity of a Supreme Court opinion is only one dimension affecting the interpreting public. The more novel the Supreme Court decision, the more likely some lower court judges will reject the Court's reasoning and the legitimacy of the decision; they may then evade it by reinterpreting its policy message. Likewise, closely divided Supreme Court decisions (a 5–4 vote) or flimsy reasoning invite evasive interpretations by lower courts.

Many Supreme Court decisions require other government agencies to alter their operations. *Brown* required school boards to desegregate their schools, *Miranda* required police to give warnings to all persons they arrested, *Roe v. Wade* required prosecutors to stop prosecuting doctors who performed abortions. The other agencies' reactions depended on their own political environment and on the interpretations that lower court judges issue. Disobeying a Supreme Court decision entails few immediate risks for other government officials. Eventually, someone may take them to a trial court, the trial court may rule against them, and an appeals court may uphold the trial court judgment. Recalcitrant officials rarely face any personal risk (such as imprisonment), and the entire process is likely to take several years, during which time the Supreme Court may alter its policy. Thus, obtaining compliance from implementing officials requires a willingness to obey based on their view that the Court's decision is legitimate and that they *ought* to obey. Moreover, if their own political constituents favor the Court's decision, implementing officials will have self-interested motives for complying; to disobey would endanger their own political future. A favorable political climate supporting implementation of the Court's decision is very important because in many cases, the implementing officials must justify the budgetary expense of doing so and overcome organizational inertia. However, sometimes a Court decision provides powerful incentives to the implementers. *Roe v. Wade*, for instance, not only legalized abortion but made abortion a profit center for hospitals and clinics. Thus, it did not take long after the *Roe* decision for abortion to become widely available.

Third, those directly affected by the Supreme Court's decisions must respond appropriately. Suspects arrested by the police must know not to talk until their lawyer has arrived; women wishing an abortion must seek ways to obtain one. If those whom the Court tries to assist display disinterest, the Court's ruling will not have its intended impact. Johnson and Canon[44] suggest that this was the short-term outcome of *Miranda*. While police grudgingly gave the warnings, many suspects continued to confess before their attorney arrived. The situation is similar when the consuming population is disadvantaged by a Supreme Court decision. In that circumstance, the targets of Supreme Court actions have strong motives to avoid or evade compliance and often do so. State legislators who stood to lose their seats in the reapportionments mandated by *Baker v. Carr*[45] were often in no hurry to comply; in many states it took additional court orders to force them to do so. Purveyors of pornography do not rush to clear their bookshelves of offensive items; they wait until they are forced to do so by the police.

The research on how quickly and how well Court decisions win compliance shows that the process is difficult. Rosenberg's[46] conclusion that Supreme Court decisions

---

[44]Johnson and Canon, supra, note 41, pp. 119–124.   [45] 369 U.S. 186 (1962).
[46]Rosenberg, supra, note 42.

have little or no measurable impact is therefore not entirely surprising. He demonstrates that the civil rights movement was already gathering steam before *Brown* and that public opinion supporting racial segregation was already crumbling. Before *Roe*, state legislatures had begun liberalizing their antiabortion statutes. Rosenberg also examines reapportionment and criminal law reforms "imposed" by Supreme Court decisions and concludes they fell short of their supporters' goals.[47] Thus, it is difficult both to assess the impact of such decisions and to conclude that the Court's decisions are decisive in establishing new policies.

There is, however, an entirely different kind of impact for which the evidence is much stronger.[48] It rests on the ability of the Court to alter the political agenda of Congress, the president, and the states. For instance, while one cannot say the Court and only the Court brought the civil rights movement to the political foreground, there is strong evidence that the *Brown* decision had a substantial impact. The Court has this influence largely because it marches to a different beat than the other branches of the government. To an enormous extent, Congress and the president are captive to two calendar cycles. One is the cycle of elections: every other year a congressional election and every fourth year a presidential election. Everyone in these two branches of government anticipates these elections. Immediately after an election, members of Congress and the president enjoy a brief window of opportunity during which initiatives are possible; that window rapidly closes as the next election approaches. The Court is largely immune to that cycle since none of its members are elected. The second calendar cycle is the budgetary cycle. Each year, Congress and the president must agree to a budget that governs all taxation and expenditure for the coming year. Since almost all government programs require substantial expenditures, all policy initiatives are bundled into the budget. Once again, the Court is immune; it plays no part in that drama.

On the contrary, the justices of the Supreme Court decide on their own which issues are important to them and issue their decisions about those issues when they are ready. Whether that is helpful or distracting to the president's program or to Congress's agenda carries no weight with the Court. The Court is a loose cannon that rolls around the deck and to which the president and Congress must accommodate.

This does not mean the Court is entirely independent of public opinion, as we see in the next section. The Court can change the political agenda only to the degree that its decision catches the attention of responsive publics. Sometimes its decisions will be lost in the din of disputes about other matters. Often, however, Supreme Court decisions alter expectations of significant portions of the political elite that other institutions are forced to respond in one way or another.

The Court's policy making thus sometimes thrusts it into the center of political controversy. Few of its decisions are accepted universally; those who stand to lose something may assert that the Court has no right to engage in lawmaking. But the Court's law- and policy-making functions are inevitable consequences of its processing of disputes.

---

[47]Rosenberg, supra, note 42.
[48]Malcolm M. Feeley, "Hollow Hopes, Flypaper, and Metaphors," *Law & Social Inquiry* 17 (1992), pp. 745–760.

Nevertheless, considerable controversy continues to swirl about its policy involvement. Some argue the Court should avoid taking an activist stance, by which they mean it should not formulate new solutions to the problems that cases present but rather should leave that function to Congress. Others, like Horowitz,[49] have argued that courts are not well equipped for policy formulation. He suggests that because courts rely entirely on litigants to present pertinent facts, they do not have enough information to form broad policy. The fact that courts in the United States operate through an adversarial process often leads to an oversimplification of issues because only two sides are represented in litigation despite the fact that most policy disputes have many dimensions. Finally, Horowitz points to the courts' difficulty in supervising the implementation of their decisions because they lack extensive administrative machinery. Many of these concerns are well grounded. In some disputes, it may seem that a legislature or administrative agency is better equipped to process the conflicting claims. On the other hand, in many instances courts may perform as well as those other legal institutions and may be more readily accessible. Many examples of the effects of the Court's policy making occurred during the eras of the Warren and Burger Courts. Such effects are well illustrated by the Court's decisions about civil rights, the rights of criminal defendants, and abortion.

SCHOOL DESEGREGATION[50]

The most dramatic intervention by the Supreme Court under Chief Justice Earl Warren into the political agenda of the president and Congress occurred as a result of its 1954 school desegregation decision in *Brown v. Board of Education*. Many school districts in the South sought to evade that decision by a variety of legal and extralegal means. The legal methods consisted of an extraordinarily long line of suits that brought to court all kinds of minute details and arcane arguments seeking to delay or reverse the Supreme Court's ruling. Each trial decision was then appealed, thus winning more delay in desegregating the schools. The extralegal means involved outright defiance of the decision. Matters came to a head in 1957 when Governor Orville Faubus of Arkansas called out the National Guard (which is ordinarily under state control) to prevent African-American children from attending Little Rock High School after a federal court had ordered the school to admit them. This presented a grave dilemma to President Eisenhower. School desegregation was not a priority of his administration; on the contrary, it seems that he personally found the Court's decision distasteful. But if he had permitted Governor Faubus to flaunt a court order and the law of the land, Eisenhower might have been opening the way for a disintegration of the country on the race issue, just as had occurred in 1860 before the onset of the Civil War. Consequently, Eisenhower took control of the National Guard and used it to protect the African-American students in their entry into the school. Eisenhower was therefore pushed into employing force to

---

[49]Donald L. Horowitz, *The Courts and Social Policy* (Washington, D.C.: The Brookings Institute, 1977).
[50] The role of the Supreme Court and lower courts is described well in David J. Garrow, *Bearing the Cross* (New York: Morrow, 1986), and Taylor Branch, *Parting the Waters, America in the King Years 1954–63* (New York: Simon & Schuster, 1988).

implement the Supreme Court's decision.[51] For at least fifteen years after *Brown*, the civil rights issue forced its way onto the agenda of presidents and Congresses, largely on the impetus of the Court's original desegregation decision. Civil rights advocates calling themselves "freedom riders" began to travel to the South in the late 1950s and early 1960s to challenge other instances of segregation. The conflicts these confrontations generated and their dissemination by the national media forced civil rights issues to a position of high priority on President Kennedy's agenda and, after his assassination, led Congress to adopt a series of new civil rights laws. Most observers agree that without the original Supreme Court decision, it would have taken longer for these issues to have reached the top of the executive and legislative agendas.

The Warren Court's desegregation decisions thus clearly bent the U.S. domestic political agenda in new directions. At the very least, the Court's decisions hastened the granting and guaranteeing of fundamental rights to the nation's African-American citizens. But court decisions alone were not sufficient to achieve this result. Grave implementation problems confronted the courts; their decisions could only be enforced by willing administrative agencies. It took many years to eliminate de jure segregation in the law books, but de facto segregation in social practice continues to persist in many corners of American life in the 1990s. As late as 1985, the *New York Times* reported African-American women being directed to the "colored" toilet in the basement of a rural southern courthouse instead of to the toilet that white women used on the first floor.[52] Likewise, in many American cities people continued to reside in neighborhoods populated mostly by their own race.[53]

RIGHTS OF CRIMINAL DEFENDANTS

The Warren Court also placed the issue of the rights of defendants in criminal cases on the political agenda. Criminal defendants have little political power. They can do little to organize themselves into an effective political interest group. The Court, however, recognized their problems in a remarkable series of decisions in the 1960s. Responding to cases that indigent defendants brought to the Court, the Warren Court decided that the constitutional guarantee of due process of law as encompassed in the Bill of Rights and the Fourteenth Amendment required courts and police to proceed quite differently in their customary treatment of defendants. As observed earlier, the Court required that all defendants be given an opportunity to be represented by a lawyer, whose services would be provided at no cost if the defendant could not afford to pay the legal fees.[54] The Court also decided that evidence gathered by an illegal search and seizure could not be used in a state court prosecution; to be admissible, evidence would have to be the product of a search authorized by a warrant.[55] Likewise, the Court ruled that due process of law required the police to refrain from questioning an arrested suspect until

---

[51]Jack W. Peltason, *58 Lonely Men: Southern Federal Judges and School Desegregation* (Urbana: University of Illinois Press, 1961), pp. 163–178.

[52]E.R. Shipp, "Across the Rural South, Segregation as Usual," *New York Times*, 27 April 1985, p. 1.

[53]Douglas S. Massey and Nancy A. Denton, *American Apartheid: Segregation and the Making of the Underclass* (Cambridge: Harvard University Press, 1993).

[54]*Gideon v. Wainwright*, 372 U.S. 335 (1963).   [55]*Mapp v. Ohio*, 367 U.S. 643 (1961).

an attorney (if requested) entered the room.[56] Finally, the Court decided that at the time of arrest the police must inform the person of his or her rights. If those rights were not read, any confession or leads given to criminal investigators could not be used against the individual.[57] These Supreme Court decisions fundamentally altered criminal procedures in the United States by placing new burdens on both criminal courts and the police, neither of which liked the constraints.

As southern school districts had done in response to the Court's desegregation ruling, some law enforcement agencies sought to evade the Court's decisions affecting defendants' rights by subterfuge and litigation. Subterfuge failed because defense attorneys challenged illegal court and police procedures. Litigation, however, has slowly succeeded in dulling the edge of the Warren Court's decisions. Particularly with respect to illegal searches and seizures, the Burger and Rehnquist Courts responded to the complaints of law enforcement agencies by adding exceptions to the rule that make it easier for the police to search persons and seize evidence without a proper warrant and still use the results in a criminal prosecution.[58] However, the reading of the *Miranda* warning when an arrest is made and the provision of free defense counsel to persons who cannot afford a lawyer have become fundamental characteristics of the criminal prosecution process in the United States.

Law enforcement agencies also went to Congress and state legislatures seeking relief from the rules regarding defendants imposed by the Supreme Court. For the most part, those legislative efforts failed. However, the Court's decisions were a major impetus for the drafting and serious consideration of a new federal criminal code that attempted to bypass some of the Court's safeguards. Some elements of that code were finally passed by Congress in the closing days of President Reagan's first term in 1984; others continued to be debated in the Clinton administration's first years.

The Warren Court's decisions strengthening the rights of criminal defendants illustrate the way some who are excluded from other legal institutions gain access to the courts. Few in society have less claim to the sympathy of legislators and administrators than criminals. The Court, in part because of its political isolation, could respond to their pleas because it saw their plight not as punishment for crime but as assaults on the rights of all Americans. Once more the political agenda was bent, and once again the Court encountered difficulty in obtaining compliance with its decisions. But no one can deny the enormous impact of these decisions on domestic political controversy.

ABORTION[59]

The Warren Court was not alone in changing the political agenda; the Burger Court also followed its own course in some of its decisions. The most notable example was its 1973 *Roe v. Wade* decision,[60] which invalidated the laws of many states prohibiting

---

[56]*Escobedo v. Illinois*, 378 U.S. 478 (1964).   [57]*Miranda v. Arizona*, 384 U.S. 436 (1966).

[58]*U.S. v. Place*, 103 S. Ct. 2637, (1983); *California v. Carney* 471 U.S. 386 (1985).

[59]The best description of the multiple political consequences of *Roe v. Wade* may be found in Barbara Hinkson Craig and David M. O'Brien, *Abortion and American Politics* (Chatham, N.J.: Chatham House, 1993).

[60]*Roe v. Wade*, 410 U.S. 113 (1973).

abortion unless the life of the woman was at risk. Until this decision, abortion had been generally prohibited, though in some states the law permitted abortion in specific circumstances. But nowhere had abortion been declared part of the constitutional right to privacy. It was the Supreme Court that interpreted the right to privacy into the provisions of the First, Third, Fourth, Fifth, and Ninth Amendments to the Constitution in a decision involving prohibition of the sale of contraceptives in Connecticut.[61] Justice Blackmun's decision in *Roe* applied the right of privacy to the issue of abortion and prohibited interference by state authorities in abortions that occurred during the first three months of pregnancy.

The Court's decision gradually aroused a tidal wave of protest. So-called right-to-life groups had not organized prior to the decision because abortion had not reached the national agenda. But after the ruling, such groups quickly organized at both the state and national levels to find ways to circumvent or reverse the Court's decision. These groups adopted an electoral and legislative strategy rather than the strategy of litigation and defiance used by opponents of school desegregation. Right-to-life groups began to intervene in congressional and state elections to defeat legislators they considered opposed to recriminalizing abortion. Beginning in 1976, Congress began restricting the use of federal funds for abortions, with the result that women on public assistance could not receive an abortion whereas those who could afford the operation could freely obtain one. The efforts of right-to-life groups appeared especially successful in the 1978 congressional races and reinforced congressional decisions to limit the use of public funds for abortions. In addition, state legislatures passed laws that sought to evade *Roe* by requiring parental or spousal permission for an abortion or by placing other obstacles in the way.[62] The abortion controversy came to play a central role in the 1984 presidential campaign, with President Reagan fervently espousing the right-to-life cause and the Catholic Church vigorously challenging the Democratic vice-presidential candidate, Geraldine Ferraro, a Catholic, to recant her pro-choice position. One of the expectations of many right-to-life groups which supported President Reagan in 1984 was that if he had an opportunity to make new appointments to the Supreme Court, he would appoint only those supporting the reversal of *Roe*. The expectation, therefore, was that *Roe* would be reversed by the Court if a new majority were appointed. That expectation was not fulfilled by the time President Bush left office in January 1993, and President Clinton named a pro-choice supporter as his first appointment to the Court.

Thus, like the Supreme Court's school desegregation decisions, *Roe* changed the political agenda of the United States. However, implementation of *Roe* presented few problems because powerful economic incentives existed for hospitals and clinics to make abortions available. On the other hand, it seems clear from reading *Roe*, that the Court gave little thought to the potentially conflicting rights of fetuses. Neither they nor their advocates were parties to the case. Nor is it likely that the Court fully anticipated the storm of controversy their decision aroused.

---

[61]*Griswold v. Connecticut*, 381 U.S. 479 (1965).
[62]Gilbert Y. Steiner (ed.), *The Abortion Dispute and the Amercan System* (Washington, D.C.: The Brookings Institute 1983).

PUBLIC OPINION AND THE SUPREME COURT

At first blush, the Supreme Court seems to operate independent of public opinion. Since the justices are not elected, they seem free from the need to curry public favor; they need not be concerned about the weekly verdict of polls indicating their popularity. Indeed, the Court does very little to create favorable opinion. It employs no "spin masters" to manipulate news about itself. Its press office is a primitive operation that provides little assistance to reporters seeking to understand its decisions, and it does not provide press releases to explain them; it also does not schedule press conferences or interviews for the justices. The Court bars television coverage of its public sessions and rigidly enforces the privacy of its decision-making conferences. Thus, it might appear as if the Court neither cares to cultivate public opinion nor is affected by it.

However, that is scarcely true. In fact, some justices are keenly aware that although they do not face the electorate, the force of their decisions depends on public willingness to obey. Instead of relying on the mystique of elections for their legitimacy, the justices depend on the mystery of the law. A decision on abortion provided an opportunity for Justices O'Connor, Kennedy, and Souter to articulate their concerns quite openly.[63] At stake was the *Roe* decision, which four of the justices appeared ready to reverse. Three of the justices feared that a simple admission that *Roe* was wrong would undermine the legitimacy of the Court. They wrote:

> . . . overruling *Roe's* central holding would not only reach an unjustifiable result under principles of *stare decisis*, but would seriously weaken the Court's capacity to exercise the judicial power and to function as the Supreme Court of a Nation dedicated to the rule of law. . . .
>
> . . . The court's power lies . . . in its legitimacy, a product of substance and perception that shows itself in the people's acceptance of the Judiciary as fit to determine what the Nation's law means and to declare what it demands. . . .
>
> . . . The Court must take care to speak and act in ways that allow people to accept its decisions on the terms the Court claims for them, as grounded truly in principle, not as compromises with social and political pressures having, as such, no bearing on the principled choices that the Court is obliged to make. Thus the court's legitimacy depends on making legally principled decisions under circumstances in which their principled character is sufficiently plausible to be accepted by the Nation.
>
> . . . the Court's duty in the present case is clear. In 1973 it confronted the already-divisive issue of governmental power to limit personal choice to undergo abortion, for which it produced a new resolution based on the due process guaranteed by the Fourteenth Amendment. Whether or not a new social consensus is developing on that issue, its divisiveness is no less today than in 1973, and pressure to overrule the decision, like pressure to retain it, has grown only more intense. A decision to overrule *Roe's* essential holding under the existing circumstances would address error, if error there was, at the cost of both profound and unnecessary damage to the Court's legitimacy, and to the Nation's commitment to the rule of law.[64]

[63]*Planned Parenthood v. Casey*, 112, S. Ct. 2791 (1992).
[64]Ibid., pp. 22, 23, and 26.

While not subject to as intensive public opinion polling as Congress and the president, some systematic research has been done on the public's view of the Court. It generally finds that the Court's public esteem rises and falls as various issues come into the news.[65] During the height of the desegregation crisis in the late 1950s and 1960s, as billboards sprouted across the country with the message "Impeach Earl Warren!," public support for the Court dipped.[66] But as that crisis faded, support for the Court once again rose. During Watergate, it rose substantially. During the late 1960s, support for the Court was substantially higher among African Americans than among southern whites, a direct reflection of the Court's role in the desegregation of public institutions. However, by the 1990s, support among African Americans had substantially declined.[67] As Caldeira and Gibson concluded, "Diffuse support for the Supreme Court is fairly substantial among whites . . . Blacks, like whites, are for the most part favorably disposed toward the Court as an institution."[68] However, public support is not unconditional. Those who are more willing to tolerate disorder for the sake of liberty are more supportive of the Court than those who place primary emphasis on order. African Americans in the age cohort most directly experiencing the Warren Court's decisions are more supportive than either older or younger African Americans.[69] Moreover, opinion leaders seem to condition their support of the Court on its decisions.[70]

Exactly how much support the Supreme Court needs in order to win compliance with its decisions remains unclear. Murphy and Tanenhaus,[71] for instance, asked respondents in 1966 about their attitude toward open housing and the sale of "indecent" magazines to adults. They then asked these respondents if they would change their mind if the Court issued a ruling opposite to their position. Very few said they would change their mind simply because of a Supreme Court decision.[72] This evidence is far from conclusive, because in the real world the Supreme Court does not act entirely alone. The support of opinion leaders is surely more important than that of the mass public because the mass public is likely to follow the lead of opinion leaders. If opinion leaders were to attack the Court continuously through the mass media, the legitimacy of the Court would surely be damaged; the justices are quite aware of this. Thus, even though they are not elected, they remain attentive to broad trends of public opinion. We cannot demonstrate by direct statements from justices that they watch public opinion, but it is noteworthy that the Court's decisions rarely stray beyond the broad spectrum of policy options that are acceptable to a large portion of the elite and mass public. The primary exception was the Court's stubborn rejection of New Deal policies during President Franklin D. Roosevelt's first term. When Roosevelt threatened to "pack" the

[65]Gregory A. Caldeira, "Neither the Purse nor the Sword: Dynamics of Public Confidence in the U.S. Supreme Court," *American Political Science Review* 80 (1986), pp. 1209–1226.

[66]Walter F. Murphy and Joseph Tanenhaus, "Publicity, Public Opinion, and the Court," *Northwestern University Law Review* 84 (1990), pp. 985–1023.

[67]James L. Gibson and Gregory A. Caldeira, "Blacks and the United States Supreme Court: Models of Diffuse Support," *Journal of Politics*, 54 (1992) pp. 1120–1145.

[68]Gregory A. Caldeira and James L. Gibson, "The Etiology of Public Support for the Supreme Court," *American Journal of Political Science* 36 (1992), pp. 640.

[69]Gibson and Caldeira, supra, note 67.   [70]Caldeira and Gibson, supra, note 68.

[71]Murphy and Tanenhaus, supra, note 66.

[72]Murphy and Tanenhaus, supra, note 66, pp. 1008–1015.

Court with new justices through legislation increasing the size of the Court, the justices changed course and Congress rejected the court-packing plan.[73]

We may conclude that public opinion is more important to the Court than its insulated position would indicate. But unlike Congress and the president, the Court does not continuously seek to manipulate public opinion nor does it test the waters before making decisions. In the long run, however, like all other institutions of American government, its strength depends on public acceptance.

Conclusion

For many observers, the Supreme Court constitutes the clearest link between the judiciary and politics. Its concern with policy making thrusts it into the middle of numerous controversies. It is, therefore, no accident that Supreme Court nominations sometimes ignite bitter partisan struggles as presidents seek to bring justices to the Court who will support administration policy. Once on the bench, the products of this political struggle often act like politicos, but of a different breed than in Congress and the White House. They follow their own agenda, craft their own solutions to policy problems, and proceed with much less overt concern for immediate public opinion. The Court's agenda is much less the product of unexpected catastrophes and much more the result of long-brewing conflicts. Like the other institutions of American government, the Court feels the constraints of the fragmentation that marks U.S. politics. Independent of Congress and the president, the Supreme Court nonetheless depends on the goodwill of the targets of its decisions to accomplish its policy objectives. Although the highest court of the land, it often has little direct influence over the judiciaries of the states or the decisions they make. It is in many ways a paradoxical institution.

KEY WORDS

judicial review	solicitor general
in forma pauperis	amicus briefs
writ of certiorari	per curiam
Rule 10	majority opinion
discuss list	justices' clerks

FOR FURTHER STUDY . . .

The flavor of Supreme Court decision making is contained in Anthony Lewis's classic account of the litigation culminating in *Gideon v. Wainwright, Gideon's Trumpet* (New York: Random House, 1964). An account of a more recent case is Barbara Hinkson Craig, *Chadha: The Story of an Epic Constitutional Struggle* (New York: Oxford University Press, 1988). A recent historical review of the Supreme Court is Bernard Schwartz, *A History of the Supreme Court* (New York: Oxford University Press, 1993).

---

[73]Gregory A. Caldeira, "Public Opinion and the U.S. Supreme Court: FDR's Court-Packing Plan," *American Political Science Review 81* (1987), pp. 1139–1153.

While the Supreme Court is quite inaccessible to casual observers—its proceedings are not televised and its members do not give interviews—its decisions are available in most college libraries. Current decisions may be obtained through Internet. Thus, you can get a feel for the manner in which the justices frame significant political issues and how they justify their decisions. For those inclined to undertake a statistical analysis of the Court's output, comprehensive data about Supreme Court decisions is available in the U.S. Supreme Court Judical Database at the Interuniversity Consortium for Political Research. Check with your instructor about how you may gain access to these data.

V

CORE INSTITUTIONS: LEGISLATURES AND ADMINISTRATIVE AGENCIES

Although people often associate only courts with the legal system, legislatures and executive agencies are also core institutions. They both play a much more active role than courts in making law. Both process disputes, although legislatures usually frame disputes as conflicts between groups rather than as grievances between individuals. Administrative agencies are as significant as courts in interpreting law.

The following two chapters are only a brief introduction to each of these core institutions; whole books could easily be devoted to them. The purpose of these chapters is to alert readers to the distinctively legal dimensions of legislatures and administrative agencies and to their special contributions to legal processes.

11

LEGISLATURES

$\mathbf{L}$egislatures are central to the legal system.[1] The statutes they adopt are the principal articulation of law in the United States. They also offer an alternative forum to the courts for obtaining remedies to disputes. Thus, they often engage in a continuing dialogue with the judiciary, as courts interpret statutes and legislatures amend the statutes in response to those interpretations. However, legislatures operate very differently from courts. When they engage in lawmaking, they deal almost entirely with collective grievances, which we shall call **conflicts,** rather than with disputes between individuals. In addition, the legislative process has no clear beginning comparable to the initiation of a civil suit or criminal complaint; consequently, the entire process of bringing conflicts to a legislature is fuzzier. It is also often more prolonged and fluid than court proceedings, and its end product is a collective statement that is often more ambiguous than court decisions. We first examine each of these characteristics of the legislative process and then discuss the relationship between legislatures and courts.

[1]This chapter presumes a general knowledge of Congress and the legislative process. For more detail, refer to general works such as John W. Kingdon, *Congressmen's Voting Decisions,* 3d ed. (Ann Arbor: University of Michigan Press, 1989); Walter J. Oleszek, *Congressional Procedures and the Policy Process,* 3d ed. (Washington, D.C.: Congressional Quarterly Press, 1989); Lawrence C. Dodd and Bruce I. Oppenheimer (eds.), *Congress Reconsidered,* 4th ed. (Washington, D.C.: Congressional Quarterly Press, 1989). Much current data on Congress may be found in Norman J. Ornstein, Thomas E. Mann, and Michael J. Malbin, *Vital Statistics on Congress 1991–1992* (Washington, D.C.: Congressional Quarterly Press, 1992). For state legislatures, see Samuel C. Patterson, "State Legislators and the Legislatures," in Virginia Gray, Herbert Jacob, and Robert B. Albritton (eds.), *Politics in the American States,* 5th ed. (Glenview, Ill.: Scott, Foresman, 1990).

The Legislative Process

THE FOCUS ON CONFLICT

At one time, legislatures handled grievances of individuals by grants of divorce, incorporation, and other so-called private laws. This rarely occurs today. Almost all legislative proposals are public bills that address the problems of entire categories of people. The legislature's focus on conflicts rather than disputes has many consequences. One result is that individuals who have a grievance have little chance of getting a law passed to remedy their problem unless they combine their grievance with those of others; those individuals are much more likely to take their grievance to a court. The social institution that performs the task of aggregating grievances is the interest group. Without interest group support, most grievances would not win the attention of a legislature. Interest groups are thus the principal gatekeepers to legislatures and provide a sort of certification that a problem has a more general scope.

A second consequence of the focus on conflict is that almost all legislative business is public. Whereas most litigation involves private disputes, the aggregation of disputes into social conflict drives them into the public sphere. The focus on conflict seems to push legislative activity so far into the political realm that some people do not even classify such activity as part of the legal system.

Finally, conflicts often have longer histories than individual disputes. They frequently originate as disputes between individuals or between individuals and a public agency. When no satisfactory resolution is found through informal dispute-processing arenas, administrative procedures, or litigation, the disputes develop into a broader conflict. This process often takes a long time.

THE LACK OF CLEAR ORIGINS OF LEGISLATION

The conflicts that legislatures process may be on the agenda for many years before any action is taken. For instance, national health insurance was first proposed by President Harry S. Truman in 1945. It was adopted in a limited manner in the Johnson administration, as the Medicare program for senior citizens in 1965 and the Medicaid program for those on welfare in 1966. It did not surface again in a serious way until Bill Clinton made it a centerpiece of his presidential campaign in 1992, and it then became the focus of congressional debate in 1994. Similarly, the Clean Air Act of 1990 had its origins as far back as 1977 when the previous clean air law was adopted; it took an unusual conjunction of political forces led by George Bush to win its approval.[2] Likewise in the states: when New York adopted a new set of rules in 1980 for dividing property after divorce, it was acting on proposals that had been before the legislature since the early 1970s.[3]

---

[2]Richard E. Cohen, *Washington at Work: Back Rooms and Clean Air* (New York: Macmillan, 1992).
[3]Herbert Jacob, *Silent Revolution: The Transformation of Divorce Law in the United States* (Chicago: University of Chicago Press, 1988), pp. 123–125.

It is usually very difficult to identify the originator of a piece of legislation. Many will claim credit—those who first proposed it, those who worked to make it a plausible solution to a problem, and those who finally were in a position to assure its passage. In the course of this long process, the problem being addressed is often redefined. It may be narrowed, as in the case of the national health insurance plan that emerged from Congress as health insurance for the aged and medical assistance for the indigent in 1965 and 1966. It may be broadened, as in the case of child abuse legislation that moved from a national law to promote child abuse research and stimulate state treatment facilities to a law that regulated treatment of severely handicapped newborns.[4] Legislation is therefore often less focused than litigation. Not only does it address broader social conflicts, but its target problem is often shifting and unclear.

THE FLUIDITY OF THE LEGISLATIVE PROCESS

The legislative process has well-defined steps that a bill must follow to be adopted into a law. But this highly structured process disguises a considerable fluidity resulting from the fact that there are many more participants in the legislative process than in litigation, that many of these participants enter and exit the decision-making process in a seemingly random way, and that diverse external influences impinge on legislatures.

Legislatures generally are large bodies whose members always represent a geographic constituency. Except for local legislative bodies, such as city councils, the districts legislators are supposed to represent are large and diverse, often covering an entire state. This situation has many consequences for the legislative process. The size of legislatures produces a large pool of participants for every decision. Most organizations with more than a handful of participants impose a hierarchical structure on their members, with the result that most perform routine tasks while important decisions are reserved for those at the top. However, this is not the case with American legislatures. They operate with little hierarchy because of their representative character. Each member has a single vote; this equality leads to large numbers of legislators being involved in important decisions. Although the legislative leaders possess some perquisites that provide them additional influence, their position is one in which they bargain for, rather than demand, support.

Because all members of legislatures have an equal vote, theoretically all may involve themselves to the same extent in every proposal. Of course, in practice this does not happen. Legislators specialize according to their constituents' interests, their personal concerns and experiences, and their committee assignments. Nevertheless, every legislator has an opportunity to participate actively on every issue. Often they simply follow a party leader, someone else from their own region, or an acknowledged expert in voting on bills outside their area of expertise. To others, the recommendation of a legislative committee is persuasive. In many instances, legislators with no previous record of interest in a bill will become actively involved for a brief period and then withdraw again; such intrusions may exert considerable influence on the language of the bill or

[4]Barbara J. Nelson, *Making an Issue of Child Abuse: Political Agenda Setting for Social Problems* (Chicago: University of Chicago Press, 1984).

the likelihood of its passage. Sometimes, the whole body of a legislature will follow a committee's recommendations; often, however, some legislators who are not on the committee will actively intervene in the floor debate to have the bill amended or defeated. Likewise, a bill endorsed by the Speaker of the House of Representatives may pass, but there is always a chance that it will be defeated.

The easy entry and exit of legislators during the consideration of a bill is prevented in some countries by a strong party system that imposes a quasi-hierarchical discipline on legislators despite their nominal equality. American legislatures, however, typically have only a rudimentary party organization. Most are organized along partisan lines, with Republicans sitting on one side of the chamber and Democrats on the other, and leadership positions go to the party with the most members. However, the leaders do not have power to force their party members to follow their lead in the consideration of legislative proposals. They cannot exclude a member from a debate, and they cannot prevent members from making proposals that upset delicate compromises hammered out among the leaders. The leadership also cannot force members to vote in support of their positions; they generally cannot even force members to be present for the votes. For instance, President Clinton's first budget passed by only one vote because many members of his own party voted against it. When Congress considered the North American Free Trade Agreement (NAFTA) three months later, the Democratic majority whip opposed the president's position, as did other Democratic members; NAFTA passed only with substantial support from the Republican "opposition."[5] Such party disunity is not uncommon in American legislatures. This is quite different from the legislative process in England, for instance, where a proposal by the prime minister is almost always adopted as law because the prime minister can impose discipline on party members.

Legislators take their role as elected representatives seriously. As Fenno has suggested, they listen to constituents, although they pay closer heed to those who have supported them politically than to the undifferentiated general public.[6] The diversity of the legislator's districts more often liberates rather than constrains them. This is partly the result of fluidity in the composition of the inner group of a legislator's strongest supporters over the course of his or her career. However, it also results from the fact that no district has a single interest so strong that it dictates every vote. On most issues, legislators can find support for almost any position from some element of their constituency; on many, most constituents either do not care or do not know how their representative votes. Consequently, legislators enjoy considerable discretion; on most votes they either act like **delegates,** following whatever portion of their constituency they wish to indulge or they can act like **trustees,** following their own consciences.[7] However, if we compare them to judges, legislators are much more sensitive to constituency pressures.

The contrast to judges is made stark by legislators' sensitivity to external events. Although legislatures have much more control over their agendas, their control is not absolute. Natural disasters, upheavals in a foreign country, disturbances in foreign

[5]*Congressional Quarterly Weekly Report 51,* 20 November 1993, pp. 3174–3185.
[6]Richard F. Fenno, Jr., *Home Style: House Members in Their Districts* (Boston: Little, Brown, 1978).
[7]Ibid. Also see Darrell M. West, *Congress and Economic Policy Making* (Pittsburgh: University of Pittsburgh Press, 1987).

money markets, and other unexpected developments surface on legislative agendas much more rapidly than on court dockets. Legislators respond to these influences because of their perceptions of their constituents' concerns. In addition, the legislature as a whole is sometimes driven to consider an issue raised by maverick members who use their privileges to force a vote that some colleagues might prefer to avoid. Thus, like judges, legislators sometimes work on issues they have not selected and would prefer to neglect.

Fluidity of legislator participation and its consequences are a fundamental fact of legislative activity in the United States. They flow from basic characteristics of governmental structure and political practice. On the one hand, it is a consequence of the representative character of American legislatures. On the other, it is supported by the lack of party discipline and the absence of other hierarchical devices in the legislative body.

Thus far, we have discussed only the fluidity of participation in the legislative process by *members* of legislatures. This fluidity is compounded by an equally fluid entry and exit of outsiders. Both the federal and state constitutions require that bills be signed by a chief executive before they become law. This requirement is a ticket admitting presidents, governors, mayors, and many of their subordinates into the legislative process.

The entry of executive officials into legislative activity admits persons who often have different priorities. For instance, in the United States it is quite common for the chief executive to belong to one party while the legislature (or one portion of it) is controlled by another. At the national level, the president's party had a minority in at least one house in more than half the congresses since the end of World War II.[8] Moreover, chief executives respond to different pressures than legislators because they are elected by larger constituencies. A president must worry about the whole nation's economy, rather than a single district's cotton or tobacco crop or textile mill; governors must keep an eye on their more rural constituencies in addition to their state's large metropolitan areas. Consequently, even after a legislature passes a bill, it remains problematic whether it will receive the chief executive's signature and become law. At the national level, every president since the end of World War II has vetoed more than a dozen bills during each term of his office.[9] In many states, governors intrude even more emphatically in the legislative process, for many have the power to change bills that are sent to them, requiring the legislature to override this amendatory veto if the legislature is to have its way.[10]

The chief executive's role in the legislative process is a wedge allowing many more outsiders to enter the process. The entire executive branch of the government plays an active role in legislative activity. Many proposals for laws originate with executive agencies. Legislators also routinely look to administrative agencies for information

[8]Ornstein et al, supra, note 1, pp. 41–42. In the states, split party control is also common; see Patterson, supra note 1, pp. 173–175.
[9]Ornstein et al, supra, note 1, p. 158.
[10]Thad L. Beyle, "Governors," in Gray et al, supra, note 1, pp. 224–226, 233–235.

about the potential effects of their proposals. Committee hearings to consider new and revised government programs routinely begin with presentations by executive officials and bureaucrats. Their stakes are extraordinarily high because the scope of their work and, perhaps, their livelihood depend on the outcome of legislative deliberations. In addition, administrators often have the most detailed information about the issue legislators seek to address and possess a close knowledge of existing legal provisions; they often best understand the likely consequences of suggested amendments to the language of existing statutes. It is, therefore, not surprising that they sometimes even participate in the mark-up committee sessions at which legislation is drafted. Thus, a large number of anonymous bureaucrats add to the fluidity of the legislative process.

THE IMPACT OF ELECTORAL AND BUDGETARY CYCLES _____

Legislative agendas are molded by two forces that are foreign to courts: the electoral cycle and the budgetary cycle. Both of them have wide-ranging consequences for the way legislatures create laws.

The **electoral cycle** is fundamental to the legislative process. Congress, for instance, finds it much easier to consider controversial legislation during the first twelve months after an election than during the next year. By January of an even-numbered year, when all of the House of Representatives and one-third of the Senate face election in November, Congress finds itself distracted by its members' need to campaign for reelection. Members are increasingly absent to raise campaign funds and electioneer in their home districts. They also find it important to posture for the media, which may make compromise more difficult. Members of Congress may be particularly concerned about having to register their vote on issues that might prove unpopular with substantial numbers of their constituents so near an election; such ballots are more easily obtained earlier in their term because most constituents who are opposed to their representatives' vote may have forgotten about it by the time of the election. As a consequence, votes on sensitive issues are sometimes delayed until after an election. Courts, on the other hand, are almost completely insensitive to the electoral calendar.

The electoral cycle reinforces the partisan tinge that is typical of almost all legislative actions. With legislators divided between two parties, bipartisanship is the closest that American legislatures approach to the disinterested stance expected of courts. Of course, legislatures are not designed to be disinterested; their purpose is to represent and reflect their constituents' interests, and that often requires partisanship. As elections draw near, each party seeks to distinguish itself from the other in order to give its candidates an advantage on election day, and partisanship becomes harsher.

Legislatures must likewise respond to the **budgetary cycle.** Every governmental unit operates within a budgetary calendar, a fiscal year for which appropriations must be made by the legislature. For the federal government, the fiscal year runs from October 1 through September 30. Congress must begin considering appropriations in early January and finish the task by early fall. States generally use different fiscal years and some operate on two-year cycles. Regardless of the details, however, the budgetary cycle periodically forces legislatures to confront policy choices. Existing programs must be given new funds; an opportunity automatically arises each year either to terminate or to expand a program. Because there are strong pressures to balance the budget (a constitutional mandate for state and local governments), or at least to reduce the deficit, existing programs provide stiff competition to new ones for the limited available revenues.

Legislatures consequently spend a great deal of time on budgetary matters. Moreover, many policy decisions are transformed into fiscal issues because the budgetary cycle has the unrelenting effect of forcing legislators to reexamine issues that had appeared settled during a previous round of legislative attention. This effect was dramatically demonstrated during the first year of the Clinton administration. President Clinton came into the White House with a long list of domestic programs he wanted to initiate; one of the key elements was a plan to boost the economy with a package of public expenditures that were to provide new jobs. In addition, a centerpiece of his agenda was a plan to provide health care insurance for every American. However, the election had also increased the visibility of deficit reduction as an issue at the same time many voters vehemently opposed raising new taxes. The need to bring the federal budget into closer balance repeatedly molded consideration of all other spending initiatives. The economic expansion package failed to win Congressional support, his first budget passed by only a single vote, and the health care plan was delayed until 1994 when it became embroiled in the congressional election.

All of the characteristics we have described make the legislative process quite uncertain. When a president or governor sends legislative proposals to the legislature, no one can be sure they will pass. Indeed, there is a high probability that they will *not* pass without amendment. Whether a legislature will address a conflict and the solution it adopts is always problematic. When the legislature finally passes a law, its language is often ambiguous; that ambiguity reflects the compromises required to win passage, but it may create difficulty when administrators begin to implement the law. This stands in sharp contrast to the way courts address disputes. Court decisions are rarely compromises. They typically address narrow problems with a comparatively high degree of precision. Even though there is considerable uncertainty in the judicial process, the sources and dimensions of that uncertainty are quite different as we saw in earlier chapters.

THE END PRODUCT

Laws are the most significant products of legislatures, for the legal system.[11] Courts, as we have seen, also make law; the next chapter shows that administrative agencies likewise participate in law making. The statutory product of legislatures, however, has some distinctive characteristics.

Courts make law in the course of interpreting existing statutes and constitutional provisions in the context of specific disputes. Legislatures make law by formulating general prescriptions. These prescriptions usually are extensions, not interpretations, of existing norms. Consequently, the form of statutory law is quite different from court-made law.

---

[11]Laws, of course, are not legislatures only products. Legislators play a very important role in processing disputes between government agencies and constituents and in providing services for constituents.

Consider, for example, the language of the Child Abuse Prevention and Treatment Act of 1974, shown in Figure 11.1. This act established a National Center on Child Abuse and Neglect, provided it with a set of activities, and defined child abuse. Other portions of the law (not reprinted here) ordered the establishment of an Advisory Board on Child Abuse and Neglect, specified how federal funds were to be allocated to state agencies, and authorized specific levels of expenditures for each of the following four years.

Certain features of this act stand out. One is that its language is thoroughly prescriptive; no descriptions of existing programs intervene. The law says that the secretary of Health, Education, and Welfare[12] "shall" engage in a variety of activities and is "authorized" to spend money in their support. A second feature of this law is that it stands alone, with little accompanying interpretation. There is a documentary trail consisting of committee reports and references to floor debates, but the interpretations that can be drawn from it are more problematic than those that accompany court decisions. Committee reports are often partisan documents; floor debates usually contain contradictory statements by various members giving inconsistent reasons for favoring the bill. After its passage, the committee in charge of the bill may issue a **legislative history,** which purports to provide an authoritative account of the intent underlying the new law, but that history is not voted on and may reflect the desires of the law's sponsors rather than the full nuances of the entire legislative process. By contrast, when courts make law, they do so through opinions that justify and explain the law they are creating. Those opinions occasionally are also ambiguous when reflecting divisions on the court, but usually they are more coherent than legislative debates and more authoritative than legislative histories.

Consequently, many statutes are ambiguous. In addition, because they are the product of legislative compromises, they often contain intentionally vague language. In the Child Abuse Prevention and Treatment Act, for instance, proponents compromised with Nixon administration officials by excluding a provision naming the administrative agency within the Department of Health, Education and Welfare that would house the new program, instead obtaining a separate letter of agreement from the administration stating that the program would be housed in the Office of Child Development.[13] This agreement, however, did not have the force of law. The ambiguity of this legislative intent became sharper in 1981, when Congress considered renewing the program. It almost fell victim to President Reagan's first slash at domestic welfare programs as he sought to reduce government spending and lower taxes. The program was saved when supporters traded their votes on an energy proposal desired by southern legislators in exchange for southern conservative support for the child abuse program.[14]

The difficulties ascertaining legislative intent in a statute has often frustrated judges. Although Justice Antonin Scalia has perhaps been most scathing in his scorn of official legislative histories,[15] this concern has not been limited to judicial conserva-

---

[12]When a separate Department of Education was created in 1979, this official became secretary of Health and Human Services.
[13]Nelson, supra, note 4, p. 116.   [14]Ibid., p. 119.
[15]See, for instance, his concurring opinion in *Taylor v. U. S.*, 110 S. Ct. 2160 (1990).

An Act to provide financial assistance for a demonstration program for the prevention, identification, and treatment of child abuse and neglect, to establish a National Center on Child Abuse and Neglect, and for other purposes.

Be it enacted by the Senate and House of Representatives of the United States of America in Congress assembled, That:

This Act may be cited as the "Child Abuse Prevention and Treatment Act."

THE NATIONAL CENTER ON CHILD ABUSE AND NEGLECT

Sec. 2. (a) The Secretary of Health, Education, and Welfare (hereinafter referred to in this Act as the "Secretary") shall establish an office to be known as the National Center on Child Abuse and Neglect (hereinafter referred to in this Act as the "Center").

(b) The Secretary, through the Center, shall—

(1) compile, analyze, and publish a summary annually of recently conducted and currently conducted research on child abuse and neglect;

(2) develop and maintain an information clearinghouse on all programs, including private programs, showing promise of success, for the prevention, identification, and treatment of child abuse and neglect;

(3) compile and publish training materials for personnel who are engaged or intend to engage in the prevention, identification, and treatment of child abuse and neglect;

(4) provide technical assistance (directly or through grant of contract) to public and nonprofit private agencies and organizations to assist them in planning, improving, developing, and carrying out programs and activities relating to the prevention, identification, and treatment of child abuse and neglect;

(5) conduct research into the causes of child abuse and neglect, and into the prevention, identification, and treatment thereof; and

(6) make a complete and full study and investigation of the national incidence of child abuse and neglect, including a determination of the extent to which incidents of child abuse and neglect are increasing in number or severity.

DEFINITION

Sec. 3. For purposes of the Act the term "child abuse and neglect" mean the physical or mental injury, sexual abuse, negligent treatment, or maltreatment of a child under the age of eighteen by a person who is responsible for the child's welfare under circumstances which indicate that the child's health or welfare is harmed or threatened thereby, as determined in accordance with regulations prescribed by the Secretary.

Figure 11.1
Child Abuse Prevention and Treatment Act, Pub. L. No. 93-247, 88 Stat. 4 (1974)

tives. The difficulties were also described by Justice William J. Brennan as the Supreme Court was attempting to understand what Congress had intended by including a reference to the "program or activity" of an educational institution in a law prohibiting sex discrimination. In his dissenting opinion to *Grove City College v. Bell*, Brennan wrote:

> The voluminous legislative history of Title VI is not easy to comprehend, especially when one considers the emotionally and politically charged atmosphere operating at the time of its enactment. And there are no authoritative committee reports explaining the many compromises that were eventually enacted, including the program specific limitations that found their way into Title VI. Moreover, as might be expected, statements were made by various Members of Congress that can be cited to support a whole range of definitions for the "program or activity" language. For every instance in which a legislator equated the word "program" with a particular grant statute, there is an example of a legislator defining "program or activity" more broadly.[16]

Even though politics plays a dominant role in the legislative lawmaking process, as Justice Brennan recognized, it would be wrong to assume that legal technicalities are entirely overlooked. Legislatures necessarily address the ways judges will interpret the statutes. There is always a possibility (and in many instances a probability) that someone will challenge the statute in court; administrators and private citizens will then be bound by the court interpretations of the law. Consequently, legislatures try to write statutes using language familiar to courts and employing terms that will force judges to implement them in the way the legislature intended. When legislatures fail to do this (and this happens with some frequency), courts may interpret the law in a way that the majority in the legislature did not intend.

To guard against such a possibility, legislatures employ lawyers to write their bills so that the drafts will conform as much as possible with existing statutes and current legal usage. Many legislatures have special offices for drafting legislation. The desire to avoid misconstruction of statutes by judges has the unfortunate consequence of making statutory language extraordinarily stilted and saturated with legal jargon.

The legislative product thus has several distinctive characteristics. It is unremittingly prescriptive. It is often full of ambiguity and sometimes contains contradictions borne of the compromises needed to obtain the vote required for adoption. However, a statute is also, in part, the product of specialized drafters who endow it with much legal jargon in an attempt to innoculate it from judicial misinterpretation.

---

[16]*Grove City College v. Bell*, 104 S. Ct. 1211, 1228–1129 (1984).

Relations Between Legislatures and Courts

Legislatures and courts have a continuing relationship. Although this relationship often results in the court's affirmation of the legislature's intent, it is sometimes tense.[17]

Some of the statutes legislatures adopt become the occasion for later litigation as the laws create rights and obligations that in turn create disputes. For example, the Americans with Disabilities Act (ADA) of 1990 forbade most forms of discrimination against those with disabilities and required making a wide range of public facilities available to those with particular disadvantages. Before this law, those confined to wheelchairs had no legal recourse when denied public transportation, and those discharged from their employment because of their disability had no legal grounds to sue their former employer. The passage of ADA opened a floodgate of grievances long felt by the disabled. Some of those grievances came to legislators and executive officials who had to provide funds for making public facilities universally accessible. Others, however, led to court actions. For instance, one such action involved an employer's right to discriminate against an otherwise satisfactory worker for obesity.[18]

At other times, legislatures and courts disagree over the interpretation of statutes. Such a dispute initiated a series of heated congressional debates in 1989, when the Supreme Court, which had become more conservative through appointments made by President Reagan, restrictively interpreted Title VII of the Civil Rights Act of 1964. In a series of decisions that, in part, overturned longstanding interpretations of the law, the Court made it increasingly difficult for workers to win employment discrimination suits.[19] President Bush defended those interpretations, invoking the specter of quotas for minorities if they were not upheld, but the Democratic majority in Congress vigorously sought to repeal them by enacting new legislation that clarified Congress's intent. A bitter legislative struggle ensued, occupying more than two years. With great effort, Congress passed a bill, only to have President Bush veto it. Just before the 1992 election, Congress passed a new version of the bill with provisions that President Bush found acceptable. Throughout the controversy, however, it was clear that Congress would make every attempt possible to reverse the Court's decisions.

This was also part of a continuing dispute with the Court over civil rights legislation that began in the early years of the Reagan administration when the Supreme

---

[17]Historical accounts of the relationship between the Supreme Court and Congress may be found in Walter F. Murphy, *Congress and the Court* (Chicago: University of Chicago Press, 1964); and John R. Schmidhauser and Larry L. Berg, *The Supreme Court and Congress: Conflict and Interaction 1945–1968* (New York: Free Press, 1972). More recent events are reflected in Roger Handberg and Harold F. Hill, Jr., "Court Curbing, Court Reversals, and Judicial Review: The Supreme Court Versus Congress," *Law & Society Review 14*, (1980), pp. 309–322, and Thomas G. Walker and Deborah J. Barrow, "Funding the Federal Judiciary: The Congressional Connection," *Judicature* 69 (1985), pp. 43–50.

[18]"U.S. Says Disabilities Act May Cover Obesity," *New York Times*, 14 November 1993, Sec. 1, p17.

[19]See, *Wards Cove v. Antonio* 490 U.S. 642 (1989); *Patterson v. McLean Credit Union*, 491 U.S. 164 (1989); *Price Waterhouse v. Hopkins* 490 U.S. 228 (1989); *Martin v. Wilks* 490 U.S. 755 (1989); *Lorance v. AT&T Technologies* 490 U.S. 900 (1989). Also involved were *Library of Congress v. Shaw* 478 U.S. 310 (1986); *Crawford Fitting Co. v. J.T. Gibbons* 482 U.S. 437 (1987); *West Virginia University Hospitals v. Casey* No 89-994 (1991); and *Equal Employment Opportunity Commission v. Arabia American Oil Co.* No 89-1838 (1991).

Court gave a narrow interpretation to Title IX of the Education Amendments of 1972[20] in *Grove City College v.Bell*. The dispute arose when Grove City College, a small liberal arts school in Pennsylvania that adhered to a Christian and libertarian philosophy, refused to sign an Assurance of Compliance—required by the federal government as a condition for receiving government funding—indicating that it did not discriminate among its students on the basis of gender. The college refused to sign the assurance because it felt it was an unwarranted meddling in the school's affairs. In fact, the college did not receive any direct federal funds, but 140 students were receiving federal tuition-assistance grants. Although no allegation was made that Grove City College discriminated against women, the college refused on principle to sign the required document. The courts, therefore, had to decide whether all aid to the college (including the grants to its students) could be cut off because of this refusal. The trial court ruled for the college; the court of appeals decided in favor of ending all aid, including student assistance, in the absence of the assurance. Finally, the dispute reached the Supreme Court. The majority held that Grove City College had no reason for not signing the assurance. However, the Court also decided that only grants to the financial aid office and not to any other part of the college's program (or to the students themselves) could be withheld because of the school's noncompliance.

The case turned on what Congress had intended by including in the law the words "program or activity," as Justice Brennan's dissent quoted above indicates. The dispute over the language was not trivial. If the Supreme Court's interpretations were sustained, colleges that did discriminate could do so with little fear of losing needed federal funds as long as the discrimination occurred in some program that used few of those funds. For instance, if a college discriminated in admissions, only federal aid to the admissions office would be endangered, even though the entire institution was then discriminatory. Civil rights and feminist organizations as well as many members of Congress were furious with the Court's interpretation. The Reagan administration, however, welcomed the decision, because it minimized governmental interference in otherwise private educational institutions. The fight to overturn the *Grove City* decision and the subsequent decisions narrowing the prohibition against job discrimination occupied much time and energy in Congress from 1984 to 1992.[21]

The *Grove City* case illustrates how legislatures and courts influence each other. Statutes that legislatures adopt create entitlements that give rise to disputes. Some of these disputes are brought to the courts, which often reinforce the legislatures' intent. However, in some cases, courts interpret the law in ways contrary to the intent of many legislators who voted for the law. After such an interpretation, the legislature often tries to change the law once more with amendments that reinstate their original intent. Thus, in many instances the law is not what either the legislatures or courts alone declare but the result of a long exchange between the two.

Another area on which courts and legislatures meet concerns their staffing and budgets. Staffing is an issue of considerable tension between the federal courts and Con-

---

[20]Pub. L. No. 92–318.
[21]For the course of this conflict, see *1991 Congressional Quarterly Almanac* (Washington, D.C.: Congressional Quarterly Press, 1992), pp. 251–261.

gress, since the courts are entirely dependent on Congress (and the president) for both the number of judgeships and who will fill them. Some judges make covert efforts to influence judicial nominations; this is best documented for the Supreme Court.[22] Open efforts to influence the president and Congress may take the form of endorsements after a nomination has been made. However, through such organizations as judicial councils in the states and the Judicial Conference of the United States for federal courts, judges lobby for budget requests and other legislation concerning the operation of the courts. Unlike judicial appointments, budgetary allocations and organizational issues rarely become hotly disputed, although the outcome of such requests may reflect tensions arising from court rulings interpreting controversial legislation.[23]

Legislative Lawmaking

When we examined appellate courts in Chapter 9, we noted the controversy over the lawmaking activities of these courts. Such judicial activism is decried by some who believe it intrudes on what they perceive to be the legitimate function of legislatures. But, as we have noted, some critics of judicial activism also fear that judicial lawmaking is marred by insufficient information. It is useful to examine similarly the legislatures' role in lawmaking.

There is no controversy about the appropriateness of lawmaking by legislatures; that is what they are supposed to do. The fact that legislators are elected to make laws bestows legitimacy to their endeavors. Their ability to perform their representative function fully, however, may be questioned. Legislators in the United States have enormous constituencies. In the 1990s, House of Representatives' members, for instance, represented constituencies with an average of more than half a million inhabitants. As we have already noted, these congressional districts comprise a large number of conflicting interests, many of which do not win a voice in Congress either because their representative disagrees with their positions or because they have not made their demands heard. To some degree, interest group activity fills the void that is left by imperfections in the constituency system, but imperfections nonetheless remain.

Laws and the policies contained in them are sometimes flawed by the same informational handicap that affects judicial policymaking. This occurs even though legislatures are much more active in seeking information than are courts. Much of the information used to justify new laws and determine their content comes from committee hearings. Many witnesses at these hearings relate particular incidents that echo the stories told by witnesses in court trials. In addition, committees typically employ experts to collect evidence that focuses on the general characteristics of a problem rather than on the idiosyncratic traits emphasized by other witnesses. When facts are missing, committees fund studies to find them. In Congress, such inquiries produce authoritative studies of problem areas about which no such knowledge had previously existed; the extent of

---

[22]Lawrence Baum, *The Supreme Court*, 4th ed. (Washington, D.C.: Congressional Quarterly Press, 1993), pp. 35–36.
[23]Cf. Walker and Barrow, supra, note 17.

this search for information is indicated by the size of legislative staffs. In 1989, Congress had more than 3300 staff members serving on congressional committees in addition to the 10,000 persons working for the Congressional Budget Office, General Accounting Office, Library of Congress, and the Office of Technology Assessment. An additional 13,700 persons worked for individual members of Congress and in leadership offices. If these seem like large numbers, it must be remembered that in the 1989 session, Congress dealt with more than 6600 bills and processed a federal budget of $1222 billion.[24] Many state legislatures also have sizeable staffs, although on a much smaller scale than that of Congress.

Despite such research efforts, much legislation is based on poor information. Legislative debates are marked more by the telling of "horror stories" than by a cold analysis of statistical evidence. In many instances, sufficient information does not exist to make an informed judgment about the best remedy for the problem at hand. This was particularly highlighted in the debate over health care reform during the first years of the Clinton administration. President Clinton proposed, and Congress considered, an enormously complex plan; estimates of its effects on various segments of the population and on the health industry remained at best educated guesses. It was a good example of how the information base available to legislatures is quite different from that used by courts, but nevertheless sometimes cannot provide all necessary answers. Thus, like the courts, legislatures operate under severe informational constraints.

Conclusion

The legislative process that produces statutes is very different from the judicial process that interprets and, sometimes, creates laws. Unlike the courts, legislatures focus almost exclusively on social conflict rather than individual disputes. The legislative process incorporates greater fluidity; its outcome in the United States is also more uncertain, for it lacks the huge number of routine (and quite predictable) decisions that characterize much of the judicial process. Partisanship plays a large and legitimate role. The end products of the two processes are also different. Statutes tend to be broadly drafted; case decisions are usually quite focused and precise. However, lawmaking in both arenas sometimes suffers from the absence of adequate information.

KEY WORDS
conflict	electoral cycle
delegate	budgetary cycle
trustee	legislative history

FOR FURTHER STUDY . . .

The atmosphere of deal-making and compromise that pervades Congress is well described by Richard E. Cohen, *Washington at Work: Back Rooms and Clean Air* (New York: Macmillan, 1992). The interaction between Congress and the courts in the context of a specific issue—abortion—is explored by Barbara Hinkson Craig and

[24]Ornstein et al, supra, note 1, pp. 124–125, 151, 172. The figure for the budget is that indicated for "budget authority."

David M. O'Brien, *Abortion and American Politics* (Chatham, N.J.: Chatham House, 1993). For more detail on the legislative process itself, refer to the citations noted in footnote 1 of this chapter.

Many libraries have copies of the *U.S. Statutes at Large* or state session laws; these volumes contain those statutes passed by Congress and by state legislatures. Examine a recent statute that has been described in the media for its organization, language, and specific provisions. Compare the statute with the media's description and analysis of how it was passed. Perhaps the most convenient source for media analysis of the maneuvering that led to passage of laws by Congress may be found in *Congressional Weekly*, published by Congressional Quarterly. Still more detail may be found in the *New York Times* and the *Washington Post*.

12

ADMINISTRATIVE AGENCIES

L ife in late-twentieth-century America takes place in a dense underbrush of administrative agencies. Even in small towns, telephone books contain a long list of public agencies; in large cities, the list fills many pages and these agencies occupy dozens of office buildings. They range from bureaus with very precise functions, such as the municipal water department or the weather service, to ones with broad mandates, such as police departments and welfare agencies. Each has a fixed place in the legal system.

Administrative agencies perform three functions for the legal system. Their principal role is to implement laws and policies as enacted by legislatures and interpreted by courts. Their second role, one that has recently become increasingly prominent, is to make policy decisions and issue legal regulations that supplement the lawmaking of legislatures and courts. Third, administrative agencies often play a courtlike role in settling disputes. We examine each of these functions separately by comparing the ways administrative agencies operate with the ways courts and legislatures work.

Implementation of Law and Policy

The primary purpose of administrative agencies is to implement the laws and policies that legislatures and courts have mandated. They collect taxes, organize a military force, enforce the criminal code and parking and traffic regulations, inspect water, food, drugs, and a host of other substances, operate schools, universities, prisons, and hospitals, and engage in the myriad other tasks common to contemporary government. What they do and how they do it is determined by law.

Much of the work of administrative agencies simply involves the delivery of routine services about which there is normally little controversy. Thousands of clerks, for instance, process monthly social security checks that senior citizens receive on the first of every month; every school day, tens of thousands of teachers go to their classrooms to teach their pupils. Ordinarily, no one questions their work as long as everything goes according to routine. However, there is considerable potential for disputes and conflict even in such routine operations. A mistake or a new policy may stop payments of social security benefits to some recipients; a teacher may decide to begin class with a prayer that offends some parents, or parents may claim that their children's classrooms are not equipped as well as others. Thus, important distributional decisions lurk in the routine operations of administrative agencies and they breed disputes that must be resolved.

In addition, agencies enjoy considerable discretion in the way they administer their programs. Both Congress and the courts have been loathe to micromanage agencies, because neither is equipped to respond to the changing circumstances that face the agencies. This discretion embraces not only the actions agencies take but also their decision not to act. For instance, if an agency decides not to deliver a service a statute mandates, little can be done by those who would have received it. Courts often decline to mandate agency action and Congress has only very blunt weapons, such as withholding all appropriations or passing a new, more compelling mandate, and both take much time and effort. When an agency decides to go its own way, if it is careful to observe legal technicalities and has at least some political support, it may succeed for a long time.

Such circumstances produce a high potential for political conflict; they do not occur often because those appointed to run agencies usually are committed to its mission. However, some political circumstances breed intentional administrative inaction. Cornell Clayton[1] describes one set of such circumstances for the Reagan and Bush administrations (1981–1993). Facing a hostile Congress (the Republicans controlled only the Senate and only for four of the twelve years), Presidents Reagan and Bush pursued a policy of appointing people antagonistic to the programs their administrations opposed but could not persuade Congress to terminate. They were, for instance, quite unenthusiastic about the civil rights laws that prohibited racial, gender, and age discrimination. Their appointees to the Equal Employment Opportunities Commission (EEOC) simply failed to investigate or prosecute many of the complaints that came to them.[2] Likewise, the Civil Rights Division of the Justice Department, headed by a notorious opponent of civil rights enforcement, reduced the number of enforcement suits from twenty-eight in the last year of the Carter administration to just three in the first four years of the Reagan administration.[3] This inaction produced much friction with Congress. However, the complainants in the cases that EEOC and the Civil Rights Division blocked had little recourse.

---

[1]Cornell W. Clayton, *The Politics of Justice: The Attorney General and the Making of Legal Policy* (New York: M.E. Sharpe, 1992).
[2]*Congressional Quarterly Weekly Report*, Vol 47, No. 44, 4 November 1989, p. 2952; B. Dan Wood, "Does Politics Make a Difference at the EEOC?," *American Journal of Political Science* 34 (1990), pp. 503–530.
[3]Clayton, supra, note 1, p. 203.

GATEKEEPERS

Like all organizations, administrative agencies use gatekeepers to regulate their flow of business. In many circumstances, they want to encourage utilization of their services, but in others, they want to keep out unwanted clients.

Administrative agencies employ specially designed routines to regulate the flow of demands for their services. When they slam the gates closed, it is difficult for would-be clients to pry them open again. One example of this occurred during the late 1970s and early 1980s, when the Social Security Administration rejected as many as 120,000 applications for disability benefits, contrary to its rules.[4] Most of the individual applicants lacked the resources to file their own lawsuits to reverse the denial; one estimate is that only 6 percent of those denied went to court.[5] Eventually, a lawsuit cosponsored by the attorney general of New York and the Legal Aid Society won reconsideration for those involved. However, before the 1992 court order, the Social Security Administration and Justice Department officials of the Reagan and Bush administrations had pointedly ignored court decisions for more than ten years; one Justice Department official was quoted as saying appellate court rulings were "merely a weather vane showing which way the wind is blowing."[6]

However, the Social Security Administration situation is exceptional. Access to administrative agencies is usually simple and direct, because administrative agencies want clients just as businesses want customers. Most administrative agencies strive to make their services readily available because their record in providing service often determines their ability to grow or survive. Thus, it usually takes no more than a telephone call to receive a public service, whether it be a police officer to check a suspicious car parked in front of one's house or an employee from the city water utility to monitor a suspected leak. In many other cases, agencies require slightly more elaborate procedures, such as filling out a simple form that provides information used to determine eligibility for the service; this can usually be done without outside help.

In a minority of cases, people dealing with an agency find it helpful to hire a facilitator, often an attorney. For instance, to open a business, one ordinarily needs a building permit, occupancy certificate, merchant's license, employer's identification number, and sales tax certificate from a number of different agencies; it is usually helpful to assign these tasks to a lawyer who is familiar with each agencies' requirements. However, this situation is contrary to the normally open stance of administrative agencies, which reflects their dependence on clients for support. Unlike courts and legislatures, which want to restrict the number of demands made on them, many administrative agencies seek as many clients as possible to justify expanding their budget and staff.

---

[4]Robert Pear, "U.S. to Reconsider Denial of Benefits to Many Disabled." *New York Times*, 9 May 1992, p. A1.
[5]Ibid.
[6]Ibid.

DECISION MAKING IN THE IMPLEMENTATION PROCESS

The internal process between applying for a document or service and obtaining it is a mystery to most clients. To ordinary citizens, it may seem that their request for service drops down a dark chute and emerges untouched by a visible hand. Bureaucracies work in a less public arena than courts and legislatures, and public rituals play a much smaller role. Thus, when a mother applies for aid to dependent children, she goes to an ordinary office building, follows the signs to a large waiting room, registers with a receptionist, and takes a seat until a clerk calls her name. She then sits in front of a desk where a clerk takes the relevant information, and tells her to wait several days for a response. None of the grandiose ritual of the courtroom or of a legislative debate exists. Unlike judges, bureaucrats usually do not wear a distinguishing uniform, and their work area is an ordinary desk or counter. They make little effort to distance themselves from their clientele.

However, bureaucratic routines follow their own, less visible, rituals, which are prescribed by rules that govern almost every aspect of their work. In fact, as Max Weber pointed out, it is a defining characteristic of bureaucracies that they make decisions according to set rules rather than whim or personal relationships.[7] This is evident in the most common transactions with agencies. For instance, a postage stamp costs the same for every customer. Likewise, to borrow a book from a public library, certain rules determine eligibility and the length of time one may keep the book. One's appearance is irrelevant; even if the librarian is a relative, the rule determines whether the book can be borrowed for seven days or four weeks. The clerk may get into trouble by allowing a friend or relative to keep a book longer than the rule specifies. Thus, bureaucratic rules prescribe the same blindfolded treatment as judicial procedure does in court.

The rules governing administrative procedures have their roots in law. As we shall see, distinctive procedures govern the proclamation of administrative rules. If agencies do not follow their rules, clients may sue them and contest any unfavorable action the agency took. Agency officials ordinarily prefer to follow the rules because it protects their decisions from reversal and themselves from reprimand.

Adherence to rules is a habit administrative personnel learn early on the job. Except for top-level policy makers, agency staff predominantly consists of career civil service employees who got their job by taking a competitive examination and are protected from summary dismissal. Many work in public service their entire lives and learn early in their careers to follow accepted procedure. Most do not have significant experience outside government service where they might have learned to be audacious. They rarely have political patrons to protect them if they violate the rules. They keep their jobs until retirement or until their agency is dismantled, and serve through many changes in political leadership. Thus, bureaucrats are often deeply attached to their agencies and to the rules that protect their routine and their careers; their allegiance is to the rule book.

The rule book routinely specifies qualifications that make certain people eligible for an agency's services and others not; favoritism is prohibited. For instance, children

---

[7]Max Weber, *On Law in Economy and Society* (Cambridge, Mass.: Harvard University Press, 1954).

must be of a given age before school officials allow them to attend public school; usually they must also reside in the school's area. Likewise, applicants for unemployment benefits must meet certain specifications, such as having previously worked and being willing to take another job, in order to qualify.

Other qualifications also act to limit agency services to particular socioeconomic groups. Sometimes the very nature of the service or its location determines who will use it. In theory, everyone may use the library, walk in the parks, ride the streets, and pay for a bus ride. But many of these services are what economists call "collective goods"— they are really available only to those who are located where the services are provided. Moreover, some social and economic circumstances help special groups of clients use certain facilities. For instance, although a dock at a public lake may be available to the entire public, only those with boats can avail themselves of it. Only those who read use libraries, and only those who fly use airports. Thus, although administrative rules may appear to provide universal services, the intrinsic character of the service limits the clientele to those possessing specific traits.

Such limited eligibility is the consequence of legislative decisions that usually represent responses to particular interest groups or to the perceived needs of distinct groups. Many groups obtain special treatment and services by legislative lobbying. For instance, state fish and game departments provide special services to people who fish and hunt, and veterans' agencies cater to former members of the armed forces. Such agencies have close relationships to their clientele because their mission is explicitly defined in ways that limit its social and economic scope.

As implementers of policy set by higher authority, public agencies are somewhat insulated from immediate political pressures, but not as much as courts. Like courts, they are much less sensitive to electoral cycles than legislatures. However, budgetary cycles are important in the life of public agencies. Many agencies feel the hot breath of legislators every fiscal year as they go to appropriations committees to justify their budgetary requests; those hearings also provide an opportunity for committee members to ask questions about the agency. This procedure is particularly stressful because a cut in funds may mean loss of positions for staff who would otherwise continue their careers in the agency.

Thus, implementation is a rule-bound process in which the law (as enforced by court decisions) specifies how agencies will dispense their services. Agencies may do only what legislatures have authorized, and they must follow the procedures specified both by statutes enacted by the legislature and by court decisions interpreting the statutes.

Administrative Rule Making

Law and politics lurk in the background during the routine operations of administrative agencies; they are more prominent when agencies issue regulations. Agencies publish such regulations because legislatures have delegated to them the task of formulating detailed rules to govern the circumstances under which they operate. Recall, for instance, the controversy described in the previous chapter over Grove City College's refusal to sign an assurance that it did not discriminate against women. The requirement for such an assurance did not come directly from Title IX of the Education Amendments of 1972 as passed by Congress; rather, it was in the regulations issued by the Department of Education, which implemented the law. The regulations specified that college students could qualify for federal financial assistance only if their institution signed an Assurance of Compliance declaring that it did not discriminate in any aspect of its operations even if it received no direct federal funds.[8] The controversy arose because of this additional requirement; Grove City College, because of religious beliefs, did not permit women to participate in certain activities. It wanted neither to change its practices nor to deny its students federal loans. The power to make such administrative rules is delegated from the legislature to the administrative agencies. It is permitted because Congress cannot address all the details involved in administering a policy. However, when agencies engage in **rule making,** they must adhere to a special set of rules specified by a branch of law called **administrative law.**

Administrative law has both constitutional and statutory roots. When regulations are challenged in courts, judges must determine that constitutional rights and due process have been respected if the regulations affect private or property rights. Consequently, an administrative regulation cannot require persons to forfeit their right of freedom of speech or their right to own property no more than a congressional statute may. Additional legal requirements on administrative regulations have been established by Congress and state legislatures specifying the procedures agencies must follow when they issue regulations. These are parallel to (but much looser than) the due process requirements at court hearings. Federal agencies are bound by the provisions of the **Administrative Procedures Act of 1946,** which has been amended many times since its adoption. Similar laws adopted by state legislatures govern the rule making of state and local administrative agencies.

The procedures required by the Administrative Procedures Act and by parallel state laws seek to reproduce in administrative rule making some of the characteristics of lawmaking by legislatures.[9] One such requirement is openness; administrative regulations may not be formulated or issued secretly. However, the process by which this openness is attained only partly mirrors legislative procedures. Legislatures use committee hearings to obtain information and public comment; there is a hearing and comment process in the administrative sphere. When an agency wishes to issue a regulation, it first publishes a draft in an official gazette, such as the *Federal Register*. It then invites public comments that are submitted in writing; sometimes, the agency holds public hearings at which interested parties may testify. On controversial matters, such as the Baby Doe regulations described in Chapter 1, thousands of comments are received by the agency issuing the regulation. Such comments and hearings often result in a revision of the proposed regulations, but this need not occur. As long as the agency

---

[8]C.F.R. § 106.2(g)(1), (h) (1982).
[9]Cornelius M. Kerwin, *Rulemaking: How Government Agencies Write Law and Make Policy* (Washington: CQ Press, 1994).

permitted public comment, it will have satisfied the public notice requirement of administrative law.

A second requirement of rule making is that the rule be reasonably related to its purpose. Consequently, agencies are required to build a record that shows the regulation is one way of achieving its objectives. Courts have been very lenient in giving agencies leeway in choosing how to implement statutes.[10] The rules agencies adopt need not be the best way to administer a program to pass judicial muster; they simply need to be a reasonable way. Neither the mandate for public comments nor the requirement of reasonableness necessarily deters agencies from passing almost any rule they wish, but they need to be careful to observe the correct procedures which in turn opens the process to considerations that may deflect them from their original intentions.

In addition, the officials issuing the rule may not appear to profit privately from them. For instance, an official in the Department of Agriculture may not participate in the formulation of rules governing milk price supports if he or she owns a dairy farm, nor may an Environmental Protection Agency official issue a regulation affecting an industry in which he or she owns stock.

These requirements have many indirect consequences for administrative agencies and those affected by them. They lend an aura of legitimacy to administrative regulations, because agencies can claim the rules are the result of public participation. The procedures by which they are issued may appear to be fairer than if they were promulgated without prior public notice. In addition, the requirement that public notice be given alerts potential political opponents. In many instances, the most powerful constraint activated by these requirements comes from legislators who threaten the agency with retaliation unless the proposed rules are changed to accommodate the preferences of groups the legislators support.

The final adoption of administrative rules, however, takes place with as much privacy as shields the decision-making process of appeals courts. Few procedural constraints inhibit bureaucratic rule making at this final stage. After public comments have been collected, bureaucrats write any revisions of the regulation they feel are necessary. When their work is done, they publish the binding regulation in an official gazette.

Administrative regulations have considerably greater force behind them than many court decisions. The implementation of court decisions ordinarily depends on voluntary compliance or the cooperation of an administrative agent. For instance, when a court orders a municipality to stop discharging sewage into a river, it depends on the city's willingness to obey; in the extreme event that the city refuses, a contempt order may be issued against the mayor or some other official, but this, too, must be executed by an independent official such as the sheriff. Courts simply do not have their own enforcement agents.

Administrative agencies can enforce their regulations directly. When Grove City College refused to file an Assurance of Compliance, the Department of Education cut off federal financial assistance to students enrolled at the college. When utilities violate regulations specifying procedures for building or operating nuclear power plants, the Nuclear Regulatory Commission may withhold the utilities' operating permit. After the

---

[10]Cf. *Chevron v. Natural Resources Council*, 104 S.Ct., 2778 (1984).

Three Mile Island nuclear accident, this happened not only to the utility operating the Three Mile Island facility but to several others as well. Likewise, if an unemployed worker fails to report to the employment office as scheduled, the unemployment compensation agency may simply stop making payments until that person complies with its rule.

Of course, disputes arise over the legitimacy of administrative regulations and their enforcement, and these generally go to court. The agency's commitment to the law usually forces it to abide by court decisions even if they run counter to the agency's policy preferences.[11]

GATEKEEPERS IN THE RULE-MAKING PROCESS

Gatekeepers play a conspicuous role in the rule-making activities of administrative agencies. Because ordinary citizens are usually not aware of these activities, only persons with extraordinary resources are likely to be directly involved in the rule-making process.

The prominence of gatekeepers in rule making stems from bureaucratic routines that have the effect of keeping the process out of the public eye and relatively inaccessible. For instance, the *Federal Register,* in which agencies disclose their intent to issue a new regulation, contains nothing but notices of proposed and final rules and other legal proceedings; it is a "newspaper" that no average person reads. Consequently, the only people who learn about newly proposed rules are those with a special interest in government regulations who take the time to monitor the *Federal Register* or hire someone else to do so. The news media do not assist ordinary citizens in following regulatory activities because they rarely report them. Since there is much less drama to an announcement in the *Federal Register* than at a congressional committee hearing, it is the hearing that obtains media coverage. Exceptions, such as the Baby Doe regulations, may draw thousands of comments, but for every such exception are several hundred proposed regulations that attract almost no attention from the general public.

The low visibility of most notices to issue regulations gives interest groups a prominent role in administrative rule making. Many such groups maintain offices in Washington, D.C., and state capitals, and at least one staff member specializes in monitoring proposed regulations and alerting the groups' membership, thereby allowing the groups to mobilize testimony and political support.

Mere awareness of agency intent does not suffice for effective participation in the rule-making process. One must also be able to understand the proposed regulations, which are usually written in even more obtuse legalese than statutes. The regulations involved in the *Grove City College* case, for instance, define recipients of federal financial assistance in these terms:

> Any public or private agency, institution, or organization, or other entity, or any
> person to whom Federal financial assistance is extended directly or indirectly, or

---

[11]But note the circumstances that led the Social Security Administration to ignore many court orders requiring it to restore benefits it had denied, as discussed above.

through another recipient, and which operates an education program or activity which receives or benefits from such assistance.[12]

This peculiar linguistic style arises from the agencies' fear that courts will misinterpret their regulations unless they are very precise and so that those who are affected by the regulations will know what they must (or must not) do. However, only lawyers, and often only those who specialize in the work of a particular agency, have the skill to decipher the regulatory proposals.

In addition, the location of the hearings on a proposed rule (if hearings are held) makes it difficult for people who are not professionally involved to appear. Because most federal agencies have their headquarters in Washington, those who wish to testify at a hearing must go there. The same difficulty exists with state agencies because many are located in their state capital, which in most instances is not the state's central metropolis. This lack of physical proximity also promotes the use of gatekeepers.

The principal gatekeepers to the federal administrative rule-making process are Washington lawyers specializing in administrative matters who are hired by interest groups. This situation favors people and organizations with substantial resources, as is the case in litigation, because they can afford the specialized legal services required for representation before administrative rule makers. Thus, interest groups and large corporations routinely comment on proposed administrative rules. Since they also have substantial political influence, administrative agencies pay attention to their comments and suggestions. Ordinary citizens rarely participate.

The rule-making process deals with a different set of circumstances than do courts or legislatures. Courts, we have seen, mostly handle disputes involving pairs of litigants or small numbers on each side. Even class action suits typically have large numbers only on the plaintiff's side. Legislatures, on the other hand, typically handle broad conflicts with very large segments of the population on each side of the issue. Administrative regulations are never as narrow as the decisions coming from ordinary lawsuits; they always deal with whole segments of the population. However, the issues are more narrowly drawn than in legislatures. Agencies rarely face the broad social and political conflicts that typify much of the work of legislatures.

Consider, for instance, the issuance of regulations by the Department of Transportation, a federal agency, regarding the installation of passive restraining devices (such as air bags) for drivers and passengers in automobiles. In 1984, Elizabeth Dole, the Secretary of Transportation, issued a regulation that delayed requiring the installation of these devices by automobile manufacturers for eighteen months to give the states a chance to pass laws mandating seat belt use. The regulation specified that if enough states passed such a law so that two-thirds of the population of the United States were required to use seat belts, manufacturers would not have to install passive restraints.[13] The Department of Transportation issued this regulation pursuant to a law passed by Congress requiring it to mandate the installation of passive restraints under certain cir-

---

[12]34 C.F.R. § 106.31(a) (1982).
[13]Irwin Molotsky "U.S. Sets '89 Date for Car Air Bags But Gives Choice," *New York Times*, 12 July 1984, pp. A1, 18.

cumstances. The congressional statute dealt with the much broader problem of highway safety, of which the issue of passenger restraints was only a part. The regulation dealt with the entire automobile industry rather than individual consumers as the typical court case does.

Politics plays a very large role in the formulation of administrative regulations. Although the regulations are often formulated by career civil servants, these bureaucrats work under the direction of politically appointed supervisors who are ultimately responsible to an elected official. In the federal government, for instance, Reagan and Bush appointees substantially altered the direction of administrative policies by issuing regulations that fit more closely with the president's preferences for deregulation and assisting the private sector than had been the case in previous administrations. Presidents Reagan and Bush required every agency to submit its proposed regulations to the Office of Management and Budget, a White House agency, for review and approval.[14] The substance of these new regulations was thus directly related to Reagan's election in 1980 and the resurgence of the Republican Party in Congress. Similarly, quite different regulations emerged from the Clinton administration.

Consequently, the evenhanded neutrality that is supposed to characterize the implementation of regulations does not govern the rule-making process. In rule making, partisan allies of the president (or, at the state level, of the governor) enjoy a decided advantage. The political process determines both the agenda of agencies and the direction of the rule making. Agencies consequently respond to many of the same agenda-setting forces that influence Congress. For example, they must be sensitive to the electoral cycle. Decisions are more likely to be made immediately after an election than just before, when the future of the administration may be in doubt. Likewise, incumbents who lose an election may try to rush through administrative regulations before the inauguration of their successor in order to place their preferences in the law books before leaving office. Officials in the Bush administration did this after Bush's defeat in November 1992; dozens of regulations were hurried toward adoption. One of the first acts of the Clinton presidency was to rescind any proposed regulations that had not yet been published in the *Federal Register*.[15]

On the other hand, social and economic forces usually have only an indirect impact on the rule-making process. Agencies do, of course, respond to social and economic conditions. When a crisis arises—as with the sudden influx of Haitian refugees in 1992—the agency in charge is likely to respond with a new set of regulations. However, the exact timing of the regulatory response and the nature of the new policy depends on political rather than social or economic factors. The Bush administration, concerned with potential disruption that a wave of immigration would create in Florida, the costs involved, and the impact on the 1992 presidential election, declared that it would intercept refugee boats on the high seas and turn them back to Haiti. No

[14]Terry M. Moe, "The Politicized Presidency," in John E. Chubb and Paul E. Peterson (eds.), *The New Direction in American Politics* (Washington, D.C.: The Brookings Institute, 1985), p. 262.
[15]Martin Tolchin, "Last Minute Bush Proposal Rescinded." *New York Times*, 23 January 1993, p. A10.

such action had been taken against Cuban refugees, who were perceived far more favorably by the Bush administration.

Administrative Adjudication

Administrative decisions produce many disputes. Some decisions deny services to clients, others may provide services at a lower than expected level. Many agency decisions impose regulations for worker and product safety, consumer health environmental protection, land use, air and water quality, and a myriad of other purposes. In the first instance, all of these are the product of legislative decisions that some "private" behaviors need to be regulated for the public good. The imposition of those regulations, however, leads to many disputes about whether they are imposed fairly in a particular circumstance. The stakes are often high for the targets of regulation. Abiding by the regulations may close businesses and cost individuals their livelihood. Disputes arising from them, however, do not usually go directly to regular courts; agencies handle these disputes themselves in **quasi-judicial proceedings.** They are quasi-judicial because they have many of the characteristics of trial courts, and their decisions, much like trial decisions, may be appealed to an appellate court. However, the agencies lack some of the most important characteristics of real courts: they do not have a court's independence, their decision makers are not full-fledged judges, and their proceedings are less formal.

As was true for court cases, disputes that reach administrative tribunals represent only a small portion of all such disputes. Many alternative dispute-processing procedures are used to deal with such cases. Some disputes disappear because one of the parties exits, as occurs in a labor dispute when a company goes out of business or takes its manufacturing to another country. In other instances, a disputant simply decides to surrender to the agency. Many people on welfare, for example, decide that fighting the agency is futile, and they instead comply with what they feel are unfair or unreasonable requirements. In still other cases, disputants and agencies negotiate a settlement. During the Reagan administration, for instance, the Environmental Protection Agency decided to seek negotiated settlements for most of its industrial pollution complaints; the same was done by the Occupational Safety and Health Administration. However, mediation and arbitration are rarely used to avoid administrative adjudication, because few mechanisms exist to bring in a third party other than the quasi-judicial administrative judge who presides over the adjudicatory proceeding.

The disputes that go to administrative adjudication range as widely as those that go to courts. Some involve small amounts of money (although they may not be trivial to the claimants); others concern large stakes. Many involve only the immediate disputants and have little or no policy consequence. Others are like test cases in court, challenging administrative policies in fundamental ways. Many private disputants in these proceedings are one-shotters, but repeat players are also prominent.

DISPUTES IN ADMINISTRATIVE TRIBUNALS

One of the most striking characteristics of **administrative tribunals** is that they are located in the agency that is a party to the dispute.[16] For instance, the Social Security Administration issues regulations about disbursing disability benefits; on the basis of these regulations, its staff decides who qualifies for benefits and who is denied. Those who are denied or who receive less than they expected must go to an administrative hearing official attached to the Social Security Administration to challenge the agency's decision.

In addition to administrative tribunals within regular administrative agencies such as the Social Security Administration or the Department of Education, the federal government and many states have independent agencies whose function is to administer regulatory statutes, but which are not under the direct supervision of the president or governor. Examples include the Federal Communications Commission, which regulates the radio and television industries, the Securities and Exchange Commission, which monitors stock exchanges and brokerages, and the National Labor Relations Board, which watches over labor-management disputes. These agencies also issue rules and make decisions based on those rules. However, it is possible for private parties to bring disputes to them, as in the case of labor unions complaining about a company's labor practices or businesses that complain about union picketing. Like the tribunals in mainline administrative agencies, those in the independent agencies are attached to the agency that issued the rules.

Perhaps the term "tribunal" is misleading, because those who hear appeals of an agency's decisions typically work in the agency. At one extreme, the official hearing the appeal may be the same person who originally issued the decision; at the other is a specially designated **administrative law judge** who is attached to the agency.

The identity of the decision maker affects his or her autonomy, but only to a degree. No administrative adjudicator is as autonomous as are trial judges. Most are committed to the agency's goals and are monitored by the agency's chief administrators for efficiency and adherence to agency policies. Consequently, it is very difficult to win reconsideration of a decision if the basis of the appeal is that the petitioner considers the policy wrong. Most successful appeals are those that show the original decision was a mistaken application of the agency's rules.

Most appeals are heard by ordinary agency staff. They may be the original decision maker's supervisors. They have no special training, no particular detachment from the agency's mission, and no social distance from the original decision maker. However, in the federal government, an agency may employ an administrative law judge. Administrative law judges are legally trained and win their positions through a competitive civil service examination.[17] They have more than the ordinary protection against dismissal or disciplinary actions, but they are employed by the agency in which they do all their work; thus they remain subject to considerable administrative pressure. Other agencies employ personnel designated as administrative judges who do not enjoy any special protection.

[16]Lief H. Carter, *Administrative Law and Politics: Cases and Comments* (Boston: Little, Brown, 1983) 188–210.
[17]Donna Price Cofer, "The Question of Independence Continues: Administrative Law Judges within the Social Security Administration," *Judicature* 69 (1986), pp. 228–235.

The autonomy possessed by decision-makers in administrative adjudication has been a matter of considerable controversy.[18] On the one hand, being able to appeal to a disinterested judge is a fundamental component of due process and of popular perceptions of fair hearings. On the other hand, agencies need to pursue the missions mandated by statute; they argue they cannot do so if they are mired in endless litigation. The conflict is reflected in the hearings that the Immigration and Naturalization Service holds on requests made by illegal immigrants to be admitted to the United States based on their need for political asylum. The administrative judges who make these decisions are under strong pressure to limit immigration; immigrant groups, on the other hand, urge their compatriots' admission. Lacking the structural autonomy that courts provide their judges, administrative judges usually are much more vulnerable to political pressure.

Another hallmark of administrative adjudication is its relative informality. Administrative hearings are similar to court proceedings but lack many of their rigid rules. Although those representing petitioners are specialists, they need not be lawyers, and courtroom rules of evidence do not apply. In many instances, agencies keep proceedings as simple as possible to facilitate petitioners' presentation of information and to avoid the costs that greater formality often brings.

In these less formal hearings, a designated officer or group of officials hears the evidence presented by both sides and makes a decision that is as binding as a court decision; like a court decision, it may be appealed to another tribunal. One example of these informal hearings is the way an allegation of student plagiarism would be handled at a public university. Typically the university adopts a rule manual governing the proceedings; the student must be notified of the charge, a hearing is held at which both the accuser and the accused may offer testimony, and the professor hearing the evidence then renders a written decision. If the original decision upholds the allegation of cheating, the decision and the penalty imposed may be appealed to a board that often is composed of both professors and students.

Several characteristics of the student disciplinary proceeding are typical of other informal administrative proceedings. Attorneys rarely appear in the first hearing before the professor. The rules are not very specific about how the hearing should proceed. It usually takes place in the professor's office, no one is sworn, none of the courtroom rules of evidence apply, and no record of the proceeding is made. It is possible that the professor hearing the evidence may also be the professor who has discovered the alleged plagiarism. The professor makes the initial decision of innocence or guilt and imposes a penalty, but the allowable range of penalties is specified by the university's rules.

Students who feel the professor has been unfair at the hearing may take their case to the appeals board, which will hear it in its entirety rather than simply ruling on the record; in legal parlance this is a **de novo proceeding.** The appeals hearing is more formal. Both the accused student and the professor are more likely to be represented by attorneys. The professor now has the single role of accuser and would not double as judge. The board makes a finding of guilt or innocence and sets the penalty.

[18]Ibid., Donna Price Cofer, "Bureaucratic Efficiency vs. Bureaucratic Justice: Administrative Law Judges in the Social Security Administration," *Judicature* 71 (1987), pp. 29–35.

Although this appeals hearing is more formal than the original proceeding, it still is much less formal than a court trial. It does not use court rules of evidence but does make a written record. The board's powers are specified in substantial detail by the governing regulations. Still further appeals are possible, both within the administrative structure of the university and, eventually, to a regular law court.

The informality of the academic disciplinary proceeding is justified on several grounds that are quite generally applied to administrative adjudications. One justification is that the special circumstances of the parties should be accommodated as much as is consistent with maintaining each person's fundamental rights. In the university setting, the professor's role as teacher should not be undermined by an extremely adversarial process. At the same time, the proceeding recognizes the importance of maintaining academic standards. Another justification for the informality is to assure that the agency's special expertise—in this case the university—be given proper weight. Professors are perhaps best able to detect plagiarism and judge the impact of such misconduct on their courses.

Other instances of administrative adjudication may be much more formal than an academic hearing on plagiarism, but they follow the same principles, compromising some of the features of the adversarial process of a trial court to accommodate the special circumstances of the agency. In a 1970 ruling,[19] the Supreme Court laid out ten procedural ingredients of administrative due process. As summarized by Paul Verkuil,[20] they included:

1. Timely and adequate notice
2. [The opportunity] to confront adverse witnesses
3. Oral presentation of arguments
4. Oral presentation of witnesses
5. Cross-examination of adverse witnesses
6. Disclosure to the claimant of opposing evidence
7. The right to retain an attorney
8. A determination on the record of the hearing
9. A statement of reasons for the determination and an indication of the evidence relied on
10. An impartial decision maker

However, Verkuil's research showed that many administrative programs provided only some, or even none, of these procedures. Moreover, in subsequent decisions, the Supreme Court has refused to require rigid observance of these standards, preferring to judge each case individually and giving considerable weight to administrators' need to have flexibility in carrying out their mandate. In many cases, administrative tribunals deal with complicated technical matters. Hearings before the Food and Drug Administration, for instance, require weighing evidence on chemical and biological processes;

[19]*Goldberg v. Kelly*, 397 U.S. 254 (1970).
[20]Paul Verkuil, "A Study of Informal Adjudication Procedures," *University of Chicago Law Review* 43 (1976), p. 739, quoted in Carter, *supra*, note 16, p. 125.

hearings before the Nuclear Regulatory Commission require an understanding of nuclear physics and nuclear engineering. Adjudicatory proceedings of such agencies recognize the agency's expertise by allowing the application of different rules of evidence than in court and by permitting agency personnel to participate in the decision-making process. However, the higher the stakes, the more likely that attorneys represent the concerned parties. In every case, formal rules previously published by the agency are applied; they generally include such rudiments of due process as adequate notice to those accused of violating agency rules, an opportunity to present evidence on their behalf, and a formal decision that can be appealed on substantive and procedural grounds to a higher administrative tribunal or regular court.

GATEKEEPERS

When acting like courts, administrative agencies act as their own gatekeepers. No outside official like the police or prosecutor screens cases before they go to an administrative tribunal. Rather, screening occurs within agencies because they possess both informal and formal ways of handling disputes. When a complaint originates within an agency, someone in the agency determines whether the case warrants formal proceedings based on the case's importance and the sufficiency of evidence. Even when a complaint originates outside an agency, as for instance, when someone wants to appeal the denial of welfare benefits the agency retains considerable control over whether the case reaches the formal hearing stage; a superior official may simply admit a mistake and grant the original request.

Almost every agency enjoys discretion in deciding whether a dispute should be heard formally or settled informally. The range of informal procedures is enormous. The university professor, for instance, may decide to avoid a formal confrontation by simply giving that student a lower mark on the paper or examination at issue. Alternatively, the instructor may informally warn the student that should further suspicious behavior occur, a full hearing will be convoked. The professor may also informally obtain a confession and require that the paper be rewritten or the examination retaken. Similar options are available to almost all administrative agencies. Indeed, they dispose of most disputes informally because convening hearings costs time and money and often results in bad feelings between agencies and their clientele. Individuals and corporations accused of violating administrative regulations also often prefer an informal settlement for similar reasons. Such settlements are less expensive in both transaction costs and penalties, and they avoid unfavorable publicity for the violator.

Attorneys play a subsidiary role as gatekeepers to administrative tribunals. When they are involved, they may counsel clients about the costs of fighting the agency. Attorneys also often provide defendants in these cases with expert knowledge about the penalties an agency is likely to impose and the procedures that must be followed if the client wishes to proceed to a formal hearing. In many cases, attorneys specializing in administrative law have previously worked for agencies and know both their rules and staff. Such attorneys play an important role in keeping trivial disputes out of agency adjudication proceedings.

GAINING COMPLIANCE WITH ADMINISTRATIVE RULINGS

Administrative agencies sometimes enjoy a favored position over courts in winning compliance with their decisions. In many instances, the party that loses an administrative hearing depends on the agency for an essential service. If the losing party refuses to comply with the ruling, the agency may take direct action, such as assessing a fine or withholding its benefits. A student found cheating may be expelled from the university; a stockbroker found guilty of violating the regulations of the Securities and Exchange Commission may be excluded from trading in stocks and bonds; a bank found to have violated banking regulations may be unable to borrow from the Federal Reserve Bank or may be taken over by the Federal Deposit Insurance Corporation.

Even when an agency must go to court to enforce its penalties, it usually obtains compliance because of the violator's dependence on the agency. Court hearings on penalties require the agency to justify its penalties on both substantive and procedural grounds and provide the accused with another opportunity to present a defense. If the agency eventually wins court approval of its sanctions, most losing parties have little choice but to obey, not only because they may be held in contempt of court but also because they need the agency's services.

Politics plays a much more prominent role in administrative adjudications than in judicial proceedings, despite the fact that administrative judges are civil servants with almost as much insulation from political pressures as courtroom judges. The most important channel for political influence on administrative adjudication is the upper leadership of the agencies, which is politically appointed and responsible to an elected official. This leadership exerts its influence in several ways. First, the top agency officials issue the regulations that give rise to disputes; thus they choose the issues to impose on their clients or the businesses they regulate. They also decide which violations to pursue and which to forgive.

In addition, political ties between administrators and alleged violators of their regulations sometimes play a more visible role in the administrative process than in judicial proceedings. Although it is illegal for an administrator to favor those with whom he or she has political connections, some administrators move freely between jobs in government agencies and positions in regulated industries. These political connections sometimes prove helpful to clients during the informal stages of administrative regulatory enforcement, before a public complaint is filed.

Economic and social forces play a secondary role in the administrative process; they provide the context that produces the problems administrators address. For example, one cannot understand banking regulations without being aware of economic conditions nor understand the operation of welfare programs without knowing the social circumstances in which they operate. However, neither social nor economic factors have a direct effect on the ways administrative regulations are imposed through adjudicatory proceedings; these are more strongly influenced by existing law and the policy preferences of those in power.

Conclusion

Administrative agencies have the broadest mandate of any of the core institutions of the legal system. In addition to their unique function implementing laws, they also play significant roles in rule making and in adjudicating disputes that arise under those rules. The law they make and adjudicate has a subordinate status to legislation, but it is much more voluminous and detailed.

Different conditions govern each of the three functions of administrative agencies. Implementation of law is often the least political, since most programs administered by government agencies are uncontroversial most of the time. Rule making parallels legislative activity to some degree, and because it creates new rules, it provokes intense interest and lobbying from affected groups. Administrative adjudication is a weak counterpart to trial courts; it uses some courtroom procedures but is much less autonomous and much more subject to political influence than are courts. Hence, administrative institutions, while exercising functions similar to those of legislatures and courts, must be understood on their own terms rather than simply as mirror images of these other core institutions.

It may appear contradictory to think of administrative agencies as "rule-bound" when they implement policy and adjudicate disputes, but free to pass almost any rule they want in their rule-making role. That paradox lies at the heart of the administrative process as it has been structured in the United States. Constraints on administrative agencies are both judicial and political. Regular courts may insist that policy implementation and dispute processing by administrative agencies hue close to their statutory authority and the rules they have issued. The effectiveness of judicial control, however, rests on the ability of aggrieved parties to complain to courts and of courts to intervene expeditiously; as we have seen in previous chapters, the ability of courts to perform those functions is limited. Political constraints are often significant. Chief executives, themselves elected officials, appoint heads of agencies and often have the power to restructure them; legislatures may rebuke runaway agencies by passing more precise statutory language or penalize them by stripping their budgets during the appropriations process.

The increasing prominence of administrative agencies in making and implementing law and adjudicating resulting disputes is one of the most notable trends of the late twentieth century in American politics, and it has troubled many observers. Because administrative agencies are at least one step removed from the political constraints inherent in popular democracy, their power holds frightening potential. Agencies' quasi-judicial functions give them additional powers that courts may be unable to control because of the volume of cases that flow through administrative channels. And, unlike courts, administrative agencies are able to follow through on their adjudicatory decisions by implementing them without reference to another agency. Thus, executive branch administrative agencies have powers that neither a legislature nor a court can match. Those powers have the potential of transforming the legal system from a court-centered process to one that is administration-centered.

KEY WORDS

rule making	administrative tribunal
administrative law	administrative law judge
Administrative Procedure Act of 1946	de novo proceeding
quasi-judicial proceeding	

FOR FURTHER STUDY . . .

A notable critique of the powers of administrative agencies is Theodore J. Lowi, *The End of Liberalism* (New York: W.W. Norton 1969). Two more recent examinations of the role of administrative agencies in the American legal process are Christopher F. Edley, Jr., *Administrative Law: Rethinking Judicial Control of Bureaucracy* (New Haven: Yale University Press, 1990), and Cass R. Sunstein, *After the Rights Revolution: Reconceiving the Regulatory State* (Cambridge: Harvard University Press, 1990).

To peek into the complexities of the administrative process, select a local agency and list the programs it administers. Choose one of those programs and read the statute that authorizes it and the administrative rules that govern it and try to observe proceedings that handle its complaints. For instance, do this with your city's planning agency, the state agency that issues drivers' licenses or a federal agency, such as the post office.

VI

CONCLUSION

A frequent response to social problems in the United States is "There ought to be a law!" That response reflects an innocent belief that problems disappear once laws are adopted. However, as we have already seen in other contexts, the legal system does not immediately respond to new initiatives. Indeed, passing a law may be only the first of many steps required to implement new policy and to produce desired results.

In the next chapter, we examine the difficulties encountered in implementing new policies through the legal system. We do so in the context of two areas that affect broad elements of the population: divorce and crime control. In the epilogue, we briefly explore some of the challenges that face the legal system in the United States in the coming decades.

13

THE LIMITS OF LAW

Law is a powerful instrument, so powerful that almost all political activity revolves around the desire to harness the law to the needs of particular interests. The law has, as we have seen, both majesty and force. Its majesty comes from its roots in symbols such as the Constitution, legitimate authority of legislatures, the grandeur of the presidency, and the mystique of courts. Its force derives from the threat of loss of property, imprisonment, and even death for those who violate it.

Yet it is easy to exaggerate the law's influence, for despite its majesty and force, it is often overwhelmed by social inertia, economic conditions, and political disagreements. These constraints do not always prevent people from using the law to their own purposes, but they frequently lead to warped results. They also produce much impatience with government and law as a remedy for social ills. In this chapter, we examine two examples of such constraints to shed light on why law seems to fail. Our examples come from recent changes in divorce law and criminal codes. These two areas of law are quite different because one plays on the field of private law and the other on the field of public law. They illustrate both unique and common problems of implementing change through law.

There are many reasons why law may not produce its intended results.[1] As we have repeatedly seen, the law interacts with social, economic, and political forces. When these elements reinforce the law's impulse, the law is much more likely to have its intended effect. As Rosenberg shows, the attempts to eliminate racial discrimination by law faltered on the deep-seated racial prejudices held by many Americans; neither court decisions like *Brown v. Board of Education* nor legislative acts like the Civil Rights Act of 1964 eliminated it from American society.[2] Similarly, the attempt to outlaw con-

---

[1]The best treatment, although limited to implementation of court decisions, is Charles A. Johnson and Bradley C. Canon, *Judicial Policies: Implementation and Impact* (Washington, D.C.: Congressional Quarterly Press, 1984). A more pessimistic assessment is Gerald N. Rosenberg, *The Hollow Hope: Can Courts Bring about Social Change?* (Chicago: University of Chicago Press, 1991).

[2] Rosenberg, supra, note 1, pp. 39–172.

sumption of alcoholic beverages in the United States through the passage of the Eighteenth Amendment was a resounding failure because it ran counter to the social norms of many people. Even under the totalitarian regime of the Soviet Union, attempts to liberate Moslem women in Soviet central Asia by legislative fiat in the early 1920s stumbled on the resiliency of social customs. Soviet laws proved unable to raise the status of women overnight; it took many years to change the social practices that bound women to an inferior position.[3] Thus, to estimate the likely success of a law it is essential to examine the social, economic, and political context in which the law operates.

The normative context of a law is also important. Law has symbolic and normative implications as well as instrumental meaning. It conveys a sense of cultural norms; its endorsement of those norms often has value independent of its behavioral effects. For instance, Gusfield, in his classic study of the origins of Prohibition, argues that the Eighteenth Amendment reinforced the values of white rural Protestants who felt threatened by the foreign values carried by immigrants who entered the United States at the end of the nineteenth century.[4] Prohibition reinforced nativist values even though consumption of liquor did not disappear. Similarly, laws prohibiting discrimination on the basis of sexual preference in the United States are important to gay men and lesbians because they signify an end to official disapproval of their life-style, but at the same time they arouse intense opposition from those who believe such life-styles are immoral. The result is that while some practices may change, some attitudes remain unchanged or even become hardened by the change in law.

Another reason that law may have a limited effect is that, as already discussed, it often harbors ambiguities. Statutes usually arise from conflicts between groups; those conflicts are not fully resolved by the passage of a law but are papered over by compromise. Nor are appellate court interpretations always clear. Court cases sometimes produce ambiguous law because they deal with specific situations that have limited applicability. When another dispute occurs under different circumstances, people may be uncertain about the law's effect. Thus, the law's ambiguity leads to mixed results; some see this as failure, but to others it appears as partial success. For instance, while Soviet authorities failed to change local customs in their Moslem areas immediately, their new laws encouraged some Moslem women to break away from tradition, and the laws did eventually help alter that society's structure. Similarly, while racial discrimination in the United States continues many years after court and legislative actions outlawed them, the lives of African Americans are much less hampered by official discrimination in the 1990s than in the 1950s.

Institutional factors, such as the way a law is communicated to the public, also affect a law's success. To be effective, it must be communicated to those whose lives it will alter. As we saw in Chapter 2, many remain uninformed about the law. The gatekeepers we discussed earlier play an important role in communication. The more the law operates in a densely populated field of social networks, the more likely its substance is communicated to those who need to know about it.

[3]Gregory Massell, "Law as an Instrument of Revolutionary Change in a Traditional Milieu: The Case of Soviet Central Asia," *Law & Society Review* 2 (1968), pp. 179–228.
[4]Joseph R. Gusfield, *Symbolic Crusade: Status Politics and the American Temperance Movement* (Urbana: University of Illinois Press, 1963), esp, pp. 55–57.

Finally, to understand the process of compliance, we need to examine the incentives and punitive sanctions a law provides and the potential barriers to bringing these incentives or sanctions into play. Where sufficiently large incentives exist, it is likely that those who benefit will use the law. When the law relies solely on sanctions, its efficacy will depend on the likelihood that the sanctions will be applied and whether they are sufficiently severe to deter violations. As many criminologists have argued, certainty and severity are required for sanctions to have their intended effect.[5]

The operation of these factors in determining the law's ability to achieve its intended result will become apparent as we examine the reforms in divorce law and the criminal code that occurred during the 1970s and 1980s. These two examples suggest that mere passage of a law often does not alter behavior but does have important consequences.

Divorce Law Reform

Since 1966, a quiet revolution has occurred in family law in the United States as divorce laws have been changed in every state.[6] Over two decades, every state adopted no-fault grounds for divorce, by which one spouse need no longer allege that the other spouse committed a marital offense such as adultery or extreme cruelty. Many states have also changed their child custody laws, removing the presumption favoring mothers during the early years of childhood and often providing for joint custody.[7] Finally, most states have changed the rules for dividing a family's property. In many states, "alimony" has been replaced by "maintenance," enforcement of child support payments has been tightened, and both the definition of the property to be divided between spouses and the criteria for its division have been fundamentally altered.[8] Since 1966, we have thus seen extraordinary changes in the law of divorce.

THE OBJECTIVES OF REFORM

The varied objectives of the divorce law reformers are difficult to identify because the reforms were accomplished with little public visibility. They occurred while most public attention was focused on other political causes: civil rights, the Vietnam war, Watergate, student unrest, and state tax revolts. Although divorce reform did not merit the headlines associated with these other issues, at least six objectives are apparent. As we shall see, those objectives were sometimes in conflict with one another.

---

[5]See, for example, Franklin E. Zimring and Gordon J. Hawkins, *Deterrence* (Chicago: University of Chicago Press, 1973); and Jack P. Gibbs, *Crime, Punishment, and Deterrence* (New York: Elsevier, 1975).
[6]For a more detailed examination of the process by which divorce laws changed, see Herbert Jacob, *Silent Revolution: The Transformation of Divorce Law in the United States* (Chicago: University of Chicago Press, 1988).
[7]This presumption was called the "tender years" doctrine. See Fran Olsen, "The Politics of Family Law," *Law & Inequality, 2* (1984), pp. 13–19.
[8]These provisions are outlined in Timothy B. Walker and Linda D. Elrod, "Family Law in the Fifty States: An Overview," *Family Law Quarterly 26* (1993), pp. 319–421.

Encouraging Family Stability

Few divorce reformers were social radicals. They did not wish to promote alternative lifestyles but rather held solidly middle-class values about families and often spoke about the need to strengthen family life. For instance, in 1965 a New York State legislative resolution establishing the Joint Legislative Committee on Marriage and Family Law began with the following words: "WHEREAS, it is the public policy of this state to recognize marriage as . . . the foundation of family life; . . . the state has profound interest in preserving the family as the basic unit of society. . . ."[9] Likewise, in 1966 the California the Governor's Commission on the Family stated that the goal of their proposal was "to further the stability of the family."[10] Such sentiments accompanied almost every effort to alter divorce laws during this period.

Protecting Children

Because most reformers recognized the potentially severe effects of divorce on children, they hoped their proposals would reduce the possible harm. Many were concerned with maintaining consistent parental figures. One influential set of mental health professionals argued strongly for allowing only mothers to retain custody, regardless of almost any intervening condition, in order to protect the bond between parent and child.[11] However, as concern over single parenting increased, reformers began to favor joint custody in the hopes that fathers would maintain contact with their children. Other reformers were principally concerned with providing an adequate financial base for children and thus sought to strengthen the machinery for enforcing the payment of child support by fathers.[12] Common to all of these efforts was the belief that the suffering of children caused by divorce should be minimized.

Treating Spouses Equally

At the same time divorce laws were being changed, feminist organizations became more active. Most of the changes we have described were not the result of lobbying by groups such as the National Organization for Women (NOW), but the growing number of women legislators, the prohibition of sex discrimination by a number of federal statutes, and increasing litigation about sexual equality, contributed to a rising concern for equality in divorce. In 1979, the Supreme Court decided that an Alabama statute which provided for alimony to wives but not to husbands violated the equal protection clause of the Fourteenth Amendment.[13] This decision was widely interpreted by state legislatures as requiring gender neutrality in divorce laws. It led some states to remove statutory preferences for the mother in child custody determinations. In other states, such as New York, it spurred the revision of laws governing the division of property be-

---

[9]State of New York, Report of the Joint Legislative Committee on Matrimonial and Family Laws (1966), Legislative Document No. 8, p. 1.

[10]State of California, Report of the Governor's Commission or the Family (December 1966), p. 5.

[11]Joseph Goldstein, Anna Freud, and Albert J. Solnit, *Beyond the Best Interests of the Child* (New York: Free Press, 1973). See also Phoebe C. Ellsworth and Robert J. Levy, "Legislative Reform of Child Custody Adjudication: An Effort to Rely on Social Science Data in Formulating Legal Policies," *Law & Society Review 4* (1969), pp. 167–233.

[12]Judith Cassetty (ed.), *The Parental Child Support Obligation* (Lexington, Mass.: Lexington Books, 1983).

[13]*Orr v. Orr*, 440 U.S. 268 (1979).

tween spouses.[14] In many a spirited debate arose between the advocates of "equal" and "equitable" **property divisions.** Equal division mandated a fifty-fifty split of all property belonging to the couple. Equitable division required judges to take into account such factors as the length of the marriage, the age, health, and earning capacities of the spouses, and their respective contributions to the property in order to arrive at a fair distribution. The common strand uniting the reformers was a desire to treat spouses more equally, which in practice meant the law should treat women more favorably than it had in the past.

REDUCING CONFLICT

Divorce has a bad reputation. It smacks of distrust, double-dealing, and conflict. One of the principal objectives of the supporters of **no-fault divorce** was to reduce the intensity of the conflict. By removing the adversarial character of divorce proceedings, these reformers hoped to defuse some of the conflict surrounding them. Some hoped lawyers would be largely avoided and divorces would be negotiated through mediation. Many reformers also sought to surround the divorce process with conciliation services that could save some marriages and take the sting out of many divorces.[15]

REDUCING FRAUD

Divorce in the early 1960s almost routinely involved fraud and perjury. In New York, for example, one could not obtain a divorce without proving adultery, and many divorcing couples staged the adultery to provide the evidence courts required. The husband would arrange a tryst, and on a prearranged signal a photographer "burst" into the room to take pictures that could be used as the required evidence of adultery. Some states, like Nevada, had more liberal divorce statutes but still required legal residency. Those who could afford the trip flocked to such divorce havens and fraudulently declared themselves residents. In other states, the plaintiff invented incidents "proving" extreme cruelty. The consequence was that divorce became an embarrassment to the courts and the legal profession. One of the strongest motives among many reformers was to remove the causes of this corruption by bringing the law into line with social reality. If divorce statutes were liberalized, the reformers reasoned, the incentives for fraud would be removed.

ACHIEVING LEGAL UNIFORMITY

A final goal that motivated many reformers was to make divorce laws uniform throughout the United States. They argued that the requirements for a divorce should not depend on where a couple resided. Complicated questions of law arose when spouses lived in different states, owned property in several places, and when one parent moved with the children from one state to another. Consequently, a massive effort was undertaken by the National Conference of Commissioners on Uniform State Law to draft a law

[14]Jacob, supra, note 6, p. 124.
[15]Both of the earliest reform proposals—in New York and California in 1966—featured conciliation services. They already existed in such other states as Wisconsin.

that all states might adopt. In 1970, the conference promulgated the Uniform Marriage and Divorce Act, which it hoped the states would follow.[16]

MEASURES OF SUCCESS AND FAILURE

These six goals were in potential conflict. Treating parents alike would not necessarily improve the situation of children. Reducing conflict by eliminating fault grounds for divorce might make it more difficult for women, who were often not equal partners, to achieve equality. The quest for uniformity risked adopting the lowest common denominator among state divorce statutes, which would make it difficult to treat marital property as belonging to the couple rather than to individual spouses. Making divorce easier through establishment of no-fault procedures might undermine rather than strengthen family ties. Such potential inconsistencies made it unlikely that all six goals could be achieved.

Twenty years after the reforms were initiated, most observers agreed that only a few of the objectives of divorce law reformers had been even partially attained, despite a frenzy of legislative activity.[17] Both the successes and the failures are instructive in understanding the limits of law.

SUCCESS IN REDUCING FRAUD

One of the principal successes of divorce law reform was the reduction of perjury in divorce actions. The most visible change occurred when New York abandoned adultery as the sole ground for divorce and added abandonment, imprisonment of one spouse for more than three years, or a legal separation of two years as grounds for divorce.[18] All of these grounds, except agreed upon legal separations, still required a showing of fault; nevertheless, the need to commit perjury was considerably reduced. Fewer divorcing spouses found it necessary to go to Nevada or Mexico to obtain a quick divorce; many could divorce without stating any grounds at all by agreeing to a two-year separation. However, the fastest route to a divorce was through a showing of "cruel and inhuman treatment," and the evidence used to sustain that charge frequently remained less than completely true.

Many other states also added no-fault grounds to their divorce statutes but often encumbered them with a lengthy waiting period. Impatient couples were tempted to lie about their proof of one of the remaining marital offenses to obtain a divorce more quickly. The incentive to perjure testimony was fully removed only in states such as California, where no-fault divorce became the only legal option, or in other states where the waiting period for a no-fault divorce was as brief as that for any procedure. In California, it took only sixty days to obtain the decree and another six months for it to become final.[19] Other states adopted similar conditions.[20]

---

[16]On the politics of the diffusion of no-fault, see Jacob, *supra*, note 6, pp. 62–103.
[17]Cf. Stephen D. Sugarman and Herma Hill Kay (eds.), *Divorce Reform at the Crossroads* (New Haven: Yale University Press, 1990).
[18]Laws of New York, 1966, Chapter 254.
[19]California Statutes, 1969 ch. 1608, tit. 3 §§4504, 4508, and 4514.
[20]Jacob, supra, note 6, pp. 80–103.

The little available evidence points to a drastic reduction of fraud in divorce proceedings after the reforms were enacted. Two indicators are particularly suggestive. The first is the decrease in divorce proceedings in such previous havens as Nevada. That state's divorce rate dropped from 23 per 1000 population in 1965 to 14.2 per 1000 twenty years later, even though the national rate increased sharply during the same period.[21] This evidence, however, does not support the hypothesis that fraudulent migratory divorces have been eliminated, because Nevada's divorce rate remained the highest in the nation and was still almost three times that of California. We can only infer from these statistics that fraud had been reduced. The other evidence is the sharp decrease in articles about divorce fraud in legal publications. Whereas fraud and perjury were denounced on a regular basis during the 1960s, almost no legal scholars mentioned the problem in the 1980s.

Success in reducing fraud was not the consequence of harsher penalties or increased enforcement. Rather, the law succeeded because it eliminated most of the incentives for perjury since it was no longer necessary to lie to obtain a speedy divorce.

A More Limited Success—Gender Equality

Although legislatures and courts rewrote divorce laws deleting unnecessary references to gender and encouraging clients, lawyers, and judges to treat women equally, there is considerable evidence that these efforts had only limited success. For instance, although **child custody law** theoretically became gender-blind, physical custody continued to be assigned to mothers in the vast majority of cases, although the proportion has declined since 1974. In 1974, approximately 1 in 8 families were headed by single fathers; in 1990, the proportion had grown to almost 1 in 5.[22]

It is probably fair to assume generally that fathers and mothers in the United States have approximately equal affection for their children. Consequently, one would expect that because the law does not express a preference for maternal custody, custody decisions would fall more equally between parents. However, strong social norms intervene.[23] It still seems "natural" to most people that mothers should be the primary caretakers of their children. Although many divorced mothers work, most judges perceive caretaking to be more burdensome to fathers. Moreover, many fathers do not feel comfortable being the primary caretaker of their children. Consequently, there is often no dispute about custody; fathers often do not think about having custody, and most attorneys counsel that it is best if mother had custody.[24] As a result, physical custody is usually awarded to mothers by default. A court dispute over custody arises in perhaps only 15 percent of all divorces. Mothers win approximately two-thirds of these disputes; in

[21]U.S. Bureau of the Census, *Statistical Abstract of the United States, 1985* (Washington, D.C.: Government Printing Office, 1985), p. 82; Ibid. 1992, p. 93.

[22]Daniel R. Meyer and Steven Garasky, "Custodial Fathers: Myths, Realities, and Child Support Policy," *Journal of Marriage & the Family 55* (1993), p. 77.

[23]Jane Hood and Susan Golden, "Beating Time/Making Time: The Impact of Work Scheduling on Men's Family Roles," in Patricia Voydanoff (ed.), *Work & Family: Changing Roles of Men and Women* (Palo Alto, Calif.: Mayfield, 1984), pp. 133–143.

[24]Herbert Jacob, "The Elusive Shadow of the Law," *Law & Society Review 26*, (1992) pp. 565–590.

addition, in a small proportion of cases, fathers obtain custody without a court dispute by the mother's agreement.[25]

More evidence of the incomplete sexual equality achieved through revised divorce laws can be found in the financial outcome of divorce, which often leads to the impoverishment of women and children. Many employers do not tolerate the flexibility a primary caretaker requires to provide children with after-school supervision, care during illness, or transportation to the various doctor, dentist, and many other appointments that mark childhood. The financial consequences are stark for women. Using data for the period 1967 to 1981, Duncan and Hoffman report that women suffered approximately a 30 percent decrease in their income unless they remarried, while men experienced a 15 percent increase after a divorce.[26] This occurred despite the fact that Congress passed additional federal legislation in 1984 and 1988 requiring states to establish child support guidelines and requiring employers to send child support payments directly to court if an employee-parent falls behind the payment schedule.[27]

The obstacles to equal financial treatment of divorcing spouses lie in both economic circumstances and social norms. The economic fact in most divorces is that because the family has little property to divide, any division yields little for the woman. In addition, in those states in which equal property division is mandated, the family home may be lost because it must be sold to allow a division of the family's assets. Where equitable division is the law, the sale of the family home is often delayed until the children finish high school, after which the proceeds are divided.

Moreover, social norms reinforced the former husband's economic position to the detriment of that of his former wife. Following their own perception of community standards, few judges award even as much as half of a man's income for maintenance and child support even though the woman has more than half of the expenses of the broken family. The problem is summarized by Chambers:

> Recall that child support for a parent taking care of two children is typically set at 33 percent of the noncustodial parent's net earnings, but that the custodial parent needs around 80 percent of the family's former total income to maintain the prior standard of living.[28]

Finally, the social circumstances that often lead men to more lucrative careers than women made it possible for divorced men to recover financially more rapidly. Typically, the ex-husband continued his career while the ex-wife was forced into the labor market

[25]These estimates are based on a very limited number of studies; no national estimates exist. See Lenore J. Weitzman and Ruth B. Dixon, "Child Custody Awards: Legal Standards and Empirical Patterns for Child Custody, Support, and Visitation after Divorce," *University of California at Davis Law Review 12* (1979), pp. 515–517. More recent evidence indicates that the number of custody awards to men is increasing but remains a small percentage. See Meyers and Garasky, supra, note 22.

[26]Greg J. Duncan and Saul D. Hoffman, "Economic Consequences of Marital Instability," in Martin David and Timothy Smeeding (eds.), *Horizontal Equity, Uncertainty, and Economic Well-Being* (Chicago: University of Chicago Press, 1985), p. 434. See also Saul D. Hoffman and Greg J. Duncan, "What Are the Economic Consequences of Divorce?" *Demography 25* (1988), pp. 641–645.

[27]In 1984 the new provisions were in the Child Support Enforcement Amendments and in 1988 in the Family Support Act. See Ann Nichols-Casebolt, "The Economic Impact of Child Support Reform on the Poverty Status of Custodial and Noncustodial Families," in Irwin Garfinkel, Sara S. McLanahan, and Philip K. Robins (eds.), *Child Support Assurance* (Washington, D.C.: Urban Institute Press, 1992), pp. 190–191.

[28]David Chambers, *Making Fathers Day* (Chicago: University of Chicago Press, 1979),p. 268.

for the first time and often had to accept a low-paying job because she had a resume marked by gaps as she took time to care for her small children and possessed few skills valued by the employment market.

Economic circumstances and social norms alone are not sufficient to explain the law's inability to provide more substantial equality in the treatment of men and women in divorce. The drafting of the laws was also flawed by inadequate information. There are no national statistics detailing the variety of circumstances that exist among divorcing couples, and few of the state legislatures that dealt with property division and child support issues commissioned their own studies. Consequently, the only information legislators possessed was fragmentary empirical studies, "horror" stories collected by proponents, and their own experiences as matrimonial lawyers or interested citizens. The horror stories of mistreated wives (or, occasionally, husbands) were the most influential data but did not carry enough information for legislators to anticipate the many difficulties in implementing more equal legal treatment of ex-spouses. Legislators thus crafted few instruments that could effectively enforce more equal treatment of men and women or protect the status of children. None devised procedures for monitoring the situations facing ex-spouses between the divorce and the maturity of their children. Unlike any other highly industrialized country, the United States continued to rely entirely on private transfers of money and largely voluntary payments to those dealing with divorce.

Finally, the movement toward equality was hampered by disagreements over the meaning of equal treatment. New York's legislature was deeply divided on this issue during the 1970s and finally passed a statute that called for equitable distribution of marital property. Although the law specified ten conditions that should be considered in property division, ultimately the definition was left to the judge in each contested case.[29] In Wisconsin, as in New York, a bitter legislative struggle over distribution of marital property divided the women legislators and pitted progressives against conservatives.[30] As a consequence of these divisions and the legislative compromises they occasioned, many details about the law remained in dispute. For instance, there was no consensus about whether a homemaker's role should be considered a financial contribution to the marriage and, if so, how to evaluate it. Likewise, there was no formula for calculating the child support required to put the caretaker on an equal basis with the noncustodial parent.

Thus, economic circumstances, social norms, naivete about the difficulties involved, and characteristics of the lawmaking process combined to hinder equality between men and women in divorce matters. The new laws did improve the condition of women, for women received a larger and more secure claim to marital property, and improved the conditions of child support. Nevertheless, divorce usually remained more hazardous for women than for men. Without fundamental changes in the position of men and women in the United States, reforms in divorce law alone could not provide the desired equality.

It would be a mistake to declare the drive toward more equal treatment of men and women in divorce a complete failure. On many fronts, small changes occurred in the

[29]Jacob, supra, note 6, pp. 123–125.
[30]Martha L. Fineman, "Implementing Equality: Ideology, Contradiction, and Social Change—A Study of the Rhetoric and Results in the Regulation of the Consequences of Divorce," *Wisconsin Law Review 1983* (1983), pp. 789–886.

1970s and 1980s. Women were no longer deprived of property accumulated during the marriage simply because its title was held in the man's name. The man's pension funds routinely became part of the assets women shared. Although far from perfect, child support enforcement improved during the 1980s. In addition, both fathers and mothers were increasingly awarded joint legal custody of their children even though mothers often retained physical custody.

THREE CASES OF FAILURE

Three goals sought by many reformers clearly eluded them. The changes in matrimonial law did not markedly reduce conflict, did not create a uniform structure of divorce law throughout the United States, and did not protect children.

Reduction in conflict was one of the aims of those who advocated no-fault divorce. They reasoned that the need to demonstrate one spouse had committed a marital offense only aggravated the tensions that accompanied most divorces. The California reformers went farthest in this respect; they not only eliminated all grounds for divorce, they required only that a couple establish "irreconcilable differences which have caused the irremediable breakdown of the marriage."[31] In addition, the term "divorce" was replaced in the law by "dissolution of marriage," and the action was begun by the neutral petition, "In re the Marriage of . . . " rather than by the adversarial complaint styled as "*Jones v. Jones.*" Few other states, however, followed California's lead. Indeed, most simply added no-fault divorce to the array of fault-grounded divorce procedures.

The consequence of these reforms seems to be that less conflict is displayed in the divorce action, but the fighting has shifted to disagreements about property division and child custody. Once again, there are few sure indicators of these trends. The most convincing is perhaps the failure of voluntary mediation to capture a large portion of the divorce market. Mediation by mental health professionals and attorneys had been touted as a way to minimize conflict in the divorce process. The mediator would emphasize face-to-face negotiation in which the couple would attempt to meet their long-range needs. When children were involved, more attention would be paid to developing a new relationship between the ex-spouses, leading separate lives, while recognizing their continuing contact with one another because of their children. This was perceived to be a sharp alternative to obtaining a divorce through attorneys who negotiated between themselves and sought to protect the rights of their clients and maximize their clients' gains.

However, despite considerable efforts, mediation did not attract a strong following. The best estimate is that less than 2 percent of all divorces in 1981 were mediated;[32] we do not know whether this figure significantly grew since then. The only mediation efforts that became widely accepted were those mandated by courts. Thus, in an increasing number of places couples who had child custody conflicts were forced to go to a court-appointed mediator. Such mediation efforts, however, often bordered on arbitration, because the couple had little freedom to develop their own solutions. Working un-

[31]California Statues, 1969 ch. 1608, tit. 3, §4506(1).
[32]Jessica Pearson, Maria Luchesi Ring, and Anne Milne, "A Portrait of Divorce Mediation Services in the Public and Private Sector," *Conciliation Courts Review 21* (1983), p. 10.

der extreme time pressures, court mediators often proposed solutions that divorcing parties felt coerced to accept. In New York, a conciliation bureau was attached to divorce courts when the divorce reform was adopted, but it was quickly abandoned.

On the other hand, there seems to be more conflict over property settlements. This may be the consequence of new laws that require equal or equitable distribution. The ambiguities of these laws occasion many conflicts as each party attempts to maximize his or her share of the divorce settlement.

Because divorce is inherently full of conflict, perhaps the hope that legal reforms would reduce it was unrealistic. Harmony may not be possible when "irreconcilable differences" exist. Changing the legal form and ritual may not affect the underlying tensions that lead to the divorce.

Another failure of the divorce law reform movement was its inability to establish a uniform structure of matrimonial law in the United States. Much of the impetus for the reform came from legal scholars and practicing lawyers who placed a premium on uniformity.[33] Beginning in the mid-1960s, they worked through the **National Conference of Commissioners on Uniform State Laws,** a hybrid private-public institution established at the end of the nineteenth century, to produce a model marriage and divorce act. Since its founding, the conference had been composed of commissioners from each of the states and had been financed largely by state appropriations. Although a uniform marriage and divorce law was a goal of the conference since its founding, its principal successes were in commercial law, with its proudest achievement the Uniform Commercial Code, which formed the basis of commercial law in every state.

In 1966, the conference obtained private funding from the Ford Foundation to develop a uniform marriage and divorce law. It established a special committee that worked on this problem for more than three years. The final product, approved by the conference in 1970, adopted no-fault as the process by which divorce should be obtained and included many innovative provisions regarding marital property and child custody. However, the Uniform Marriage and Divorce Act met with immediate resistance. The Family Law Section of the American Bar Association denounced the act as soon as it was promulgated. For three years, the American Bar Association withheld its endorsement of the conference's proposal.[34]

In the meantime, states turned to divorce law reform in their own ways, considering but not slavishly following the suggestions of the conference. Many states retained fault grounds for divorce. By 1985, divorce law had changed fundamentally throughout the United States, but it had not become uniform; each state still insisted on its own special provisions.

The failure to achieve uniformity in divorce law is a consequence of both the legal and political structures of the United States. Divorce law is state law. It is deeply rooted in local traditions on matters such as child custody and property rights. Over many decades, each state had woven its own web of matrimonial law that includes elements of civil procedure, property law, and domestic relations law. State legislators perceived

[33]Jacob, supra, note 6, p. 68.
[34]Jacob, supra, note 6, pp. 70–79; Harvey L. Zuckman, "The ABA Family Law Section v. the NCCULS: Alienation, Separation and Forced Reconciliation over the Uniform Marriage and Divorce Act," *Catholic University Law Review* 24 (1974), pp. 61–74.

the task of superimposing a uniform law that had its origins in other customs and practices as having insurmountable difficulties. They feared such uniformity would create confusion rather than certainty. Indeed, the task seemed so intimidating that most legislatures did not even attempt it. Another roadblock to uniformity was that divorce law, unlike commercial law, is practiced by local lawyers who rarely have professional contact with their counterparts in other states. Strong centralizing forces are required to pass uniform legislation in all the states. In other legal areas, uniformity has been effected when the federal government provided financial incentives or when powerful private interests that spanned state borders supported uniformity. In divorce law, there was little incentive to abandon local provisions for the sake of national uniformity.

A third failure was the hope that divorce reform would reduce the potentially severe effects of divorce on children. The law was indeed changed to establish the "best interest of the child" as the standard for custody rather than the "tender years" doctrine that had usually awarded custody to mothers. The reformed law also more frequently promoted joint, rather than single, legal custody of children, and legislatures adopted new procedures for collecting child support.

The outcome of these initiatives, however, was ambiguous. Joint custody has become more common, especially in California.[35] However, the standard of living for children continues to decline after divorce,[36] although perhaps not as much as before. We have already seen that women's living standards usually fall and that child support payments are often grossly inadequate. In addition, despite the new legislation, child support awards were lower in new divorces in 1985 than in 1978.[37]

Other aspects of children's welfare after divorce are equally difficult to evaluate. The dominant view among child psychologists in the mid-1980s was that children do best when they can relate to two parents. Yet despite the new laws providing for joint custody, many fathers fade from their children's lives after divorce.[38] On the other hand, many mothers remarry and stepfathers are more common. An entirely new vocabulary has been created describing these households as "blended," "reconstituted," or "remarried" families. There is, however, no systematic broad-based evidence that permits a definitive evaluation of the welfare of children in these circumstances.[39] A fair summary may be that the new laws make divorce easier, allow parents and children to escape from oppressive relationships, and attempt to promote financial support of children from parents, but they may not protect children from paying a steep price for their parents' problems.

---

[35]Eleanor E. Maccoby and Robert H. Mnookin, *Dividing the Child: Social & Legal Dilemmas of Custody* (Cambridge, Mass.: Harvard University Press, 1992).

[36]Frank F. Furstenberg, Jr., and Andrew J. Cherlin, *Divided Families: What Happens to Children When Parents Part* (Cambridge, Mass.: Harvard University Press, 1991), pp. 45–61.

[37]Andrea H. Beller and John W. Graham, *Small Change: The Economics of Child Support* (New Haven: Yale University Press, 1993), p. 34.

[38]Frank F. Furstenberg, Jr., Christine Winquist Nord, James L. Peterson, and Nicholas Zill, "The Life Course of Children of Divorce: Marital Disruption and Parental Contact," *American Sociological Review* 48 (1983), pp. 656–668.

[39]The evidence is briefly summarized in James H. Bray and E. Mavis Hetherington, "Families in Transition: Introduction and Overview," *Journal of Family Psychology* 7 (1993), pp. 3–8.

EFFECTS ON FAMILY STABILITY

It is difficult to separate the effect of social forces on family structure from the effect of law. Divorce rates continued to increase during the 1970s and remained at a high level thereafter. States that liberalized divorce later had no less of an increase than those in the forefront of the changes. As far as we can tell, the new laws had very little effect on the divorce rate of most states.[40] Moreover, the high divorce rates characteristic of the United States since the 1970s is not associated with a sharp rise in alternative lifestyles. Most people who got a divorce did not move into communes; rather, they remarried.[41]

One cannot conclude the new laws had no impact or that they damaged family life in the United States. For instance, Caplow and his associates found that in Muncie, Indiana, families were happier and fought less in the 1970s than in the 1920s. He speculates that contemporary families are happier because easy divorce makes it possible to escape unsatisfactory marriages.[42] In addition, no-fault divorce laws help reduce the stigma that was once attached to divorce. When divorce was inextricably linked to serious misbehavior such as adultery, it was widely condemned. Now that divorce is associated only with "irremediable breakdown," it no longer evokes such strong sentiments.

SUMMARY

Divorce law reform presents a mixed record of success and failure. When no conflicting social, economic, or political forces intervened—as in the effort to reduce fraud and perjury—considerable change occurred. However, the reformers'other goals were stymied to some degree by obstacles. Some—such as achieving legal uniformity—ran counter to the federalism of American politics that gives entrenched local interests insurmountable power. Other goals—such as gender equality—were hindered by deeply ingrained social norms and practices. Still others—such as protecting children— foundered on both economic constraints and insufficient knowledge of the underlying social context for well-designed legal intervention.

All the reforms operated in a relatively sparsely populated field of supporting (or opposing) social structures. People obtaining a divorce had few connections with others undergoing the same process except through their attorneys. As we saw in Chapter 6, such attorneys do not constitute a highly specialized subset of the legal profession and do not have a highly developed communications network. In most places, no clientele groups of children, women, or men existed to advocate protection of their special interests. Finally, divorce law operated in a field devoid of public bureaucracies that might otherwise be the center of facilitative communications. Courts were the only public organization consistently involved, and they were not in a position to promote the new

---

[40]Harvey J. Sepler, "Measuring the Effects of No-Fault Divorce Laws across Fifty States: Quantifying a Zeitgeist," *Family Law Quarterly* 15 (1981), pp. 65–102; Alan H. Frank, John J. Berman, and Stanley F. Mazur-Hart, "No-Fault Divorce and the Divorce Rate: The Nebraska Experience—An Interrupted Time Series Analysis and Commentary," *Nebraska Law Review* 58 (1978), pp. 1–99.
[41]Andrew J. Cherlin, *Marriage, Divorce, Remarriage* (Cambridge, Mass.: Harvard University Press, 1981).
[42]Theodore Caplow et al., *Middleton Families: Forty Years of Change and Continuity* (Minneapolis: University of Minnesota Press, 1982), pp. 116–135.

laws because they do not interact with litigants in the same way that bureaucracies interact with clients.

Criminal Code Reform

At the same time state legislatures were revising divorce laws, they substantially changed the sentencing provisions of their criminal codes. They intended their revisions to address a number of problems that attracted attention during this period.

THE GOALS OF SENTENCING REFORM

Criminal code reform focused on a variety of goals. Two were paramount: (1) to reduce the threat of prison unrest that seemed to have been bred by the perception of unfairness and uncertainty in sentencing; and (2) to reduce crime by imposing harsher sentences, thus keeping criminals off the street for a longer period of time.

Reformers recognized the widespread perception that **indeterminate sentences** both were unfair and created unnecessary uncertainty. Indeterminate sentences were those in which the judge would set both a minimum and maximum incarceration period, but left it to a parole board to determine exactly how long a convict would remain in prison, as long as the term did not exceed the maximum. This form of sentencing was designed to provide flexibility with the hope that it would allow prison authorities to reward prisoners who showed evidence of rehabilitation.

Such flexibility resulted in substantial variations in sentences for similar crimes. On the one hand, the law allowed a wide range of minimum and maximum sentences for each offense. This led some judges to assess short sentences while others imposed much longer ones for the same offense. In addition, a convict's adjustment to prison life often had as much influence on the length of the prison term as the original offense. When prisoners compared their sentences, they found that although convicted of the same offense, they were serving considerably different terms.

Indeterminate sentences also created great uncertainty among prisoners about when they would be released. Release almost always came before the maximum term had been served, but the exact time was subject to parole board decisions that often appeared capricious. This uncertainty seemed to contribute to prison unrest. In the 1970s, several states experienced prison riots. The most publicized was the 1971 uprising at the Attica prison in New York, which lasted three days and cost thirty-seven lives. The official report on that rebellion concluded that "by 1971 conditional release and parole had become by far the greatest source of inmate anxiety and frustration."[43] Thus, rather than helping prison officials control inmates, the indeterminate sentence system bred prison unrest.

[43]*Official Report of the New York State Special Commission on Attica* (New York: Bantam, 1972), p. 98, reprinted in Martin L. Forst, "Sentencing Disparity: An Overview of Research and Issues," in Martin L. Forst (ed.), *Sentencing Reform: Experiments in Reducing Disparity* (Beverly Hills, Calif.: Sage, 1982), p. 23.

The second major problem sentencing reforms sought to address was the rising crime rate that began in the mid-1950s. It attracted enormous attention in the media and among elected officials.[44] Fear of crime and the inadequacy of prison policies was spotlighted in George Bush's 1988 presidential campaign, with the campaign ad featuring menacing men marching through revolving gates of a prison. It became a focus of congressional action in 1993 and 1994, with the long-awaited passage of the "Brady" gun control bill and consideration of many other crime control measures. Officials struggled to devise measures to combat both the reality of crime and its perception by the general public. One remedy that appeared especially attractive was to imprison offenders for longer periods to keep them off the streets; evidence seemed to be mounting that prisons were unsuccessful in rehabilitating offenders. This view was given much currency by a review of a large number of studies on the rehabilitative effect of prison published by Martinson in 1974.[45] Martinson showed studies which purported to demonstrate the success of rehabilitative programs were methodologically flawed. Rather, the weight of the evidence suggested that large numbers of those released before they had served their full terms were later returned to prison because they had violated the conditions of their parole or committed another offense. Prisons had become turnstiles that made little visible contribution toward rehabilitating criminals. Such conclusions spurred legislators to redesign the law's sentencing provisions to designate incapacitation rather than rehabilitation as the principal purpose for sending offenders to prison.

However, as with divorce law, the reformers sought to promote many potentially contradictory goals.[46] Civil libertarians sought to reduce the arbitrary power of parole boards; they also often wanted to decriminalize certain behavior, such as possession of marijuana. However, they did not necessarily oppose rehabilitation as a goal or prison educational programs that promoted it. Many law enforcement officials wanted to reduce the crime rate by keeping known criminals in prison; they did not have much faith in rehabilitation and considered educational programs in prison a waste of money. They were joined in these sentiments by many citizen groups who feared the growth of crime. Still others saw prison as an opportunity to exact retribution from criminals; for them, the purpose of imprisonment was simply to punish offenders. However, the punishment needed to fit the offense, and every offender should be treated equally. This was the theory of so-called "just desserts."[47] In addition, many law enforcement officials were appalled at the widespread practice of plea bargaining. It seemed to observers that many offenders were receiving more lenient sentences than they really deserved simply because they managed to strike a good bargain. These critics of different aspects of exist-

---

[44]An analysis of crime and official responses to it in American cities in the 1970s may be found in Herbert Jacob, *The Frustration of Policy: Responses to Crime by American Cities* (Boston: Little, Brown, 1984).

[45]Robert Martinson, "What Works—Questions and Answers about Prison Reform," *The Public Interest* (Spring 1974), pp. 22–54.

[46]See Forst, supra, note 43, pp. 9–34; Richard A. Berk, Harold Brackman, and Selma Lesser, *A Measure of Justice: An Empirical Study of Changes in the California Penal Code, 1955–1971* (New York: Academic, 1977), pp. 273–300; Andrew von Hirsch, *Doing Justice: The Choice of Punishments* (New York: Hill & Wang, 1976).

[47]Andrew von Hirsch, supra, note 46, pp 45–58, 143–150.

ing penal policies sometimes joined forces even though they disagreed on fundamental issues, because they shared a commitment to change existing practices.

ATTEMPTED SOLUTIONS

In response to these concerns, Congress and state legislatures adopted a variety of changes in criminal codes. A particular state's reform depended on a combination of factors, including the character of existing law and the priorities of political leaders and interest groups.

One reform involved the replacement of indeterminate sentences with "flat" or **determinate sentences**.[48] Maximum and minimum terms were replaced with a single figure. Except for a small adjustment that could be made by prison officials to reward good behavior, the length of the sentence could not be changed once imposed by the judge. By 1983, nine states had adopted determinate sentencing that eliminated the possibility of early release by a parole board.[49]

Another change adopted by some states was to require **mandatory sentences** for certain offenses. In 1973, the New York legislature, on the urging of Governor Nelson Rockefeller, passed a law imposing harsh sentences on drug dealers; the law prohibited the reduction of charges through plea bargaining in many instances. A somewhat similar law passed by the Massachusetts legislature was directed at persons arrested for gun possession; such persons automatically incurred a prison sentence. In Michigan, mandatory sentences were established for anyone convicted of possessing a firearm while committing another felony. Forty other states had set mandatory sentences for violent crimes by 1983.[50]

A third alteration of the criminal code sought to make prison sentences uniform throughout each state. Commissions were created to establish **sentencing guidelines** that set the exact sentence to be given for each crime and permitted only small variations for specified reasons. Thus, a slightly lighter sentence could be given if extenuating circumstances accompanied the crime, and a slightly longer sentence could be imposed if the circumstances of the crime were aggravated or if the offender had a previous criminal record. By 1993, nine states used such guidelines for all or part of their criminal court systems, and others were considering them.[51]

These reforms were aimed at different elements of prison and crime problems. Determinate sentences sought to reduce uncertainty about a prisoner's release date and, therefore, reduce prison unrest. Mandatory sentences were designed to curb plea bargaining and increase the number of offenders sent to prison. Both reforms and sentencing guidelines were intended to reduce disparities in sentences given to offenders who committed identical offenses.

[48]Wesley G. Skogan, "Crime and Punishment," in Virginia Gray, Herbert Jacob, and Robert B. Albritton (eds.), *Politics in the American States*, 5th ed. (Glenview, Ill.: Scott, Foresman, 1990), p. 389.
[49]*Setting Prison Terms* (Washington, D.C.: U.S. Department of Justice, Bureau of Justice Statistics, 1983), pp. 2–3.
[50]Ibid. An account of the changes in New York, Massachusetts, and Michigan may be found in Malcolm M. Feeley, *Court Reform on Trial: Why Simple Solutions Fail* (New York: Basic Books, 1983), pp. 118–138.
[51]Michael Tonry, "Sentencing Commissions and Their Guidelines," in Michael Tonry (ed.), *Crime and Justice: A Review of Research 17* (Chicago: University of Chicago Press, 1993), p. 141.

CONSEQUENCES OF LEGAL CHANGE

Unlike divorce law reforms, sentencing revisions were addressed to a densely populated field of practitioners who immediately knew of the changes. Prosecutors, judges, and prison officials were bound by their oaths of office to observe the new regulations in their decisions. Thus, the process of decision making changed to some degree with the new laws. In California, indeterminate sentences were replaced with determinate ones, and the entire sentence-setting process shifted from an independent agency called the Adult Authority to the courts. As in some other states, the parole board was simply abolished.[52]

Sentencing, however, was not an insulated activity of the courts. It had intricate connections with police and prosecutorial procedures because plea bargaining was one way of handling the overwhelming number of cases produced by high crime rates. In addition, prison authorities were sensitive to the consequences of changed sentencing procedures if those procedures limited the ways they could maintain security or if they substantially increased prison populations without commensurate programs to build new facilities. Because of these complexities, some of the provisions of the new laws were evaded and others produced unanticipated and undesired results.

In California, the new determinate sentencing law, while shifting authority away from the abolished Adult Authority, did not always enhance judges' power, and prosecutors continued to dominate the sentencing process.[53] On the other hand, sentences pronounced by judges became drastically shorter because the new law authorized sentences based on the actual time inmates commonly served rather than on the symbolically long sentences everyone knew would not be served. This shift from symbolically long to realistically short sentences brought immediate pressure on the California legislature to amend the new statute to provide for longer sentences. Both this development and the prisons' new inability to release inmates early produced prison overcrowding. Prison unrest did not disappear. Rather, prison tensions now focused more on racial conflict than release dates.[54]

Mandatory sentence laws had other consequences. In New York, defendants on drug charges facing stiff prison sentences and barred from plea bargaining more often insisted on a full trial.[55] This created long backlogs of cases awaiting bench and jury trials, and defendants, who pursued technical faults in their cases more systematically, more often won dismissal of their charges on the grounds that evidence had been obtained il-

---

[52]The following draws heavily from Sheldon L. Messinger and Phillip E. Johnson, "California's Determinate Sentencing Statute: History and Issues," *Proceedings of the Special Conference on Determinate Sentencing, Boalt Hall School of Law, University of California, Berkeley, March 1978* (Washington, D.C.: U.S. Department of Justice, National Institute of Law Enforcement and Criminal Justice, Law Enforcement Assistance Administration, 1978), pp. 13–58; Feeley, supra, note 50, pp. 139–147; and Jacqueline Cohen and Michael H. Tonry, "Sentencing Reforms and Their Impact," in Alfred Blumstein et al., *Research on Sentencing: The Search for Reform* 2 (Washington, D.C.: National Academy Press, 1983), pp. 305–459.
[53]Jonathan D. Casper, David Brereton, and David Neal, "The California Determinate Sentence Law," Paper presented at the annual meeting of the Midwest Political Science Association, Chicago, April 1983.
[54]Some of the consequences of these reforms are discussed in Franklin E. Zimring and Gordon Hawkins, *Prison Population and Criminal Justice Policy in California* (Berkeley, Calif.: Institute of Governmental Studies Press, 1992).
[55]Feeley, supra, note 50, pp. 124–128.

legally. Consequently, fewer defendants were convicted in the three years following the passage of the new law than in the preceding three years.[56] However, most of those convicted were sent to prison with longer sentences than had been the case before.[57] Thus, both desired and undesired changes occurred. However, if the law's architects had hoped to solve New York's drug problem with the law, they palpably failed, as drug trafficking in New York continued at a seemingly unabated pace. After a brief unsuccessful run, the law was repealed in 1979.[58]

Mandatory sentencing laws for weapons offenses also were a mixed success. Massachusetts enjoyed a three-year drop in armed robberies after its tough sentencing law took effect; thereafter, however, the armed robbery rate again increased.[59] The law caused more cases to go to trial and led to a larger number of dismissals and acquittals than had occurred when plea bargaining and nonprison sentences were permitted. In Michigan, the mandatory sentencing law produced even fewer changes, as judges and prosecutors simply evaded its provisions by substituting non-weapons charges for many arrested with a gun.[60]

Convicts in federal courts also faced mandatory guidelines designed both to make sentencing more uniform and to ensure harsh sentences for drug offenses. Federal judges, however, soon chafed at the guidelines' rigidity. Many bitterly resented imposing what appeared to them to be unduly harsh sentences on occasional drug users. By 1993, some simply refused to handle such cases.[61]

The causes for the limited success of the new sentencing laws lie in the complex situation that faced officials as they sought to implement them. The laws did not reduce the resources defendants brought to trial but rather induced their more vigorous use. Faced with probation or a short prison sentence, defendants had previously often agreed to plead guilty in exchange for a light sentence. When the new statutes offered no possibility of probation and mandated a certain sentence, or when plea bargaining was not permitted, defendants decided to do everything possible to obtain an acquittal or dismissal; some succeeded.

Other unanticipated consequences were caused by independent economic and political developments. The new laws were implemented just as an increasing number of state prison systems came under attack for overcrowding and other deficiencies that federal courts held were in violation of the constitutional prohibition against cruel and unusual punishment. Many prison systems came under court orders to enlarge their facilities or release inmates.[62] Simultaneously, taxpayers in many states sought to reduce expenditures and taxes. Thus, both prison officials and sentencing judges felt substantial pressure to ease the flow of prisoners into penitentiaries at the same time the laws they were administering caused them to send more convicts to prison for longer periods

[56]Feeley, supra, note 50, p. 126.   [57]Feeley, supra, note 50, p. 124.
[58]Feeley, supra, note 50, p. 128.   [59]Feeley, supra, note 50, pp. 130–136.
[60]Milton Heumann and Colin Loftin, "Mandatory Sentencing and the Abolition of Plea Bargaining: The Michigan Felony Firearm Statute," *Law & Society Review* 13 (1979), pp. 393–430.
[61]Robert Reinhold, "A Judge Who Challenges the System," *New York Times*, 24, October 1993, p. A18.
[62]As of June 1990, approximately one of seven state correctional institutions were under a court order to remedy overcrowding. See James Stephan, *Census of State and Federal Correctional Facilities, 1990* (Washington, D.C.: U.S. Department of Justice, Bureau of Justice Statistics, 1992), p. 1.

of time. On balance, the number of prisoners in state and federal institutions increased significantly after the new laws despite the contrary pressures.[63]

The effect of these laws on the incidence of crime was unclear. Official crime rates fluctuated but public fear of crime remained unabated, and experts were divided over whether the new laws had caused the decline which occurred. Police and court officials tended to take credit when the crime rate fell. Criminologists, however, pointed out that most or all of the decline might be due to the decrease in the size of the youthful population most likely to engage in crime. In addition, even when official crime rates were falling, as they did in 1992, public fear of crime increased, fed by incessant media publicity of particularly brutal offenses.

SUMMARY

The new sentencing codes had a substantial effect on the criminal prosecution process. They accomplished some of their goals: they reduced disparities in sentences, lengthened prison terms, and reduced the discretion of judges, prison officials, and parole boards in determining sentences. Other goals, however, were not so clearly achieved. We cannot know whether decreased crime rates were a product of new laws or of fundamental population shifts. They appeared to have no effect on fear of crime. Moreover, prison riots continued to occur sporadically. In addition, the laws had some unintended consequences. They increased the burdens on courts because fewer defendants pleaded guilty and thus more full trials were necessary. They increased pressure to build new prisons, and in some instances, led to a larger number of dismissals and acquittals. Thus, one may conclude that even when laws are addressed to public officials rather than the general public, achieving policy goals through legal change is far from simple.

Conclusion

The power of law to achieve social change is limited. A law's implementation depends on myriad factors, including knowledge of the law, the social consensus supporting or opposing it, the informal and official mechanisms existing to enforce the law, and the incentives and sanctions available to promote compliance. But judging the power of the law is not a simple exercise of totaling these factors.

The power of the law is often ambiguous because the law itself is full of ambiguity. As pointed out earlier in this book, law is the product of political coalitions. Many laws grow out of compromises that intentionally obscure their purpose; one can almost always find legislative supporters of a law who disagree about its purpose. Consequently, it is too glib to say that a law has not met its goal, because laws usually have several goals and they may be inconsistent.

In addition, law has symbolic as well as instrumental functions. A law that is not fully enforced may not be all its proponents desire, but it may be better than no law at

---

[63]Bureau of Justice Statistics, "Historical Statistics on Prisoners in State and Federal Institutions, Yearend 1925–86" *Report* (Washington D.C.: U.S. Department of Justice, Bureau of Justice Statistics, 1988).

all. The simple presence of a prescription on the statute books confers legitimacy on a group's claims, and the group may use it to win voluntary concessions from its opponents without going to court or seeking administrative action. Such symbolic value is difficult to assess but would be foolish to deny.

It is unclear whether the inclination of Americans to seek legal remedies for their problems is effective. Indeed, their continuing recourse to getting a new law passed or going to court to use existing laws seems to indicate popular confidence in the efficacy of the legal system. The legal system apparently rewards its users frequently enough to encourage them to return. It is rightfully feared and admired.

KEY WORDS

property division
no-fault divorce
child custody law
National Conference of Commissioners
  on Uniform State Laws

indeterminate sentence
determinate sentence
mandatory sentence
sentencing guidelines

FOR FURTHER STUDY . . .

For a more detailed account of divorce law reforms, see Herbert Jacob, *Silent Revolution: The Transformation of Divorce Law in the United States* (Chicago: University of Chicago Press, 1988). A series of essays reviewing twenty years of divorce reform are presented in Stephen D. Sugarman and Herma Hill Kay, *Divorce Reform at the Crossroads* (New Haven: Yale University Press, 1990). For a wide-ranging discussion of the potential costs and benefits of incarceration, see Franklin E. Zimring and Gordon Hawkins, *The Scale of Imprisonment* (Chicago: University of Chicago Press, 1991).

14

EPILOGUE

Americans have an ambivalent relationship with their legal system. Publicly, most Americans profess pride in it, and they seemingly rush to use it. Yet, American newspapers are filled with criticisms of the courts and other legal institutions. If Americans love their legal system, it is affection tinged with foreboding.

Apprehension about the future is perhaps the trademark of the twentieth century's last decade. On New Year's Day 1990, the United States seemed to stand triumphantly over the crumbling Soviet Union as the Cold War ended. The Berlin Wall had fallen and each of the Eastern European countries had rejected its old regime. All of them were eagerly seeking to reestablish a rule of law like that in the United States. However, before the decade was half over, the end of the Cold War began to look like a mixed blessing. Domestic troubles loomed larger than ever for the United States: the budget deficit hampered efforts to address residual racism, health care, welfare, crime, and economic competitiveness. The legal system, like all American institutions, had come under a cloud of disappointed hopes.

In this new global environment, the legal system faces severe challenges. It is confronted by a crisis of confidence, tested by impatience with disorder, and challenged by a new world order that asserts international norms superior to those of the American polity.

The Crisis of Confidence

Confidence in American political institutions has been uniformly low in the last third of the twentieth century. As Figure 14.1 shows, few Americans reported "a great deal of confidence" in "the people in charge of running" Congress, the presidency, and the Supreme Court. Confidence in the White House fluctuated from a low of 11 percent in 1976 (when President Gerald Ford was running a losing campaign against Jimmy Carter) to a high of 42 percent in 1984, the second year of Ronald Reagan's presidency.

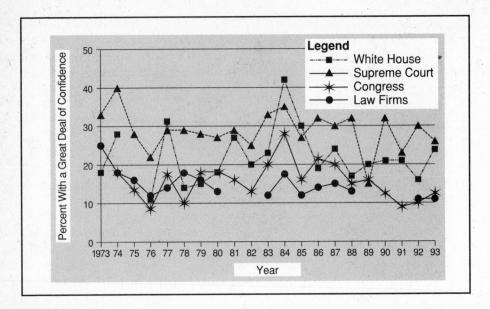

Figure 14.1
Confidence in Core Institutions
Source: Harris Poll, as reprinted in Kathleen Maguire, Ann L. Pastore, and Timothy
Flanagan (eds.), *Sourcebook of Criminal Justice Statistics, 1992* (Washington, D.C.:
U.S. Department of Justice, Bureau of Justice Statistics, 1993), p. 164.

The glow from the first years of the Reagan presidency lifted confidence in Congress as
well, but in general, it recorded lower levels than the White House. Institutions most
closely related to the legal system—the Supreme Court and lawyers—fared both better
and worse. The Supreme Court generally won the highest ratings in these polls; law
firms received by far the lowest. However, in 1993, none of the four institutions could
claim that more than one-fourth of the American people regarded them with great confidence.

The low standing of the legal profession is particularly noteworthy. As seen in the
previous chapters, lawyers are the linchpin of the legal system. They perform essential
duties at every turn of the legal process. Yet lawyer-bashing has become a public sport.
Hardly a week goes by in the pages of newspapers like the *New York Times* without unfavorable stories about lawyers. The public's estimation of their honesty and ethical
standards is scarcely higher than that of politicians. In a 1992 Gallup poll, only 18 percent of respondents rated lawyers as very high or high in ethics and honesty; the figures
for U.S. senators and representatives were 13 and 11 percent, respectively. By contrast,
27 percent rated journalists' ethics and honesty as very high or high, while 52 percent
rated medical doctors as high or very high.[1]

---

[1]Kathleen Maguire, Ann L. Pastore, and Timothy J. Flanagan, *Sourcebook of Criminal Justice Statistics, 1992*
(Washington, D.C.: U.S. Department of Justice, Bureau of Justice Statistics, 1993), p. 168.

Confidence in local judges is somewhat lower than that in police officers and prosecutors,[2] not altogether surprising, given the succession of scandals that have rocked urban court systems. In Chicago, two series of trials, theatrically labeled Greylord and Gambat, convicted more than a dozen judges of bribery and related charges; similar scandals rocked the judiciary in Miami,[3] Philadelphia,[4] Atlanta,[5] and San Diego,[6] as well as several other cities between 1987 and 1992.

The Crisis of Effectiveness

Many Americans show little patience with "legal technicalities" that are the trademark of the rule of law in the United States. In the face of threats of street crime, the right to be secure against unreasonable searches and seizures, guaranteed by the Fourth Amendment to the Constitution, is under constant attack, as are other ingredients of due process of law, such as the right not to incriminate oneself, the right to a lawyer, and protection against double jeopardy. For instance, when Chicago public housing projects became shooting fields with innocent bystanders being gunned down daily, the chief of the Chicago Housing Authority ordered police to sweep through the projects, enter all apartments, and search for weapons—all without evidence that any particular apartment had illegal weapons. Eight months later, a federal court ruled those sweeps were unconstitutional. In defense of his policy, the housing chief said that "he would rather be damned for doing something" than stand idly by.[7] Another example of the desire to catch criminals overriding concerns for civil liberties were proposals by the Bush and Clinton administrations to preserve the ability of law enforcement officials to eavesdrop on private communications. Both President Clinton and President Bush recommended a procedure by which law enforcement agencies could penetrate whatever privacy codes commercial firms provided for electronic communications.[8] Hardly a day passes without an expression of impatience with constitutional guarantees that are seen as unduly cumbersome.

Lack of public support for due process "technicalities" is not new. Using national surveys in the late 1970s, for instance, McClosky and Brill found that 58 percent of the general public did not support the prohibition against double jeopardy,[9] and almost half of the public supported convicting persons on the basis of evidence collected illegally.[10]

Tentative support for the courts, particularly at the local level, comes at the same time there is growing awareness of the legal system's limitations in dealing with con-

[2]Ibid.

[3]"4 Florida Judges Are Indicted in Federal Corruption Inquiry," *New York Times*, 25 September 1991, p. A16.

[4]"9 Philadelphia Judges Criticized," *New York Times*, 9 August 1987, p. A38.

[5]Prentice Palmer. "2 Traffic Judges Named in '86 Probe of Ticket Fixing Suspended for a Month," *Atlanta Constitution*, 9 October 1987, p. A24.

[6]Mark Platte, "Attorney's Gifts to Judges, Verdict Being Investigated," *Los Angeles Times*, 10 April 1992, p. B1.

[7]Matt O'Connor, "Judge Blocks CHA Sweeps for Weapons" *Chicago Tribune*, 15 February 1994, Sec. 2, p. 1.

[8]William Safire, "Sink the Clipper Chip," *New York Times*, 14 February 1994, p. A17.

[9]Herbert McClosky and Alida Brill, *Dimensions of Tolerance: What Americans Believe about Civil Liberties* (New York: Russell Sage Foundation, 1983), p. 163.

[10]Ibid., p. 164.

temporary social problems. The problem of crime, as we have seen, is not solved by anything the courts have done or foreseeably can do. They struggle to keep up with the flow of cases the police bring them. If an enlarged police force were to produce more arrests, courts would be still more likely to pursue shortcuts to full trials. Indeed, popular solutions to the crime problem may be no solution at all. In 1994, many states as well as the federal government considered adopting a provision commonly known as "three strikes and you're out." According to this proposal, those convicted of three serious offenses would receive life sentences without possibility of parole. The first experience with such a plan, however, indicated important limitations.[11] With the defendants facing life sentences, fewer are likely to plead guilty; by demanding a trial, they have hope they will escape conviction. That would increase the work load of trial courts quite out of proportion to the number of third-time offenders, since many first-time and second-time offenders would demand trials. Second, it may make apprehension of offenders considerably more dangerous as they forcibly resist arrest when facing a third conviction; some might choose to shoot it out with the police rather than surrender, since they would have little to lose. Even if only a small percentage did this, police work would become much more dangerous, since the police would never know when they were about to confront such a desperate person.

Similar difficulties confront civil courts. Domestic relations courts can do little to strengthen family ties; at best they create truces in family wars. Reducing the use of contingent fees for lawyers in personal injury cases, as one prominent group of lawyers has suggested,[12] may reduce litigation costs, but it may also reduce access to courts for those who cannot afford to pay attorney fees on anything but a contingent fee basis. Civil suits are often filed by those who feel unjustly treated, but the long delays, high costs of litigation, and uncertain results do not produce a sense of justice. Instead, they often create a perception that civil justice is a game of chance.

One indicator of the move away from the protections inherent in due process procedures used by courts is the push toward alternative dispute resolution (ADR) forums for many cases, especially those perceived by lawyers and court officials as minor. To some degree, the move to ADR appears voluntary, as both parties to a dispute seek to find less expensive, more flexible, and quicker paths to resolving their differences. An example is the employment of arbitration by commercial disputants who are on a fairly equal plane. However, many referrals of disputes to arbitration and mediation are anything but voluntary. For instance, claimants against their stockbrokers and insurers typically discover they have signed a standard agreement written by the stockbroker or insurer that routinely channels disputes to arbitration under conditions in which the complainant has little influence over the choice of the arbitrator or the rules of arbitration. Such claimants might, of course, have refused to sign the agreements when they first began using the broker or insurance company, but they would have been denied those companies' services, because the arbitration clauses are usually not negotiable. Similarly, disputants in a divorce case increasingly find that before they can obtain a

[11]Timothy Egan, "A 3-Strike Law Shows It's Not as Simple as It Seems," *New York Times*, 15 February 1994, p. 1.
[12]Peter Passell, "Windfall Fees in Injury Cases Under Assault," *New York Times*, 11 February 1994, p. 1.

trial they must attempt mediation with a mediator they do not choose and who may push them to a solution they do not prefer. In both instances, dissatisfied disputants may still go to court, but the unwanted arbitration or mediation will have consumed time and money, and it often places them in a less favorable position than they previously occupied.

It may be true that claimants' demands for substantive justice can be satisfied by out-of-court alternatives. Although it is difficult to measure, and no widespread attempts to do so yet exist, it is quite conceivable that claimants do as well in mandated mediation and arbitration as when they litigate. They may even receive the remedy quicker than if they relied on the courts. However, the outcomes may be different in two significant ways. First, as repeatedly stressed, disputants often file their cases in court to strengthen their negotiating position, eventually settling out of court. Interposing arbitration or mediation between the private negotiations and an eventual court filing alters the balance between parties. It distances court action, which in turn becomes less of a threat. It may also lead to the employment of different standards than those a court would impose. Thus, in terms of what claimants receive, the outcomes may be substantially different if an alternative forum is required before cases may come to court.

A second way outcomes in alternative disputing forums may differ is in the delivery of procedural justice. One of the strengths of voluntary mediation and arbitration is that disputants have control over the choice of the third-party participant and the norms that will be applied to their dispute. However, such choices are often not preserved in mandatory arbitration or mediation. Those elements of procedure which produce a sense that disputants receive procedural justice may be lacking in mandatory alternative forums, with the result that large portions of the population will feel they are denied the justice being delivered to other, more powerful, sectors.

Internationalization of Norms

National borders confine the legal system and process described in this book. As the title indicates, it is about law and politics *in the United States*. International norms, however, are beginning to penetrate national boundaries in ways that pose potential threats to the law and legal process as Americans know them. In Europe, national legal processes are increasingly subject to the jurisdiction of the European Court of Justice and the European Court of Justice on Human Rights, which enforce norms that transcend national boundaries. In the United States, the first omen of such a phenomenon became visible in the debate over the North American Free Trade Agreement (NAFTA) and discussions over the General Agreement over Trade and Tariffs (GATT). Under both agreements, standards the United States imposes may be challenged before international bodies with no further recourse to U.S. courts or other legal proceedings. Under GATT, for instance, regulations that require certain kinds of labels for food products may be declared unfair impediments to free trade; the use or prohibition of additives to food products may also be forbidden. Under NAFTA, requirements for environmental protection may similarly be declared unfair trade practices.

The imposition of international standards drastically alters the balance of power among disputants. If they have insufficient influence to alter the treaties as they are negotiated or ratified by the Senate, they lose their second chance at recourse that the courts normally provide. Moreover, the interpretation of these treaties often lies with international bodies composed of officials chosen under quite different procedures than judges, and the means to influence these tribunals also is different.

How quickly such internationalization will proceed and how far it will go is impossible to predict. However, in the past, law followed the paths beaten by the marketplace. It is, therefore, likely that as economies become increasingly internationalized, legal processes will follow. Thus, some of the distinctiveness of the American legal process may gradually erode as new international forums and norms become more common.

Future Challenges

Each of these crises poses serious challenges to the American legal system. We do not offer solutions to these problems; rather, we propose that the way of thinking promoted by this book will enable officials to devise workable solutions and will allow the public to evaluate their proposals.

The model this book has used is simple. First, we defined the legal system in a very broad yet quite specific way. Second, we repeatedly called attention to the need for an empirically reliable understanding of phenomena and sensitivity to the role of norms.

Defining the legal system as extending beyond courts to their gatekeepers and users and also to the legislative and administrative processes is important in devising responses to future challenges. Changes in one part of the system affect the other segments; that, indeed, is the working definition of a system. However, too often policy makers are surprised by unanticipated consequences in seemingly unrelated places caused by their alterations. The first reports[13] of increased resistance to arrest caused by a sentencing policy of "three times and you're out" are a classic example of an unanticipated consequence that could have been predicted had policy makers considered the potential consequences of their changes as broadly as we urged in this book. A broader consideration does not imply paralysis, since it is certain that every action will have consequences elsewhere in the legal system. Rather, it allows policy makers and the public to evaluate the consequences intelligently. It may be rational to prefer sending three-time convicts to prison for life even if police work becomes riskier or if it requires adding judges and other court personnel to deal with increased demands for full trials. However, it is never rational to adopt such policies without considering the consequences.

Our analysis also focuses on ascertaining the facts. It sounds simple, but throughout this book we noted that our knowledge is quite limited. Our count of crime is flawed in fundamental ways; we still possess only a limited understanding of the circumstances that lead people to commit crimes. We do not keep adequate court records, so we can-

---

[13]"Victim Prevents Felon from Taking 3d Strike Under Law," *Chicago Tribune*, 1 May 1994, Sec 1, p. 12.

not routinely ascertain how many people receive particular kinds of sentences for specified crimes. Court records are even more rudimentary in civil courtrooms; courts do not routinely collect information that allows us to understand how remedies are distributed among different segments of the population for particular sets of grievances. We know next to nothing about how informal disputing processes work and how they distribute remedies.

This lack of knowledge is unlikely to be remedied in the foreseeable future. Policy makers readily dismiss complaints about the lack of knowledge as special pleading of academics for research funds. However, in an age where computer simulations seek to chart the future course of the economy or predict the likely outcome of a new health care policy, without better information we are fated to grope our way in darkness through the labyrinth of the legal system as we seek to implement improvements. As in all fields of endeavor, the adage of statisticians applies: "garbage in, garbage out"; analyses based on poor data produce unreliable results.

Our examination of the legal system repeatedly emphasized norms and values. Law incorporates preferences; it elevates one set of values over others and advantages one segment of society over competitors. It is an instrument of control and domination. Therefore, one must always inquire about who benefits and who becomes handicapped as the legal system changes. There are always winners and losers, although it need not be a zero-sum game in which one person's gains are the other person's losses. Rather, as we suggested, benefits and costs are distributed in complex ways over a large network of institutions and individuals. Once the winners and losers are identified, people may refer to their own preferences and decide whether the outcome is acceptable. Thus, people must often decide about the equity of outcomes. For instance, is it fair that early claimants in a massive injury incident like that created by the use of asbestos receive punitive damages while others do not, or is it an acceptable way of imposing a civil penalty on the defendant corporation for its carelessness? Is it fair that attorneys receive large fees for personal injury cases that are sure winners, or is any unfairness offset by their consequent ability to assist others who face uncertain odds of winning? Is the deprivation caused to relatively poor claimants by mandatory arbitration an acceptable tradeoff for greater efficiency and larger profits for insurance companies? Such questions must be asked, and the answers depend on preferences, not facts.

Finally, the stress on values emphasizes the importance of seeing the legal system's problems in their political context. Action in the political arena permits interests to impose their value preferences in acceptable ways, because politics is a legitimate way to declare winners and losers. Thus, politics routinely imposes values on courts that judges are obliged to accept. The choice of values is always political. Consequently, the link between law and the political arena does not simply consist of the ways judges and other officials reach their offices or the consequences of judicial decisions on other officials. At its very heart, the legal system is linked to the political arena because the political arena selects the values that become embedded in substantive and procedural law.

INDEX

Abel, Richard L., 121, 127, 128
abortion, 4, 24, 78, 190, 232-233
Abraham, Henry J., 202
adjudication, 45-46
administrative law judges, 267-268
administrative tribunals, 267
administrative agencies, as core institutions, 14, 146-147, 256-272
administrative regulation, 28
adversarial process, defined, 17
adversarial legalism, 9
Albert, Lee, 149
Albritton, Robert B., 241, 292
Allen, Frances A., 201
amicus briefs, 152-154, 223-224
Anderson, Jill K., 45
Andreasen, Alan R., 63
appellate courts, 200-213
    case load of, 204-205
    error correction by, 200-201
appellate judges,
    background of, 209
    selection of, 209-212
Apple Computer Inc., 69-71
Applebohm, Paul, 181
arbitration, 45
Austin, John, 6
Baby Jane Doe, 3-5, 12
bail, 167-168
Baker, Liva, 21
Baker v. Carr, 189
Baker, Lynn A., 49
bar. See, lawyers
Barrow, Deborah J., 251, 253
Barry, Ruback R., 89
Barry, Kathleen, 8
Bates, v. State Bar of Arizona, 128
Baum, Lawrence, 205, 207, 253
Beller, Andrea H., 288
bench trial, 171
Berg, Larry L., 251
Berk, Richard A., 291

Berke, Richard L., 111
Berman, John J., 289
Berry, Jeffrey M., 13, 143, 147
Best, Arthur, 63
Beyle, Thad L., 245
Birnbaum, Jeffrey H., 147
Black, Donald, 6, 117
Blackstone, William, 6
Blasi, Vincent, 202
Blumstein, Alfred, 94, 293
Boland, Barbara, 164, 165, 172, 173
Bork, Robert, 225-226
Bowen v. Kendrick, 153
Brackman, Harold, 291
Branch, Taylor, 230
Bray, James H., 288
Brenner, Saul, 219
Brereton, David, 293
Brieland, Donald, 8
Brill, Alida, 299
Brodeur, Paul, 186
Bronner, Ethan, 152, 226
Brown, Michael, 107, 115
Brown v. Board of Education, 190, 214
Brown, Mark, 172
Bullock, Charles S. III, 33
Bush administration, 14, 15, 134, 257
Caldeira, Gregory A., 154, 216, 217, 223, 235
California v. Carney, 232
Campbell, Bruce, 178, 207, 227, 228, 277
Cantor, David, 96
Caplovitz, David, 65, 66
Caplow, Theodore, 289
Cappaletti, Maruo, 209
Carlin, Jerome E., 124
Carp, Robert, 210
Carter, Lief H. 8, 267, 269
Cartwright, Bliss, 205
case law, 27
    defined, 7
Casper, Jonathan D., 174, 293
Cassetty, Judith, 280

Cellis, William III, 212
Chada v. INS, 27
Chambers, David, 284
Chambliss, William, 94
Cherlin, Andrew J., 288, 289
Chevron v. Natural Resources Council, 262
Cifelli, Anna, 186
civil law, 30
civil courts, 175-196
Clayton, Cornell W., 257
clerks, in Supreme Court, 221
Clinton administration, 14
Cloward, Richard A., 96
Coats, James, 95
Cofer, Donna Price, 267, 268
Cohen, Richard E., 144, 242, 254
Cohen, Lawrence E., 96
Cohen, Jacqueline, 94, 293
commerce clause, 26
commercial litigation, 68-72
common law, 29
    defined, 7
Conklin, John E., 95
Conley, John M., 177
Conly, Catherine H., 164
consent decrees, 150
contingent fee, 131, 178
Coser, Lewis A., 41
courtroom workgroup, 169-170
courts, as core institutions, 15
Couzens, Michael, 108
Craig, Barbara Hickson, 28, 73, 77, 232, 236,
    254
Crawford Fitting Co. v. J. T. Gibbons, 251
crime, 86-99
crime statistics, 107-110
crime, and politics, 111-112
criminal law, 30
criminal courts, 163-175
criminal defendants, Supreme Court decisions
    about, 231-232
Culver, John H., 212
Curran, Barbara A., 55, 56, 57, 179, 180
Damaska, Mirjan R., 38
David, Martin, 284
Davies, Thomas Y., 201, 206
Davis, Patricia, 105
debtor-creditor disputes, 63-68
Denton, Nancy A., 231
DeParle, Jason, 174
depositions, 179
deterrence, 93-97, 163-164
Diamond, Shari, 17

Diamond, Irene, 8
Dickhut v. Norton, 33
Dienes, Thomas C., 73
Dingwall, Robert, 51
discuss list, 216-217
disputes, 10-11
    transformation of, 159-161
dispute processing, 41-84
    and commercial litigation, 68-72
    and consumer credit, 63-68
    and legislatures, 242
    arenas, 44-58
    by courts, 157-177
dispute resolution. See, dispute processing.
dispute processing, and legislatures, 242
divorce, 60-63, 184-186, 279-290
Dixon, Ruth B., 284
Dodd, Lawrence C., 241
domestic violence, 89, 90
Downing, Rondal, 192
Dubois, 192, 194, 211
due process, 32
Duncan, Greg J., 284
Easton, David, 6
Ebener, Patricia, A., 176
Edley, Christopher F., 273
Edgewood Independent School Dist. v. Kirby,
    212
Egan, Timothy, 300
Eisenstein, 9, 89, 93, 124, 168, 170, 171, 198
Ellsworth, Phoebe C., 280
Elrod, Linda D., 279
Emery, Robert E., 49
Emmert, Craig F., 207, 208, 211
Engel, David, 85, 160, 161
Engel, David M., 85
Epstein, Lee, 151, 152, 153, 154, 155
*Equal Employment Opportunity Commission v.
    Arabia American Oil Co.*, 251
equity, 29
Erickson, Kai T., 138
Escobedo v. Illinois, 21, 232
Evans, Daryl, 5
Faux, Marian, 76, 189, 190
Feeley, Malcolm M., 93, 166, 167, 228, 292,
    293, 294
Fellows, Mary Louise, 50
felony, defined, 165
    treatment of, by criminal courts, 167-
    171
Felson, Marcus, 96
Felsteiner, William L. F., 44, 176
Fenno, Richard F., Jr., 244

Fineman, Martha L., 284
Fisk, Margaret Cronin, 121
Flanagan, Timothy J., 87, 89, 93, 95, 108, 111, 112, 113, 164, 166, 172, 173, 202, 298
Flemming, Roy B., 9, 167, 170, 198
Flood, John A., 123
Forst, Martin L., 290
Frank, Alan H., 289
Freud, Anna, 280
Friedman, Lawrence M., 9, 19, 29, 38, 99, 103, 205
Friedman, Leon, 78, 80
Frost, Edward, 120
Frumer, Louis R., 34
Furstenberg, Frank F. Jr., 288
Fyfe, James J., 116, 117
Galanter, Marc, 33, 57, 59, 69, 83, 121, 122, 123, 180
Garasky, Steven, 283
Garfinkel, Irwin, 284
Garrow, David J., 230
gatekeepers, in administrative agencies, 258, 263-266, 270-271
    defined, 11-13
    in the legislative process, 242
gatekeeping, by lawyers, 118-119
    by police, 107-116
Gates, John B., 153, 154, 155, 197, 204
Gibbons v. Ogden, 26
Gibbs, Jack P., 21, 41, 279
Gibson, James L., 235
Gideon v. Wainright, 214, 231
Gilboy, Janet A., 169
Gleser, Goldine C., 138
Glick, Henry R., 208, 211
Goldberg v. Kelly, 269
Golden, Susan, 283
Goldman, Jerry, 147
Goldman, Sheldon, 122, 194, 205, 209
Goldstein, Joseph, 280
Gollop, Frank M., 51
Goodstein, Lynne, 174
Gottshall, Jon, 210
Graham, John W., 288
grand jury, 169
Gray, Virginia, 143, 147, 241, 292
Greatbatch, David, 51
Greenberg, Martin S., 89
Greenwood, Peter W., 97
Gren, Bonnie L., 138
grievances, 42-43
Griswold v. Connecticut, 76, 233

Grossholtz, Jean, 8
Grossman, Joel B., 152
Grove City College v. Bell, 250, 252, 261
guilty plea, 166, 169-170; also see, plea bargain
Gusfield, Joseph R., 278
Haggard, Ernest A., 45
Hall, Jay, 50
Hall, Kermit L., 225
Handberg, Roger, 251
Hanson, Roger, 183
Harris v. Forklift Systems, 48
Hastie, Reid, 17
Hawkins, 94
Hawkins, Gordon J., 51, 94, 279, 293, 296
Hazard, Geoffrey C., 30
Heinz, Anne M., 12
Heinz, John P., 119, 124, 126, 140, 146, 147
Henry, M. L. Jr., 194
Henshel, Richard L., 50
Hensler, Deborah, 176
Hentoff, Nat, 5
Herhige, Robert R. Jr., 72
Hetherington, E. Mavis, 288
Heumann, Milton, 294
Hill, Harold F. Jr., 251
Hirsch, Andrew von, 291
Hoffman, Saud D., 248
Holzman, Harold R., 97
Hood, Jane, 283
Horowitz, Donald L., 230
Hostetler, John A., 9
Howard, J. Woodford, 201, 205, 213
Hrebenar, Ronald J., 143
indictment, 169
injunction, 29
INS v. Chadha, 215
interest groups, as gatekeepers, 11, 12-13
    as gatekeepers to appellate courts, 151-155
    to legislatures, 144-145
    to administrative agencies, 146
    to trial courts, 148-151
    before Supreme Court, 223-224
Jackson, Bruce, 94
Jacob, Herbert, 6, 12, 25, 48, 49, 53, 56, 61, 89, 93, 107, 112, 113, 117, 126, 168, 170, 171, 192, 198, 241, 242, 279, 281, 282, 283, 284, 287, 291, 292, 296
Janda, Kenneth 147
Johnson, Charles A., 153, 154, 155, 197, 204, 227, 228
Johnson, Phillip E., 293

judges, appointment of, 15
    removal of, 195
    selection of, 192-194
judicial review, by state supreme courts, 208
juries, in civil cases, 183
    in criminal cases, 171
justices, appointment of Supreme Court, 224-
    227
Kagan, Robert A., 9, 205
Kalish, Carol H., 97
Kalman, Laura, 224
Kaupen, Wolfgang, 49
Kay, Herma Hill, 282, 296
Kerwin, Cornelius M., 261
Keynes, Edward, 189
Kidder, Robert L., 9, 25
Kingdon, John W., 241
Kluger, Richard, 189
Kneale, Dennis, 70
Kohlberg, Lawrence, 49
Kornhauser, Lewis, 47, 61
Kritzer, Herbert M., 9, 45, 59, 181, 198
Krygier, Martin, 177
Kutchinsky, Berl, 49
Ladinsky, Jack, 63
Lamb, Charles M., 33
Land, Kenneth C., 96
Landis, Jean M., 174
Landon, Donald D., 127, 140
Larson, Erik, 70
Laumann, 140
Laumann, Edward O., 119, 124, 126, 140, 146
Lavin, Marvin, 97
law, defined, 6, 7-9, 18, 21-25
    distinctiveness of American, 36-37
    layers of, 26-35
    shadow of, 47-48, 61, 69
Lawrence, Susan E., 155
lawyers, advertising by, 128
    disciplining of, 128
    education of, 120-121
    gatekeeping by, 11, 12, 128-139
    in large firms, 122-124
    in solo practice, 124
    regulation of, 127-128
    specialization by, 125-127
    women, 121-122
legal process, defined, 17-18
legal aid offices, 132
legal profession. See, lawyers
legal process, defined, 7, 17-18
legal system, defined, 7, 9-16, 18
legal culture, 9

legislatures, as core institutions, 13-14, 241-
    254
legitimacy, 11
    and civil proceedings, 176-177
    and criminal courts, 164
    and the law, 21-23
    and trial courts, 196
Lehne, Richard, 28
Lehnen, Robert J., 90
Lemmon, John Allen, 8
Lesser, Selma, 291
Leventhal, G. S., 23
Levine, Felice J., 45
Levy, Robert J., 280
Lewin, Tamar, 129
Lewis, Anthony, 236
Library of Congress v. Shaw, 251
Lind, E. Allen, 176
Lineberry, Robert L., 12, 113
Lipson, Leon, 83, 121
litigiousness, 82-83
Littlefield, Neil O., 63
Loftin, Colin, 294
Lorance v. AT&T Technologies, 251
Lowi, Theodore J., 146, 273
Luckenbill, David F., 96
Luker, Kristin, 73, 75
Lyon, Jeff, 3
McClosky, Herbert, 299
McGuire, Kevin T., 222
McIntosh, Wayne V., 83
McLanahan, Sara S., 248
McNeil, Kenneth, 63
McQuiston, John T., 116
Macaulay, Stewart, 58, 67, 69
Maccoby, Eleanor E., 184, 288
Maccoun, Robert J., 176
Maguire, Kathleen, 87, 89, 93, 95, 108, 111,
    112, 113, 164, 166, 168, 172, 173,
    174, 202, 298
Mahanna, Paul, 164
Malbin, Michael J., 241
Mann, Coramae Richey, 174
Mann, Thomas E., 241
Mapp v. Ohio, 231
Marbury v. Madison, 215
Marquardt, Jeffrey, 51
Martin, Elaine, 209
Martin, Susan E., 94
Martin v. Wilks, 251
Martinson, Robert, 291
Maruffo, Michele, 30
Marvell, Thomas B., 204, 206

Massell, Gregory, 278
Massey, Douglas S., 231
Mather, Lynn, 53, 85, 159, 197
Maxfield, Michael B., 90
Mayhew, Leon H., 57
Maynard, Douglas W., 167
Mazur-Hart, Stanley F., 289
Meadow, Robert G., 132, 178
mediation, 45, 62
Melnick, R. Shep, 148, 149
Menkel-Meadow, Carrie, 132, 178
Mentschikoff, Soia, 45
Merry, Salley E., 45
Merryman, John H., 36, 38
Messinger, Sheldon L., 293
Meyer, Daniel R., 283
Miller, Richard E., 41, 43, 56, 58, 63, 85
Miller, Randall K., 189
Milne, Ann, 286
Miranda v. Arizona, 20-21, 25, 34, 37, 214, 232
Miranda warning, 22
misdemeanor, defined, 165
Mishler, William, 220
Miyazawa, Setsuo, 83
Mnookin, Robert H., 47, 61, 184, 288
mobilization, of law, 11
Moe, Terry M., 265
Molotsky, Irwin, 264
Murphy, Bruce Allen, 224, 227
Murphy, Walter F., 235, 251
Nader, Laura, 59, 63
Nader, 63
Nardulli, Peter, 9, 170, 198
Navasky, Victor S., 124
Neal, David, 293
negotiation, 44-45
Nelson, Barbara J., 243
Nelson, Robert L., 119, 140, 146, 147, 248
Nevin, John R., 63
New York v. Quarles, 37
Newman, Stephen A., 5
Nichols-Casebolt, Ann, 284
Niemi, Richard G., 143
Nimmer, Raymond. T., 128
Nixon v. U.S., 214
Nord, Christine Winquist, 288
O'Barr, William M., 177
O'Brien, David M., 73, 77, 232, 255
O'Connor, Matt, 299
O'Connor, Karen, 153, 222
Ohlin, Lloyd E., 96
Oleszek, Walter J., 241

Olsen, Fran, 279
Olson, Susan M., 150, 225
Olson, Mancur, 13
opinions, by appellate courts, 206
Oppenheimer, Bruce I., 241
oral argument, before Supreme Court, 218
    in appellate courts, 206
Ornstein, Norman J., 241, 254
Ostrom, Brian, 183, 189
Pacelle, Richard L., 218
Palay, Thomas, 122, 123
Palmer, Prentice, 299
Par, Robert, 258
Passell, Peter, 300
Pastore, Ann L., 109, 111, 113, 164, 202, 298
Patterson, Samuel C., 241
Patterson v. McLean Credit Union, 251
Pearson, Jessica, 286
Peltason, Jack W., 231
Pennington, Nancy, 17
Penrod, Steven D., 17
Perry, H. W. Jr., 214, 217, 219
Petersilia, Joan, 96
Peterson, James L., 288
Planned Parenthood v. Casey, 234
Platte, Mark, 299
plea bargain, 170, 175
Podgorecki, Adam, 49
police, 103-117
police-civilian relations, 113-114
police, as gatekeepers, 11-12, 103-117
policy making, by appellate courts, 207-212
    by trial courts, 196-197
political crimes, 94
political process, defined, 7, 18
Porter, Mary Cornelia Aldis, 212, 213
Powell, Michael J., 130
preliminary examination. See preliminary hearing
preliminary hearing, 168
Price Waterhouse v. Hopkins, 251
privacy rights, 76-77
private law, 31
probation, 173
procedural justice, 22-23
public opinion, and the Supreme Court, 234-236
public law, 31
public defender, 167
Quinlen, Karen, 208
Quinney, Richard, 92
rape, spousal, 8
Rau, William, 50

Reagan administration, 4, 12, 14, 15, 133, 134,
        221, 257
Reaves, Brian A., 111
recidivism, 173
regulations, defined, 6
Reinhold, Robert, 294
Reiss, Albert J., Jr., 57, 88, 90
remedies, in civil cases, 180-182
repeat players, 57-59, 67-69, 90-91, 180
Resnik, Judith, 176
Rich, Michael J., 113
Richey-Tracy, Lisa, 210
Ring, Maria Luchesi, 286
Roberts, Penny, 191
Robins, Philip K., 284
Robinson v. Cahill, 28
Rodau, Andrew J., 70
Roe v. Wade, 73, 76, 154, 214, 232
Roosevelt, Franklin Delano, and appointment
        of judges, 15
Rosenberg, Gerald N., 227, 228, 277
Rosenblum, Victor G., 6, 121
Rosenthal, Douglas E., 136, 137, 178
Ross, H. Laurence, 63, 136, 137, 188, 189
Rottman, David, 183
Rowland, C. K., 151, 210
Royko, Mike, 65
Rubenstein, Jonathan, 114
Ryan, John Paul, 166, 167
Safire, William, 299
Salisbury, Robert H., 119, 146, 147
Sarat, Austin, 41, 43, 49, 56, 58, 85, 205
Scheingold, Stuart A., 117
Schmidhauser, John R., 251
school desegregation, 230-231
Schulhofer, Stephen J., 166, 171
Schur, Edwin, M., 74
Schwartz, Bernard, 221, 236
Segal, Jeffrey A., 215, 220, 222
Seidman, David, 108
Sepler, Harvey J., 289
Serrano v. Priest, 28
settlements, in civil cases, 183
Shapiro, Susan, 90
Sheehan, Reginald S., 210, 220
Shipp, E. R., 231
Silbey, Susan S., 45
Silverman, Robert A., 50
Simon, Rita J., 50
Skogan, Wesley G., 90, 99, 292
Skolnick, Jerome H., 114, 116, 117
slow plea, 170
Smeeding, Timothy, 284

Smigel, Erwin O., 123
Sobol, Richard B., 19, 182
social control, 87
        and law, 41-42
        and police, 103-107
        by appellate courts, 213
        by criminal courts, 163, 167
        by trial courts, 195-196
        in divorce cases, 62-63, 186
        in bankruptcy, 187
        in civil proceedings, 176
solicitor general, 217, 221-222
Solnit, Albert J., 280
Sones, Ronald, 164
Songer, Donald R., 204, 205, 210, 220, 225
Spaeth, Harold J., 215, 219, 220, 222
Staidl, Tracy Lynn, 51
Stanley, Harold W., 143
statutes, defined, 6
statutory law, 27
Steele, Erick H., 128
Steiner, Gilbert Y., 77, 233
Stern, Gerald M., 19, 138
Stevens, Robert B., 121
Stewart, James B., 71, 72, 135
Stidham, Ronald, 210
Sugarman, Stephen D., 282, 296
Sullivan, Joseph F., 105
Sunstein, Cass R., 273
Supreme Court, 214-237
        agenda of, 215-218
        and political arena, 224-236
        decision making, 218-224
        impact of decisions, 227-236
Susmilch, Charles, 63
Taggart, William A., 189
Talarico, Susette, 178
Tanenhaus, Joseph, 235
Tapp, June Louin, 45, 49
Tarr, G. Alan, 212, 213
Taylor v. U.S., 248
Taylor, Gary, 201
test cases, 148-150, 152
Thomas, Clive S., 143
Tolchin, Martin, 265
Tonry, Michael, 94, 172, 292, 293
torts, 31
Traut, Carol Ann, 207, 208
Trost, Cathy, 105
Truman, David B., 13, 155
Trubek, David M., 63
Tyler, Tom R., 11, 23, 174, 176
U.S. v. Place, 232

Uelmen, Gerald F., 222
Unger, Roberto Magabeira, 6
Uniform Crime Reports, 107-108
United States v. Nixon, 78, 80
Van Houtte, J., 49
Verkuil, Paul, 269
victimization surveys, 108-110
victimless crimes, 88, 91-92
Vinke, P., 49
Voydanoff, Patricia, 283
Walker, Jack, 143, 147
Walker, Timothy B., 279
Walker, Thomas G., 251, 253
Walsh, Edward, 191
Wanner, Craig, 60
Wards Cove v. Antonio, 251
Warner, Lynn, 164
Wasby, Stephen L., 201, 227
Watergate, 78-82
Watson, Richard, 192
Waxner, Michael, 34
Weber, Arnold R., 186
Weber, Max, 259
Webster, v. Reproductive Services, 154
Weiss, R. H., 23

Weitzman, Lenore, 284
Welch, Edward P., 191
West Virginia University Hospitals v. Casey, 251
West, Darrell, M., 244
Westcott, Davird R., 89
Westinghouse Electric Corporation, 71-72
Wheeler, Stanton, 83, 121, 205
Will, Hubert L., 72
Williams, Martha, 50
Wilson, James Q., 12, 105
Winget, Carolyn, 138
Wold, John T., 212
Wolfgang, Marvin E., 108
Wood, B. Dan, 257
Worthington, Rogers, 95
Wright, John R., 154, 216, 217, 223
writ of certiorari, 216-217
Yngvesson, Barbara, 53, 85, 159
Young, Warren, 172
Zawitz, Marianne W., 108
Zeisel, Hans, 17
Zemans, Frances Kahn, 6, 9, 11, 121
Zill, Nicholas, 288
Zimring, Franklin E., 51, 94, 279, 293, 296
Zuckman, Harvey L., 286